Praise for *Helen Keller: A Life*

"Much of Herrmann's fascinating story describes the tensions swirling around Keller throughout her life, including the often humiliating efforts to prove she was a saint or a fraud. . . . Herrmann's biography takes us far beyond Keller's childhood drama to explore her equally remarkable life as an adult."
  —Ron Charles, *Christian Science Monitor*

"*Helen Keller* is a superbly balanced book—but not so balanced that it drains all the blood out of its subject. . . . Herrmann is a master at weaving the crucial details and interesting minutiae of this varied and energetic life into a seamless story."
  —Stephanie Zacharek, *Newsday*

"Herrmann's portrait of Keller is both fully embodied and unflinchingly candid."
  —Mary Loeffelholz, *Boston Sunday Globe*

"We meet an entirely unexpected Helen Keller—a woman with deep if concealed ambivalence toward her self-sacrificing teacher; a political radical; and a woman longing for romantic love and the fulfilled sexual life of a woman."
  —Joan Mellen, *Philadelphia Inquirer*

"Perhaps the most intimate biography [of Helen Keller]. [Herrmann] gives her back her sexuality [and] imbues her with a true humanity. . . . *Helen Keller: A Life* has some of the texture and the dramatic arc of a good novel."
  —Dinitia Smith, *New York Times*

Helen Keller

ALSO BY DOROTHY HERRMANN

Anne Morrow Lindbergh

S. J. Perelman: A Life

With Malice Towards All

Helen Keller

A Life

DOROTHY HERRMANN

The University of Chicago Press

Reprinted by arrangement with Alfred A. Knopf, Inc.

The University of Chicago Press, Chicago 60637
The University of Chicago Press, Ltd., London
Copyright © 1998 by Dorothy Herrmann
All rights reserved. Originally published 1998
University of Chicago Press Edition 1999
Printed in the United States of America
04 03 02   6 5 4 3 2

Library of Congress Cataloging-in-Publication Data

Herrmann, Dorothy.
Helen Keller : a life / Dorothy Herrmann.
p.   cm.
Includes bibliographical references and index.
ISBN 0-226-32763-9 (paperback: alk. paper)
1. Keller, Helen, 1880–1968. 2. Blind-deaf women—United States
Biography. 3. Blind-deaf women—Education—United States.
I. Title
HV1624.K4H47 1999
362.4´1´092—dc21
[B]
99-23242
CIP

⊛The paper used in this publication meets the minimum requirements
of the American National Standard for Information Sciences—Permanence
of Paper for Printed Library Materials, ANSI Z39.48-1992.

ays

Helen Keller is fellow to Caesar, Alexander, Napoleon, Homer, Shakespeare and the rest of the immortals. . . . She will be as famous a thousand years from now as she is today.

—MARK TWAIN

I found that of the senses, the eye is the most superficial, the ear the most arrogant, smell the most voluptuous, taste the most superstitious and fickle, touch the most profound and the most philosophical.

—DIDEROT

Contents

Contents

Preface

THREE DECADES AFTER her death in 1968, Helen Keller, who over-
came blindness and deafness to become a symbol of the indomitable
human spirit, remains a legendary figure. Through her unquenchable zest
for life and learning — and her strength and courage — she was able to transcend her severe disabilities. In a society fearful of limitation and mortality,
she is an enduring icon, a woman who, by her inspiring example, made disability seem less threatening.

William Gibson's 1962 film *The Miracle Worker*, which portrayed Helen
Keller's childhood relationship with her teacher Annie Sullivan, was so
compelling that most people are only familiar with this early part of Helen's
life. The poignant scene at the water pump in which Patty Duke, who
played Helen, cries "wah-wah" as she feels the rushing water and Annie
spelling the word into her hand both celebrated Helen's emergence as a
knowing human being and condemned her to eternal childhood in our
imagination. "She remains not quite seven years old for many of us . . . ,"
writes a woman who like most of us becomes teary-eyed every time she
watches the celluloid Helen at last understand that everything has a name.

But the real Helen Keller did grow up and live a life that was more problematic than her inspiring childhood. The existence she shared with the

tormented, half-blind Annie Sullivan was turbulent—with its intrigues, doomed marriages and love affairs, and battles against physical and mental infirmity, not to mention constant struggles to earn a living. Triumphant as well as tragic, their life together might be considered an epic of the disabled that rivals any real-life or fictional drama involving nonhandicapped people.

My biography provides a chronological account of Helen Keller's long, eventful life, a life that would have crushed a less stoic and adaptable—as well as less protected—woman. It also deals with the controversies surrounding her. In her lifetime Helen was either venerated as a saint or damned as a fraud. One of the most persistent questions had to do with her relationship to the fiercely devoted woman through whom she largely expressed herself. Was Annie Sullivan "a miracle worker," or a domineering, emotionally troubled woman who shrewdly realized that exploiting a deaf-blind girl of average intelligence was her key to fame and fortune? Was she merely an instrument through which Helen's "brilliance" could manifest itself? Or was Annie herself the genius, the extraordinarily gifted and sensitive one?

What was the nature of Helen's strange, sensorily-deprived world? Was it a black and silent tomb, like being buried alive, as we imagine? And why was Helen so cheerful about her disability, appearing in public as the soul of radiance and altruism? Was this her real self that emerged at age seven after she was transformed by language from a savage, animal-like creature into a human being? Or was it a false persona that the driven Annie Sullivan had manufactured for her to appeal to the public, one that was modeled after Elsie Dinsmore and other children in Victorian literature?

The final chapter deals with how Helen's life might have been different had she not been dependent on only one teacher. Although she would have enjoyed a more normal existence, Helen's close relationship with Annie Sullivan and her other companions did not completely account for her constricted life as a deaf-blind woman in the mid-twentieth century. Famous as she was, she remained a victim of society's ambivalent attitude toward the disabled. On the one hand, she was sentimentalized and turned into the perfect symbol of a handicapped person; on the other hand, because she was disabled, the public tended to dismiss her often astute opinions on politics and social conditions.

Behind Helen Keller's public image of shining crusader for the blind was a woman who was forced to live an abnormal life from the time she lost her sight and hearing at nineteen months until the day she died, at eighty-seven. Because of the severe nature of her disability, the puritanical time in which she lived, and the self-interest of her handlers, she was never permitted to marry. To communicate with the outside world, she relied on women who knew the manual finger language and who led her everywhere and helped her with her daily tasks. For almost her entire life, these females, some of whom were jealous and scheming and had their own ideas about the proper lifestyle of a handicapped woman, were the key to her existence, even though all her life she yearned for a hearing-sighted woman's traditional life, for romance and sex, a husband and children. "If I could see," she once said bitterly, "I would marry first of all."

Several years ago, I began my quest to find Helen Keller, who, as much as she is admired by the hearing-sighted, as well as the deaf-blind and blind, is nevertheless regarded as "a plaster saint." To my surprise, I discovered that whenever I mentioned to anyone that I was working on her biography, inevitably I would be told one of those "Helen Keller jokes" that have been circulating for years among schoolchildren and other devotees of sophomoric humor. Had I ever heard the one about Helen scorching her fingers as she tried "to read" a waffle iron? Or the one about the peculiar method of discipline employed by her mother, Mrs. Keller, which was to rearrange the furniture whenever Helen acted up? These jokes reflect the teller's dread of incapacity, his own or anyone else's. They also point out something about the life of Helen Keller, a woman whose severe handicaps aroused people's fears about the prospect of their own disability to the point where they ceased to regard her as a person and either adulated her or invented sick jokes about her.

Who was Helen Keller?

As I soon discovered, the search to find the woman behind the legend proved a daunting challenge for a biographer. As a child reading about her in school, I remember trying to simulate her world by donning a blindfold and plugging my ears, but even as I stumbled around my suddenly unfamiliar house, I knew that I could never enter the silent blackness that I imagined was her whole world. I could rip off my blindfold and earplugs whenever I chose, and besides, I already knew the meaning of words.

After beginning work on my biography of her, I would attempt similar experiments, realizing, as I thankfully reentered the world of light and sound, that for Helen Keller there was never any choice. In contemplating and writing about her life, I could not help asking myself how I would react if I became blind and deaf. Would I go insane? Commit suicide? Or would I, like Helen Keller, find meaning and joy in life through my other senses?

With the help of many people, some of whom were deaf-blind or blind themselves, I was to discover the real Helen Keller, and she was a complex and enigmatic person, anything but "a plaster saint." Beautiful, intelligent, high-strung, and passionate, Helen might have lived the life of a spoiled, willful, and highly sexed woman had not the nature of her disability and her dependency on Annie Sullivan forced her into an entirely different existence, one in which she had to subjugate her own personal happiness as a female for the good of people afflicted like herself and other minorities.

Today, when a "visually or hearing-impaired" person makes newspaper headlines if he or she climbs a mountain, wins a beauty contest, or does anything extraordinary, but, sadly, in daily life, still faces negative preconceptions and prejudices, the search for Helen Keller may offer new insights into the nature of society's relationship to disability, and will perhaps prompt us to examine our fears about our own normalcy.

Helen Keller

CHAPTER 1

Helen

IN A SUNLIT, sound-filled room, the deaf-blind Helen Keller sat inconsolably beside the deathbed of Annie Sullivan, her teacher and virtually lifelong companion. Annie had died minutes before, and Helen was consumed with grief. Annie had been more than her friend; she had been her "other self," the woman to whom she owed her very life. Fiery, intemperate, and above all, indomitable, it had been twenty-one-year-old Annie, a dark-haired Irish orphan raised in a poorhouse, who had transformed a wild child who smashed plates and kicked people into one of the most celebrated women of her time, an embodiment of hope and courage to millions of disabled people around the world.

Since that moment at the wellhouse at the Keller home in Tuscumbia, Alabama, in 1887, where Helen was transformed from something a little more than a beast into a human being, both women had become world-famous. Immense crowds gathered whenever they lectured or appeared on the vaudeville stage, and even presidents, kings, queens, and popes deferred to them. For many persons, meeting Helen Keller was akin to having a religious experience. It was like an encounter with an angel. And almost invariably people were moved to tears.

Helen had sat beside her teacher for the past eight hours, her sensitive fingers on Annie's emaciated chest, painfully aware of her labored breathing. And then of her death rattle. And finally, when it was all over, of the sudden drop in temperature in her hand. For almost half a century, that hand, which had been her warm, pulsing lifeline to the world, was now cold and lifeless.

Her friends drew Helen aside so that Annie's body could be prepared for her funeral. But there was another reason they desired her out of the room as quickly as possible. They feared for her sanity. For years, people were aware of Helen's dependence on Annie and wondered if she would be able to survive without her.

An hour later, as Annie Sullivan's body was to be removed to a funeral parlor, Helen was led back into the room for her last farewell to the woman whom she still reverently called "Teacher," even though by this time she was fifty-six.

She was still, in the opinion of many, a beautiful woman. She was tall and shapely, with regular, almost perfect features and blue eyes that were the color of the sky on a perfectly clear day. Her eyes, which from the time she was nineteen months old had never seen a sunrise, a rainbow, or a human face, were luminous, as if they fathomed the inmost secrets of life and death. But Helen's family had lived in dread that the public would discover that her eyes were artificial. For medical and cosmetic reasons, they had been removed and replaced with glass ones.

In her youth, before the advent of her prosthetic eyes, she was considered even more fetching. Her porcelain complexion was clear and smooth, and she had a luxuriant mane of chestnut hair that cascaded down her back. Her figure was voluptuous; she had large breasts, small hips, and lovely, shapely legs. Because of her severe disabilities, her physical attributes, which were considerable, were usually not mentioned. People, when they met her, were quick to point out her spiritual beauty, comparing her to "a religious figure imagined by some Italian primitive or a Cimabue virgin, infinitely touching in her simplicity." "Physically she was large for her years, and more fully developed than is the every-day girl of her age," wrote a man who met her when she was fourteen, quickly adding that "she had come straight from the hands of God, and for fourteen years the world and the flesh and the devil had not obtained possession of her."

With her hands outstretched, Helen began to grope her way toward the body of her beloved teacher. Or rather she lurched forward, her body constantly broken by shivers and convulsive movements that appeared to be caused by nothing that was apparent to those present. The strange quivers and jolts corresponded to the world of vibrations and sensations to which she was acutely sensitive.

Reaching Annie's body, she bent down and reverently stroked the face that she had worshiped but never seen. Instantly she knew it was not the same. The features were fixed, waxen. All of Annie's warmth and vitality were gone. She recoiled in horror.

"It's not Teacher!" she cried in the broken, metallic, and mechanical voice that few people could comprehend. "It's not Teacher!"

For nearly fifty years the two women had enjoyed a friendship that was as all-encompassing as the most passionate love affair between a man and a woman. Commenting on their affinity for one another, friends compared the duo to Romeo and Juliet or Orpheus and Eurydice. Richard Watson Gilder, a famous poet and critic of the period, upon reading Annie's account of her first meeting with Helen in Tuscumbia, remarked that it would take a William Blake to paint the picture of those two souls rushing toward each other. Like the relationship between most couples, their alliance had been a complicated interplay of power and dependence. Although Annie came to rely on Helen's fame to provide their livelihood and on her seemingly tranquil disposition to lift her out of her dark moods, it was Helen, with her afflictions, who appeared to the world as the helpless one.

As her hands mournfully explored Annie's face for the last time, Helen feared that she could not survive without the woman who had been her savior and bridge to the world.

THE VIVID SMELL of bananas, the strangely comforting warmth of a burn, the vibrations from an object falling suddenly — even the eternal grayness and silence — meant nothing to the child who had no sight or hearing, no thought or language.

Helen Adams Keller did not always inhabit this strange, unreal world. She was born a normal, hearing-sighted infant, on June 27, 1880, in Tuscumbia, a small rural town in northwestern Alabama. For almost two halcyon years, her childhood was like most other people's. Some years later, when she was in her early twenties, she made an attempt to reconstruct that period of her life, her account embellished by an editor who had been employed to make her peculiar existence understandable to the hearing-sighted public. It was filled, she said, with the light of long summer days and the chirping sound of birds, of feeling lost "in a great green place, where there were beautiful flowers and fragrant trees," and of "seeing flakes of light flitting among the flowers," which perhaps were birds or butterflies. But the truth was that Helen Keller never remembered seeing even a sliver of light or hearing birdsong. What she recalled privately to a friend was rubbing her distraught young mother's face until the skin sloughed off in patches.

An account of Helen's first months must come from her mother, Kate Adams Keller, and other relatives. It was reported that at six months she could say "How d'ye" and "tea, tea, tea." She also knew the meaning of the word "water," which she pronounced "wah-wah." When she was a year old, she took her first steps, attracted, she was told later, "by the flickering shadows of leaves that danced in the sunlight on the smooth floor." Her vision was excellent. She could spot needles and buttons on the floor that no one else in the family could find. She was a precocious child, with soft golden curls, pale blue eyes, and a quick intelligence that she had inherited from her mother.

Kate Keller, then twenty-three, doted on her young daughter, and her intense maternal absorption was perhaps not surprising, given that by the time of Helen's birth, she had realized that her marriage was a mistake. A tall, statuesque blonde with periwinkle blue eyes and a porcelain complexion, Kate was twenty years younger than her husband, Captain Arthur Henley Keller, with whom she had little in common. A friend once bluntly described Captain Keller as "a gentleman farmer who loved to direct rather than work" and "a man of limited ideas and ability." But these lacks seem to have been offset by the fact that he was a raconteur as well as a good-natured, hospitable neighbor who was respected in the community. He was also a hunter, who, as Helen admitted later, "next to his family, loved his dog and his gun." Above all, Captain Keller was a loyal Southerner who had proudly served as a captain in the Confederate Army. He believed all things southern were noble, and that Negroes, although he would never be deliberately unkind to them, were not human beings.

Captain Keller had two grown sons from his first marriage, to Sarah E. Rosser of Memphis, who had died in 1877 at age thirty-eight. Kate got along fairly well with the younger boy, William Simpson, who was a teenager, but she had difficulty coping with James, who was in his early twenties and bitterly resented her. Only nine years older than him, she sensed that he was furious with his father for marrying her only a year after his mother's death.

Before her marriage to the captain, Kate had been a Memphis belle who had been pampered and protected by her father, Charles W. Adams, who was a brigadier general in the Confederate Army. But Kate, unlike her

Kate Adams Keller, Helen's mother, and Captain Arthur Henley Keller, her father. Captain Keller was the editor of the local newspaper.

husband, was not a dyed-in-the-wool Southerner. Although she seldom mentioned them in the provincial postbellum society of Tuscumbia, she had illustrious northern roots. Her father had been born in Massachusetts and was related to the famous Adams family of New England. Later he moved to Arkansas and fought on the side of the South when the Civil War broke out. Her mother, Lucy Helen Everett, was related to the celebrated New England clergyman and orator Edward Everett, who had spoken on the same platform at Gettysburg with Abraham Lincoln, as well as Edward Everett Hale, the famous author of "The Man Without a Country," which strengthened the Union cause, and to General William Tecumseh Sherman. When the Civil War ended, Kate and her family had moved to Memphis, Tennessee.

Marriage at age twenty-two to the forty-two-year-old captain ended Kate's luxurious existence. No longer did she live the carefree life of a pampered southern lady. Instead, this once indulged beauty was plunged into a rugged and primitive existence that was not unlike a pioneer woman's. As she discovered to her dismay, her jovial husband, like most of the southern gentility during the tumultuous postbellum period, was struggling to make ends meet. Although a member of a distinguished southern family, Captain Keller, a former lawyer, was forced to earn a living both as a cotton plantation owner and as the editor of a weekly local newspaper, the *North Alabamian*. In 1885 his fortunes had taken an upturn when President Grover Cleveland appointed him U.S. marshal for the Northern District of Alabama. Still money was scarce, and Kate had to raise her own vegetables, fruit, and livestock. There were black servants to help run the plantation, but she did most of her own work, starting at dawn. To further cut down on expenses, she made her own butter, lard, bacon, and ham. She never complained publicly about her husband's shortcomings, attempting to sublimate her regrets about the marriage by becoming an ardent woman suffragist and finding refuge in books and other intellectual pursuits. She also found the time to cook and tend her flower garden, of which she was intensely proud. It was said that she raised the most beautiful roses that people had ever seen outside of a greenhouse. It was also said that she went for days without speaking to her husband.

Even Helen's name became a matter of dispute. When she was born, Kate wanted to name her "Helen Everett," after her mother. The name Helen means "light," and the frustrated Kate liked to imagine that her little girl's life would be unlike her hard, frustrating one, full of the brightness of the day. The obstinate captain would not hear of it. He wanted to name the baby "Mildred Campbell," after a cherished ancestor, but finally he relented. At the baby's christening, however, he conveniently forgot the name that his wife wanted to call the child and told the minister that she was to be named "Helen Adams."

The house where the Kellers lived in Alabama was a simple, white clapboard house that was built in 1820 by Helen's grandparents, David and Mary Fairfax Moore Keller. David was the son of Caspar Keller, a native of Switzerland who had immigrated to Maryland and owned large tracts of land in Alabama. (Ironically, another of Helen's Swiss ancestors was the first teacher of the deaf in Zurich. He later wrote a book about their education.) Helen's grandmother Mary was a daughter of Colonel Alexander Moore, one of Lafayette's aides who was present at Lord Cornwallis's surrender at Yorktown, and a second cousin of Robert E. Lee.

The Kellers' house, which was the second to be built in Tuscumbia, was of Virginia cottage construction. Located on a 640-acre tract, its grounds included English boxwood trees, magnolia, mimosa, and a magnificent water oak with a crepusculated trunk that would become Helen's favorite tree and provide her with a thrilling tactile experience every time she climbed it. The house itself, as well as many of the surrounding trees and fences, was covered with an abundance of English ivy, inspiring its owners to call it "Ivy Green."

In the South it was a practice to build a cottage near the main house as an annex for occasional use. After the Civil War, the captain built such a small dwelling forty feet from the house; he used the cottage as an office to keep his plantation books. To his son James's dismay, no sooner had his first wife, Sarah, died than he had the office refurbished as a bridal suite. After their marriage, he and Kate lived there for a while. For the as yet undisillusioned Kate, it was a secluded, romantic place, the couple's privacy ensured by a screen of climbing yellow roses and honeysuckle.

It was in this structure, known as "The Little House," composed of one large room with a lovely bay window and a smaller room, that Helen was born and where she lived with a nurse until the time of her illness.

In February 1882, when Helen was nineteen months old, she developed a severe congestion of the stomach and brain. The nature of her ailment, which was called "brain fever" by the doctors of the period, remains a mystery to this day. Some modern doctors believe it was scarlet fever, a contagious disease that is caused by a hemolytic streptococcus, while others are of the opinion that her symptoms were more indicative of meningitis, an inflammation of the delicate membranes that cover the spinal cord and brain. In any event, for several days the family doctor thought she would die. But the fever gradually subsided, and the child fell into a deceptively

"Ivy Green," the Keller house in Tuscumbia, Alabama. Helen Keller was born in the small cottage at the right.

The pump behind Helen's birthplace, where she learned her first word—"water." She learned twenty-nine more words that first day.

quiet sleep. Her eyes, however, continued to pain her. They felt "so dry and hot" that, as she later recalled, she kept them turned "to the wall, away from the once-loved light, which came to me dim and yet more dim each day." Believing their little daughter cured, the Kellers rejoiced. Only when Kate passed her hand before the baby's eyes and they did not close and she rang a dinner bell and Helen did not respond, did they realize that the illness had left her deaf, blind, and mute. She was living in a world where there was neither light nor sound. Medical tests would later reveal that she could perceive neither light nor objects and that she was completely deaf, possessing neither bone nor air conduction in either ear.

"I was too young to realize what had happened," she wrote many years later. "When I awoke and found that all was dark and still, I suppose I thought it was night, and I must have wondered why day was so long coming. Gradually, however, I got used to the silence and darkness that surrounded me and forgot that it had ever been day."

Helen Keller's severe handicap was rare. It has been estimated that since the beginning of the twentieth century there have been only fifty men and women in the world who have completely lost their sight and hearing in infancy or early childhood. Fewer numbers of blind-deaf mutes have been recorded in previous centuries. The great majority were killed in infancy by their relatives, a practice that exists today in many areas of the world, particularly in Asia and Africa.

For centuries, the blind, as well as the deaf-blind, were regarded as monsters, to be killed as quickly as possible. In ancient Greece, blind children were taken to mountaintops and left to starve to death or be eaten by wild animals. In Rome, a parent of a sightless child could buy a small basket in the marketplace in which to put their visually impaired offspring before throwing him or her into the Tiber. Other early societies sanctioned the selling of blind children into slavery or prostitution, and in the Orient, blind women were routinely forced to become prostitutes. Even in Europe, blind children were often thrown into the streets by their parents to beg for a living.

The deaf-blind, in particular, were regarded by their parents as pariahs, a retribution for their own sins. Even for a loving mother and father, they were almost impossible to handle. As a result of their intense frustrations at not being able to communicate, deaf-blind children, or "children of the silent night," as the blind commonly refer to them, throw temper tantrums, scratching, biting, hitting, and pinching other people. Helen Keller was no exception. No one had the heart to discipline her. She was willful and quick-tempered by nature and tyrannized the household. She smashed dishes and lamps, plunged her hands into people's plates. On one occasion she dashed into the parlor in her red flannel underwear and pinched her Grandma Adams, chasing her from the room. Helen could neither see nor hear other people's reactions and had no idea of the pain she inflicted. Her parents' tears and recriminations had no effect on her. She was regarded by her relatives "as a monster," and at least one of them suggested to Kate Keller that she was "a mental defective" who would be far better off in an institution. But Kate would not hear of it. Helen clung to her mother's skirts all day, and Kate's intense suffering was obvious to her friends and family— she had the most sensitive mouth they had ever seen, as if every line of her tragedy were etched upon it.

"Fate ambushed the joy in my heart when I was twenty-four and left it dead," Kate once confided to a friend.

Kate Keller was in an excruciating position. She had adored the darling Helen who could speak and hear, but after her daughter's defects were confirmed medically, she experienced a bewildering array of emotions: hurt pride, guilt, sadness, and often a wish for the child's death. She felt helpless about how to deal with Helen's destructive behavior.

Kate Keller continued to resist the idea of putting Helen away, even though she was getting harder to handle with each day. The Kellers by then had a second child, a girl named Mildred, who was five years younger than her sister. A jealous Helen overturned the cradle. The baby might have died if Kate had not caught her before she fell on the floor. A short time later, Helen locked her mother in the pantry for several hours and cut off the black corkscrews of the child of the family cook who had been instructed to keep her entertained. Once Helen's wet apron caught flame as she held it in front of the fire, and a nurse quickly threw a blanket over her, putting out the fire.

By this time Helen, who felt a need to communicate with other people, had learned a primitive way to communicate by crude signs: To say "no," she shook her head; "yes" was indicated by a nod. If she wanted her mother to make ice cream, she mimicked the motion of the freezer and shivered as if she were cold. To indicate her father, she made the motion of putting on glasses; for her mother, she laid her hand against her face; and for her sister Mildred, she sucked her thumb.

"I cannot recall what happened during the first months after my illness. I only know that I sat in my mother's lap or clung to her dress as she went about her household duties," she later wrote in *The Story of My Life*. "My hands felt every object and observed every motion, and in this way I learned to know many things."

CHAPTER 2

Laura

L AURA DEWEY BRIDGMAN WAS BORN a normal infant on
December 21, 1829, in Hanover, New Hampshire. Her parents were
prosperous farmers, who, according to their neighbors, were both
temperamental and high-strung people, possibly because Laura had convulsions in infancy. When she was two, she and her two older sisters
became ill with scarlet fever. Laura's sisters died, and although Laura survived, she lost her sight and hearing. Medical tests would later reveal a complete loss of hearing in both ears and that her only feeling was one of
vibrations. In addition, she could not speak, and her senses of smell and
taste were impaired. Unlike other children, she could be made to swallow
the foulest-tasting medicines without a grimace. Laura was forced to make
her adjustment to life with only one of the principal contact senses, the
sense of touch.

Her parents eventually taught the nervous, physically frail child how to
sew and braid and to make crude signs for what she wanted. She might have
continued her uncomplicated existence as a "wild child" had she not interested Dr. Samuel Gridley Howe. A handsome, black-bearded medical doctor who had fought in the Greek War of Independence, Howe had become
the first director of the first school for the blind in the United States in 1831.

Helen

Before her illness Helen had made signs for everything, and alt[h]
she could say a few words, such as "wah-wah" and "tea, tea, tea," Kate
thought this habit was responsible for her slowness in learning h[ow to]
speak. After the illness, when the family was dependent on signs to co[mmu-]
nicate with her, this natural tendency to gesture stood Helen in good [stead.]
How much she could understand from this method of communicat[ion is]
difficult to determine, but at five she could sort and fold the laundry a[s it]
was ironed, distinguishing her own clothing from the other family m[em-]
bers'. She knew when Kate was dressed to go out and begged to accom[pany]
her. By this age she also had realized that she was different from other [peo-]
ple and that her mother and other people did not use signs as she did [but]
spoke with their mouths. "Sometimes I stood between two persons [who]
were conversing and touched their lips," she later recalled. "I could[n't]
understand, and was vexed. I moved my lips and gesticulated frantic[ally]
without result. This made me so angry at times I kicked and screamed u[ntil]
I was exhausted."

The frustration at not being able to express herself intensified as He[len]
grew older. Her outbursts increased to the point where they were occurr[ing]
hourly. The Kellers were mystified. Helen was almost six, and if they co[uld]
not manage her at this age, when she was still a little girl, how would th[ey]
handle her when she reached her full growth and sexual maturity? S[he]
would be capable of doing real physical harm to herself and others, an[d]
Kate Keller brooded that her child's severe disability would make her esp[e-]
cially vulnerable to a sexual assault, as she recalled with horror the storie[s]
about southern women who had been raped by Union soldiers durin[g]
the Civil War. Kate's attitude toward sex could be considered fanatical[.]
Whether it was because of her own disappointing marriage, in which she
was forced to bear children for a man she did not love, or her guilt at having
produced a severely disabled daughter, she was puritanical about sex to the
point of obsession.

One day, as Kate was cradling her exhausted child in her arms, she
remembered a piece she had once read by Charles Dickens, her favorite
author. It was about Dickens's own experience of visiting America and
meeting Laura Bridgman, an ethereal deaf-blind young woman who had
become educated. The solution to Helen's problem, if one existed, might
lie with a young woman who had once shared her child's cruel fate. But was
Laura as severely afflicted as Helen? Kate Keller wondered. And how, precisely, had her teachers broken through to her? Would their methods work
with a child who was as violent and intractable as Helen?

Although he was an idealist and a humanitarian, the school, ironically, was not his idea—it had been the brainchild of his friend Dr. John Dix Fisher, a Boston medical student who had recently returned from a visit to the first school for the blind in Europe, L'Institution National des Juenes Aveugles. The National Institution for the Blind, as it was called in the United States, had been founded in Paris by the young intellectual Valentin Hauy in 1784, a few years before the French Revolution.

The new school that Fisher wanted to found in Boston, however, existed largely in his imagination—it had no buildings, students, or director.

Howe had absolutely no experience in the education of the blind and was an odd choice for the job. Yet as one of his biographers has observed, "he so combined poetic insight, the fiery zeal of a prophet, sound scholarship and business acumen that any philanthropic enterprise was bound to prosper in his hands."

Upon his appointment as director, Howe immediately set sail for Europe, visiting all the major institutions for the blind to see what he could learn from their methods of education. He found "much to admire and copy, but also much to avoid." Rather than being prepared for an independent adult life, the blind were treated as objects of charity. Nothing was being done to advance their cause as a class, and there was also a shocking shortage of embossed books and supplies.

In the eighteenth century, one of the favorite subjects for philosophers investigating the nature of intelligence was a metaphysical inquiry on whether a blind person, restored to sight, could recognize the objects he or she knew solely through touch. Another tantalizing subject for discussion was whether it was possible for anyone to be educated who lacked the two principal senses, sight and hearing. In the early nineteenth century, in the United States, there later appeared such a person, a deaf-blind eighteen-year-old woman named Julia Brace, who was enrolled at the American Asylum for the Education and Instruction of the Deaf and Dumb in Hartford, Connecticut; Thomas Hopkins Gallaudet had founded the asylum in 1817. Efforts to teach Julia proved futile, undoubtedly because her education did not start until her late teens, and many people doubted whether it was possible ever to educate a deaf-blind person.

Howe met Julia shortly after he became director of Fisher's school, which by then was named the Perkins Institution and Massachusetts Asylum for the Blind.* After observing her, he concluded the attempt to break

* In 1877 the word "School" replaced "Asylum," and in 1955 the name was shortened to Perkins School for the Blind.

Samuel Gridley Howe, 1859,
American reformer and the
first director of the Perkins
Institution for the Blind

through to such a person "should not be abandoned, though it had failed in her case as well as in all that had been recorded before."

Five years later, as he gazed on the blank face of deaf-blind seven-year-old Laura Bridgman at her parents' New Hampshire farmhouse, he was presented with the daunting challenge himself. Fascinated by the child's almost unique disability and moved by her predicament, he convinced her parents to let him take her to his school.

Howe began Laura's education by handing her ordinary objects such as a key or a spoon, with their names pasted on them in raised letters. Next she was permitted to feel the word in raised letters on a separate piece of paper. Some weeks elapsed, and Laura still did not realize the point of the exercise. Then, suddenly, she realized that it had a purpose. The word *spoon* in raised type meant a spoon, and if she wanted a spoon, she could use the sign instead of the spoon to indicate what she wanted. Next Howe and her teachers taught her the manual finger alphabet of the deaf, which had first been used in France in the early part of the eighteenth century. It was originally brought from Spain, where it was reportedly invented by Trappist monks to converse with one another while not breaking their vow of silence. Soon, to Howe's delight, Laura was learning simple nouns, verbs, and then adjectives.

When news of Howe's remarkable achievement spread, both student and teacher achieved world renown. Among those persons who were fascinated by Laura Bridgman was the novelist Charles Dickens, who met the pale, delicate thirteen-year-old at the Perkins Institution in South Boston on his first visit to the United States, in 1842, and recorded his impressions in his *American Notes:*

> . . . blind, deaf, and dumb; destitute of smell; and nearly so of taste . . . a fair young creature with every human faculty, and hope, and power of goodness and affection, enclosed within her delicate frame, and but one outward sense—the sense of touch. There she was, before me; built up, as it were, in a marble cell, impervious to any ray of light, or particle of sound; with her poor white hand peeping through a chink in the wall, beckoning to some good man for help, that an Immortal soul might be awakened.
>
> Long before I looked upon her, the help had come. Her face was radiant with intelligence and pleasure. Her hair, braided by her own hands, was bound about a head, whose intellectual capacity and development were beautifully expressed in its graceful outline, and its broad open brow; her dress, arranged by herself, was a pattern of neatness and simplicity; the work she had knitted, lay beside her; her writing-book was on the desk she leaned upon.—From the mournful ruin of such bereavement, there had slowly risen up this gentle, tender, guileless, grateful-hearted being.
>
> Like other inmates of that house she had a green ribbon bound round her eyelids. A doll she had dressed lay near upon the ground. I took it up, and saw that she had made a green fillet such as she wore herself, and fastened about its mimic eyes. . . .

The fear, as well as the wonder, that Laura Bridgman aroused in Dickens and other Victorians was closely associated with a fear of death. For centuries the blind and the deaf-blind had been viewed by the hearing-sighted as symbols of darkness, of returning "to the black limbo from which we came." In the Talmud, the blind were referred to as the living dead. A Talmudic command urged that upon meeting a blind person, one must quickly murmur the same benediction as was said on the death of a relative.

An equally powerful fear that the deaf-blind aroused was the fear of being buried alive, a not unfounded fear in the centuries prior to the practice of modern embalming. This method, in which body fluids are replaced by chemicals, was to be invented in Washington, D.C., in 1856, fourteen

Laura Bridgman with one of her teachers, Mary Swift, c. 1845

years after Dickens's visit to the United States. It later became widespread during the Civil War, which made it possible for thousands of dead Union soldiers to be preserved for the long trips north to their families. The new process, however, did not erase the age-old dread of waking up six feet under. Most wills of the period contained a clause specifying that the family of the deceased make sure that a loved one had in fact expired. To ensure that this was the case, many people often stipulated that a finger be amputated before the coffin was closed. If there was no scream, grieving relatives could be assured that they were indeed burying a corpse. Others insisted on more ghoulish extremes: of being decapitated, or having their hearts removed.

For Charles Dickens, Laura's living entombment, prior to Dr. Howe's intervention, was a gruesome reminder of the premature death of his lovely, high-spirited sister-in-law Mary Hogarth. Although in seemingly perfect health, Mary had had an undiagnosed heart condition. She had fallen ill one night after returning from the theater and died the following day in his arms. She was seventeen years old, and five years later, on the bright January morning in Boston when Dickens had met Laura, he had still not recovered from her death. As he had held the dead Mary in his arms, his life and fictional world had been altered forever.

IF CHARLES DICKENS VIEWED Laura Bridgman as a resurrected woman who had escaped the fate of his sister-in-law Mary, other distinguished Victorians regarded her as an object for scientific scrutiny. As Elisabeth Gitter pointed out in her article "Deaf-mutes and Heroines in the Victorian Era," "as a real girl, Bridgman became a living laboratory for research into the existence of innate ideas; she was studied, poked, prodded and discussed not only by Howe, but by an array of scientists and pseudo scientists that included the psychologists G. Stanley Hall and Wilhelm Wundt; the philosopher, Francis Lieber; the phrenologist, George Combe; and prominent oculists and aurists; even Charles Darwin was interested in her. At the same time, however, she was mythologized in the writings of Howe and other admirers as a redemptive angel, whose sufferings would touch the most hardened hearts, whose instinctive 'innocence and purity' were exemplary and whose rescue by Howe from spiritual darkness movingly reenacted the Christian drama."

Although Howe was loath to admit it, his pupil never lived up to his expectations. As she had never heard anyone speak, Laura never learned idiomatic English. After eight years of study, the disappointed Howe was privately forced to concede that Laura was "without so much acquaintance with language as a common child of six years."

Howe was disappointed that Laura never learned to speak. Perhaps she would have been taught to articulate had he personally taken the time to teach her. By this time, however, too many other humanitarian causes and projects were competing for his attention; he was absorbed with the education of the blind and the mentally retarded as well as with prison reform, the plight of the mentally ill (with his friend Dorothea Dix), and the antislavery movement. In 1843 he married Julia Ward, an aristocratic young woman from a wealthy New York banking family. Unlike his paternalistic relationship with the deaf-blind mute Laura, who, in the paintings of the period, was portrayed as dangling contentedly from his knee, his marriage to a hearing-sighted woman who was to become a leading advocate of woman suffrage was destined to be an unhappy one. As Julia admitted many years later to one of their daughters, "Life with a Comet-Apostle was not always easy." Nevertheless, in the end, his wife managed to overshadow him, writing new words to an old song and titling it "The Battle Hymn of the Republic," after their visit to a Civil War battleground. Today the protean idealist, humanitarian, and reformer Howe is largely forgotten, except by special-education teachers who remember him as one of the fathers of American special education and one of the first advocates for inclusion of handicapped children in regular classes.

Yet, even without Howe's help, Laura, to her credit, was determined to verbalize her feelings. If she was unable to speak, at least she could make noises, and eventually she learned to make at least sixty monosyllabic sounds, by which she addressed her teachers and friends, as well as the words she did manage to learn. Three years after Dickens's visit to Perkins, the sixteen-year-old Laura was becoming so verbally boisterous that she was in danger of destroying the idealized image of a rescuing angel that Howe and Dickens, who equated her with his latest fictional creation, the "gentle, tender, guileless" Little Nell, had created for her. Howe and her teachers pleaded with her to be more quiet and ladylike, and she promised to behave in a manner that was befitting her image as a secular saint. However, she finally rebelled against them, spelling into their hands the ultimate rebuke, "God gave me much voice!" Fearful of both their reputations, Dr. Howe then had no choice. He convinced Laura that if she felt like being vocal, she should go into a closet and close the door; then she could be as "repulsive" and "uncouth" as she pleased.

This rowdy side of her character remained a closely guarded secret, and in an era in which shy or mute, unworldly females were celebrated in the work of Charles Dickens; Alfred, Lord Tennyson; and Wilkie Collins, Laura was the epitome of the pure and virtuous—and suffering and saintly—woman. By this time she had reached age twenty-one and become one of the most famous women of her time as a result of Dickens's description of her in his *American Notes*, which was published in 1842, shortly after he had met her at Perkins. A highly accomplished needlewoman, her beautiful crocheting and lacework, which she sold to visitors with her attached autograph, were highly sought after. Since there was always a ready sale for Laura's handicrafts, Howe, who could be a shrewd businessman when the occasion demanded it, urged her to speed up her production of crocheted mats and other fancy articles, often at the expense of her fragile health.

In Europe it was customary to display blind pupils in public exhibitions, a practice Howe deplored, although he found that to raise money for his school and to change the public's attitude toward the blind, it was necessary to exploit them. On weekends in Boston, if a citizen found himself without anything to do, he could always amble over to the Perkins Institution, where he could marvel at blind children reading, writing, and giving musical concerts. Glossy green ribbons were tied over the children's eyes to convince the cynics in the audience that they were not cheating.

Dr. Howe devoted the first Saturday of each month to a public exhibition, of which Laura was the star attraction. One of her feats was to thread with her tongue a needle fine enough to carry 120-gauge threads. As she was world-famous, usually several hundred people mobbed the small schoolroom to gaze on her face and to speculate about her unimaginable world. This was a strenuous ordeal for Laura. An avid exerciser who rode horseback and routinely walked six miles a day when in good health, she often became so agitated before the Saturday exhibitions that it was necessary for her teachers to take her on a longer walk than usual.

With the exception of her Pygmalion, Dr. Howe, whom she worshiped until his death in 1876, she continued to distrust men, although she remained a conventionally feminine woman, preoccupied with fashion and her looks. She loved pretty dresses and finery and gravitated toward visitors who were well dressed. Her female teachers found it uncanny that she knew when they were wearing a different coat, even though it was one of the same cut, color, and fabric. They also found it remarkable that she knew who they were when they passed her in the hall. She could estimate the age of her visitors by feeling the wrinkles around their eyes. She could also tell someone's frame of mind by touching his or her face and could detect a person's degree of intelligence by the tonicity of the muscles of the hand. According to a doctor who later studied her, "she possessed a remarkable sense of direction and was so sensitive to vibrations that when the bell of the Perkins Institute malfunctioned, she who had never heard it ring missed its vibrations."

Like many blind people, she hated dirt and dust, which dull the sensitivity of touch. She wished only clean hands to touch hers. Once, when one of the blind students emerged from a room with a dustpan and began spelling to her with dirty fingers, Laura stopped her quickly by pounding the following letters into her hand: "W-A-S-H Y-O-U-R D-I-R-T-Y P-A-W-S!"

Laura went through at least five teachers, many of whom quit after several months of being with her day and night. The constant physical and mental strain of being cooped up with such a helpless, dependent person was overwhelming, and one teacher suffered a mental breakdown. Laura did not seem perturbed by the constant change in personnel. After her last teacher left, Laura's formal education ended, although Dr. Howe asked some of the blind female students at Perkins to spell to her at certain hours.

As celebrated as Laura was, she simply could not function outside the Perkins Institution. Whenever she was returned to her residence in New Hampshire, she became homesick to the point of becoming physically ill, starving herself until she was brought back to Perkins. As the years and decades rolled on, her fame diminished, and she was forgotten by the outside world that had once flocked to Boston for a piece of her exquisite handiwork. For many years she occupied the same room at the school, a small, elderly, wraithlike woman with wire-rimmed, tinted glasses who would remind later generations not of an angel, but of a forbidding figure in a Gothic tale.

In 1889, when Helen Keller was nine years old, Laura died at age sixty of pneumonia at the Perkins Institution, where she had spent her entire life. From age seven she had been the object of almost every conceivable type of

Laura Bridgman threading a needle with her tongue, c. 1885

study: educational, linguistic, medical, and psychological as well as theological. As soon as the medical world learned she was dead, doctors from Harvard Medical School immediately performed an autopsy. The postmortem findings were disappointing. After careful examination, the doctors of the period concluded that aside from some underdevelopment of the areas that control visual and auditory functions, Laura's brain differed "from other brains with which it may be compared to no remarkable degree." Her unfathomable inner world, which scientists and theologians believed might contain the keys to the true nature of communication and language, as well as the origin of the human soul, remained a mystery.

KATE KELLER FELT a sense of hope as she reread the account of Dr. Howe's education of Laura Bridgman in Dickens's *American Notes*. But her elation soon gave way to sorrow. This was 1887, and Howe had been dead for more than ten years. Undoubtedly, Laura's education had been a fluke, a brilliantly successful experiment that could not be replicated.

Meanwhile, chaos continued to reign at Ivy Green, with its clipped boxwood gardens and fragrant rose arbors. Helen continued her campaign of terror against her family, gobbling food from other people's plates at meals and hurling silverware and china across the dining room whenever someone tried to discipline her. She often assaulted members of her family and the servants, physically hurting them. These violent outbursts were usually followed by crying spells and physical exhaustion, as well as an amnesia for the cause of her violent behavior.

The Kellers desperately sought a medical solution to her problems. Although they had already taken Helen to numerous oculists in Alabama and Tennessee, they arranged for a consultation with a famous oculist in Baltimore who specialized in curing "hopeless" cases. Miraculously sedate during the tedious trip from Alabama, the six-year-old Helen amused herself by trailing the conductor up and down the aisles and demanding that an aunt who had accompanied them sew eyes, fashioned from two beads from her cape, on an improvised doll made of towels that had recently become her favorite toy.

The trip, however, was anything but a diversion for the frantic Kellers. After thoroughly examining Helen's eyes and ears, the doctor in Baltimore informed them there was nothing medically that could be done for her. She would never see or hear again. In his opinion, however, they should not give up hope. Helen could be taught, like Laura Bridgman.

"There's a gentleman in Washington, a short distance away, who is an expert on the problems of deaf children. Why not go to see him while you're in town. Perhaps he can help you find a school or teacher for your little girl," the doctor advised the Kellers, scribbling a name on a piece of paper and handing it to Captain Keller.

The man he advised them to see was Alexander Graham Bell.

PERCHED ON Bell's massive knee, Helen was enthralled. This stranger had taken out his pocket watch for her to feel, and she was bemused by the vibration that the clock made when it struck the hour. A burly Scotsman with a luxuriant, silvery beard and side whiskers, Alexander Graham Bell was no stranger to the world of the deaf and the deaf-blind. Bell, who had invented the telephone when he was in his early twenties, considered his real vocation to be the teaching of the deaf. His invention of the telephone in 1876 had been partly conceived in the hope that it might serve as a hearing aid.

But Bell's absorption with the deaf was not merely scientific; it was also personal. Bell's mother, Eliza, an accomplished miniature painter, was deaf and could hear only with the help of an ear tube. Bell's adored, sweet-faced wife, Mabel, was also deaf. She had lost her hearing at five, when she had become ill with scarlet fever. Distraught that his bright little girl could not speak, her father, Gardiner Hubbard, a prominent and well-to-do Boston patent attorney, sought help for her at the school Thomas Gallaudet had founded in 1817 in Hartford, the American Asylum for the Education and Instruction of the Deaf and Dumb.

To his dismay, at Gallaudet's school Hubbard was advised that his daughter should learn the standard sign language, which had been invented by the French monk Abbé de l'Épée a hundred years earlier. Hubbard was determined that Mabel would learn to speak like other people and enlisted the aid of Samuel Gridley Howe, who believed in the oral method, which he had seen used successfully by the deaf in Germany twenty years before. Together they started an oralist school, the Clarke Institution for Deaf-Mutes in Northampton, Massachusetts, in 1867. It was the beginning of a revolution in the education of the deaf, as the "sign language" schools that Gallaudet advocated—like Bell, he had a deaf mother—were swiftly being replaced by oralist institutions.

Like Howe and Hubbard, Bell was a staunch advocate of oralism. As a prominent teacher of the deaf, he was invited to visit Clarke several times, and impressing Hubbard, began privately tutoring the sixteen-year-old Mabel. They married a few years later. Few people thought of Mabel, who was by then an accomplished lip-reader, as being deaf, although her speech, even with the oral method, made it difficult for people first meeting her to understand her. This did not matter in the slightest to Bell, who was enamored of his wife. "The value of speech is in its intelligibility, not its perfection," he once said of her articulation. As his biographer points out, "In their love the Bells found deliverance, Alec from his temperamental constraint, Mabel from her physical handicap." Although Bell knew finger spelling and used it with his mother, he could speak freely with Mabel. "It is no uncommon occurrence for my husband to talk to me perhaps for an hour at a time of something in which he is interested," she once wrote proudly. "It may be on the latest geographical discoveries . . . some abstruse scientific problem in gravitation. . . . Very rarely do I have to ask him to repeat."

During his lifetime millions of people revered Bell as a great friend of the deaf. Ironically, today many of the hearing-impaired view him as "an enemy" and "something of an ogre." In 1880, at the International Congress of Educators of the Deaf at Milan, Bell, a zealous advocate of oralism, had used his authority to exclude deaf teachers from voting, and the use of sign language was officially prohibited in the schools. For many in the deaf community, Bell's edict had disastrous consequences. Previously, using sign language, many had achieved high goals, writing books and entering public life. Now they were forbidden to use their own natural language and expected to use English only, a trend that prevailed until the 1980s. As a result, many bright deaf children became less literate and educated than those generations who had used signs.

AS HER TINY FINGERS felt the vibrations of Bell's watch strike the hour, Helen was, of course, unaware of the battle between the proponents of sign language and the believers in oralism, in which she herself would one day play an important part. She only knew that he was able to instantly understand her rudimentary signs, and she "loved" him at once. His touch seemed tender and sympathetic. "But I did not dream," she wrote many years later, "that interview would be the door through which I should pass from darkness into light." Had she known Bell's clinical observations of her, perhaps she would not have gravitated toward him so instantly. According to his biographer, Bell thought her well-formed face "chillingly empty," unlike the expressive faces of most normal six-year-olds that reflect a distinct personality.

Keeping his feelings to himself, Bell suggested that the Kellers write Michael Anagnos, who had become the director of the Perkins Institution following the death of his father-in-law, Dr. Howe. As it turned out, Anagnos, a Greek who was married to Howe's eldest daughter, Julia Romana, was aware of Helen's case. One of the Kellers' friends who was studying in Boston had mentioned her to him months earlier, and Captain Keller had written Anagnos the previous year, making a tentative inquiry as to whether he thought Helen could be helped. Anagnos's reply is unknown, but encouraged by Bell's suggestion, Keller wrote again to Anagnos, this time asking him to send a teacher to Tuscumbia who was versed in the techniques that Dr. Howe had used to bring Laura Bridgman in contact with the outside world.

After receiving Keller's letter, Anagnos looked over the list of his recent graduates for a possible teacher. One name instantly leaped to mind, even though she had absolutely no experience as a teacher, either of the hearing-sighted, the blind, or the deaf-blind. Only twenty years old, she herself suffered from trachoma, a viral eye disease that had left her partially blind for many years. Despite her visual impairment, she was his star graduate, the class valedictorian who had spent time with the aging, reclusive Laura and who was well versed in Howe's methods of educating her.

From personal experience he knew that she was tempestuous, passionate, idealistic, argumentative, and flamboyant, as well as brilliant and persevering. Her name was Anne Sullivan.

CHAPTER 3

Annie

NNIE SULLIVAN LIVED in a world that was almost as much of a wasteland as Helen Keller's. Annie's childhood had been marked by poverty. Her parents were illiterate immigrants from Limerick, Ireland, who, like vast numbers of their fellow Irishmen, had flocked to the United States during the years that followed the great famine of 1847, in which millions of people had starved to death. Among old, aristocratic American families during that period, the Irish were considered the most despised social group, described by Henry Cabot Lodge as "an idle, quarrelsome, and disorderly class, always at odds with the government," yet easily exploitable as cheap, unskilled labor. Many of the new Irish immigrants eked out a livelihood by digging ditches or working as hired men.

Upon his arrival in America, Thomas Sullivan, Annie's father, an alcoholic, intemperate young man, immediately went to work as a hired hand on a farm in Feeding Hills, Massachusetts, not far from Springfield, where his older brother had already settled. With Thomas Sullivan was his slender young wife, Alice Chloesy, who, unlike her husband, had a vivacious and charming disposition. She was little more than a girl when Annie, whom she christened Johanna, was born in squalid poverty on April 14, 1866, in Feeding Hills. Four more children followed, and whether it was because of the unsanitary conditions resulting from the Sullivans' poverty or because Alice herself suffered from tuberculosis, all but one was sickly. Annie's sister Ellen died of brain fever at age five, a brother Johnny in infancy, and Jimmie, the fourth child, was born with a tubercular hip. Only Mary, the next to youngest, was strong and healthy.

Shortly after Ellen's birth, Alice fell against the kitchen stove, disjointing the pipe. The stove crashed against her, crushing her legs and hip. From then on she could walk only with the aid of crutches.

When Annie was five, she developed trachoma, a chronic, contagious conjunctivitis marked by inflammatory granulations on the lid and cornea, which is the transparent front portion of the eyeball. Until 1937, when sulfa drugs were discovered to be an effective treatment, this dreaded eye disease was the cause of more blindness in the world than any other single infection.

"She would be so pretty if it were not for her eyes" were the first words Annie could remember hearing.

Distressed by her daughter's clouded eyes, which had once been a luminous blue like her own, Alice consulted a neighbor, who advised bathing them in geranium water. Annie remembered her mother's "long thin fingers plucking the leaves from a geranium that bloomed in the window." That was one of her last memories of her mother, who died of tuberculosis at age twenty-eight, when Annie was eight years old.

"Mother had been taken from the bed and laid on a table made of boards covered with a bedspread," Annie told her biographer Nella Braddy Henney shortly before her own death in 1936.

> She had on a brown dress which I knew very well. I had seen it many times, wrapped up in tissue paper in one of the bureau drawers. There was a square of the cloth bordered with white on her breast. In the middle of it was a word made of pieces of white cloth. I knew that the word was Jesus. Round her neck was a green ribbon with a silver cross that almost touched her hand, which rested on her stomach. Her other hand lay very straight by her side on the board. Her hair was in two braids wound round her head. I thought it was beautiful. One of the women told me to touch it if I wanted to. It felt soft, not cold like her face. I began to sob violently, I did not know why. A woman whom I did not know gave me a penny and told me to run down to the store and buy myself a stick of candy. I threw the penny on the floor. I did not know why any more than I knew why I was sobbing. . . . I don't remember anyone speaking to me, or anything that happened afterwards, until my father, Jimmie, Mary and I were together in a big, black carriage. And I was furious with Jimmie because he wouldn't give me his place

Anne Sullivan, age twenty-one, August 1887

by the window so that I could watch the horses. He began to cry, saying I hurt him, and my father struck me sharply on the side of my head. A fire of hatred blazed up in me which burned for many years.

The family had no money to pay for Alice's funeral, and she was buried in potter's field. Two years later, Thomas Sullivan abandoned his children, and Annie never learned what became of him until she was an old woman. She had no wish to locate her father, as he had beaten her so frequently and severely that her mother used to help her hide from him. Following his disappearance, Mary, who was healthy and lovable, was sent to live with an aunt, but ten-year-old Annie and five-year-old Jimmie, after briefly living with some of their father's somewhat prosperous relatives who were tobacco farmers, were sent to the poorhouse at the State Infirmary in Tewksbury, Massachusetts. Because of their handicaps, their father's family did not want the burden of raising them. Annie was not only half blind, she was also defiant and unmanageable. Although his personality was more appealing, Jimmie was in deteriorating health. Pale and emaciated, he had a tubercular growth, which was the size of a teacup, on his hip. Like his mother, he could walk only with the aid of a crutch.

The children entered the poorhouse on February 22, 1876, and found themselves in an endless, waking nightmare. Of the twenty-seven foundlings received that year, not one child had survived. This statistic was perhaps not surprising, as abandoned children like Annie and Jimmie were permitted to mingle freely with older patients with highly contagious diseases. The children's first night in the almshouse was spent in a small enclosure at the end of the ward that served as the "dead house," where corpses were wheeled to wait for burial. The place swarmed with rats, mice, and cockroaches. "Jimmie used to tease the rats with long spills of paper made from the pages of the *Police Gazette* and used to shriek with delight when one of them leapt into the room and frightened the patients," Annie later recalled.

In May, three months after they entered the poorhouse, as Annie was helping her crippled brother dress one morning, he began to cry. Later she was to write a heart-wrenching account of his final illness:

> . . . Jimmie tried to stand up by his bed but couldn't. He fell backward and screamed terribly. The matron, or someone else, came and took off his clothes. He pointed to the bunch on his thigh, which seemed larger than I had ever seen it. He kept saying over and over, "It hurts, it hurts." The next

thing I remember is the doctor bending over him. . . . Once he put his hand
on my shoulder and said, "Little girl, your brother will be going on a journey soon." . . . An indescribable feeling of terror swept over me. It was as if
sharp cruel fingers gripped my heart. The pain made me beat out at the
doctor like a little child in a rage. He seized my arms roughly and threatened to send me out of the ward. I controlled myself instantly.

I must have been sound asleep when Jimmie died, for I didn't hear
them roll his bed into the dead house. When I waked, it was dark. . . . Suddenly I missed Jimmie's bed. The black, empty space where it had been
filled me with wild fear. I couldn't get out of bed, my body shook so violently. I knew the dead house was behind that partition at the end of the
ward, and I knew that Jimmie was dead. . . . I got up and ran to the dead
house. I lifted the latch and opened the door. . . . It was all dark inside. I
couldn't see the bed at first. . . . Then I crept to the side of the bed and
touched him! Under the sheet I felt the little cold body, and something in
me broke. My screams waked everyone in the hospital. Someone rushed in
and tried to pull me away; but I clutched the little body and held it with all
my might. Another person came, and the two separated us. They dragged
me back to the ward and tried to put me in bed; but I kicked and scratched
and bit them until they dropped me upon the floor, and left me there.

The next day, after the staff made Annie promise to behave, she was permitted to see Jimmie again. The attendant put her in a chair next to the bed
that contained his corpse and then lifted the sheet.

The light from the half-window fell upon the bed, and Jimmie's little white
face, framed in dark curls, seemed to lift from the pillow. Before they could
stop me, I jumped up and put my arms around him and kissed and kissed
and kissed his face — the dearest thing in the world — the only thing I have
ever loved. I heard a voice saying, "Come away now. You can see him again
after breakfast. You must control yourself. It doesn't do any good to make a
fuss." I believe I hated that voice as I have not hated anything else in the
world. I went out quietly, I sat down beside my bed and wished to die with
an intensity that I have never wished for anything else.

After returning from her brother's burial at the poorhouse's cemetery,
Annie sat down beside her bed and her brother's bed, which had been put
back in its place. Once more, she "longed desperately to die. I believe very
few children have ever been so completely alone as I was. I felt that I was
the only thing that was alive in the world. The others meant nothing to me.
Not a ray of light shone in the great darkness which covered me that day."

Annie stayed at the almshouse for four years, living among unwed mothers and men who tried to molest her. One, a giant of a man with deformed fingers called Beefy, supervised the dining room, and he was in the habit of fondling her and the other attractive women as they went in and out for meals. "Beggars, thieves, whores, what do you expect? Broiled chicken and lobster, I suppose, and cream cheese from the dairy of heaven. One more word and I'll throw you out," he screamed at the women who complained about the tasteless food.

It was at the almshouse that Annie developed what a friend would later characterize as "a queer fascinated antagonism for men." Although she turned over a bucket of hot tea on Beefy when he tried to assault one of her friends, she was attracted to some of the other deranged male inmates. One was a crazy young man named Jimmie Burns, who ran errands for the asylum. Even though she knew he was mentally unbalanced, she was thrilled by the sound of his deep masculine voice speaking to her and allowed him to kiss her. Despite the warning of friends that he was dangerous, she decided to meet him again. But this time, when she became frightened of him and refused to yield to his advances, Jimmie pulled out a long bread knife he had stolen from the bakery. Only the quick intervention of a male inmate, who knocked him to the ground and told her to run, saved her from being raped and perhaps knifed to death.

While she was in the poorhouse, two operations were performed on her eyes at an outside hospital. They were unsuccessful, and her lack of vision continued to plague her. She saw practically nothing except "bright colors dancing in a perpetual and bewildering procession." More unsuccessful operations followed. When she returned to the almshouse, she resumed her play with the other children, many of whom were covered with syphilitic sores.

Years later, she spoke of herself in that inhumane institution as "a small, incidental figure in a great canvas of human misery. . . . The world of the disinherited is one of strangeness, grotesqueness and even terribleness, and a close recital of the doings of its inhabitants reveals an almost new universe." Her experience at Tewksbury had convinced her "that life is primarily cruel and bitter . . . and I doubt if life or for that matter eternity is long enough to erase the terrors and ugly blots scored upon my mind during those dismal years from 8 to 14."

In the almshouse, many of Annie's friends were "daughters of joy," as the Victorians discreetly called prostitutes. One of them told her that blind people could be educated at special schools. To Annie, that seemed like an impossible dream, until one day she learned that members of the State Board of Charities, appalled by the sensational tales circulating in Massachusetts about conditions at the State Infirmary, were conducting an investigation. Reportedly, the paupers' corpses were being sold for bookbinding and shoe leather and the living inmates were indulging frequently in sexual relations, thereby producing additional foundlings by the dozens and adding to the taxpayers' burdens. Somehow the inmates managed to learn the name of the head investigator, a Frank B. Sanborn. When the committee members arrived, Annie, whose vision was so blurred that she could not distinguish one person from another, flung herself into their midst, crying, "Mr. Sanborn, Mr. Sanborn, I want to go to school!"

Someone asked what was wrong with her, and Annie replied that she couldn't see very well. Then someone else asked her how long she had been in the poorhouse, but she could not remember how many years she had stayed there. Sometime later a woman came to the almshouse and told her she was going away to school. In October 1880, when Annie Sullivan was fourteen and Helen Keller three months old, Annie was transferred to the Perkins Institution and Massachusetts School for the Blind in Boston, where she learned to spell and read Braille. She was ungrateful to the people who had delivered her from her horrific situation and was homesick for her friends at the poorhouse. The two calico dresses that someone had given her when she left the State Infirmary seemed shabby in contrast to the stylish new clothes worn by the Perkins girls, and she seethed with anger every time they ridiculed her in class for her poor spelling and other mistakes. They also made it clear that they looked down on her because she was Irish. Feeling lonelier than ever, night after night she cried herself to sleep. Despite their poverty, her accepting female friends at the poorhouse had been worldly and colorful, and they had kept her enthralled with their stories, as she later told her biographer, of "trysting in courtyards, lovemaking in closets, drunkenness, amours of people that frequented sinister alleys like cats, and children begotten and abandoned on door-steps, or otherwise disposed of. There was nothing I did not hear broadly discussed in gutter-language." In contrast, the blind girls at Perkins seemed like nuns, "sweet, virginal and inexperienced." As for her teachers, she distrusted them even more than she disliked the girls and believed nothing they told her. "My mind was a question mark," she also confided to her biographer. "The years at Tewksbury had opened mental windows and doors, pushed back concealing curtains, revealed dark depths in lives of human beings which would have remained closed to a more happily circumstanced child. All my experiences had unfitted me for living a normal life. I soon became aware that I was different from people around me. I learned quickly and thought myself superior to the other girls."

After an argument with a teacher, she was nearly expelled from Perkins, and it was only through the intervention of some of the teachers who liked her despite her obvious faults that she was permitted to stay on as a pupil. What is more important, after several years at the school, she had a protector, Michael Anagnos, the current director. At first the middle-aged, amiable Greek had found Annie irritating, like everyone else. Dr. Anagnos was absorbed with establishing a library as a memorial to his deceased father-in-law, Dr. Howe, which later became the largest library of blindiana in the United States, as well as establishing the first kindergarten for the blind in the country, and had little patience with such a thorny and difficult student. Still, Anagnos could never bring himself to send her back to Tewksbury. He correctly sensed that Annie's recklessness and anger masked a highly intelligent and sensitive nature. Besides, like many other men whom she would charm in the future, he was fascinated by her. Impertinent, amusing, a coquette, she flattered him, making him feel significant and youthful.

Michael Anagnos's support of Annie Sullivan was not accidental. As her biographer was to point out, "All of her life she has made more enemies than friends, but she has never been in a crisis when she did not have at least one friend sympathetic enough to understand her position and strong enough to make her secure in it."

One of the few people at Perkins with whom Annie had any rapport was Laura Bridgman. When Annie entered the school four years after Howe's death, Laura was a woman of fifty. The school was run on the cottage plan, and for some time Annie was in the same cottage with Dr. Howe's most famous pupil. By that time, Laura, who had become deeply religious, seldom ventured out of her room, and Annie never forgot the sight of her, "sitting beside her window quietly like Whistler's mother as we know her in the picture, with her sightless eyes turned towards the sun, a frail woman with fine features and delicate hands which wove their way in and out through the intricacies of beautiful needlework."

Like all the other blind girls, Annie learned the manual alphabet to communicate with Laura. People familiar with this alphabet, which employs simple movements of the fingers of one hand, can spell with amazing speed, easily translating the essence of a conversation or a lecture to a deaf-blind person. The two women often sat together, and Annie spelled into Laura's hand the news of the day, gossip, and other things she thought might interest her. Although she liked Laura and found her intelligent, even if she was something of an oddity, she privately felt that Dr. Howe had made a mistake in allowing her to become the object of scientific experimentation. People viewed Laura as a curiosity rather than a human being.

One summer, when the school closed for several months, as it did every summer, Annie found a job in a local rooming house. One of her fellow lodgers told her about an oculist he thought might help her. She consulted the doctor, and he referred her to the Massachusetts Eye and Ear Infirmary. Within a year, two operations were performed on her eyes. When she recovered from the last one, she could see well enough to read normally for restricted periods of time. However, her sight was not good enough to permit her to attend a regular school.

Although there were still lumps and ridges on her eyes, and her sight was still not clear, for the first time in her life she could read. "She had always been able to see enough to have a sense of perspective and distance," her biographer reported, "and because of the raised Roman type which was then in use at the Perkins Institution, she found reading easy, so easy, in fact, that she does not remember learning it, but she does remember that, drunk and delirious with her new power, she swept into the newspapers, stealing them after the teachers."

During this time, the members of the State Board of Charities assigned Annette Rogers, an elderly, cultivated woman, to assist Annie financially. Like many Bostonians of the period, Miss Rogers prided herself on her philanthropy. Her house on Beacon Hill was filled with rare books, flowers, paintings, and rugs, and as Annie surveyed her new benefactor's elegant, richly furnished dwelling, she became fond of elegant clothes. One of her teachers, Cora Newton, remembers Annie "asking one moonlight winter night permission to model in the snow in the quadrangle after the reading hour." According to Miss Newton, she was "a graceful, full-sized figure clothed in a low-neck, short-sleeved, long-train evening gown; the hair arranged in heavy coils high on the head, and a long curl over the shoulder. It was interesting to watch her skillful work in making an artistic expression of what she evidently hoped to be and have."

Annie also began experimenting with her name in an attempt to make it sound more aristocratic. One of her friends told her that Mansfield was a name used by many wealthy Irishmen, and she adopted it as her middle name, using it for many years.

Although she was obviously drawn to the world of the cultivated upper class, she scorned one well-to-do woman in Boston whose patronage might have been beneficial. Julia Ward Howe, who by then had survived her husband by many years, was one of the nation's most celebrated citizens when Annie entered Perkins. Her prominence lent an aura of distinction to the school, and many famous people, including Oscar Wilde, came to visit it and to pay homage to her. Julia herself was fifty years older than Annie, but neither her age, celebrity, nor her progressive opinions awed the insolent young woman. Once Annie unsuccessfully tried to organize a boycott of the Saturday morning readings for Perkins students that Julia held at her home, in which she personally read them passages from the *Iliad* in a voice that a friend once described as "richly musical and modulated to the tone of high society." Annie was baffled by Julia Ward Howe's championship of woman suffrage. "You don't need a vote to raise hell!" she once said apropos of "Mother Jones," the aggressive leader of the mineworkers. "You need convictions and a voice!" Julia and her aristocratic, self-satisfied daughters always made her uneasy. She felt that she was being patronized by women she knew looked down on the Irish, and she retaliated against the Howes by responding in a hostile and aggressive manner.

Annie attended Perkins for six years, graduating as class valedictorian in 1886, in a ceremony attended by Julia Ward Howe and the governor of Massachusetts. As she sauntered to the center of the platform after the governor read her name, Anne "Mansfield" Sullivan was exultant. She felt jubilant not because she was at last graduating from Perkins, where she had often felt ill-at-ease, but because she was wearing a white muslin dress with elbow sleeves and three ruffles edged with Valenciennes lace. Mrs. Sophia Hopkins, the widow of a New England sea captain who was also Annie's house mother at Perkins, had copied the dress from the design of one that had been worn by twenty-two-year-old Frances Folsom, who had just married the fifty-year-old president Grover Cleveland. Cleveland, who during the presidential campaign did not deny the allegation that he was the father of an illegitimate daughter, had become Frances's guardian after the death of her father, who had been his former law partner. The wedding of the corpulent, middle-aged president and his pretty young guardian captured the public imagination to the point where the prying press had no qualms about pursuing the couple on their honeymoon with spyglasses.

It was the first time any president had been married in the White House, and it was the first time Annie Sullivan had ever had a white dress, as well as white slippers and a pink sash. She had been thrilled when Anagnos himself told her that she bore a striking resemblance to the fetching Frances. As Annie later recalled, that morning, as Mrs. Hopkins piled Annie's glossy dark hair on the top of her head and with her curling iron made little

Julia Ward Howe, c. 1900

ringlets at her temples like Mrs. Cleveland's, "I gazed at my reflection speechless with delight. I *did* look like the Bride of the White House."

Later, when she was back in her small room at the school, putting away her finery, she wished that she could wear beautiful, expensive dresses every day. "The thought of Mrs. Hopkins' kindness brought tears to my eyes. How good she was! And how much the lovely things must have cost! The thought of money brought me back to reality. . . . One must have money to buy pretty things. What could I do to get money? Here I was twenty years old, and I realized that I did not know a single subject thoroughly. I could not possibly teach, and I had no urge to teach. I knew better than I had six years ago how abysmal my ignorance was."

At twenty, Annie still had no idea of how to earn her living. Should she apply for a job washing dishes in Boston, as one of her friends suggested? The only idea that appealed to her was selling books from door to door, but a blind friend, who had taken a similar job, rapidly dissuaded her from it. At Perkins, along with the other blind students, she had been taught to crochet shawls and mats, but she loathed doing handiwork. "Sewing and crocheting are inventions of the devil," she once said. "I'd rather break stones on the king's highway than hem a handkerchief." Besides, even if she were a skilled needlewoman, like Laura Bridgman, there was no money in it. People had snapped up Laura's handiwork because she was a deaf-blind mute who happened to be one of the most famous women of her time, while Annie wasn't even blind anymore and was a nobody.

That summer she went to Cape Cod with Mrs. Hopkins, as she did almost every summer, and wandered along the beach and wondered what to do with her life. Then, on August 26, 1886, she received the following letter from Michael Anagnos:

My Dear Annie,

Please read the enclosed letter carefully, and let me know at your earliest convenience whether you would be disposed to consider favorably an offer of a position in the family of Mr. Keller as governess of his little deaf-mute and blind daughter.

I have no other information about the standing and responsibility of the man than contained in his own letters; but, if you decide to be a candidate for the position, it is an easy matter to write and ask for further particulars.

I remain, dear Annie, with kind remembrances to Mrs. Hopkins,

Sincerely your friend,
M. ANAGNOS

When Annie read Anagnos's letter, the first thing that flashed through her mind was that she had no idea of how to teach a deaf-blind mute. Undaunted, however, she decided to return to Perkins in the fall to prepare herself for the job, reading the detailed accounts that Howe and his assistants had made about their work with Laura Bridgman. As she pored over the records, she was again seized with self-doubt, wondering if it would be possible for her, a young woman barely out of her teens who knew nothing about the education of such a person, to duplicate their achievement. But when she told Anagnos about her reservations, he amazed her by saying that he had every faith in her. He was certain that she could teach the Keller child if she made up her mind to do it. It was not until January 1887, however, after both he and Annie were convinced of her qualifications, that Anagnos wrote Captain Keller, recommending her for the position and stressing her intelligence, moral character, and literary ability. When Anagnos received an immediate reply from the captain, Annie was ecstatic. In his letter, Captain Keller said that he would be willing to pay her twenty-five dollars a month, which she considered an excellent salary for a teacher who knew nothing about teaching and had no desire to be one.

When Annie set forth for Tuscumbia two months later, in early March 1887, there was no thought in her mind that she was embarking on a mission. She was a poverty-stricken young woman of twenty who had to earn her living, and she thought teaching a spoiled and willful deaf-blind child was the only job she could get.

Although her vision was restored, her eyes were still slightly crossed. A few days before she left for Alabama, she had another eye operation to correct the defect, which was paid for by Annette Rogers, her Beacon Hill benefactress. Mrs. Hopkins and Anagnos, who had loaned her the money for the train fare and given her a garnet ring as a good-bye present, took her to the station. She was carrying with her a doll that the Perkins students had bought for Helen. Laura Bridgman herself had dressed it. A devout Baptist, she had handed it to Annie with spelled-out advice about Helen's future religious education, giving her a note for Helen that was addressed to "My dear sister in Christ."

Annie had never traveled before, but she felt "brave and independent," convinced that she could take care of herself. But as the train pulled away from the station and the familiar figures of Anagnos and Mrs. Hopkins receded into the distance, she felt terrified. "It was the first time I had been in a sleeping-car. I did not know what to ask for, or how to order a meal," she later recollected. But Mrs. Hopkins had thoughtfully provided her with a lunch, so that she was spared the ordeal of going to the dining car, and the porter showed her how to button the curtains and put out the light in her compartment.

When her train arrived in Washington, D.C., Annie was dismayed to discover that the train she expected to take to Tuscumbia had left an hour before. The next train would not leave until tomorrow morning, and the friend whom Anagnos had arranged to meet her train in Washington advised her to go to a hotel.

"I don't know how to register at a hotel!" she told him hysterically. "I have never been in a hotel in my life!"

Anagnos's friend escorted her to a hotel, where he registered for her, and she was given a room. After lunch, he escorted her on a sight-seeing tour of the nation's capital. As she gazed at the fashionably dressed women on the streets, the clothes-conscious Annie felt dowdy and out of place. One glance at her plain dark blue dress and black satin and red velvet bonnet, and anyone could see that she was "a country cousin." The only fashionable clothes she wore were her brand-new high-buttoned shoes, which, as it turned out, were too small and tight.

They had not gone more than a few blocks when her feet began to throb. Barely managing to limp past the White House, she had to retreat to her hotel. After bathing her feet in cold water and washing her face, she lay down on her bed and sobbed herself to sleep. In the middle of the night she woke with an intense pain in her right eye, the one on which she'd had the operation. Inflamed by her weeping, it resembled "a red-hot coal." Her feet, too, were swollen, so puffy that she could not put on her high-buttoned shoes. At that point her courage "flew out the window, and I was seized with an uncontrollable fit of crying. I got out my old felt slippers and put them on—there was nothing else to do."

The next morning, after a sleepless night, she was on her way again. On the train from Chattanooga to Knoxville, she wept so continuously that the conductor asked her when she handed him her ticket if "any of her folks were dead." After changing trains several times, she finally arrived in the rural town of Tuscumbia on Wednesday evening. The thought flashed through her mind that she was "more than a thousand miles from any human being I ever saw before." Nevertheless she was not sorry that she had come all that distance. "The loneliness in my heart was an old acquaintance," she wrote Mrs. Hopkins. "I had been lonely all my life. My surroundings only were to be different."

Kate Keller and her older stepson James were in a carriage at the station to greet her, as well as a crowd who had collected to see "the Yankee girl who was going to teach the Keller child." When Mrs. Keller spoke, Annie felt relieved. "There was so much sweetness and refinement in her voice," she later recollected, also noting that Mrs. Keller's periwinkle blue eyes had a "brooding sadness" to them. And she was surprised to find that her future employer was only ten years older than herself.

Annie thought that Mrs. Keller looked shocked as she gazed at the future teacher of her child, with her inflamed eye and felt bedroom slippers, although she was too well bred to mention her bedraggled appearance.

As the Kellers drove Annie to her new home, she observed that the small town of Tuscumbia was more "like a New England village than a town; for the roads—there were no streets—were lined with blossoming fruit trees, and the ploughed fields smelt good. . . . When Mrs. Keller pointed out her house at the end of a long, narrow lane, I became so excited and eager to see my little pupil that I could scarcely sit still in my seat. I felt like getting out and pushing the horse along faster."

Then at last she reached the house. It was March 3, 1887.

A child was standing on the porch.

Annie descended from the carriage and quickly walked up the steps.

"There was Helen standing by the porch-door, one hand stretched out, as if she expected someone to come in," she wrote to Mrs. Hopkins.

> Her little face wore an eager expression, and I noticed that her body was well formed and sturdy. For this I was most thankful. I did not mind the tumbled hair, the soiled pinafore, the shoes tied with white strings—all that could be remedied in time; but if she had been deformed, or had acquired any of those nervous habits that so often accompany blindness, and which make such an assemblage of blind people such a pitiful sight, how much harder it would have been for me. I remember how disappointed I was when the untamed little creature stubbornly refused to kiss me, and struggled frantically to free herself from my embrace. I remember, too, how her eager, impetuous fingers felt my face and dress and bag which she insisted on opening at once, showing by signs that she expected to find something good to eat in it. Mrs. Keller tried to make Helen understand by shaking her head and pointing to me that she must not open the bag, but the child paid no attention to these signs, whereupon her mother forcibly took the bag from her. Helen's face grew red to the roots of her hair, and she began to clutch at her mother's dress and kick violently. I took her hand and put it on my little watch and showed her that by pressing the spring she could open it. She was interested instantly, and the tempest was over. Then she followed me upstairs to my room and she helped me remove my hat, which she put on her own head, tilting it from side to side, in imitation, I learned afterwards, of her Aunt Ev.

By "nervous habits," Annie meant "blindisms," physical manifestations of nervousness and a desire for stimulation that are commonly observed in the blind. According to an authority on the subject, those symptoms include "an inane swaying of the head, often accompanied by a vacant and meaningless smile; rubbing the eyes or even gouging them for considerable periods of time; shaking the hands before the eyes (in the case of those with some vision); nervously twitching the hands or other parts of the body; swaying or reeling the body; constantly running the hand over objects and a restless pacing back and forth in a limited area."

Annie Sullivan, despite her own struggle against blindness and exposure to the sick and handicapped, was repelled by obviously afflicted people. As her biographer pointed out, "If Helen had been deformed or repulsive this story would have had the same beginning, but it is unlikely that it would have had the same ending."

Expecting to find a physically frail child like Laura Bridgman, Annie was relieved to discover that this was not the case:

> Somehow I had expected to see a pale, delicate child—I suppose I got the idea from Dr. Howe's description of Laura Bridgman when she came to the Institution. But there's nothing pale or delicate about Helen. She is large, strong, and ruddy, and as unrestrained in her movements as a young colt. She has none of those nervous habits that are so noticeable and distressing in blind children. Her body is well-formed and vigorous, and Mrs. Keller says she has not been ill a day since the illness that deprived her of her sight and hearing. She has a fine head, and it is set on her shoulders just right. Her face is hard to describe. It is intelligent, but lacks mobility, or soul, or something. Her mouth is large and finely shaped. You see at a glance that she is blind. One eye is larger than the other, and protrudes noticeably. She rarely smiles.

Annie's plan to win the child's love—"I shall not conquer her by force alone"—was immediately thwarted the following day when she learned the wild and tyrannical nature of her pupil. When Annie tried to discipline her, Helen assaulted her, knocking out one of her front teeth.

Undaunted, Annie persisted in attempting to teach Helen to spell. This process had begun soon after her arrival at the Keller household when she had first given Helen the doll that Laura had dressed for her and spelled the word *doll* into her hand. It was the first word that she had tried to teach her. But Helen's response was anything but gracious. She thought Annie was trying to snatch the new doll away and had a temper tantrum. The second word Annie tried to teach her was *cake*, which she spelled into Helen's hand when she gave her a piece. Although Helen repeated the finger movements, she did not seem to grasp that they meant anything.

One morning, at the breakfast table, these two equally quick-tempered and obstinate personalities met in yet another collision. Appalled by Helen's table manners, Annie refused to allow Helen to eat from her plate, as she did from those of other members of her family. Helen went into one of her rages. After asking the bewildered Kellers to leave the room, Annie locked the door and kept on eating her breakfast while Helen, emitting strange, unearthly screams, flung herself on the floor, and then tried to jerk Annie's chair out from under her. When this attempt to unseat Annie failed, she became curious and got up off the floor to determine what Annie was doing.

I let her see that I was eating, but did not let her put her hand in the plate. She pinched me, and I slapped her every time she did it. Then she went all round the table to see who was there, and finding no one but me, she seemed bewildered. After a few minutes she came back to her place and began to eat her breakfast with her fingers. I gave her a spoon, which she threw on the floor. I forced her out of the chair and made her pick it up. Finally I succeeded in getting her back in her chair again, and held the spoon in her hand, compelling her to take up the food with it and put it in her mouth. In a few minutes she yielded and finished her breakfast peaceably. Then we had another tussle over folding her napkin. When she had finished, she threw it on the floor and ran toward the door. Finding it locked, she began to kick and scream all over again. It was another hour before I succeeded in getting her napkin folded. Then I let her out into the warm sunshine and went up to my room and threw myself on the bed, exhausted. I had a good cry and felt better.

Annie realized that if she were to break through to Helen, she had to get her away from her family. She broached the subject of being alone with her pupil, and to her surprise the Kellers agreed. Captain Keller suggested that they use the small annex near the house, where he and Kate had stayed shortly after their marriage and where Helen was born. Helen and Annie could stay in the large room, while a child servant would occupy the small one and run errands for them. The furniture in the annex was rearranged so that it would be unfamiliar to Helen, and she was taken to it after a ride so that she would think she was in a strange place. Helen's family were allowed to visit them every day, but they were not to make their presence known to their daughter.

As Annie noted, their first day at the annex was a disaster:

She was greatly excited at first and kicked and screamed herself into a sort of stupor; but when supper was brought she ate heartily and seemed brighter, although she refused to let me touch her. She devoted herself to her dolls the first evening, and when it was bedtime she undressed very quietly; but when she felt me get into bed with her, she jumped out on the other side, and nothing that I could do would induce her to get in again. But I was afraid she would take cold, and I insisted that she must go to bed. We had a terrific tussle, I can tell you. The struggle lasted for nearly two hours. I never saw such strength and endurance in a child. But fortunately for us both, I am a little stronger, and quite as obstinate when I set out, I finally succeeded in getting her on the bed and covered her up, and she lay curled up as near the edge of the bed as possible.

The next morning she was very docile, but evidently homesick. She kept going to the door, as if she expected someone, and every now and then she would touch her cheek, which is her sign for her mother, and shake her head sadly. She played with her dolls more than usual, and would have nothing to do with me.

Several mornings later, Helen and Annie were still at odds. Helen refused to put on the clothes Annie had given her to wear, throwing them on the floor. But Annie refused to be intimidated. Somehow she made it known to Helen that she could not have her breakfast until she was dressed. When Captain Keller looked through the window and saw his little girl in her nightgown at ten o'clock in the morning, he was so distressed that he later told his cousin that he had "a good mind to send that Yankee girl back to Boston." The cousin, however, talked him out of it, a fortuitous circumstance, as on March 20, when they were back in the main house, Anne was writing to Mrs. Hopkins:

> My heart is singing for joy this morning. A miracle has happened! The light of understanding has shone upon my little pupil's mind, and behold, all things are changed!
> The wild little creature of two weeks ago has been transformed into a gentle child. She lets me kiss her when she is in a particularly gentle mood, she will sit in my lap for a minute or two; but she does not return my caresses. The great step—the step that counts—has been taken. The little savage has learned her first lesson in obedience, and finds the yoke easy. It now remains my pleasant task to direct and mold the beautiful intelligence that is beginning to stir in the child-soul. Already people remark the change in Helen. . . .

What was the nature of this "great step"? How, precisely, was Annie Sullivan beginning to tame Helen Keller, transforming her from a savage, animal-like creature into a docile child who would become the epitome of Victorian piety and virtue? Did Annie subdue Helen by beating her into submission, as her brutal, physically abusive father had tried unsuccessfully to break her wild spirit? Although this is a distinct possibility—Annie later admitted to her biographer that she was not at all averse to "whipping" Helen if she misbehaved—it does not seem likely. The doting Kellers would have been aware that their daughter was being physically hurt, and Annie would have been dismissed.

Still, there was a nonphysical but far more effective method that Annie could employ to make Helen do what she wanted. She could refuse to spell to a child whose curiosity was beginning to be aroused by the strange rapid actions of her fingers and whose innate intelligence sensed that those darting movements might mean something. Whenever Helen acted like a savage, Annie, by stilling her hand, could instantly cast her back into solitary confinement until she behaved, condemning her once more to her dark and silent—and very lonely—tomb.

Many years after Annie Sullivan's death, Helen disclosed some of her teacher's methods. "Force was wasted on a child of Helen's temperament," she wrote, referring to herself in the third person. "Helen kept biting her nails and one day there descended upon her a human whirlwind who boxed her ears and tied her hands behind her back, thus shutting off all means of communication. It was only when her hands were tied that Helen's desire to express her thoughts became strong enough to enable her to fight her Apollyon. And she did not suffer as much as Annie who paced up and down the room, unable to read or interest herself in anything else. . . .

"There were days when Helen would not give enough attention to the lesson or observe things and movement with enough care. She loved to wear rings, and Teacher would take them from her and stand her in a corner until she felt that her pupil had endured sufficient punishment."

ALTHOUGH ANNIE'S METHODS WERE questionable by modern standards, they worked, and something akin to "a miracle," as the amazed Victorians would soon refer to it, happened on April 5, 1887. At the wellpump between the main house and the annex, Helen's "soul was set free," as she later always exultantly described the experience. That day, Annie wrote a letter to Mrs. Hopkins in which she described the actual circumstances:

> In a previous letter I think I wrote you that "mug" and "milk" had given Helen more trouble than all the rest. She confused the nouns with the verb "drink." She didn't know the word for "drink," but went through the pantomime of drinking whenever she spelled "mug" or "milk." This morning, while she was washing, she wanted to know the name for "water." When she wants to know the name for anything, she points to it and pats my hand. I spelled "w-a-t-e-r" and thought no more about it until after breakfast. Then it occurred to me that with the help of this new word I might succeed in straightening out the "mug-milk" difficulty. We went out to the pump-

house, and I made Helen hold her mug under the spout while I pumped. As the cold water gushed forth, filling the mug, I spelled "w-a-t-e-r" in Helen's free hand. The word coming so close upon the sensation of cold water rushing over her hand seemed to startle her. She dropped the mug and stood as one transfixed. A new light came into her face. She spelled "water" several times. Then she dropped on the ground and asked for its name and pointed to the pump and the trellis, and suddenly turning round she asked for my name. I spelled "Teacher." Just then the nurse brought Helen's little sister into the pump-house, and Helen spelled "baby" and pointed to the nurse. All the way back to the house she was highly excited, and learned the name of every object she touched, so that in a few hours she had added thirty new words to her vocabulary. Here are some of them: *Door, open, shut, give, go, come,* and a great many more.

Although the mystery of language was at last revealed to her, Helen never remembered anything about it. Like the rest of us, she had no idea of how she learned language, although she did not make public this revelation until long after Annie Sullivan's death. Nor did she remember anything about her battles royal with her teacher or her assaults on her relatives and the servants. In fact, she remembered practically nothing about her life before the arrival of her teacher.

"Before my teacher came to me, I did not know that I am. I was a phantom living in a no-world," she later described this period in her life, which she called "before the soul dawn." "I had neither will nor intellect. I was carried along to objects and acts by a certain blind natural impetus. . . . My inner life, then, was a blank without past, present, or future, without hope or anticipation, without wonder or joy or faith."

That Helen was mindless prior to the incident at the water pump is doubtful, however. According to an individual who was close to both women, "nothing could be more false than the notion that before Annie Sullivan went to her, she had no mind, that she is sort of an artificial construction made up of what her teacher had given her. . . . Before she had learned a word, she was using her eager, willful brain. She tried to express ideas by signs."

The seeming emergence of Helen's character at age seven poses complex questions about the development of the brain and personality, questions that are not easily addressed by science or psychology, as very few children other than Helen Keller and Laura Bridgman have completely lost their sight and hearing at such a young age. What is particularly puzzling to students of Helen Keller's life is the startling metamorphosis of her personality that occurred shortly after her revelation at the wellpump. How could a child who acted like a little savage be so swiftly transformed into a child saint? In reading Annie Sullivan's account of Helen's education, however, it becomes apparent that the Helen Keller who was released by language was by no means a paradigm of virtue. She still indulged in temper tantrums, but the gift of language had made her aware that the mysterious, outside world was a hearing-sighted one, and she had to imitate and conform to its rules if she did not want to suffer rejection and complete subordination.

A severely handicapped child who needed people to help her in a world where she was physically defenseless sometimes found it beneficial to adopt the guise of an angel, and Annie Sullivan's description of Helen's tantrum several months *after* the incident at the wellpump demonstrates that Helen's fear of losing the teacher on whom she was almost completely dependent was partially responsible for the transformation of her personality:

> There was a great rumpus downstairs this morning. I heard Helen screaming, and ran downstairs to see what was the matter. I found her in a terrible passion. I had hoped this would never happen again. She had been so gentle and obedient the past two months. I thought love had subdued the lion: but it seems he was only sleeping. At all events, there she was, tearing and scratching and biting Viney [the child of one of the servants] like some wild thing. It seems Viney had attempted to take a glass, which Helen was filling with stones, fearing that she would break it. . . . When I took her hand, she was trembling violently, and began to cry. I asked what was the matter, and she spelled: "Viney—bad," and began to slap and kick her with renewed violence. I held her hands firmly until she became more calm.
>
> Later Helen came to my room, looking very sad and wanted to kiss me. I said, "I cannot kiss naughty girl." She spelled, "Helen is good, Viney is bad." I said. "You struck Viney and kicked her and hurt her. You were very naughty, and I cannot kiss naughty girl." She stood very still for a moment, and it was evident from her face, which was flushed and troubled, that a struggle was going on in her mind. Then she said: "Helen does not love teacher. Helen do love mother. Mother will whip Viney." I told her that she had better not talk about it any more, but think. She knew that I was much troubled, and would have liked to stay near me; but I thought it best for her to sit by herself. At the dinner table, she was greatly disturbed because I didn't eat, and suggested that "Cook make tea for teacher." But I told her that my heart was sad, and I didn't feel like eating. She began to cry and sob and clung to me.
>
> She was very much excited when we went upstairs, so I tried to interest her in a curious insect called a stick-bug. . . . But the poor little girl couldn't fix her attention. Her heart was full of trouble, and she wanted to talk about

This photograph of Helen at age seven, in 1887, is said to be the first ever taken of her. This seems unlikely, as the Kellers had photographs made of their other two children at earlier ages. In Helen's case, if any prior photographs were made, they have not been preserved, possibly because the Kellers did not wish to recall their daughter's violent behavior prior to the advent of Annie Sullivan.

it. She said: "Can bug know about naughty girl? Is bug very happy?" Then, putting her arms around my neck, she said: "I will be good tomorrow. Helen will be good all days." I said, "Will you tell Viney you are very sorry you scratched and kicked her?" She smiled and answered, "Viney cannot spell words." "I will tell Viney you are very sorry," I said. "Will you go with me and find Viney?" She was very willing to go, and let Viney kiss her, though she didn't return the caress. She has been unusually affectionate since, and it seems to me there is a sweetness—a soul-beauty in her face which I have not seen before.

From Annie's account, it is clear that Helen had discovered that if she appeared "unusually affectionate," "sweet," with "a soul-beauty," not only her teacher, but also other people in the unknown outside world would like her and want to help her. Her violent outbursts and physical assaults, she had also learned, resulted in punishment, or worse yet, rejection by her teacher. Although in later life Helen would maintain, along with a number of psychologists, that blindness does not affect personality, she always remained keenly conscious of her disability and feared that if she did not reflect her teacher's and society's standards, people would shun or abandon her and she would be helpless. "The experience of the deaf-blind person, in a world of seeing, hearing people, is like that of a sailor on an island where the inhabitants speak a language unknown to him, whose life is unlike that he has lived," she wrote some years later of her double life as a deaf-blind woman. "He is one, they are many; there is no chance of compromise. He must learn to see with their eyes, to hear with their ears, to think their thoughts, to follow their ideals."

ALTHOUGH HELEN WAS oblivious of it, her destiny was being shaped by a driven and tormented woman. That first year in Alabama, Annie lost her patience and courage numerous times, but it wasn't the prospect of breaking through to Helen that was her greatest challenge. It was coming to terms with her own turbulent nature, her persistent restlessness, which, as she wrote to Mrs. Hopkins, "overflows my soul like a tide, and there is no escape from it. It is more torturing than any physical pain I have ever experienced. . . . I pray constantly that my love for this dear child may grow so large and satisfying that there will be no room in my heart for uneasiness and discontent."

Annie was still childlike in many respects at age twenty-one, and one of her favorite pastimes was playing with dolls. That previous summer, when

With Annie Sullivan in Tuscumbia, Alabama, 1887

she had been living at the museumlike home of Mrs. Hopkins's mother at Cape Cod, she had crept into the gloomy, overstuffed parlor and secretly fondled the expensive glass dolls on the mantelpiece. As she handled them, the memory of another doll, lusted after by an unwanted little girl, had come to mind. Before being deposited at the poorhouse, when Annie had been staying at the home of her prosperous uncle, the tobacco farmer, she had found under the Christmas tree a beautiful doll with bright blue eyes and golden hair that she assumed to be her gift. On Christmas morning, when she learned that the doll was intended as a present for one of her uncle's daughters, she had burned with fury. All her life she felt cheated out of the doll—it should have been hers.

At the Kellers' she continued to play covertly with dolls, hoping that her employers would not discover her curious pastime. By then she was beginning to usurp Kate Keller's position as Helen's mother, and Helen was becoming more attached to her than to Kate. To relieve Annie of the endless burden of being with Helen night and day, and possibly as a way of thwarting her obvious possessiveness, Kate had wanted to hire a nurse. But Annie had protested, saying it was not necessary. She could easily handle all the child's needs. Helen was now sharing her bed, and when she finally fell asleep, Annie would sit before the open fire in her bedroom and croon to one of her dolls. As she sang softly to the doll, Annie imagined that it was "a child—my child, perfect in body and faculty as Helen was not, as I never had been." But Helen was not a doll, but a child, whose personality she was obsessed with molding, and soon Annie would triumphantly describe her to Anagnos as "nearer perfect than any human being I ever dreamed of."

CHAPTER 4

Helen and Annie

P HANTOM" WAS DYING. Progressively that animal-like creature was
being metamorphosed into "Helen," an eight-year-old human female who was partially fashioned from the hopes, dreams, and fantasies of a passionate and ambitious young woman who had never enjoyed a
normal childhood. To the feeble Phantom, who had just discovered an
escape from her "no-world," Annie's lithe fingers in motion on her outstretched palm were life itself. Producing a quasi-electric sensation, they
brought her words that conveyed the sense of a universe that "rang, rippled,
danced, buzzed and hummed." For Annie, the touch of her own dancing
fingers on her pupil's eager little palm was no less exalting. It also signaled a
way out.

But Phantom-Helen at this point understood only the meaning of isolated words. She had no conception of a sentence, an idea, or sophisticated
communication. Although largely self-taught, Annie Sullivan was a brilliantly intuitive teacher. She realized that if Helen was to have any chance
of mastering language, she had to invent a different method than the one
Dr. Howe had used to educate Laura Bridgman. She decided to stop
Helen's regular lessons and to treat her eight-year-old pupil as if she were a
two-year-old who had not yet learned to talk, but had begun to grasp some

of her parents' conversation. The same process by which other children learned language she felt could be used with Helen, only finger-spelling would take the place of the human voice. Annie decided to talk into Helen's hand "as we talk into the baby's ear." "I shall assume," she wrote Anagnos, "that she has the normal child's capacity of assimilation and imitation. I shall use complete sentences in talking to her and fill out the meaning with gestures and her descriptive signs when necessity requires it, but I shall not try to keep her mind fixed on any one thing. I shall do all I can to interest and stimulate it and wait for results."

Many years later, after Annie Sullivan's death, Helen was to analyze the methods by which her teacher taught her language:

> What happened at the well-house was that the nothingness vanished, but Phantom was not yet in a real world. She associated words correctly with objects touched, such as "pump," "ground," "baby," "Teacher," and she gave herself up to the joy of release from inability to express her physical wants. She was drawn to Teacher, not by any sense of obligation, but by the natural impulse of receiving from her finger-motion what her word-hunger craved, just as the infant reaches out to his mother's breast for milk. . . . But the first words which she understood was like the first effects of the warm beams that start the melting of winter snow, flake by flake, a patch here and there. After she had learned many nouns, there came the adjectives, and the melting was more rapid. Finally Teacher dropped in the verbs, one by one, sometimes in groups, but for Helen there was no connection between the words, no imagination or shape or composition. Only gradually did she begin to ask questions of the simplest kind. Earth, air, and water were quickened by Teacher's creative hand, and Phantom disappeared as life tumbled upon Helen full of meaning. . . .

After she had observed that Helen's mind was more receptive when her body could be in constant motion, Annie decided to conduct many of their lessons outdoors. "Our happiest school-room was the roadside or a field or beside the Tennessee River," she recalled.

Helen agreed. Years later, she wrote, "Long before I learned to do a sum in arithmetic or describe the shape of the earth, Miss Sullivan taught me to find beauty in the fragrant woods, in every blade of grass. . . . She linked my earliest thoughts with nature, and made me feel that 'birds and flowers and I were happy peers.' "

It was Annie who taught Helen how to distinguish flowers by their forms and odors, who taught her what a pig felt like by catching a piglet and letting the child run her fingers over the squealing animal. It was Annie who taught Helen how to touch everything gently and to stop pinching her grandmother, whom she disliked. And when the circus came to Tuscumbia, Annie made sure that Helen's experience of it was unlike any other child's. Helen shook hands with a tame bear, hugged a lion cub, rode an elephant, and felt the ears of a giraffe.

When Annie was an abandoned waif, her toys had been the rats in the almshouse, but now she seemed to be making up for the lack of a happy childhood as she taught Helen how to play. Since becoming deaf, Helen had not laughed, and as Helen later remembered, her teacher "came into the room one day laughing merrily. . . . She put the child's hand on her bright face, spelling 'laugh,' then gently tickled her into a burst of mirth. . . . She did it again and again, after which she guided Helen through the motions of romping—swinging, tumbling, jumping, hopping, skipping, and so forth, suiting her spelled word to each act."

Annie later came to believe that Helen possessed a subconscious sense of the physical world, or "the buried impressions of ages of human experience," as she described it. "If a child has seen and heard for a period of time, say, nineteen months as in Helen's case, his mind, it seems to me, must retain images of the sun, moon, trees, flowers, space, moving objects. True, the impressions are too dim to be described as images. The child may not separate them from the mass, yet they are a part of the brain's stored-up equipment."

For Annie, the rapidity with which Helen absorbed language and formed concepts of her surroundings suggested the waking from a dream. "It actually seemed to me as if she were rubbing her mental eyes and saying to herself, 'Oh yes, I saw that a long time ago!' "

Helen's amazing progress clearly thrilled Annie, as she indicated in her weekly letter to Mrs. Hopkins: "I think the most wonderful sight I have ever seen was Helen's changed appearance as her mind found release. The shining happiness of her face was remarked by everybody who saw her. Each new idea grasped was a bursting light through the gloom of the past."

In late June 1887, almost four months after she began teaching Helen, Annie sent Michael Anagnos a report on Helen's progress, in which she observed that like Laura Bridgman, Helen was "very fond of dress and all kinds of finery and is very unhappy when she finds a hole in anything she has on. She will insist on having her hair put in curl papers when she is so sleepy she can scarcely stand. . . . She knows four hundred words, not counting the numerous proper nouns. In one lesson I taught her these words, bedspread, mattress, sheet, blanket, comforter, spread, pillow. I found the next day that she remembered all but spread. . . . This will give you an idea of what a retentive memory she possesses. She recognizes instantly any person she has ever met and spells the name. Unlike Laura, she is fond of gentlemen. We notice that she makes friends with a gentleman sooner than a lady. When a gentleman is about to leave, Helen always kisses him, but will seldom kiss a lady. In fact, I think her mother and myself are the only ladies she will allow to caress her."

At the end of her letter, Annie asked for Anagnos's guidance in helping her teach Helen. He had a "store of experience," while she herself often felt "incompetent to do the work which seems to have fallen to me." But Annie was being disingenuous. As she had revealed in a letter written to Mrs. Hopkins in June, three months after she started working with Helen, she felt more than qualified to teach a deaf-blind mute. Not only was she a capable teacher, she made it clear that she was also a brilliant and inspired one. What pleasure she must have taken in the thought that her work with Helen was rapidly surpassing the achievement of the husband of her archrival, Julia Ward Howe:

> And right here I want to say something which is for your ears alone. Something tells me that I shall succeed beyond my dreams. Were it not for some circumstances that make such a dream improbable, even absurd, I should think Helen's education would surpass in interest and wonder Dr. Howe's achievement. I know that she has remarkable powers, and I believe that I shall be able to develop and mold them. I cannot tell how I know these things. I had no idea a short time ago how to go to work; I was feeling about in the dark; but somehow I know now, and I know that I know. I cannot explain it; but when difficulties arise, I am not perplexed or doubtful. I know how to meet them; I seem to divine Helen's peculiar needs. It is wonderful.
>
> Already people are taking a deep interest in Helen. No one can see her without being impressed. She is no ordinary child, and people's interest in her education will be no ordinary interest. Therefore let us be exceedingly careful what we say and write about her. I shall write freely to you and tell you everything, on one condition: It is this: you must promise never to show my letters to any one. My beautiful Helen shall not be transformed into a prodigy if I can help it.

If Annie did not want people to consider Helen "a genius," it is pertinent to raise the question why her pupil, at seven years of age, was suffering from nervous and physical exhaustion. As a result of overwork, she was becoming so anxious and distraught that in June a doctor had to be consulted, while

Annie herself, who had still not recovered from her eye operation, was also suffering from frequent headaches and insomnia. When the physician diagnosed Helen as suffering from "an overactive mind," Annie blamed Helen's eagerness to learn for her excitability, downplaying her own pushing of her pupil to excel. "And how are we to keep her from thinking?" Annie defended herself in a letter to Anagnos. "She begins to spell the minute she wakes up in the morning and continues all day long. If I refuse to talk to her, she spells into her own hand, and apparently carries on the liveliest conversations with herself. . . . We are bothered a great deal by people who tell us that Helen is overdoing, that her mind is too active (these very people thought she had no mind at all a few months ago!) . . . and they suggest many impossible and absurd remedies. But so far, nobody seems to have thought of chloroforming her, which is, I think, the only effective way of stopping the natural exercise of her faculties."

Drugging the child was, of course, out of the question, and Helen remained, as Annie put it, "all fingers and curiosity." In August, Helen's cousin Leila gave birth, and when Helen discovered that there was a new baby in the family, she began bombarding her teacher with questions about human reproduction, for which the usually unflappable Annie had no easy answers. Nevertheless, she tried as best she could to honestly answer Helen's questions. By modern standards of sex education, however, her explanations skirted the issue, reflecting the age in which she lived, as well as her own ignorance of biology:

> I do wish things would stop being born! "New puppies," "new calves," and "new babies" keep Helen's interest in the why and wherefore of things at white heat. The arrival of a new baby at Ivy Green the other day was the occasion of a fresh outburst of questions about the origins of babies and live things in general. "Where did Leila get new baby? How did doctor know where to find baby? Did Leila tell doctor to get very small new baby?" . . . These questions were sometimes asked under circumstances which rendered them embarrassing, and I made up my mind that something must be done. If it was natural for Helen to ask such questions, it was my duty to answer them. It's a great mistake, I think, to put children off with falsehoods and nonsense, when their growing powers of observation and discrimination excite in them a desire to know about things . . . "Why should I treat these questions differently?" I asked myself. I decided that there was no reason, except my deplorable ignorance of the great facts that underlie our physical existence. . . .
>
> I took Helen and my Botany, *How Plants Grow,* up in the tree, where we often go to read and study, and I told her in simple words the story of

plant life. . . . I drew an analogy between plant and animal life, and told her that seeds are eggs as truly as hens' eggs and birds' eggs—that the mother hen keeps her eggs warm and dry until the little chicks come out. I made her understand that all life comes from an egg. . . . Then I told her that other animals, like the dog and cow, and human beings, do not lay their eggs, but nourish their young in their own bodies. I had no difficulty in making it clear to her that if plants and animals didn't produce offspring after their kind, they would cease to exist, and everything in the world would soon die. But the function of sex I passed over as lightly as possible. I did, however, try to give her the idea that love is the great continuer of life. The subject was difficult, and my knowledge inadequate; but I am glad I didn't shirk my responsibility; for, stumbling, hesitating, and incomplete as my explanation was, it touched deep responsive chords in the soul of my little pupil, and the readiness with which she comprehended the great facts of physical life confirmed me in the opinion that the child has dormant within him, when he comes into the world, all the experiences of the race. These experiences are like photographic negatives, until language develops them and brings out the memory-images.

At this point in her life Annie seemed uninterested in the opposite sex, even though a local physician was attempting to court her. She spurned him, however, writing Mrs. Hopkins that she had "something better to do" than "fall in love with the good doctor":

My work occupies my mind, heart, and body, and there is no room in them for a lover. I feel in every heartbeat that I belong to Helen, and it awes me when I think of it—this giving of one's life that another may live. God help me to make the gift worth while! It is a privilege to love and minister to such a rare spirit. It is not in the nature of man to love so entirely and dependently as Helen. She does not merely absorb what I give, she returns my love with interest, so that every touch seems a caress.

Why had an attractive young woman become so absorbed in teaching a deaf-blind child that she rejected romance and sex and described her relationship with her pupil in quasi-sexual terms?

The answer lay in Annie Sullivan's voracious desire to love—and to be loved by someone—who would not desert her, like all the members of her doomed family. In late May 1887 she wrote Mrs. Hopkins, "Have I not all my life been lonely? Until I knew you, I never loved anyone, except my little brother, and I have always felt that the one thing needful to happiness is love. To have a friend is to have one of the sweetest gifts that life can bring, and my heart sings for joy now; for I have found a real friend—one who will never get away from me, or try to, or want to."

The grateful, helpless child, and later the thankful, utterly dependent woman would never desire to be free of her. Years later, Helen would describe the day of her teacher's arrival in Tuscumbia on March 3, 1887, as "my soul's birthday."

WHATEVER ANNIE SULLIVAN'S MOTIVES, her experiment in breaking through to a deaf-blind mute was a brilliant success. In one of his letters Anagnos had referred to her as "a genius," a label that Annie demurely rejected. But Anagnos was right in calling her one. Her experiment in teaching Helen language was a superlative feat, combining intelligence, intuition, and stamina as well as devotion. In that first year, Helen learned nine hundred words and could write letters that far surpassed Laura Bridgman's writing at a similar age. By March 1, 1888, when she was almost eight years old, Helen knew language well enough to start a journal, which she wrote in pencil on paper fitted over a grooved writing board in a script called "square hand." An entry reads:

> I got up, washed my face and hands, combed my hair, picked three dew-violets for Teacher and ate my breakfast. After breakfast I played with my dolls for a short time. Nancy was cross. Cross is cry and kick. I read in my books about large, fierce animals. Fierce is much cross and strong and very hungry. After supper I played romp with Teacher in bed. She buried me under pillows and I grew very slow like tree out of ground. Now I will go to bed.
>
> HELEN

By the end of their first year together, Annie was spelling into Helen's hands stories from the *Iliad* and the *Odyssey*, Charles Lamb's *Tales of Shakespeare*, as well as Shakespeare's plays and the Bible. She felt that it was better for a child to read a profound work "in all its power" than to have a teacher select passages for her. By the time she was eight years old, Helen was reading Longfellow, Whittier, and Oliver Wendell Holmes's poems.

In an attempt to form Helen's conception of life, Annie decided that she should be acquainted with only the best literature. First, she read a book carefully herself, familiarizing herself with its characters and theme, before sharing it with Helen. To her amazement, she found that Helen "grasped the essentials of a narrative almost as quickly as I did, and her perception of beautiful words and images delighted me."

Unlike other children, however, Helen never outgrew her love of fairy tales and entered the complex, real world. As Annie observed, "she seems to live in a sort of double life, in which the scenes and characters she has read are as real to her as the everyday occurrences and the people in the house." All her life she would live largely in a world of illusions, one that was peopled by heroes and villains and where good inevitably triumphed over evil. "The years have not destroyed the magic which fairy lore spreads over the work-a-day world. Fairy-land still holds enchantment for her," Annie noted many years later. "Grimm and Andersen and the *Arabian Nights* did not displace Fairy-land, they only enlarged the realm."

OUTSIDE FAIRY-LAND, in the complicated adult world of the Keller household, a subtle battle was being waged between Annie and the Kellers for the newly emerging soul of Helen Keller. The Kellers were clearly the losers, as by this time Annie had almost complete power over their daughter. She made it known to the Kellers that she was to be the only person to give Helen words, and she disliked it when Mrs. Keller, who had learned the manual finger alphabet to communicate with her child, occasionally disobeyed her request. She had also been highly annoyed when Captain Keller had called Helen away in the middle of a lesson. "You can see what a bad effect this is going to have on her development," she complained to Michael Anagnos.

As for Kate Keller, Annie rightly sensed that she was expressing her anger by withdrawing from her. Instead of realizing that Kate may have resented her usurping her maternal role, she blamed Kate's increasing aloofness on "a congenitally cold disposition" that prevented her from responding warmheartedly to anyone outside her own family.

"It was only the intellectual side of herself which Mrs. Keller permitted others to know," she reflected years later, grudgingly conceding that "she read widely, and had an excellent memory. Her conversation about books delighted me, and I learned much from her. . . . A discussion with Mrs. Keller was a test of one's metal. An error of taste offended her more than a real fault. I came to admire her delicate poise, and awkwardly tried to imitate her manner. She used to say that complaints and intrusion upon one's privacy should be made punishable offenses. Her rebuffs were not easily forgotten. She was often witty, very intelligent, inclined to exaggeration and mercilessly ridiculing people's stupidities. She was interested in politics, agriculture, birds and flowers. She had to an unusual degree the gift of swift rejoinder and vivid phrase, which I greatly envied. There was in her nature all the best elements of the Adams character with a goodly measure of their faults."

As for Captain Keller, she enjoyed listening to his entertaining stories but felt that "his mind was so constructed that it had neither shades nor depth."

Her dim view of the Kellers was shaped by the fact that they were Southerners. After Annie had learned that her new position was going to be in the state of Alabama, she had initially been opposed to the idea of going south to live in a family that had possibly been slaveholders. Although her friends had talked her into taking the job, they warned her to avoid discussions about the Civil War.

She was fairly successful in avoiding the subject until Uncle Frank, Captain Keller's brother whose sons had died fighting the Yankees, arrived from Knoxville. According to Annie, "this gentleman was as argumentative, aggressive and vindictive as I was. His comments were as a lighted match to dynamite." Before long, she and Uncle Frank were shouting at each other, and Captain Keller naturally took his brother's side, telling Annie that her unladylike behavior was "an outrageous display of prejudice and ignorance." By then equally furious at Captain Keller, she vowed to leave Tuscumbia the next day, but when she informed Kate of her plans, Kate calmed her down and persuaded her to stay. A relieved Helen helped her unpack her things, and soon Annie was so absorbed in teaching her pupil new words that she quite forgot Uncle Frank.

Anything but an obsequious employee, Annie Sullivan was constantly making rude remarks to the Kellers about their fellow Southerners. After one particularly vehement attack on their shiftlessness, Kate was driven to say, "After all, God made us, Miss Annie." But Annie quickly retorted, "If He did, He must have been thinking of something else at the time."

Although Annie eventually came to prefer the warm friendliness of the southern people to the cold, distant manners of New Englanders, she still had no use for the southern way of life. In her opinion, southern women were careless housekeepers, and Kate Keller was no exception. Her house looked "as though a hurricane has past over it, around it, and through it," she carped to Anagnos. Over the years her views on the South did not soften. "The untidy, shiftless manner of keeping house and the shabbiness of the grounds and out-houses were very distasteful to me," she told her biographer many years later. "The only things that appealed to me in the first year I spent in Tuscumbia were the delicious food in the Keller house, the cherokee hedges and thickets, Mrs. Keller's rose garden, the magnolias and mocking-birds. The poverty and wretched conditions under which the Negroes lived, their ragged children, their poor schools, their over-crowded cabins have never ceased to sicken me."

As a working woman, she was also appalled to discover that the majority of southern men would rather see their wives and daughters dead than to know they were employed. Even young southern men, she observed, admired immature and impractical girls and spoke disparagingly of females who were ambitious and wanted to make their own way in the world. "It seems to me the heights of a southern woman's ambition to dance well; and a boy leaves school when he can shoot a bird on the wing," she wrote to a friend.

Still, it had been a triumphant year, as she wrote to Mrs. Hopkins:

> I rejoice to be able to tell you at the end of the first year of my independence that I have lived peaceably with all men, except Uncle Frank, and all women, too. There have been murder and treason and arson in my heart; but they haven't got out, thanks to the sharpness of my teeth, which have often stood guard over my tongue. The arrogance of these southern people is most exasperating to a northerner. To hear them talk, you would think they had won every battle in the Civil War, and the Yankees were little better than targets for them to shoot at! But for all that they are uniformly kind and courteous, and I shall remember with gratitude as long as I live their gentleness and forbearance under conditions that tried the souls of all concerned.

The Kellers discreetly never divulged their private opinion of this thorny, difficult young woman who had entered their lives like a whirlwind. Over the years both they and their relatives were always careful to speak of Annie Sullivan in the most respectful terms. Undoubtedly, one of the reasons why they never said a word against her was that whatever her faults, however hot her temper, she had restored their lost child to them, as well as relieved them of most of the burden of her care.

The Kellers fully expressed their thanks to Annie on the occasion of their first Christmas together, in 1887. As Annie later wrote Anagnos, Kate said to her with tears in her eyes, "Miss Annie, I thank God every day of my life for sending you to us, but I never realized until this morning what a blessing you have been to us." She also reported that Captain Keller, suddenly overcome with emotion, took her hand but was unable to murmur his thanks. "But his silence was more eloquent than words. My heart, too, was full of gratitude and joy."

This was the first happy Christmas that the Kellers had been able to spend as a family, and they all would remember it as a time of love and generosity. On Christmas Eve the Tuscumbia schoolchildren invited Helen to a ceremony where underneath a blazing Christmas tree there were gifts for both her and all the other children. Helen was delighted when she was asked to personally deliver the presents. One child, however, neglected to receive a gift, and as Annie later wrote Anagnos, "She seemed very much troubled for a few moments; then, her face became radiant and she spelled to me, 'I will give Nellie mug.' The mug was one of the presents which afforded her great pleasure. She had chosen her prettiest gift and the one which had pleased her most to give a little stranger. Such an instance of self-denial so simply and so naturally done, is most gratifying in a world of selfishness."

Since Annie had observed a similarly luminous expression appear on Helen's face after she had shunned Helen for assaulting Viney, it seems unlikely that Helen's altruism was completely genuine. Possibly her giving away her mug to the hapless Nellie was not so much a generous token as it was her way of ensuring that people continue to protect her in a world where she could not take care of herself.

CHAPTER 5

"The Eighth Wonder
of the World"

H ELEN KELLER MIGHT HAVE remained one more anonymous
handicapped person had it not been for the support of two powerful men who stood to profit professionally from the world knowing
about "the miracle." One was Michael Anagnos, the director of the Perkins
Institution; the other was Alexander Graham Bell, the inventor of the telephone, whose real interest was the promotion of the teaching of speech to
the deaf in the United States.

Of the two, it was Anagnos who was largely responsible for creating the
public persona of Helen Keller, a virtuous deaf-blind prodigy. In the fifty-
sixth annual report of the Perkins Institution, which was titled "Helen
Keller: A Second Laura Bridgman" and published in 1888, he gave birth to
this legend by exaggerating Helen's accomplishments:

> But of all the blind and deaf-mute children who are under instruction,
> Helen Keller is undoubtedly the most remarkable. It is no hyperbole to say
> she is a phenomenon. History presents no case like hers. In many respects,
> such as intellectual alertness, keenness of observation, and vivacity of tem-
> perament she is unquestionably equal to Laura Bridgman; while in quick-
> ness of perception, grasp of ideas, breadth of comprehension, insatiate thirst

for solid knowledge, self-reliance and sweetness of disposition she clearly excels her prototype. . . . As if impelled by a resistless instinctive force she snatched the key of the treasury of the English language from the fingers of her teacher, unlocked its doors with vehemence, and began to feast on its contents with inexpressible delight. As soon as a slight crevice was opened in the outer wall of their twofold imprisonment, her mental faculties emerged full-armed from their living tomb as Pallas Athene from the head of Zeus.

Anagnos's report unleashed a storm of publicity. Like Dr. Howe's account of Laura Bridgman's education, his description of this astonishing child amazed almost everyone in the country. Newspapers printed carefully posed photographs of Helen reading Shakespeare or sitting demurely in a lacy white dress with her dog on a settee. More frequently, she was photographed with Annie, their pale, absorbed faces almost melding into one. By age ten Helen was world-famous. Americans and Europeans avidly followed every detail of her education, and Queen Victoria and the queen of Greece were said to be among the many thousands of awestruck persons who marveled at her phenomenal achievements. Reportedly Helen could

With her dog Jumbo. By this time Helen was world-famous.

speak fluently, play the piano, and demonstrate problems in geometry by means of her playing blocks. It was also said that she and Annie Sullivan were able to read each other's minds. After Helen had gone to sleep, Annie prepared her lesson mentally. When Helen woke up the next morning, she could recite the entire lesson to her teacher by spelling it on her fingers.

Oddly, this last, supernatural claim was the only one that had some basis in fact. According to Annie, the eight-year-old Helen had "never been told anything about death or the burial of the body, and yet on entering the cemetery for the first time in her life, with her mother and myself, to look at some flowers, she laid her hand on our eyes and repeatedly spelled, 'cry — cry.' Her eyes actually filled with tears. The flowers did not seem to give her pleasure, and she was very quiet while we stayed there."

Another bizarre but genuine claim was that both teacher and pupil were able to communicate with each other by using a type of telegraphy. As Annie explained it to Anagnos, "By means of a dot and dash system I can stand at one end of a large room and Helen on the other and by simply tapping my foot upon the floor I can transfer to her any information which I may desire to convey to her."

Alexander Graham Bell was among the many persons who was impressed by Anagnos's report. After reading it, he wrote a letter to Captain Keller, saying that Helen's education had been a brilliantly successful experiment, which was largely due to Annie Sullivan's inspired teaching methods. According to his biographer, "Bell followed the Tuscumbia 'miracle' with wonder, as did the public after Michael Anagnos sounded the trumpet. Bell himself helped to spread the news, furnishing a New York paper in 1888 with Helen's picture and one of her letters to him. He saw a wider good coming from the dazzling emergence of her mind. 'The public has already become interested in Helen Keller,' he wrote in 1891, 'and through her, may perhaps be led to take an interest in the more general subject of the Education of the Deaf.' "

In one respect, Bell stood alone among Helen Keller's admirers and celebrators. He insisted that what Annie Sullivan and Helen Keller between them had done was not a miracle but a brilliantly successful experiment. "It is . . . a question of instruction we have to consider," he wrote, "and not a case of supernatural acquirement." He interviewed Helen himself to measure that acquirement and pressed Annie Sullivan for explanations of it, especially of Helen's command of idiomatic English. From what Annie reported, he found the key in her constant spelling of natural, idiomatic English into Helen's hand without stopping to explain unfamiliar words and constructions, and in her encouragement of Helen's reading book after book in Braille or raised type, with a similar reliance on context to explain new language. This, as Bell pointed out, was the equivalent of the way a hearing child learned English. And it supported his long-standing emphasis on the use of the English language with deaf children, including the use of books.

Bell did not need Anagnos's report to convince him that Helen was a very special child. In November 1887, several months after the Kellers had consulted him about Helen's condition and after Annie Sullivan had become her teacher, he received the following letter from Helen. At the time Helen was seven years old, an age when most children are not inclined to write letters on their own initiative.

Dear Mr. Bell,

I am glad to write you a letter. Father will send you picture. I and Father and aunt did go to see you in Washington. I did play with your watch. I do love you. I saw doctor in Washington. He looked at my eyes. I can read stories in my book. . . .

Good-by,
HELEN KELLER

This was the first letter in what was to become a voluminous correspondence between Helen and Bell. She wrote him frequently, often signing her letters, "Your loving little friend, Helen Keller," which endeared her to the great inventor but not to his two hearing-sighted daughters, Elsie and Daisy. As time went on, they began to resent their father's deaf blind protégée, feeling that his friendship with her prevented him from spending any time with them.

But then how could ordinary children compete? At age ten Helen was busy raising money to bring Tommy Stringer, a poverty-stricken deaf, dumb, and blind boy from Pennsylvania, to Perkins to be educated. The appeal had begun when Helen's dog Lioness was shot by a policeman. When Helen heard the news, she said simply with charity, "I am sure they never could have done it if they had only known what a dear, good dog 'Lioness' was."

The story of her loss was published in newspapers across the country and in Europe, and people deluged her with offers of money or another dog. Helen said that she did not want another dog but would accept the

Helen Keller, age eleven (top left), with other deaf-blind students at the Perkins Institution. Tommy Stringer, the five-year-old boy whom she rescued from poverty and an animal-like existence, is at bottom right.

money on behalf of Tommy Stringer. To raise money, she wrote an average of eight personal appeal letters a day and wrote newspaper articles addressed to children as well as general appeal letters, never any two precisely alike. While other children were playing, she deliberately abstained from buying soda water and other luxuries so she might save money to give to Tommy.

Bell was deeply moved by Helen's seeming generosity and selflessness. "I feel that in this child I have seen more of the Divine that has been manifest in anyone I ever met before," he wrote to a scientific colleague. He was not alone in believing that Helen directly communicated with God. After one glance at the child's beatific face, many religious leaders felt vindicated. Darwin and the materialists were in error. This wonder child, like Laura Bridgman before her, was proof of the soul's existence.

But there was one person who did not believe Helen Keller to be divine and who dismissed Anagnos's report as sheer poppycock. Although Annie Sullivan had written Anagnos frequently from Alabama, filling his ears with glowing descriptions about Helen's love of literature, even though she was too young to understand precisely what was being read to her, and her saintly disposition ("Helen seems to grow more sweet and loving every day, if such a thing is possible"), she was aghast when she read Anagnos's exaggerations. This was not the first time that she had been upset by sensationalized reports about Helen. She was equally outraged when a reporter in the *Boston Herald* had claimed that Helen was "already talking fluently."

"Why, one might just as well say that a two-year-old child converses fluently when she says 'apple give,' or 'baby walk go,' " she fumed. "I suppose if you included his screaming, crowing, whimpering, grunting, squalling, with occasional kicks, in his conversation, it might be regarded as fluent—even eloquent.

"Nearly every mail brings some absurd statement (about Helen or myself). The truth is not wonderful enough to suit the newspapers, so they enlarge upon it and invent ridiculous embellishments. . . . I expect to hear next that she has written a treatise on the origin and future of the planets!"

After writing his first report, which had made Helen a celebrity, Anagnos had visited Tuscumbia to see this amazing child for himself. He had already received a letter from Helen in November 1887 in which she had nearly moved him to tears with such sentiments as "I do like to read in my book. You do love me. I do love you." After examining four more letters that Helen had written, he was convinced that she was not a fraud and invited her, Annie, and Kate Keller to stay at the Perkins Institution free of charge for several months. His trip to Alabama and their invitation to Perkins were not his idea, however. Unbeknownst to the Kellers, Annie Sullivan had secretly written her mentor, lamenting that she could no longer stand her monotonous life in Alabama, which was so boring she felt like joining a traveling circus, or the Kellers' meddling in their daughter's education. "If you would only find it in your heart to give your poor head a rest and come here and see if you could not induce her family to let Helen spend a few months in Boston each year, you would be doing yourself and Helen an invaluable service and affording me great pleasure," she had written Anagnos.

Their relationship was complicated. A widower of fifty who had lost his wife in 1886, the year before Annie went to Alabama, Anagnos was in a vulnerable emotional state. There is no doubt that he was bemused by this temperamental—and talented—twenty-two-year-old who alternately vamped him and then offered to be his "grown-up daughter." His favorite nickname for her was "Miss Spitfire," which he coined when she was a student at Perkins and there had been a robbery at the school. The girls whom the teachers considered to be prime suspects were called in front of an impromptu tribunal; one of these suspects was Annie, who, predictably, refused to answer any questions even though she knew nothing about the theft. She might have been expelled had Anagnos not come to her rescue by disbanding the tribunal, of which he disapproved.

Later she reported that, as they were leaving the exhibition hall where the tribunal had been held, he grabbed her arm. According to Annie, he told her:

> "Come with me, I'm going to search you. I suspect you of being the thief."
> Then he laughed loudly and said, "What would you have done, Miss Spitfire, if I had searched you?"
> "Scratch your eyes out," I instantly replied.
> "You know what happens to undesirable cats," he warned me, putting his arm around my shoulder caressingly. I decided then and there that I liked men better than women, and I have never changed my mind since.

Anagnos's remarks to Annie sounded risqué, but it is unknown whether they were lovers. Certainly, many of Annie's letters to him contain phrases that might have been written by a lovesick adolescent to her older paramour. "I wish to be near you because I love you and I am happier near you than anywhere else in the world," she once wrote him. If Anagnos returned her feelings, however, he was careful not to commit them to paper. His letters

were filled with such fatherly sentiments as "I consider you my daughter and
I take great pride in your achievements. If you were my own child, I could
hardly love you any more or be more proud of you than I am now."

Still, one wonders why he tried so hard to placate such an impossible
young woman had he not been in love with her. On his visit to Alabama,
after observing that she was overworking herself, he admonished her in a
letter, "I command you not to do more than is absolutely necessary between
now and the first of June. . . . Remember that if you break down, you cannot
be of service either to Helen or yourself."

In his report, Michael Anagnos, while paying tribute to Annie's extraordinary teaching, tried to downplay the sordid background that he knew she
was ashamed of:

> But remarkable and unparalleled as is Helen's case, that of her teacher is, in
> some points, no less noteworthy. Miss Sullivan entered our school Oct. 7,
> 1880 at the age of sixteen years. Her sight was so seriously injured as to jus-
> tify her classification with the blind. The circumstances of her early life
> were very inauspicious. She was neither rocked in a cradle lined with satin
> and supplied with down cushions, nor brought up on the lap of luxury. . . .
> An iron will was hammered out upon the anvil of misfortune. . . . Miss Sul-
> livan's talents are of the highest order. In breadth of intellect, in opulence of
> mental power, in fertility of resource, in originality of device and in practi-
> cal sagacity she stands in the first rank. . . . She undertook the task with
> becoming modesty and diffidence, and accomplished it alone, quietly and
> unostentatiously. She had no coadjutors in it, and there will therefore be no
> plausible opportunity for any one to claim a share in the origin of the archi-
> tectural design of the magnificent structure because he or she was
> employed as helper to participate in the execution of the plan.

Annie was outraged by Anagnos's feeble praise. In an instant he had
turned from a man she could idolize and flatter into a man she could truly
hate. Was he implying that she could not have broken through to Helen
had it not been for Dr. Howe's previous work with Laura Bridgman? By promoting his father-in-law's work, it was evident that Anagnos was trying to
rob her of her glory. Instead of confronting him directly, she vented her
anger in a letter to Mrs. Hopkins:

> The report came last night. I appreciate the kind things Mr. Anagnos has
> said about Helen and me; but his extravagant way of saying them rubs me
> the wrong way. The simple facts would be so much more convincing! Why,

for instance, does he take the trouble to ascribe motives to me that I never dreamed of? You know, and he knows, and I know, that my motive in coming here was not in any sense philanthropic. How ridiculous it is to say I had drunk so copiously of the noble spirit of Dr. Howe that I was fired with the desire to rescue from darkness and obscurity the little Alabamian! I came here simply because circumstances made it necessary for me to earn my living, and I seized upon the first opportunity that offered itself, although I did not suspect, nor did he, that I had any special fitness for the work.

In May, Annie, Helen, and Kate Keller started their trip north. In Washington they visited with Bell, who, according to Helen, "talked very fast with his fingers about lions and tigers and elephants." Then they were received at the White House by President Cleveland. "We went to see Mr. Cleveland. He lives in a very large and beautiful white house, and there are lovely flowers and many trees and much fresh and green grass, and he was very glad to see me." To Annie's disappointment, they did not meet her look-alike, the winsome Frances Folsom. When they met with Bell, he showed Helen a special glove he had devised, on which were written the letters of the alphabet, so that anyone could communicate with a deaf-blind person. But Annie discouraged Helen from using this apparatus. "I cannot bring myself to the mental state, where I can feel contented to allow irresponsible and unreasoning persons to have easy access to my darling's pure and loving little heart. I am sure that while I stay with her, she will never have occasion to feel the solitude of her life, and when I go, the glove, I doubt not, will add greatly to her enjoyment. But until then, I am determined to keep my beautiful treasure pure and unspotted from the world."

By this time Bell was Annie's devoted friend as well as Helen's. "It was an immense advantage for one of my temper, impatience, and antagonisms to know Dr. Bell intimately over a long period of time," Annie wrote many years later.

> I never felt at ease with anyone until I met him. I was extremely conscious of my crudeness. Dr. Bell had a happy way of making people feel pleased with themselves. . . . After a conversation with him, I felt released, important, communicative. All the pent-up resentment within me went out. . . .

The trio arrived in Boston at the end of May. In early June, Helen and Annie attended the commencement exercises of the Perkins Institution and sat beside Laura Bridgman on the platform. But people in the audience had not come to see the elderly, shriveled Laura. They were moved to tears when a smiling, robust child with chestnut brown hair and a luminous expression rose and read a poem with the fingers of one hand, spelling it into the air with the other while her teacher watched the movements and translated them aloud to the audience. According to the bedazzled Anagnos, who attended the commencement, "So rapid were the movements of her little fingers, that the three processes of reception, transmission and expression of ideas became simultaneous . . . an electric play of gestures and of features, an unconscious eloquence of the whole body, and she seemed inspired." Later Helen joined in a more mundane demonstration of clay modeling with the other Perkins students, making a honey jar for her sister Mildred and a cup and saucer for her mother.

Julia Ward Howe was conspicuously absent from the commencement exercises. Undoubtedly, Mrs. Howe's deliberate slight was triggered by her mounting suspicion that Annie was attempting to denigrate her husband's achievements. Recently the two women had become openly hostile to each other. Once, when people were complimenting Annie on her success in teaching Helen, she turned to Mrs. Howe and asked, "Can it be possible, Madam, that the almshouse has trained a teacher?" To which Julia retorted, "I would say, it has nurtured the vanity of an ill-mannered person." As for Helen, the Howes held her in the same low esteem that they did her teacher. To Maud Elliott Howe, one of Howe's daughters, Helen seemed "hoydenish" compared to the "beautiful modesty of Laura's behavior." As for Annie, Maud thought that "Anagnos has made a mistake in choosing Miss Sullivan for her teacher. . . . She has not the right feeling."

After attending the commencement exercises, Helen, Annie, and Kate spent the rest of the summer with Mrs. Hopkins on Cape Cod. Although Annie had a miserable summer—a perpetual malcontent, she was irritated by the fact that many of the people who had patronized her now wanted to be her friend—Helen had a wonderful one. Ever since she had read about the ocean in one of her books, she was "filled with wonder and an intense longing to touch the mighty sea and feel it roar." Unprepared for the action of the waves, she was relieved when "the sea, as if weary of its new toy, threw me back on the shore, and in another instant, I was clasped in my teacher's arms. Oh, the comfort of the long, tender embrace! As soon as I had recovered from my panic sufficiently to say anything, I demanded: 'Who put salt in the water?' "

By December they were back in Tuscumbia, where Helen continued to learn new words and studied arithmetic, geography, zoology, and reading.

Their studies were frequently interrupted, as Annie's eyes were bothering her again and she decided to have medical treatments in Boston that summer. When she had told Mrs. Keller of her plans, Kate wept and claimed that she was too busy taking care of Mildred to devote any time to Helen. The only solution was to hire a substitute companion from Perkins while Annie was in Boston.

This was the first time that Annie and Helen were ever apart. Only one letter has survived from this separation of three and a half months, and it is one of the few letters that Helen Keller ever wrote that one can be fairly sure was unedited or uncensored, as all her letters were scrutinized by either her companion or an editor before being mailed. It revealed her love for—as well as dependency on—her teacher. "I read in my books every day. I love them very, very, very much. I do want you to come to me soon. I miss you so very, very, very much. I cannot know about many things when my dear teacher is not here. I send you five thousand kisses, and more love than I can tell. . . . From your affectionate little pupil, Helen A. Keller."

In the fall they returned to the Perkins Institution in South Boston, where Helen continued to be treated as a guest of the school, rather than a regular pupil, who was permitted to avail herself of its impressive resources, including a large library of embossed books and a taxidermy collection of bird and animal specimens through which the blind learned about the natural world. Although Annie remained her primary teacher, she received instruction from other Perkins teachers in basketry, clay modeling, and music. She also mastered French, reportedly learning it in three months' time without the aid of a French textbook or dictionary in Braille. In 1890 she continued to amaze the already awestruck Anagnos by writing him a long letter in French while he was traveling in Europe. He later commented, "With all my faith in the vastness of her abilities, I was not quite prepared to believe that she would succeed in accomplishing in three months what no child in America in full possession of his faculties would be expected to do in less than a year."

But then Anagnos was the last person who needed to be convinced of Helen's extraordinary abilities. Like Bell, he had received a number of charming missives from her, containing protestations of love, which were signed, "Your loving little friend, Helen A. Keller" or "Your darling child, Helen A. Keller." One, incorporating phrases in French, had especially touched him. It was written shortly after Helen had made a visit to the kindergarten for the blind.

Mon cher Monsieur Anagnos,

I am sitting by the window and the beautiful sun is shining on me. Teacher and I came to the kindergarten yesterday. There are twenty-seven little children here and they are all very blind. I am sorry because they cannot see much. Sometime will they have very well eyes? Poor Edith is blind and deaf and dumb. Are you very sad for Edith and me? . . .

Signed Au revoir,
From your darling little friend,
HELEN A. KELLER

These heart-wrenching letters, which Annie made Helen rewrite until they were correctly spelled and phrased, appeared to have accomplished their goal. In his next annual report of the Perkins Institution, which was published in 1889, Anagnos devoted 146 pages to Helen, and his praise was more extravagant than ever. "Helen's mind seems almost to have created itself, springing up under every disadvantage, and working its solitary but

Helen Keller with Michael Anagnos, 1891. The queen of Greece wept when Anagnos, visiting his native land, read her a description of a rose garden that Helen had written to him in a letter.

resistless way through a thousand obstacles. . . . She is the queen of precocious and brilliant children, Emersonian in temper, most exquisitely organized, with intellectual sight of unsurpassed sharpness and infinite reach, a true daughter of Mnemosyne." As for her speech that no one could understand, he wrote that "verily her articulation is well-nigh perfect. She unloosed her tongue . . . and angels 'forgot their hymns to hear her speak.' " Her compositions "sparkle with perfect crystallizations of fancy's blossoms, which are sometimes huddled in clusters upon the blazing page. . . . It is no exaggeration to say that she is a personification of goodness and happiness. . . . Of sin and evil, of malice and wickedness, she is absolutely ignorant. She is as pure as a lily of the valley, and as innocent and as joyous as the birds of the air or the lambs in the field. No germ of depravity can be detected in the soul of her moral constitution, even by means of the most powerful microscope. To her, envy and jealousy are utterly unknown. She is in perfect harmony and on the best of terms with everyone."

Perhaps because her character suffered in comparison, Anagnos did not describe Annie Sullivan's work in nearly as glowing terms. "She had no uncertain problems to solve, no untried experiments to make, no new processes to invent, and no trackless forest to traverse," he wrote. "Her course was clearly and definitely indicated by the finger of the illustrious liberator of Laura Bridgman. His glorious achievement stood before her like a peerless beacon."

Annie was furious when she read Anagnos's words. How dare he tell the world that she could never have broken through to Helen had it not been for Howe's achievement. And why did he persist in writing such drivel about Helen when he knew that she despised it? In her view, the only reason was so that he could pander to the gross curiosity of a sensation-loving public. "If these statements are correct is it not the height of presumption to ask teachers and philosophers to read twenty pages of matter on a subject which was exhausted some forty years ago by the illustrious liberator of Laura Bridgman! For surely it is these people we wish to interest and not the ignorant masses. I would rather be shot than gratify the idle curiosity of a *news loving public*," she wrote him angrily, "and dear friend, I think you will understand me when I say, that it puzzles me to know why I deserve especial congratulations for following a course which *was clearly and definitely indicated* by another. Do you not think it would be better and juster to let Dr. Howe's glorious achievements to stand as the *goal*, beyond which it is not possible for his successors to attain?"

Anagnos wrote her a long reply, in which he tried to both soothe her wounded feelings and defend the work of his father-in-law. "Has anyone thought of using a way or process differing from his in order to reach an entombed soul? Has it ever occurred to you to convey information to Helen's mind through her toes or the back of her head or her nose? You may say that Dr. Howe did not invent the manual alphabet or the raised letters, nor did he construct any unknown or uncommon conveyance for reaching Laura's mind. No, certainly he did not. Neither did Christopher Columbus form the Atlantic Ocean or invent the sails of the ships which were fitted out for his perilous voyage in search of a vast continent. . . ."

In his opinion, it had not been wrong for him to publicize Helen's case. Society would benefit from knowing about her education and progress: "True, there are persons who prompted by mere curiosity, ask all sorts of questions in a thoughtless manner; but these, I am glad to say, are few as compared with the vast army of intelligent, thoughtful, considerate and well-educated men and women, who are seeking information for higher and better purposes than the gratification of a morbid desire for novelty and excitement. . . . I am aware that your annoyance increases in proportion to the spread of the knowledge of the uncommon talents of your pupil; but you and everyone else have to follow the example of sweet patience set by the little Heroine herself and to make the best of the inconvenience. . . . The admiration and earnestness with which people follow Helen's progress is creditable to their intelligence and do honor to our civilization."

Eventually Annie and Anagnos patched up their disagreement and resumed their correspondence. But their friendship was soon coming to a bitter end, and Helen would be the one who would suffer.

IN MARCH 1890, a nine-year-old Helen Keller, who had never said a comprehensible word except for baby talk before her illness, sat spellbound as she gripped the fingers of Mary Swift Lamson, a former teacher of Laura Bridgman, who had just given her some thrilling news. Mrs. Lamson had recently returned from a trip to Scandinavia, and what she was spelling into Helen's hand made the child feel "on fire with eagerness." Mrs. Lamson's fingers were telling her that in Norway she had seen a deaf-blind mute girl named Ragnhild Kaata, who had been taught to speak with her lips. The instant she learned about Ragnhild, Helen resolved that she, too, would learn to speak. She began pressuring Annie to find someone to teach her, and after much prodding, Annie took her to see Sarah Fuller, principal of the Horace Mann School for the Deaf in Boston. According to Miss Fuller, Annie originally had been opposed to the idea, adamantly informing her on two previous occasions, when the subject of Helen's learning to speak came up, that she did "not want her to speak, the voices of deaf children are not agreeable to me," and that Mrs. Keller agreed with her.

Now that she finally had Annie Sullivan's permission, Miss Fuller began to teach Helen herself by passing Helen's hand lightly over her face and letting her feel the position of her tongue and lips when she made a sound. Helen imitated her motions, and in an hour had learned six elements of speech: M, P, A, S, T, I. She was thrilled when with the greatest of effort, she uttered her first connected sentence: "It is too warm." Unfortunately, no one, with the exception of Sarah Fuller and Annie Sullivan, could understand a word of what she was saying.

"Her voice was to me the loneliest sound I have ever heard, like waves breaking on the coast of some lonely desert island," reported one of Howe's daughters in perhaps the most vivid description ever written of Helen Keller's flawed speech.

After the lessons concluded, Annie continued to teach Helen herself. But Helen's voice still was incomprehensible to most people, even though she and Annie continued to work on it. "Many times," one of Helen's cousins later said, "it was necessary for Helen to put her sensitive fingers in Teacher's mouth, sometimes far down her throat, until Teacher would be nauseated, but nothing was too hard, so Helen was benefited."

While she was taking speech lessons, Helen learned to read other people's speech by placing her middle finger on the nose, her forefinger on the lips, and her thumb on the throat of the person with whom she was communicating, so that she could "hear" what they said. Around this time she largely discarded the manual alphabet as a medium of communication with strangers, although she and Annie continued to use it exclusively as their secret language.

As Helen later discovered to her deep regret, it was Sarah Fuller's methods that doomed her chances of ever speaking normally. "The tragic fact is that Teacher and Miss Fuller blundered at the beginning by not developing my vocal organs first and then going on to articulation," she later wrote in *Teacher*, her tribute to Annie Sullivan. "It was not until Mr. Charles White, a distinguished teacher of singing at the Boston Conservatory of Music, gave me speech lessons during three summers, out of the goodness of his heart, that Teacher and I realized our initial mistake—we had tried to build up speech without sound production!"

The tremendous effort of learning to speak took its emotional toll on Helen. Nervous and high-strung, she became even more excitable and restless after her fruitless lessons with Mrs. Fuller, alarming everyone when she had a fainting spell on her return to Tuscumbia. Although Annie encouraged her to rest, she still had not recovered when she returned to Perkins in the fall, and it was to everyone's relief that by the spring of 1891 her health was finally restored. Reported Anagnos: "She has grown amazingly fast in body and mind alike. . . . She is now 5′2″ in height and of symmetrical figure and weighs 122 pounds. Her physique is magnificent. . . . Her head is finely formed and decked with beautiful brown hair falling in luxuriant curls over her pretty shoulders."

Anagnos's association with Helen was as paternalistic as his father-in-law's relationship had been with Laura Bridgman. "Yes, darling, to me it will be one of the great pleasures of my life to take you in my lap and hear you speak," he often told her.

Ever since her arrival in Boston, Helen had been deluged with invitations to the homes of wealthy, philanthropic citizens who considered it a social coup to have the deaf-blind child attend one of their occasions. A smiling, sweet-faced Helen graced many of their functions, accompanied by a scowling Annie, who usually scorned her hosts, as they made her feel as though she were Helen's handmaiden. Once, when she sensed people were snubbing her, she snatched away the celebrity guest in a huff and boarded a train for home, even though the party was far from Boston and she had no money. A conductor saw to it that they got home safely. Another time, when Helen alone received an invitation to a party, she refused to go with her, which meant that Helen had to decline the invitation, even though it was from one of the most powerful members of Boston society.

The list of Annie Sullivan's enemies was growing longer. At the Perkins Institution, many of the teachers were whispering behind her back. Some complained that Annie and her special student, who were not subject to the rules of the school, were receiving preferential treatment. They could obtain equipment and supplies denied the other pupils. Other teachers spread more insidious rumors. Since no other teacher of the deaf-blind had ever been able to duplicate Annie's spectacular results with Helen, it was said that she was not a "miracle worker" but a "liar."

On May 17, 1890, the *Boston Daily Journal* published an interview with Annie in which she brushed aside Perkins's contribution to Helen's education. "Helen is not a regular pupil at the Perkins Institution, being under the care of a private teacher there," she told a reporter. "I have the whole charge of her, and my salary is paid by her father." Outraged, the Perkins trustees immediately charged her with ingratitude.

After realizing that her words had sounded rash, she fired off an uncharacteristically diplomatic letter of apology to the board of trustees:

. . . The truth is that the advantages Helen Keller has had at the Institution during the past year have done more to develop and broaden her mind than any training I could possibly have given her in years, alone. And, much as Helen is indebted to the Institution, I am much more so, for, as you know, I was educated there, and since Helen has been in my charge I have been encouraged constantly by its Director, Mr. Anagnos. And without the help of my Institution friends, the work would have seemed an impossibility to me. It was farthest from my mind to speak lightly of my obligations to my school; and I beg that though you blame me for indiscretions, you will not blame me for ingratitude. . . .

She also wrote separately to Anagnos, enclosing the interview and her letter to the board of trustees "in the faint hope that it will help you to judge me kindly, or at least fairly, in this matter. At any rate, it will prove to you that I did all that I could to correct the false impression given in that miserable interview."

At the upcoming commencement exercises, Helen had been scheduled to demonstrate her ability to speak. As a punishment to Annie for her indiscreet remarks, the trustees canceled her participation, making the excuse that it would look as though they were taking the credit for teaching her to talk. Although undoubtedly furious at this latest rebuke, this time Annie did not voice her objection. According to her biographer, her interview with the *Boston Daily Journal* was the last time she spoke to a reporter for publication. Still, she managed to take her revenge on Perkins by postponing writing a detailed account of Helen's last two years for the annual report, even though Anagnos pleaded with her to furnish him with a full record. She kept putting him off, pleading that her eyesight was so poor that it was impossible for her to write it, a debatable excuse, as she later confessed to her biographer that "I sometimes used them [her eyes] as an excuse for getting out of doing things that I didn't want to do." Eventually, however, she gave into Anagnos's demands and wrote her account.

ON NOVEMBER 4, 1891, Helen sent Anagnos a birthday present, a gift that she soon would bitterly regret. It was a story that she had spelled on her Braille slate, and in her accompanying letter, she described it as "a little story which I wrote for your birthday gift." Her story was titled "The Frost King," and it was all about King Frost, who "lives in a beautiful palace, far to the north, in the land of perpetual snow." Anagnos was charmed with the story and printed it, along with her letter, in the Perkins alumni magazine, *The Mentor*. At the same time, it was reprinted in *The Goodson Gazette*, a weekly publication of the Virginia Institution for the Education of the Deaf and Dumb and Blind. As given to hyperbole as Anagnos, the editors deemed it "without parallel in the history of literature." Unfortunately, it was soon brought to their attention that Helen's delightful little story was similar to Margaret T. Canby's "The Frost Fairies," which had appeared in her children's book, *Birdie and His Fairy Friends*.

An upset and humiliated Anagnos was forced to insert the following retraction in the annual report that was published several months later:

> Since this report was printed, I have received evidence through the Goodson Gazette of Staunton, Va., that the story by Helen Keller, entitled "King Frost," [sic], is an adaptation, if not a reproduction, of "Frost Fairies," which occurs in a little volume "Birdie and His Fairy Friends," by Margaret T. Canby, published in 1873. I have made careful inquiry of her parents, her teacher and those who are accustomed to converse with her, and have ascertained that Mrs. Sophia C. Hopkins had the volume in her possession in 1888, when Helen and her teacher were visiting her at her home in Brewster, Mass. In the month of August of that year the state of Miss Sullivan's health was such as to render it necessary for her to be away from her pupil for a while in search of rest. During the time of separation, Helen was left in the charge of Mrs. Hopkins, who often entertained her by reading to her, and though Mrs. Hopkins does not recollect this particular story, I presume it was included among the selection. No one can regret the mistake more than I.
>
> M. ANAGNOS

When Anagnos, who was not fluent in the manual language, questioned a terrified Helen through an interpreter, she told him that when she had written "The Frost King," she believed that it was an original story. She insisted that she had no recollection of having read Mrs. Canby's story. She wrote despairingly in her diary in late January 1892:

> Someone wrote Mr. Anagnos that the story which I sent him as a birthday gift and which I wrote myself, was not my story at all, but that a lady had written it a long time ago. The person said her story was called "Frost Fairies." I am sure I never heard it. It made us feel so bad to think that people thought we had been untrue and wicked. My heart was full of tears, for I love the beautiful truth with my whole heart and mind.
>
> I thought about my story in the autumn, because teacher told me about the autumn leaves while we walked in the woods. . . . I thought fairies must have painted them because they are so wonderful, and I thought, too, that

King Frost must have jars and vases containing precious treasures because I knew that other kings long ago had, and because teacher told me that the leaves were painted ruby, emerald, gold, crimson and brown; so I thought the paint must be melted stones.

In the second volume of the Helen Keller *Souvenir*, which would later be published in Dr. Bell's *Volta Review*, Annie Sullivan presented her side of the controversy:

As I myself never read this story or even heard of the book, I inquired of Helen if she knew anything of the matter, and found that she did not. She was utterly unable to recall either the name of the story or of the book. Careful examination was made of the books in raised print in the library of the Perkins Institution, to learn if any extracts from this volume could be found there; but nothing was discovered. I then concluded that the story must have been read to her a long time ago, as her memory usually retains with great distinction facts and impressions which have been committed to its keeping.

Annie then went on to say that Mrs. Hopkins had a copy of the book, and when she and Helen had spent the summer with Mrs. Hopkins at her home on Cape Cod, Mrs. Hopkins recalled having read Helen stories from *Birdie and His Fairy Friends.*

Anagnos appears to have been appeased by this explanation until late February, when one of the Perkins teachers told him about a conversation she had with Helen in the Perkins front parlor. According to the unidentified teacher:

Helen said to me, "Did you ever write a story out of your own head?" I replied I might have done so in composition class. Helen said, "I do not mean that. I mean did you ever write a story out of your own head?" I then tried to tell her that there were different ways of composing; that it could be in the form of a story or a poem or a letter. I then asked, "Did you ever write a story out of your own head?" She said, "Once I wrote a story King Frost from Frost King, but it was not exactly that." I said, "Someone read it to you?" She said, "Yes." I asked, "Who?" Her answer came promptly, "Teacher." I spelled with my fingers. "Teacher," for I could not believe my ears. She said, "Yes." I then asked, "Last summer?" She said, "No, last fall." I said, "In the mountains?" She said, "No, in my own home." I said, "Was it from a little book called 'Birdie and his friends,—fairy friends?" She said, "I think so—it was something about birdie." I said, "I thought it was Mrs.

Hopkins who read it to you." She said, "Yes?—No." I said, "It was teacher herself who read it to you?" She replied, "Yes" and added what I understood to be this: "Teacher says I must not get mixed up, that Mrs. Hopkins read it to me when I was little."

Many years later Annie Sullivan would confess to her biographer that it was folly to leave Helen completely in the hands of another person, citing the example of a relative who had upset all her plans for instructing Helen in religion. The malleable Helen, it seemed, could be easily influenced by any person who could communicate with her.

When the Perkins teacher informed Anagnos about this startling conversation, he confided that it was almost as painful as his wife's death.

Although initially siding with Helen, Anagnos was now persuaded that "a court of investigation" should be instigated. Helen was charged with plagiarism and deliberate falsehood. As for Annie, he humiliated her by sending her a questionnaire in which she was asked a number of questions about Helen and "The Frost King." The first one read, "What does Helen say about the story? Does she claim that it was original to her?" to which Annie gave an answer that he undoubtedly did not want to hear, as it presented a more realistic picture of Helen's capacities:

I cannot say positively whether Helen has, or has not a clear idea of the difference between original composition and reproduction. I do not know certainly that she has ever had an original idea. If she has not, of course, she cannot have a clear conception of what is meant by original composition. But supposing that she has been conscious of the birth of ideas in her own brain, it is not probable, I think, that she makes any wise discriminations between such ideas and others which she has unconsciously absorbed in her reading. . . . Please have it plainly understood by all seekers for further information regarding Helen's story that this is the last statement which I shall make in relation to it, and believe me.

Yours truly,
ANNIE M. SULLIVAN

Helen and Annie were brought before Anagnos and eight school officers, four of whom were blind. Then Annie was asked to leave her and, as Helen later wrote, she was questioned and cross-questioned "with what seemed to me a determination on the part of my judges to force me to acknowledge that I remembered having had 'The Frost Fairies' read to me. I felt in every question the doubt and suspicion that was in their minds, and

I felt, too, that a loved friend was looking at me reproachfully, although I could not have put all this into words. The blood pressed about my thumping heart, and I could scarcely speak, except in monosyllables. Even the consciousness that it was only a dreadful mistake did not lessen my suffering. . . . As I lay in bed that night, I wept as I hope few children have wept. I felt so cold, I imagined I should die before morning, and the thought comforted me. I think if this sorrow had come to me when I was older, it would have broken my spirit beyond repairing."

Four members of the investigating committee rejected Helen's protests of innocence, and four voted to believe her. It was up to Anagnos to break the tie, and he cast a deciding vote in her favor.

Why would the administrators of a school for the blind, who prided themselves on their humane attitudes, subject a severely disabled twelve-year-old to this type of inquisition? Even if Helen had deliberately plagiarized Margaret Canby's book, she was still a child, and children, whether or not they are disabled, have been known to cheat. Undoubtedly, they were punishing her for failing to live up to the image they had created for her, an image of a courageous, handicapped genius that had little to do with the real Helen Keller but one that had brought world fame to their school. Then, too, her deception had discredited the Perkins Institution and Michael Anagnos himself. By this time Anagnos's promotion of himself as the educator of Helen Keller had convinced many people that she would never have been "delivered from cruel fate" had it not been for Perkins. To prove to some of his colleagues who doubted Helen's brilliance that she was in fact "a prodigy," he had no choice but to demand a full investigation of the truth. As Dr. Edward Waterhouse, a subsequent director of Perkins, was to point out many years later, "The extraordinary events of Helen's life undoubtedly raised doubts in many minds. Some professional jealousy probably existed among the teachers of Perkins not actually involved in Helen's education. . . . A great deal was at stake. The credibility of reports that had been widely read both at home and abroad was undoubtedly shaken. The reputation of Perkins, especially those of Anne Sullivan and Mr. Anagnos, were assailed. Some sort of 'official' investigation was probably unavoidable."

As Dr. Waterhouse suggested, it also seems likely that Helen was not the real target. Even before Helen's confession to the Perkins teacher, Annie's enemies, who included envious teachers and the powerful Julia Ward Howe herself, had been hoping that she would blunder. For years she had counted on Michael Anagnos to defend her against her detractors. But now it was obvious that he wished the world to view himself—and not her—as

Helen's liberator, and his support—and possibly his romantic ardor—had evaporated.

That day, Helen, in her unlit, noiseless pit, sensed his estrangement. "When I went into the room where Mr. Anagnos had so often held me on his knee, and, forgetting his many cares, had shared in my frolics, and found there persons who seemed to doubt me, I felt there was something hostile and menacing in the very atmosphere, and subsequent events have bourne out this impression," she later wrote. "For two years he seems to have held the belief that Miss Sullivan and I were innocent. Then he evidently retracted his favorable judgment, why I do not know."

Although Helen, Annie, and Anagnos would meet occasionally during the next few years, the friendship was over. Shortly after Helen and Annie left the Perkins Institution, Anagnos began a whispering campaign against them, impugning their integrity. "And after we, of our own will and contrary to Mr. Anagnos's wish, had left the Institution finally, he declared and continued to declare to one person and another his opinion that we were one or both guilty," Helen wrote in an uncharacteristic display of anger some years later. "Once at the Kindergarten for the Blind in the presence of several friends, one of whom reported the matter direct to us, he said, 'Helen Keller is a living lie.' Another friend went straight to him from us and demanded explanation. He did not deny that he had said that thing, but reported that my teacher had taught me to deceive. . . . That was the wrong Mr. Anagnos did my teacher. That was the untruth he told of me."

Was Anagnos justified in calling Helen "a living lie"? Helen's many defenders included Margaret Canby herself, who graciously forgave her the plagiarism, but nevertheless pointed out in a letter to Annie Sullivan that there were several other instances where Helen had appropriated passages from her other stories. Despite these adaptations or copies, Mrs. Canby insisted that Helen's ability to recall a story that had been spelled into her hand three years earlier was proof of her astonishing tactile memory and "phenomenal" power of concentration. "What a wonderfully active and retentive mind that gifted child must have!" Mrs. Canby wrote admiringly. "To have heard the story once, three years ago and then to have been able to reproduce it so vividly, even adding some touches of her own in perfect keeping with the rest, which really improves the original, is something very few girls of riper age with every advantage of sight and hearing and even greater talents of composition could have done so well."

There is little doubt that it was Annie, not Mrs. Hopkins, who had read Mrs. Canby's book as well as her other tales to Helen. Once the plagiarism was discovered, she panicked and lied about having any knowledge of them. Nevertheless, neither she nor Helen deliberately set out to deceive Michael Anagnos. "The Frost King" scandal was not so much a case of deliberate fraud as it was a fault inherent in Annie Sullivan's teaching methods in which she encouraged a deaf-blind child to use visual and auditory images for which she had no firsthand sensory knowledge.

Many years later, Pierre Villey-Desmeserets, a professor of literature at the Caen Faculty of Letters in France who had been blind from earliest childhood, would present a compelling argument that verbalism or word-mindedness had been responsible for "The Frost King" debacle:

> Helen Keller is, to a singular degree in a person of such keen intelligence, constantly the dupe of words, or rather the dupe of her dreams. Wordiness, unreal emotion and, in the worst sense of the term, literature occupy a disconcerting place in her writing. . . . Helen Keller did not allow her mind the time . . . to obtain all the direct impressions that she might have had for these words that she had too easily assimilated. . . . Whole phrases, either read in Braille or from the hand of her teacher, kept coming frequently both in her conversation and in her writings, and these phrases, which she did not recognize as borrowed ones, she believed were her own. . . . At twelve years of age, she published as her own, with the best faith in the world, a little story which was little more than a reproduction, in certain parts word for word, of a tale read to her a few years previously. She had lost all recollection of that reading and could not remember it again.

Helen was devastated by "The Frost King" episode. For years, every time she wrote a letter, she spelled the words into her hand to make certain they were her own, not words she had read in a book. Significantly, her autobiography, *The Story of My Life*, begins with these words: "It is with a kind of fear that I begin to write the history of my life. I have, as it were a superstitious hesitation in lifting the veil that clings about my childhood like a golden mist. . . . When I try to classify my earliest impressions, I find that fact and fancy look alike across the years."

Five short years after her amazing breakthrough, Helen Keller was still in chains. Her new jailers were the very people who purported to help her communicate with the outside world, but who fought to possess her as if she were an exotic specimen. Completely helpless, a true victim, she had emerged from her lightless, quiet dungeon to enter a society that accepted a handicapped person only if he or she was physically unrepulsive, intellectually and morally superior, and heroic about their affliction.

CHAPTER 6

"Angel Child"

I N HER WORLD of gray silence, Helen began to sense the complicated personality of the young woman with whom she was communicating by code. As she entered adolescence, she became aware that her vibrant, endearing Annie was subject to frequent spells of melancholia, in which she did strange things, such as hiding for hours in the woods or under a boat on the shore. She also indulged in spending sprees, buying extravagances she could ill afford. Among Helen's early memories was going with her teacher to a shop in Boston, "where she was so captivated by a handsome velvet fur-lined cape that she fell for it and spent her slender salary on it."

Helen tried to explain away Annie's wild mood swings, blaming her pessimism, restlessness, and immoderate behavior on her unhappy childhood. When Helen was nine, Annie had told her about her serious visual problems—one eye saw more than the other and both could not focus normally—but she knew nothing about her teacher's years in the poorhouse. Annie had told her only that she came from a poor Irish family and her brother was dead. She would not learn Annie's dark secret until she was fifty and Annie, sixty-four, and it was only then that Helen understood why she had "occasionally felt alone and bewildered by her peculiarities."

In the beginning, their relationship was an unequal one, and Annie wielded almost complete power over her pupil. In all aspects of Helen's life,

86

her authority was not to be questioned. Early in their relationship, Annie had decided that Helen must read only the classics. Once when she caught her reading *The Last Days of Pompeii*, a potboiler of the period, she was furious, pounding into her hand, "Caught, discovered, trapped!" When she spied Helen smelling flowers when she should have been writing poetry, she compared her "to a calf without a spark of expression on your face" and refused to speak to her for the remainder of the day. And when Helen proved hopelessly inept as a sculptress—an art, along with writing, in which Annie herself was gifted—she slapped her face with the cold, wet clay.

Helen made excuses for Annie's abusive conduct. "However, there was an indescribable dearness about Teacher which caused her to repent easily of her cross behavior and call herself the worst names she could think of," she wrote fondly many years later. "She came to me soon after the tempest and said, 'Do forgive me Helen! I can never imagine you as deaf-blind—I love you too much for that. But I should remember that you are a human being, and I shouldn't be so ambitious as not to let you relax now and then.'"

Helen also noted that Annie "could not submit to any fate if it meant defeat for us. . . . Every morning she would brace herself with a resolve that the day would pass happily for us both, and often as she watched the sunset, her eyes absorbing its lovely hues, her heart was filled with a sense of work well done; but sometimes a composition I wrote did not please her, or I could not solve a problem in geometry, or some other stupidity angered her—it seemed as if a thundercloud passed over me."

Yet Helen remained deeply appreciative of the woman who was her magical link to a universe she could neither see nor hear. "She made every word vibrant to my mind—she would not let the silence about me be *silent*," she later observed. "She kept in my thought the perceptive, audible, and other qualities of every object I could touch. She brought me into sensory contact with everything we could reach or feel—sunlit summer calm, the quivering of soap bubbles in the light, the songs of birds, the fury of storms, the noises of insects, the murmur of trees, voices loved or disliked, familiar fireside vibrations, the rustling of silk, the creaking of a door, and the blood pulsing in my veins."

Annie brought the world into Helen's eager hand, and the child, and later the woman, would remain touchingly grateful. Instinctively, she understood and accepted the moody and insecure young woman who "moved among the fires of creation that bring normal personalities out of unpromising materials." Although her teacher's obsessive pursuit of perfection puzzled Helen, she sensed that Annie had high goals for her, whether

Helen reads Annie Sullivan's lips with her fingers, c. 1894.

or not they were realistic, and felt guilty when she failed to live up to Teacher's expectations. "From bits of talk I caught on her fingers, I know that in her mind there were lovely visions, now radiant, now dimmed through disappointment of an 'angel child,' 'a maiden fair and full of grace,' 'a young woman pleading the cause of the unfortunate with a natural voice' and other images whose non-realization makes tears start to my eyes."

As she grew older, Helen came to believe that Annie's fanatical pursuit of excellence stemmed from her love of physical beauty. "Annie Sullivan was born for refined surroundings, fastidious living, artistic and intellectual self-expression," she later wrote. "She was proud of work as embodying the dignity of man and could not bear to see it ill done. An ugliness in human beings or in places afflicted her, deformity repelled her, although her compassionate heart was ready to minister to its victims. . . . She was so sensitive to comely faces, splendor in landscapes, and beauty in art that sometimes she actually shed tears. It wounded her to have a handsome vase or a daintily carved statuette broken, just as if it were alive. . . ."

Like Helen, Annie was completely mortified by "The Frost King" debacle. It had tarnished both their public images, the ones she had so painstakingly created of Helen as the "angel child" and of herself as the "miracle worker." Neither she nor Helen ever wanted to return to the Perkins Institution, although Annie, hoping for a rapprochement, still occasionally corresponded with Anagnos. For months they hid out in Tuscumbia, only to discover that even in the isolation of rural Alabama, they made good news copy. The newspapers were reporting that Helen was a "wreck," "broken down mentally and physically," "given over to melancholy," and "dwelling constantly on the thought of death." Although they both denied the report, it was obvious to Annie that Helen was despondent, and Annie temporarily halted their regular lessons. As an antidote to her own anxiety and depression, she sought release in hair-raising horseback rides through the woods. As Helen later observed, "Teacher was wounded by the impeachment of my honesty by those who would not recognize that all children, blind or seeing, learn to put their ideas into words by imitation and assimilation, and she was embarrassed, as she had so often been, by the remembrance of her own imperfect education."

"I was very glad to get in the country for a while . . . then I collapsed," Annie wrote to John Hitz, Bell's secretary, in November 1892. "Helen was very complaining. . . . The excitement of the last few weeks in Boston had overtaxed her strength; but we thought the pure mountain air and perfect quiet would soon restore her health and spirit. But the days passed and we failed to see any change in her. She remained pale and listless—taking very little interest in her surroundings. Even her books were neglected. She would sit in the same place for hours without speaking and in every way was so unlike her own bright self that a great anxiety took possession of my heart. . . . I have tried several times to persuade her to write to Miss Canby; but without success. She seems to shrink from any reference to the sad experience with which that kind lady's name is connected."

Traumatized by the plagiarism charge, Helen, in the midst of a conversation or a letter she was writing, would spell to Annie, "I am not sure it is mine." To help restore her self-confidence, Annie persuaded her to write a brief account of her life for the children's magazine *Youth's Companion*. "I wrote timidly, fearfully, but resolutely, urged on by Teacher who knew that if I persevered, I should find my mental foothold again and get a grip on my faculties," she later wrote in *The Story of My Life*. Nevertheless, her piece, titled "My Story," which was published in the January 4, 1894, issue, begins with this disclaimer: "Written wholly without help of any sort by a deaf and blind girl, twelve years old. . . ."

In 1887, Alexander Graham Bell had founded and endowed the Volta Bureau in Washington, D.C., "for the increase and diffusion of knowledge relating to the deaf" with the Volta prize money he had received from the

French for the invention of the telephone. But not even the publication of the *Helen Keller Souvenir* in 1892 by his prestigious *Volta Review*, in which there appeared a complete account of Helen's education, could restore their self-esteem. In an attempt to set the record straight, Margaret Canby's story and Helen's were printed in their entirety. There were also statements by Helen and Annie, as well as a poem written by Miss Canby. Dedicated to Helen, it expressed the author's faith in her honesty and integrity.

Helen's loveliness was one of her chief assets, and Annie had let Hitz arrange for some new, carefully posed studio photographs in the hope that they would sway public opinion. The results were gratifying, but then photographs of Helen were usually flattering. She was extraordinarily photogenic, and in the several thousand photographs that would be made of her during her long life, she seldom looked unattractive, or, for that matter, disabled. Annie thought that one picture, with Helen's "head bent slightly downwards," looked exactly like St. Cecilia. She instructed Hitz to send it to Anagnos "with my compliments." Anagnos's reaction, as he gazed at the image of the angelic girl he had helped make world-famous, is unknown. Possibly he did not acknowledge the receipt of the photograph because the draft of Helen's autobiographical sketch for the *Companion* that Annie had previously sent him did not mention his or Perkins's contribution to her education.

In the summer of 1893 Helen and Annie traveled to Washington for the second inauguration of President Cleveland and then visited Niagara Falls, where Helen was amazed by the "water that I felt rushing and plunging with impetuous fury at my feet. It seemed as if it were some living thing rushing into some terrible fate. One feels helpless and overwhelmed in the presence of such a vast force."

Then, with Alexander Graham Bell as their personal guide, Helen and Annie visited the 1893 World's Columbian Exposition in Chicago. They stayed three weeks at the exposition, which was a celebration of the discovery of the New World four hundred years before and a testimony to the scientific and artistic progress of the nineteenth century. Helen created a sensation as she was escorted through the fabulous White City, which was composed of some 150 glistening white buildings of classic Greek style that were built by the leading architects of the period and surrounded by a beautiful man-made lake.

Stardom has been called the intersection of personality with history, and Helen Keller's rise to fame coincided with the dawn of modern communication. People flocked to gaze at this famous deaf-blind girl whose

Age thirteen, c. 1893

breakthrough into the daylight of language and consciousness and knowing was every bit as astonishing as the fabulous recent invention of her companion, one that enabled a person to talk with his family, friends, or business associates over large distances. In the early 1890s, the telephone system was still in its infancy. Only 200,000 to 300,000 people in the United States owned a telephone, for which Bell had received a patent in 1876. The initial link in the national network, between New York and Boston, had been put into service in March 1884. On October 18, 1892, Bell had opened the first telephone line from New York to Chicago.

Unlike ordinary visitors, Helen was permitted to touch all the exhibits, from a Viking ship to African diamonds to French bronzes, which reminded her of "angel visions which the artist had caught and bound in earthly forms." Bell himself showed her the telephones and phonographs in the Electrical Building, explaining to her "how it is possible to send a message on wires that mock space and outrun time, and like Prometheus, to draw fire from the sky."

According to one of Helen's friends, "More than anyone else, during those [early] years, it was Alexander Graham Bell who gave Helen her first conception of the progress of mankind, telling her about science." His biographer provided more detail about her scientific education, writing that

> Bell thrilled her with stories that paralleled the Greek epics she loved, Promethean tales like that of the laying of the Atlantic cable. One day he placed her hand on a telephone pole and asked her what it meant to her, then explained that the wires it carried sang of life and death, war and finance, fear and joy, failure and success, that they pierced the barriers of space and touched mind to mind throughout the world.
>
> But Bell's mind, and Helen's through his, responded to nature too. Once, beneath an oak, he placed her hand on the trunk, and she felt the soft crepitation of raindrops on the leaves. Then, on another day, he went with her to Niagara Falls and put her hand on the hotel window pane so that she could sense the thunder of the river plunging over its shuddering escarpment.

Bell had defended Helen and Annie during "The Frost King" incident, telling their detractors that "our most original compositions are composed exclusively of expressions derived from others." According to his biographer, "he also observed that Anagnos had 'failed to grasp the importance of the Frost King incident' and that 'a full investigation will throw light on the manner in which Helen has acquired her marvelous knowledge of language—and do much good.' "

For the vast crowds at the World's Columbian Exposition, there were several other side attractions besides a chance encounter with the famous Helen Keller strolling arm-in-arm with the equally celebrated Dr. Bell. A visitor to the exposition, apart from admiring Daniel Chester French's sculpture *Republic*, symbolizing America, and Mary Cassatt's mural for the Women's Building, could enjoy a meal at one of the new-fashioned restaurants that were entirely self-service and called "cafeterias" or "conscience joints," as they were nicknamed by some customers who were on their honor to tally up their own bills. At these modern eateries they could order Adolph Coor's prize-winning Golden Select beer or a treat of caramel popcorn and peanuts, with the vaguely exciting name of Cracker Jack. Then, after finishing their meal, they could ride in a strange-looking contraption called the Ferris wheel, the brainchild of inventor George W. G. Ferris, in which dozens of passengers stood in each of the thirty-six boxes attached to a giant wheel 250 feet in diameter and were carried up and around the wheel.

Another diversion was a female dancer, "Little Egypt," who shocked the ladies in the audience by wearing silk trousers and doing an undulating "hoochee-coochee dance."

Perhaps the biggest draw at the exposition was German weight lifter Eugene Sandow, who had been causing yawns in a vaudeville show in New York until he had been brought to Chicago by Flo Ziegfeld amid clouds of ballyhoo. After announcing that any female in the audience who contributed three hundred dollars to charity could feel Sandow's bulging muscles, Ziegfeld opened a brand-new show in which the strong man lifted pianos, let horses trample on him, and wrestled drugged lions. It was the showman's first great promotional success. Sandow's vaudeville mighty-man feats were so successful that by the following year, when he was photographed wearing only a fig leaf as he strained to topple a pillar, he was one of the best-known people in the United States.

Had it not been for the financial generosity of several philanthropists whom Annie and Helen were cultivating, Helen would have met with a similar fate as Sandow, parading her exotic disability before an avid public.

When Helen was studying at Perkins, Captain Keller had lost his job as U.S. marshal from North Alabama after Benjamin Harrison, a Republican, defeated Grover Cleveland, a Democrat, in the 1888 presidential election. In desperate financial straits, he had written to Anagnos, demanding that he be granted entire control of his daughter's income from whatever source. He also wrote that he would have no choice but to exhibit Helen for money if he found no other way to meet his obligations.

A few years before, B. F. Keith, who had joined forces with E. F. Albee in 1885 to create the most powerful of the vaudeville chains, had offered to pay Helen five hundred dollars a week to appear on his circuit. The only reason that Helen was not exhibited like P. T. Barnum's sensational assortment of midgets, bearded ladies, and the Siamese twins Chang and Eng was because of Kate Keller's violent objections to her daughter being displayed publicly as a curiosity. As Helen reminded her sister Mildred many years later, her mother had written "a heartbroken letter to Teacher declaring that she would die before she would let this happen."

As for Annie, Captain Keller had done his best to exploit her as well. He had not paid a dollar of her salary since the day that she, Helen, and his wife had departed for Boston in June 1888. Anagnos had paid all their train fares, and as a result of his financial support, Helen and Annie were able to live at the Perkins Institution free of charge. When they had an emergency or wished a vacation, they were forced to depend on the largesse of their large circle of philanthropist friends, which by this time included John S.

Spaulding; Mrs. John Pierpont Morgan; Alexander Graham Bell and his wife, Mabel; William Wade; and Annette P. Rogers.

With Anagnos's defection, they were more dependent than ever on the generosity of the very wealthy. Fortunately, they had a major new benefactor, John S. Spaulding, an elderly bachelor who was known as "the Sugar King" of Boston and who was famous for his philanthropies (he was one of the first men in the city to give a share in his sugar company to his employees) and for his love of fetching little girls (another of his protégées was the famous child actress Elsie Leslie Lyde, upon whom he also showered boxes of roses and sweets). Helen and Annie had met Spaulding when they sponsored a tea for the Kindergarten for the Blind at the luxurious Beacon Street home of his sister-in-law. An unstinting friend, Spaulding gave them money and luxuries and loaned the impecunious Captain Keller fifteen thousand dollars. Spaulding also promised to provide for Helen for the rest of her life. According to Helen, Spaulding had wanted to send them to Europe one summer, but Annie, who was an accomplished rider, announced that she wanted a horse instead. He sent her a beautiful Kentucky saddle horse that cost three hundred fifty dollars but that was killed the following winter by a railroad train in Tuscumbia. To Helen's ire, her father collected damages but did not pay Annie the back wages he owed her.

After attending the World's Columbian Exposition, Helen and Annie stayed for three months at the estate of another philanthropist friend, William Wade. Wade was a benefactor to many deaf-blind individuals, furnishing them individually with books, bicycles, vacations, and other luxuries to alleviate their loneliness. He had originally contacted Helen when he read a letter she had written in a children's magazine in which she described her small dog. Wade felt that as a blind child, Helen needed a mastiff, and he sent her one. When the ill-fated Lioness was shot by a policeman shortly after its arrival in Alabama, Wade sent her a second mastiff, named Lion, who was soon put to death by Captain Keller after it had bitten Annie Sullivan.

Wade never forgot their first meeting in Pittsburgh, when Helen, who had a remarkable sense of smell, had recognized him instantly. "He met us at the train . . . and I recognized him at once by the tobacco he used, the scent of which had permeated the letters he sent me," she later recalled.

Fascinated by deafness, Wade published a monograph in 1901, *The Deaf-Blind,* which was the first attempt to compile a roster of deaf-blind individuals in the United States, detailing their education and accomplishments.

After observing Helen during her frequent visits to his home in Hulton, Pennsylvania, Wade concluded that she had a more loving, unselfish disposition than the fictional Little Lord Fauntleroy, whom many people found unbelievable. He wrote to Anagnos that he was convinced she was "superior even to the creation of Mrs. Burnett's pen."

At his home, Helen was taught Latin and higher mathematics by a neighbor, Rev. Dr. John D. Irons, a Presbyterian minister who was an excellent Latin and Greek scholar. "It was my wish that she should go to some good school with seeing girls of her own age, but her father was unable to pay the expenses, and our good friend Mr. Wade proposed our coming here," Annie wrote to Hitz. "Of course a school would be better in many ways; but this arrangement is better than staying in Tuscumbia. Captain Keller's affairs are far from satisfactory. Indeed I hardly see how they are going to make both ends meet this winter."

A woman who could be charming and flirtatious when it came to persuading a male to come to her financial aid, Annie convinced Bell that he should pay their way to attend conventions of the deaf. In the summer of 1894 Annie and Helen attended the meeting of Dr. Bell's American Association to Promote the Teaching of Speech to the Deaf in Chautauqua, New York. At this conference Annie was scheduled to read her paper "The Instruction of Helen Keller." Always ill at ease in new social situations and, of course, aware that many people in the audience felt she was a charlatan, she was suddenly overcome with stage fright, and Bell himself had to give the speech for her. This was undoubtedly to her benefit, as his delivery of her address amounted to his endorsement of both her as an individual and her teaching methods. Through her admirer and mentor Bell, Annie attempted to set the record straight about Helen's true personality and accomplishments:

> Much has been said and written about Helen Keller, too much, I think, has appeared in type. One can scarcely take up a newspaper or a magazine without finding a more or less exaggerated account of her so-called "marvelous accomplishments" which I believe consist only in her being able to speak and write the language of her country with greater ease and fluency than the average seeing and hearing child of her age. . . . Helen's case, because of the peculiar circumstances which attend it, appeals to our sense of wonder, and, as this is one of the deep-rooted instincts of human nature, such appeals are seldom in vain; they command the attention even of those who would fain deny the possibility of achievements which have been claimed for my pupil. It is easier for the credulous to say, "She is a miracle,

With Annie Sullivan and Alexander Graham Bell while attending a meeting of the American Association to Promote the Teaching of Speech to the Deaf at Chautauqua, New York, 1894. They are simultaneously using three modes of communication: spoken language between Annie and Dr. Bell, the manual alphabet between Helen and Dr. Bell, and lipreading between Helen and Annie.

and her teacher is another miracle," and for the unbelievers to declare, "Such things cannot be; we are being imposed upon," than to make a conscientious study of the principles involved in her education. . . .

I shall also have cause for gratification if I succeed in convincing you that Helen Keller is neither a "phenomenal child," "an intellectual prodigy," nor an "extraordinary genius" but simply a very bright and lovely child, unmarred by self-consciousness or any taint of evil. Every thought mirrored on her beautiful face, beaming with intelligence and affection, is a fresh joy, and this workaday world seems fairer and brighter because she is in it. . . .

It is Helen's loving and sympathetic heart rather than her bright intellect which endears her to everybody with whom she comes in contact. She impresses me every day as being the happiest child in the world, and so it is a special privilege to be with her. The spirit of love and joyousness seems never to leave her. May it ever be so. It is beautiful to think of a nature so gentle, pure, and loving as hers; it is pleasant also to think she will ever see only the best side of every human being. While near her, the roughest man is all gentleness, all pity; not for the world would he have her know that he is aught but good and kind to everyone. So we see, pathetic as Helen's life must always seem to those who enjoy the blessings of sight and hearing that it is yet full of brightness and cheer and courage and hope.

The speech, in which Annie also stressed one of Bell's most ardent beliefs, that "original composition without some mental preparation in the way of conscientious reading is an impossibility" was not only a success, it also helped to create a more balanced view of Helen among educators of the deaf. However, not everyone was impressed by her remarks. Observed one of her harshest critics, Francis D. Clarke, the superintendent of the Michigan School for the Deaf: "Miss Sullivan's cool assumption at Chautauqua that all Helen is, is the result of her superior teaching—struck me as the greatest exhibition of supreme vanity that I ever saw. She told me at Chautauqua that she was looking around for another blind-deaf child, in order that she could train her, and by the experiences which she had with Helen, make of her a greater wonder than Helen ever would be. I was so completely taken aback that I could not say a word."

At Chautauqua, Helen and Annie met John D. Wright and Dr. Thomas Humason, who told them that they were planning to start a school in New York City to teach oral language to the deaf. The two eager young men also gave them some thrilling news. With the new methods now available, they felt certain that Helen's speech could be made normal. Although Annie had recently come to believe that no handicapped child should be educated at a special school who could be taught in a normal environment, she agreed that Helen should attend their new school, the Wright-Humason School for the Deaf, in the hope that her speech could be improved.

On her way to New York in the fall of 1894, Annie felt suddenly hopeful. For the moment, their financial worries were in abeyance, as the lavish Spaulding was paying for Helen's tuition and all their expenses. The stinging memories of Anagnos and "The Frost King" were growing more distant with each passing day. With the right social connections, they would conquer New York as they had once conquered Boston. And Helen at last would learn to speak. In an age where beautiful diction was valued, this fourteen-year-old child, whose voice sounded like gibberish to most people, was going to talk like everyone else. And when she did speak normally, no one would ever again accuse them of being frauds.

CHAPTER 7

"It Took the Pair of You"

I N THE 1890s, people strolling in New York's Central Park were frequently startled by the sight of a beautiful, blind young woman on horseback. Smartly dressed in a fashionable riding habit, she was often observed with her short, dark-haired female companion trotting past the Dairy, where the children of the city could sip fresh milk, which was a scarce commodity, or near the herds of cows and sheep that were grazing in the nearby meadows.

With Annie, who was also an accomplished equestrienne, Helen rode daily in Central Park. In this sport, which had recently become fashionable among well-to-do women who had ignored their doctors' warnings that the sport might cause "pelvic troubles," her only restrictions were that she not be the lead rider and that their horses gallop at equal pace. For the adolescent girl, the undulating motion of the massive animal was a sensuous experience.

Helen's unique disability, as well as her fame, continued to isolate her from her peers. As the only deaf-blind student at the Wright-Humason School, she had practically no interaction with the other students, who were deaf only. Her studies included geography, French, German, and arithmetic, a subject she found boring and for which she had little aptitude.

By this time she had learned to type, using several typewriters with special keyboards and then a Remington that Spaulding bought her, which she thought "the best writing machine that is made." She seldom made a typing error, and in the words of one observer, "no one seeing her 'copy' would for a moment imagine under what dreadful difficulties it had been made."

Unlike Helen, Annie was unhappy with the new school. A constant rebel, she chafed at the thought of having to submit to its rules and regulations. "My time is wholly occupied. I like the work in a way, but I feel restive under the school routine. You may say what you will. I was never meant for a schoolmarm," she complained to Bell's secretary, John Hitz, a theatrical-looking old gentleman with a flowing white beard and a sweeping cape, to whom she wrote flirtatious letters, as she had to Anagnos, containing such sentiments as "Mon cher père knows that I love him and that is of more importance to him than anything else, I imagine."

She also confided to Hitz that she loathed the teachers' "stupidities" and their students' "plodding pursuit of knowledge." Predictably, the teachers of the deaf were outraged when they learned of her indiscreet remarks. They became even more upset when word got out that Bell was so delighted with Annie's savage critique of their teaching methods that for their next convention he had asked her to write a paper on the methods she had used to educate Helen.

Another reason for Annie's growing disillusionment with the school was that Helen was making little progress in speech and lipreading. Although Helen worked very hard to improve her voice, writing a friend that she would be "willing to work night and day if it could only be accomplished," her speech, as the bitterly disappointed Annie noted, "is no better as far as I can tell."

To still sound unintelligible to most people, when she had worked so hard to improve her speech, was an even graver setback for Helen. Although a hearing-sighted society viewed her life as a courageous battle against overwhelming disabilities, she herself accepted her blindness and deafness as natural conditions. It was her inability to speak at all intelligibly that first gave her "an awareness of the universal struggle against limitation."

Although Helen was depressed by her inability to communicate like other people, she refused to let her speech impediment isolate her from them. In New York as in Boston, she and Annie soon made many new friends, who because of Helen's fame and Annie's shrewd ability to exploit it were all very influential and wealthy people. Their new circle included Mark Twain and William Dean Howells, the most famous American writers of the period; Richard Watson Gilder, editor of *Century Magazine*; the oil magnates John D. Rockefeller and Henry H. Rogers; the famed British thespian Sir Henry Irving; Ellen Terry, Irving's leading lady and mistress, who was England's leading Shakespearean actress; and Joseph Jefferson, a celebrated American actor who was a good friend of Mark Twain.

At this point Helen made a friend who was her own age and blind. Her new companion, Nina Rhoades, was the daughter of John Rhoades, the president of Greenwich Savings Bank.

Another friend was Laurence Hutton, a wealthy dilettante who lived in Princeton and who numbered many famous people among his circle. He and his wife, Eleanor, who were instrumental in establishing a permanent fund for Helen's education, met Helen and Annie for the first time in 1895 at the home of Mary Mapes Dodge, the editor of St. Nicholas, a leading magazine for children. According to Hutton, Helen was unlike any other young woman they had ever met:

> We felt as if we were looking into a perfectly clean, fresh soul, exhibited to us by a person of more than usual intellect and intelligence, freely and without reserve. Here was a creature who absolutely knew no guile and no sorrow; from whom all that was impure and unpleasant had been kept; a child of nature with a phenomenally active mind, one who knew most things that were known to men and women of mature age and the highest culture, and yet who had no thought of evil in her heart, and no idea that wickedness or sadness exists in the hearts of others. She was a revelation and an inspiration to us. And she made us think and shudder, and think again. . . .
>
> Physically she was large for her years, and more fully developed than is the every-day girl of her age. Her face was almost beautiful, and her expression charming to behold, in its varying changes, which were always bright. Her features were regular and perfect. And she moved one to tears even when one was smiling with her. . . .
>
> She was peculiarly affectionate and demonstrative in her disposition. And she bestowed her innocent kisses upon persons of all ages and of either sex as freely and as guilelessly as the ordinary girl of fifteen would bestow a harmless innocent smile.

Helen's "sixth sense" amazed Hutton. When someone in the room asked Annie what would happen to Helen if they were to become separated, Helen, who had obviously not heard the question, pulled Annie's face to her own and kissed her on the lips. Although touched by Helen's devotion to Annie—"her absolute dependence upon that teacher is inexpressibly touching"—Hutton suspected Annie of mind control. When he quizzed her on the subject, she told him that through the unconscious movements of her fingers, she could make Helen follow her own thoughts and do what she wanted.

Although physically well developed, Helen Keller, in her midteens, was childlike in her attitudes. Although she had wept when she had first entered a graveyard, she still had no idea of death. But it was not her fault that she lived in an unreal world that was peopled with gods and goddesses and the heroic characters she read about in her Braille books. Annie, believing that Helen had suffered enough, could not bring herself to tell her about sadness and death. "She knew that men and women are now, have been, and are not; but with their going away, and where to, and why, she had not concerned herself," Hutton observed, and then speculated, "No doubt she thought, simply, that they had gone back, for a time to the sightlessness which still possessed her; back to the absence of hearing from which she suffered—although not unpleasantly—back to the condition of want of speech from which she was just emerging."

Hutton was also intrigued that Helen could correctly differentiate one sculptor's work from another and recognize each person in the room by touch even though she had met only two of them before. He was fascinated by her phenomenal tactile memory, which he attempted to explain by noting that her "powers of concentration were of course heightened and intensified by the isolation of her surroundings. She is not distracted or attracted by disturbing sights and sounds, as other mortals are; and the time we spend in seeing and in listening are spent by her in thought."

As for Hutton's estimation of Annie, it was obvious that he was unaware of the controversy that surrounded her. "The teacher interested and impressed us almost as much as did the pupil. Greater love, greater devotion, greater patience were never known. A whole life has been given up to one beautiful, unselfish object, with no hope of reward there. . . ."

When Helen drew her face to his and kissed him twice, the worldly Hutton felt that he had received a benediction.

SOME WEEKS LATER, at a gathering at the Huttons' mansion in Princeton, Samuel Clemens was introduced to the young woman he had come to the party especially to meet. Usually not impressed by other well-known people, he considered Helen to be the most remarkable woman he had ever met in his life. Although possessed of neither sight nor hearing, she instantly knew all about him and his books.

He was amazed when she inquired how he had come to adopt the nom de plume "Mark Twain," the time-honored call of the river man sounding the shallows. How could anyone who was blind as well as deaf know about a pen name, let alone the French term for it? He was completely won over when Helen felt his hair and face in a delicate, inquisitive way, put some violets she had received in the buttonhole of his coat, and kissed him when he said good-bye.

"The wonderful child arrived now, with her almost equally wonderful teacher, Miss Sullivan," Samuel Clemens recollected ten years later. "The girl began to deliver happy ejaculations, in her broken speech. Without touching anything, of course, and without hearing anything, she seemed quite well to recognize the character of her surroundings. She said, 'Oh, the books, the books, so many, many books. How lovely!'" During their first meeting Clemens told her a long story, "which she interrupted all along and in the right places, with cackles, chuckles, and care-free bursts of

With Mark Twain, 1902. The humorist later sent a photograph of himself to Annie Sullivan, signing it "To Mrs. John Sullivan Macy, with warm regard and with limitless admiration of the wonders she has performed as a miracle worker."

laughter. Then Miss Sullivan put one of Helen's hands against her lips and spoke against it the question, 'What is Mr. Clemens distinguished for?' Helen answered, in her crippled speech, 'For his humor.' I spoke up modestly and said, 'And for his wisdom.' Helen said the same words instantly—'and for his wisdom.' I suppose it was mental telegraphy for there was no way for her to know what I said."

In its own way, Clemens's life had been tragic. He had been born two months prematurely and was a sickly infant who barely survived his first two years. As a young man, he was horror-struck when his twenty-year-old brother Henry burned to death on a steamboat that exploded and caught fire.

Clemens's life was soon marred by further misfortunes. His first child, a chronically sickly boy named Langdon, died of diphtheria at twenty-two months of age after the writer had taken him out for a long ride in an open carriage and accidentally let the blankets slip off him. As he had with Henry, Clemens blamed himself for the death, confessing to his friend William Dean Howells that "Yes, I killed him," although Justin Kaplan, one of his biographers, believes that Clemens, "a lifelong guilt seeker," was no more responsible for his son's demise than he was for his brother's being on the steamboat.

After Langdon's death, Clemens became obsessed with his second child, Susy, a sensitive, timid, intelligent young woman who aspired to be an opera singer. Susy was a student at Bryn Mawr when Clemens met Helen Keller. According to Kaplan, "In everything she [Susy] did, he subjected her to demands for perfection, but he himself was vulnerable to her slightest criticism and was easily angered, pursued by a guilty sense that he had failed her. . . . As she grew older she knew he was a great man, but she was not at all sure a humorist was any better than a clown, and more and more she wanted him to be a great man in some other way. . . . She wanted him to be a moral philosopher, for example, and the author not of *Huckleberry Finn* but of *The Prince and the Pauper* and especially *Joan of Arc*."

As with Bell and his two daughters, it was easier for Clemens to idealize a powerless, dependent Helen Keller than to deal with his daughter.

In August 1896, after a triumphant world lecture tour, while Clemens was vacationing in England with his wife, Livy, he received a letter from a friend saying that Susy was ill. Livy sailed for America immediately, but it was too late. At their estate in Hartford, Connecticut, Susy died of meningitis after being in a coma for two days. She was twenty-four years old. At the very end of her brief life she became blind. In her delirium she wrote, "Mr. Clemens, Mr. Zola, Mr. Harte, I see that even darkness can be great. To me darkness must remain from everlasting to everlasting," and imagined that she was the friend of a famous deceased opera singer. Gazing out the window, she reflected, "Up go the trolley cars for Mark Twain's daughter. Down go the trolley cars for Mark Twain's daughter." According to another of his biographers, Clemens would later grasp at these words as proof of Susy's love and approval.

"It is one of the mysteries of our nature that a man, all unprepared, can receive a thunder-stroke like that and live," Clemens later wrote in his autobiography, as he remembered the day when he had been in England in his dining room, "thinking of nothing in particular when a cable-gram was put into my hand. It said, 'Susy was peacefully released today.'"

A heartbroken Clemens refused to return to the United States for Susy's funeral, rationalizing that her burial would take place long before his arrival. "All the circumstances of this death were pathetic," he wrote a friend. "My brain is worn to rags rehearsing them. The mere death would have been cruelty enough, without overloading it and emphasizing it with that score of harsh and wanton details. The child was taken away when her mother was within three days of her, and would have given three decades for sight of her."

Clemens and Livy never recovered from Susy's death. For many years they consulted mediums in a vain attempt to communicate with her.

Clemens's two surviving daughters, Jean and Clara, were far from well, as was Livy herself. Jean suffered from a strange combination of emotional and physical symptoms that doctors eventually diagnosed as epilepsy, while Clara suffered frequent nervous breakdowns. Toward the end of her life, Livy, who for several years had been mysteriously paralyzed in her youth after a skating accident, again became an invalid, suffering from asthma, hyperthyroidism, a heart ailment, and nervous prostration. The doctors— and then Livy herself—blamed the moody, irascible Clemens for exacerbating the emotional states that accompanied her heart disease, which was caused by her untreatable thyroid condition. According to Kaplan, "during the fall and winter of 1902 she was isolated in her room, and Clemens was prevented from paying her even a brief visit. On December 30, he saw her for five minutes, the first time in three months, and on their thirty-third wedding anniversary he again had only five minutes with her." He had to communicate with his wife in a private code, like the one used between Helen and Annie. "'Sozodont and sozodont and sal ammoniac synchronously pax vobiscum, S.L.C.'—by which he meant to say that he was passionately hers."

Livy died on the evening of June 5, 1904, in a rented villa in Florence, where the family had gone in the hope that a more moderate climate would help her regain her health. As Kaplan writes, when Clemens saw his wife "sitting upright in bed with the oxygen tube in her mouth, it came to him not like the thunderclap of Susy's death but as inevitable, and a portent of his own." Following their mother's death, Jean again began to suffer from uncontrollable epileptic seizures and was in and out of sanitariums before she died of a fit in her bathtub in 1909. Clara, the only daughter who would survive him, had a mental breakdown and entered a rest home in New York in 1904. As Kaplan notes, "The pattern of Livy's last years was ironically, perhaps vindictively, repeated: for a year Clemens was not allowed to visit Clara, telephone her, or even write to her."

AWARE OF HELEN'S DISABILITIES, Clemens spared her his own personal sufferings. If anything, he took pains to conceal his innate pessimism and to divert her from her handicaps, writing her letters that, when Annie translated them, made her roar with laughter. Whenever Helen visited him at his home in Connecticut, he stocked her room with what he considered the necessities for any houseguest: a bottle of whiskey and a box of cigars. Once he even offered to teach her billiards, a game with which he enjoyed a genuine love affair, often playing it all night long.

"Oh, Mr. Clemens," she said. "It takes sight to play billiards."

"Not the kind of billiards we play around here," he retorted.

Clemens's language could be coarse, but Helen loved him because he never tried to sound refined in her presence, although occasionally he would remove her hand from his lips, with the warning, "Now, Helen, I must curse."

For the rest of his life, he would be one of her greatest champions, defending her against the critics and scoffers. Once, when a mutual friend pointed out her seemingly monotonous life, he replied testily, "You're damned wrong there; blindness is an exciting business. I tell you; if you don't believe it, get up some dark night on the wrong side of your bed when the house is on fire and try to find the door."

As a writer, Clemens was fascinated by Helen's unique relationship with Annie Sullivan. He himself was a dual personality who could never reconcile the practical morality and unpretentiousness of Mark Twain with the freewheeling ambition and extravagance of Samuel Clemens, and he was fascinated by the double nature that he felt existed in many other people. In his opinion, Helen Keller and Annie Sullivan were not two separate beings, but one individual. He once wrote Helen, "You are a wonderful creature, the most wonderful in the world—you and your other half together—Miss Sullivan, I mean, for it took the pair of you to make a complete and perfect whole."

Although Clemens did not delve into the strengths and weaknesses of each half of this fabulous creature, it was clear from his letters that he was equally dazzled by Annie Sullivan. In *The Gilded Age*, he had poked fun at the nouveau riche Irish with their adopted French names to hide their origin, but from the beginning of their relationship he sensed that Annie, despite her meager education, was a highly gifted woman. "How she stands out in her letters! her brilliancy, penetration, originality, wisdom, character and the fine literary competencies of her pen—they are all there," he raved to Helen in the same letter.

In his opinion, Helen Keller, whom he believed to be a constructed woman who was composed of two disparate personalities, was the most marvelous creature of her sex since Joan of Arc.

This was no idle comparison on his part. In 1893, when Clemens had met Helen, he was deep into a book about the French peasant girl who, after hearing the voices of several saints, persuaded the French dauphin to let her lead the French troops to victory at Orléans. Joan of Arc fascinated Clemens because she was a double person like Helen/Annie and himself. One of her two personae was an uneducated country girl; the other, a military genius.

After reading that Joan, who led the French troops in male attire, had never menstruated, Clemens came to believe that "the higher life absorbed her and suppressed her physical (sexual) development." Although it is not recorded that he made a similar comment about Helen Keller, others would soon speculate that Helen sublimated her sexuality in her work, even though her femininity was far from stunted. Full-bosomed and womanly by her early teens, she obviously had started menarche at a young age.*

When Helen became sixteen and was preparing for the Harvard examination for admission to Radcliffe College, Clemens wrote a letter to Mrs.

* As a lifelong connoisseur of diseases, Clemens would have been fascinated to learn that Joan of Arc, like Helen Keller, may have suffered from a profound hearing disorder, which in Joan's case caused visual and auditory hallucinations. "I heard the voice on the right-hand side . . . and rarely do I hear it without a brightness . . . [that] comes from the same side. It is usually a great light," Joan is reported to have told her jailers, who observed that her rapturous attacks were accompanied by fits of vomiting and vertigo. These symptoms have led a number of modern doctors to conclude that she may have been afflicted with Ménière's disease, a disorder of the semicircular canals of the inner ear that is marked by recurrent attacks of tinnitus, especially in one ear, of a ringing or singing sound that some sufferers misinterpret as speech, visual disturbances, and vomiting.

With Annie Sullivan, 1898. Helen was by then eighteen, Annie thirty-two.

Henry Huddleston Rogers, the wife of the Standard Oil magnate who had been his own financial savior when he had declared bankruptcy in 1894, "for and in behalf of Helen Keller, stone blind and deaf, and formerly dumb," in which he pleaded with her "to lay siege to your husband and get him to interest himself and Mess. John D. and William Rockefeller and the other Standard Oil chiefs in Helen's case. . . . It won't do for America to allow this marvelous child to retire from her studies because of poverty. If she can go on with them she will make a fame that will endure in history for centuries. Along her special lines she is the most extraordinary product of all the ages."

It was fund-raising at its best. Unable to resist Clemens's appeal, H. H. Rogers and his wife, as well as others, contributed liberally to Helen's fund, making it possible for her to complete her college education.

As for Helen, she was immensely grateful for Clemens's support. Indeed, by 1896, Clemens and Bell were the only males on whom she could depend. In that year in which Clemens mourned the death of Susy, she herself lost two significant men in her life.

At the beginning of January, John Spaulding, the elderly bon vivant who was her major benefactor, died from a stomach inflammation that was exacerbated by chronic alcoholism. Although his illness was a prolonged one and he had ample opportunity to reconsider his last will and testament, he died without providing for Helen as he had promised. Not only were she and Annie without means of financial support, but Spaulding's heirs wanted Captain Keller to pay back the fifteen thousand dollars he had borrowed, declaring that their uncle would not lend a stranger a large amount of money without proper securities. (Spaulding's heirs eventually contributed seven thousand dollars to Helen's education fund, although, after Captain Keller's death, they tried to get back the loan from his estate.) They also insinuated that Annie had used "her charms" to influence their aged uncle to make the loan to Captain Keller in the first place. Captain Keller was unable to raise even the ten thousand dollars that Spaulding's heirs proposed as a settlement and again threatened to exhibit Helen as a way of paying off the sum.*

WITHIN A FEW MONTHS, Captain Keller, heavily in debt, died. He expired suddenly in Tuscumbia on August 19, 1896, while Helen and Annie were visiting friends in Massachusetts.

Helen's heartbroken reaction to her father's death astonished Annie. During their nine years together she had often been struck by Helen's lack

---

* The philanthropists who helped Helen pay for her education were dismayed by what they termed "the outrageous attitude" of Helen's family regarding her financial support, as was Helen herself when she grew older and realized that both her father and mother had treated her differently from their nonhandicapped offspring. Helen, who was sixteen years old at the time of her father's death, did not receive a copy of her father's will. Although she later learned from her mother that he had equally divided his property among his five children, she did not receive her share of his estate. She also learned that he had made no provision to pay Annie's back salary—a small sum of three hundred dollars a year. Her benefactors were appalled that Captain Keller's handicapped child should be left to the charity of strangers and felt that she should have her share, but Annie Sullivan would not let them intervene on Helen's behalf. When they wanted to bring suit against the Kellers to collect Teacher's back salary, she again talked them out of it, stressing that no suspicion should ever be cast on Helen's family.

of feeling toward other people, an egocentricity and an indifference that today might be labeled autisticlike traits. This lack of affect was so marked that Annie once wrote a friend that she had "come to believe that her [Helen's] peculiar limitations had dulled her emotional nature so that she did not feel as intensely as many" and later reinforced that belief by admitting to her biographer many years later that Helen had "no aptitude for emotional expression" and that when she had first come to Tuscumbia, she had to tell Helen "to hug her mother" and then report to Helen "how pleased her mother was."

But as she gazed at Helen's stricken face, Annie realized that she had misjudged her. Helen, on occasion, could be capable of powerful emotions. Immediately, on learning of her father's demise, Helen pleaded to go to Tuscumbia to be with her mother. But Kate Keller refused to let her attend the funeral, making the feeble excuse that the intense heat and humidity of Alabama in the late summer would be bad for her health. Perhaps she felt that she could not cope with her handicapped daughter at a time when she was struggling to sort out her own feelings about the husband who in life had caused her pain and unhappiness.

As Annie spelled her mother's decision into her hand, Helen began to sob. Not only was her father dead, but her family was refusing to let her share their grief. She felt more lonely and isolated than ever.

"He died last Saturday at my home in Tuscumbia," she later wrote a friend, "and I was not there. My own loving father! Oh, dear friend, how shall I ever bear it . . . ?"

Helen's only solace was in her newly discovered religion. Although Captain Keller had been a Presbyterian who was active in the church, Kate was an Episcopalian, and Helen herself had received religious instruction from the illustrious Bishop Phillips Brooks at Trinity Church in Boston, she had lingering spiritual doubts about the relationship between divine love and the material world. In the past year the Swiss-born John Hitz had become her spiritual guardian, introducing her to the writings of the famous eighteenth-century Swedish theologian, scientist, and philosopher Emanuel Swedenborg. Deeply moved by Swedenborg's accounts of the mystical visions he had experienced during his spiritual crisis when he turned away from scientific research and devoted himself to biblical study and the writing of religious philosophy, Helen had become a devout Swedenborgian. "Teacher has read 'The Immortal Fountain' to me, and as she spelled the words into my hand, I forgot my heartache, and only thought of dear father in his heavenly home, surrounded by angels, and learning all that he could not learn here," she wrote to Hitz. "So you see, what a great help those truths are to me. Oh, I have never needed them so sorely before."

ALTHOUGH SHE NEVER CONFIDED her thoughts to anyone, Annie Sullivan must have felt secretly relieved that Captain Keller was dead. For some time she had been aware that he considered her a charlatan. Once he had gone so far as to write Helen a letter that he knew Annie would read in which he stated outright that her teacher was "a fraud and a humbug." Possibly Captain Keller's skepticism stemmed from his awareness that his daughter's teacher regarded him as a poor husband and provider and was spreading rumors about his marital and financial problems. In August 1892 Annie had written Anagnos one of her seductive, gossipy letters from Fern Cliff, the Keller family's summer retreat in the mountains near Tuscumbia. It painted a miserable portrait of the Kellers' marriage:

A rare photograph of the twelve-year-old Helen with John Hitz, Alexander Graham Bell's secretary, 1892

Helen's younger brother
and sister, Phillips
Brooks and Mildred,
with a nurse, 1893

To begin with, the heat had been terrific and continuous. Soon after Helen
and I reached home there was a prolonged spell of rainy weather. The
swamps and ponds filled, the crops were nearly ruined, and sickness
became alarmingly prevalent. . . . The baby (Phillips) was very sick indeed,
and James just escaped having typhoid fever. Mildred and Helen both took
the whooping cough, and Helen's dog had the mange badly. . . . As soon as
Phillips was able to be moved we packed up our traps and came up here
only to find that our trials were just beginning. The scarcity of money made
it necessary for us to arrange to live as cheaply as possible. . . . I loaned Captain Keller thirty-five dollars and this with Helen's thirty-five I believe constituted the family income for the past two months. Mrs. Keller told me a
short time ago . . . that everything they had in the world was mortgaged.
Besides Capt. Keller is heavily in debt. Never was I sorrier for anyone in my
life than I was for poor Mrs. Keller; here she was trying to cook with a sick,
fretful baby in her arms most of the time. Every drop of water we used had
to be carried a quarter of a mile up a steep hill, and we could not get milk
for the children without walking a mile on the railroad. When Capt. Keller
found how things were, he hastened back to Tuscumbia, and left us two,
lone women here in the woods, without a protection save Eumer, a mastiff

dog. Did you ever hear of a greater outrage? We lived this way for nearly two weeks—until the election was over and the head of the family found time to bestow a thought upon his beloved family. . . . But it will not be difficult for you to understand that Mrs. Keller and her better half are not in a honeymoon state of mind as regards each other. Indeed our family life is far from pleasant. Capt. Keller's visits are not frequent and when he does come, the rest of us find the woods pleasanter than the house. Poor little Helen my heart aches for her! While I am near her, I can shield her from the knowledge of much that would distress her; but I cannot go on living this way a great while longer. . . . If they would only give me Helen, I am sure I could find away [sic] of making her life brighter than it will ever be here. . . .

Although she never mentioned it to Anagnos, Annie knew that Captain Keller was considering a new offer to exhibit Helen as if she were "a monkey" and to separate them.

CHAPTER 8

"A Born Schemer"

C APTAIN KELLER WAS NOT the only person who considered Helen and Annie's symbiotic relationship unwholesome. Shortly after his death, there was a bizarre plot to separate them. It revolved around Helen Keller's menstrual period, and the unlikely conspirators included the distinguished headmaster of a girls' school, a cantankerous millionaire, and Kate Keller.

Ever since she was a child, Helen had longed to go to college, once announcing in her crippled voice that she wanted to attend Harvard. Since Harvard did not admit women, that was out of the question, but, as she grew older, it did not seem out of the realm of possibility that she could attend its "annex" for women, which became known as Radcliffe College. Her dream was unconventional, as a college education was considered a risky venture for women in the 1890s, and most college girls were widely viewed by the public as bloodless, sexless spinsters.

Before fulfilling her dream, however, Helen first would have to attend a school that would prepare her for the college examinations. At the suggestion of a former president of Radcliffe, Helen applied for admission to the Cambridge School for Young Ladies. After initial skepticism on the part of Arthur Gilman, its director, who had proposed that Harvard start an "annex" for women, she was accepted as a pupil in October 1896. After the first six months, her little sister Mildred, with whom she now had a closer relationship following their father's death, joined her as a pupil.

Helen was sixteen years old, and this was the first time she had been exposed to hearing-sighted girls her own age. Many years later she wrote about what a wonderful experience it had been to "join them in many of their games, even blind man's buff and frolics in the snow," but the truth was that she was more isolated than ever. At the Cambridge School, unlike Perkins, few of the staff and students knew the manual finger language, and Annie was almost her sole bridge to the world.

Ironically, at age sixteen she was at the height of a beauty of which she was completely unaware. Aside from the pathos of her obviously afflicted eyes, she was handsome and well formed, with an expressive countenance, short brown hair that curled around her shoulders, and beautiful hands. "Their whiteness and delicacy and beauty of shape are delights to the eye," wrote a reporter who interviewed Helen when she was seventeen, "and the extraordinary sensitiveness of their finger-tips cannot be imagined by one who has only the usual sense of touch."

Her comely face, as well as her sensual body, might have attracted any number of men, especially men who were aroused by dependent, helpless females. But any contact with boys her own age was strictly forbidden by Kate Keller, who was revolted by the idea of her daughter marrying and becoming sexually active. Then, too, the puritanical code of late Victorian society demanded that a severely handicapped female, even one who was "the wonder of the nineteenth century," remain chaste and undefiled. And so it was clear that despite her considerable beauty, charm, and intelligence, Helen would never enjoy the life of most women of her period, with a husband who took her to Niagara Falls on their honeymoon, where they posed happily for photographs, and with children and weekly visits to the ladies' sewing circle.

Initially, Annie agreed with Gilman that Helen would spend five years at the school. However, her progress was so remarkable that after the end of the first year her course was shortened to three more years, and she was also allowed to take part of her college entrance examinations.

Although Annie had been at her side in every class, interpreting the teacher's lessons, she was not allowed to be with Helen at the examinations so as to crush the rumors that she was prompting her pupil. Gilman himself, who had learned the manual alphabet especially for the occasion, translated the questions for Helen, who was permitted to type her answers

Mildred Keller at the time
she and Helen attended the
Cambridge School for
Young Ladies, 1897

while the other students wrote in longhand. She was elated when she learned that she had passed all her subjects, including elementary and advanced German, French, Latin, English, and Greek and Roman history, and had received honors in English and German. According to an equally jubilant Gilman, "I think I may say that no candidate in Harvard or Radcliffe was graded higher than Helen in English. . . . No man or woman has ever in my experience got ready for these examinations in so brief a time. How has it been accomplished? By a union of patience, determination, and affection, with the foundation of an uncommon brain."

These spectacular marks were not replicated the following year. She did poorly, and both she and Annie blamed her deteriorating grades on the fact that she had no aptitude for the mathematical subjects that were her major course of study. Also, because of Queen Victoria's Diamond Jubilee, there was a delay in manufacturing the Braille textbooks from England that she needed to help her with her work. Annie had to read and interpret her books as well as her school lessons, and as Helen later admitted, "for the first time in eleven years it seemed as if her dear hand would not be equal to the task."

It was during Helen's second year at the Cambridge School that Annie

Sullivan made one of her spectacular blunders. Fearful that the philanthropists who were contributing funds for Helen's education would lose interest in her if she took too long to complete her preparatory course, she decided that Helen could be ready for Radcliffe in two more years, not the three that Gilman had originally suggested. She and Gilman had "an amicable difference of opinion" about the time Helen would remain at the Cambridge School, but finally Gilman agreed to Annie's demands.

On November 12, Helen, who suffered from painful menses, started her period, and to make matters worse, had "an unusually hard time with her geometry," a subject that she found difficult. When Annie put her to bed for three days, Gilman's suspicions were aroused. Helen, he was convinced, had suffered a nervous breakdown as a result of overwork.

According to Gilman, "Last week, Helen went to bed, worn out. Dr. Bell called to see me on Saturday, and we went in to see Helen. Dr. Bell told her [Annie Sullivan] of a young man of brilliant mind who had been pressed in that way, and who is now insane. But Miss Sullivan remains obstinate. Meantime Mrs. Hopkins called to see Helen and wrote to me that she was in a very bad way, and that she should at once write to Miss Sullivan that her work be made less."

In a subsequent letter to Mrs. Keller, Mrs. Gilman corroborated her husband's impressions, adding that she had been appalled by Annie Sullivan's callous treatment of a woman who was not only deaf-blind but also menstruating. "The issue between Mr. Gilman and Miss S. came about by Helen's being ill one day, and not being able to go to school," she wrote. "She was unwell and so tired she could not sit up, but as soon as she could get about, in a day or two, Miss S. took her on a long walk, from the school to Boston. The next day, they took a drive, and the day after, another long walk of equal length. She says that Helen is always sick two weeks, and yet she is willing to have her study from morning to night, and to exercise her at this rate when she ought to be placid and quiet. There is no hurry. Helen cannot look forward to the kind of life other girls have, and it would be such a cruel shame to mar her life just to gratify Miss S.'s foolish ambitions. . . . She boasts she can take Helen anywhere she chooses, and that she will remove her from our care."

When Mrs. Hopkins, Annie's former housemother at Perkins, visited Helen, she was also shocked by her condition, which she later described to Gilman as "a state of collapse. . . . So it seems to me for Helen to study all day, or be in the class-room preparing lessons, also Saturday and Sunday, working all day is more than any mortal can endure. I shall write Miss Sullivan this. Should Helen break down through study, there would be no end of denunciation, for it has often been predicted by many people."*

Mrs. Hopkins then paid a call on Annie Sullivan, with the hope of persuading her to stop overworking Helen. One look at Annie's pale face and her ailing eyes, which she had been overusing to read Helen books that were not in Braille, convinced her that Annie, too, was on the verge of a nervous breakdown. As far as the pious Mrs. Hopkins was concerned, it was Annie's own intense ambition that was driving her to push Helen, sheer folly as far as the housemother was concerned, as she reminded Annie that Helen "was not her property" and if she broke down as a result of overwork, Annie was "digging her own grave." But Mrs. Hopkins got nowhere with Helen's implacable teacher. Never one to listen to advice, Annie Sullivan threw her out of the house, telling her to mind her own business.

The old rumors circulated. Among educators of the blind and the deaf, it was said that Annie Sullivan was "a born schemer" who could not brook the slightest criticism or interference and a "publicity monger" as well. "She is nothing if not theatrical. She cannot live without newspaper notoriety," a Perkins employee reminded Gilman. "Do you not remember that when she came to me at first telling me how much she desired Helen's movements to be without attention from the reporters, she herself went directly to the Sunday papers of the very next week with a statement of my conversation with her?"

Another educator of disabled children was of the opinion that "Helen is no incident in any one's life. Miss Sullivan owes her notoriety and prominent position to the greatness of Helen Keller. Helen is not a product of Miss S.'s ingenuity or training, but on the other hand it seems to me that Miss S. has been raised by Helen's great natural abilities."

At the Cambridge School, the teachers could hardly contain their glee as they gossiped to Arthur Gilman about Annie's heartless treatment of Helen. Not only was she frequently impatient with her in class, but she also accused her of making "stupid remarks." In their opinion, Annie's lack of tolerance revealed the real source of her irritation. She was able to teach

---

* In reality, Annie Sullivan's attitude toward menstruation was a modern one and in marked contrast to her contemporaries, who, according to one authority, believed that "whenever there is actual pain at any stage of the monthly period, it is because something is wrong either in the dress, or the diet, or the personal and social habits of the individual. One ramification of this notion was that the responsibility for painful menstruation was placed squarely on the woman's shoulders. . . . Light housework was commonly—and conveniently—recommended as the best way to regulate the menses and decrease pain. Study and reading, however, allegedly drew too much energy and blood from the genital area, thereby further weakening the sufferer and potentially damaging her reproductive system."

Helen as long as the work was elementary, but now Helen was far ahead of Annie intellectually, and Annie could not keep up with her.

Even the long-suffering Anagnos broke his silence to give his side of the story. He confided to somebody who confided to William Wade, the wealthy landowner who often invited Helen and Annie to his Pennsylvania estate, that besides "The Frost King," a geographical sketch that Helen had written while she was at Perkins was copied verbatim from a book. Once, upon questioning Helen, he detected Annie spelling in her other hand.

Dr. Humason, whom Annie had always considered her friend, had the same observation. In a separate communication to Wade, he wrote that he had detected the same dishonesty in prompting Helen that Anagnos had discerned. "That settles the fact that teacher did such tricks, and I believe it now," a reluctant Wade finally had to admit.

For some time Wade had predicted that Helen could never stay in any large school or college with Annie as a companion. In his judgment, Annie had subjugated Helen for so many years that it would be impossible for her to defer to anyone else's authority concerning her, and it "would inevitably result in a blow up." As he wrote to Gilman:

> I am much disturbed that the dreaded expected has happened. When Helen and Miss Sullivan were with us that winter, there was the same fever-ish forcing. We gently remonstrated and tried all sorts of quiet, mild, effort, and at last Mrs. Wade could stand it no longer and took Helen in hand as far as physical condition went and insisted that she have more exercise. . . . In matters of Helen's general health, Miss Sullivan seems either not to know anything or she disregards them as non-essentials. She made Helen re-write long papers for the merest typographical errors, perhaps only one in five hundred words. . . . My daughter remarked apropos of Helen's study-ing, that unless she was physically very strong, she would break down at that rate. . . . Perhaps it might be best for me to write Mrs. Keller, and if it is thought best, I will tackle the job, "Bell the cat" in fact.

In subsequent letters to Gilman, Wade related that he had been stunned when Helen asked him about "the meaning of something she was reading that was a euphemistic way of saying 'rape' and on my evading reply, telling her to 'ask teacher,' she said she thought it must be 'using a woman without her consent.' I was exceedingly shocked, not at her knowledge of such mat-ters, but at her lack of the necessary knowledge that such remarks were improper to a man. I suppose you know that Miss Sullivan is—well perhaps call it 'a free-thinker' as the 'tenderest word.'"

Like Spaulding's suspicious heirs who were convinced that Annie had seduced their uncle so he would loan money to Captain Keller, Wade suspected her of using her feminine wiles to manipulate powerful men like himself and Alexander Graham Bell. "Confound it! I guess I must come out with my views of Teacher's 'freedoms with that distinguished man,' he thundered to Gilman. "I suppose Mr. Bell is *meant*, although I never saw anything amiss there, but she has been very disagreeably free with me; she has often sat down on the arm of my chair, leaning on me and in one of those giggles, punching her head onto my shoulder and all such didos. Now remember, I do not think that there was any improper intent in this, or to be the plainest—had I been the man to presume on this and take any personal liberties with her, I am very sure she would resent them instantly and hotly; but it was her confounded 'Frenchyness,' the notion that the mere *appearance* of wrong is never wrong and that prejudices on such matters are not entitled to respect."

It was a secretly titillated Wade who first made the suggestion to Gilman that they be separated:

> . . . Miss Sullivan must be separated from Helen. She certainly lacks one of
> Helen's greatest charms, rare natural delicacy of character. . . .

Emboldened by Wade's support, Gilman wrote Mrs. Keller several letters in which he suggested that she consider finding a new companion for Helen. In a letter of November 27 he told her frankly that "the time had arrived" for her to take more of a direct part in her daughter's education and requested that he be formally appointed Helen's guardian, "so that I could exert my authority with some influence. As I wrote last evening, we have no thought of underrating the great work that has been accomplished by Miss Sullivan, but at the same time," and here he finally arrived at the crux of the matter, "we must not blind ourselves to the truth that she is better adapted to the training of a girl in the beginning than of a young lady who has already far outstripped her, especially when we consider the wide social difference in their position."

As it so happened that the wealthy, socially prominent William Wade had a genteel, well-spoken daughter who was more than eager to replace the lower-class Irish Annie Sullivan.

Meanwhile, Gilman's barrage of missives had succeeded in alarming Mrs. Keller. She wrote back almost immediately that she was well aware of Annie Sullivan's shortcomings.

I thank you most sincerely for your timely warning on Helen's behalf, even more on my own. It has been unwittingly, believe me, that I have allowed her to run this risk. I hope in any case I should have too much sense to allow a daughter to be taxed beyond her strength. It is an error in judgment on her part and her inexperience in teaching is not sufficient to show her the injury being done Helen. The child does not have time to write me once a month. An immediate change must be made.

Less than two weeks later, Gilman received the following letter from Mrs. Keller in which she agreed to Helen and Annie's separation.

I have been very, very blind. This has all come about from the fact that I have not furnished the money for Helen's expenses, and I do not ever now know who has all my money. As advised, I doubt very seriously if I could have sanctioned the means, had I known, and Helen has always been so devoted to Miss Sullivan, and she was so necessary to the child, that even when her father wished to interfere, I interposed. As I understand, the money for Helen's education is subscribed each year. In the uncertain conditions of Helen's finances, would you be willing to be appointed Helen's guardian? . . . I much prefer that she should, as she expresses it, "leave," than that I have to tell her she cannot remain with Helen. . . .

That afternoon, Gilman was thrilled to receive a telegram that formally gave him the permission he had so long desired:
"You are authorized to act as Helen's guardian."
With this directive, the exultant Arthur Gilman had every reason to believe that the Cambridge School for Young Ladies could now claim exclusive credit for the higher education of the world-famous Helen Keller. But he had not counted on the wiliness of Annie Sullivan. On that same day, December 8, 1897, as Gilman was savoring his new position as Helen's guardian, Annie Sullivan happened to spy a sealed letter he had written that morning to Mrs. Keller. Possessing no scruples whatsoever about reading other people's mail, she ripped open the letter, her face growing dark with fury as she read of Gilman's plans to remove Helen from her care.

Throwing one of her tantrums, she immediately summoned Gilman and informed him that if she and Helen were to be separated, it would be "at the cost of two dead bodies." Then she announced her intention to remove Helen and her younger sister Mildred from his school that morning, becoming even more incensed when Gilman informed her that she had no right to leave with Helen, as he was now her guardian. The final insult came when he told her that Mrs. Keller had written him that "Captain Keller wished before he died to remove Helen from her teacher, and that she herself felt that she should never have allowed her authority to lapse."

The curtain was still up on the melodrama. On her way to visit friends in Boston that night, Annie considered drowning herself in the Charles River. At the last moment, however, she refrained from jumping into the dark waters. According to an ever-grateful Helen, the only reason that Annie, a lapsed Catholic, did not go through with this desperate act was that "it seemed to her that an angel laid a restraining hand upon her and said, 'Not yet.' That strengthened her to return to Cambridge the next morning and refuse to leave except by force until she had seen my sister Mildred and me."

Helen, of course, was the last person to learn of the conspiracy. The eternal pawn in other people's schemes and ambitions, she was informed about the plot via Annie's "trembling hands" on December 8, after she had dutifully finished her Greek lesson.

> "What is it, Teacher?" I cried in dismay. "Helen, I fear we are going to be separated!" "What! Separated? What do you mean?" I said utterly bewildered. She said something about a letter she had received from someone, who expressed his opinion to my mother that Miss Sullivan and I should be separated. Mr. Gilman, whom I had trusted, had done it all.

Upon learning that Annie would no longer be her teacher, Helen carried on like an insane person, refusing to sleep or eat. A good friend, Joseph Edgar Chamberlin, a noted literary critic who wrote a column for the *Boston Transcript*, persuaded Gilman to let him take both children to his farm in nearby Wrentham. One look at the sobbing young woman and it was obvious to him that she was shattered by the prospect of life without her teacher. As Chamberlin later wrote to Annie Sullivan's biographer Nella Braddy Henney, "At Wrentham I took Helen alone in my study, and told her it might soon be incumbent on her to decide whether she should stay with Annie or go away from her with her mother. She said to me, 'Uncle Ed, if I have to decide between my mother and Teacher, I will stay with Teacher.' This decided me as to my own sympathies in this case."

Meanwhile, Annie Sullivan, having abandoned the idea of suicide, had mustered her forces. And they were mighty ones. First, there was Mrs. Keller, to whom she sent a telegram. "We need you" was all it said. Then she wired Alexander Graham Bell, who, upon reading her telegram, immediately dispatched the ever-sympathetic Hitz from Washington. Last but not least, the aid of Mrs. Laurence Hutton, their principal fund-raiser whom Annie privately loathed, was enlisted. Moved by the women's plight, Mrs. Hutton immediately wrote Gilman a letter, in which she accused the distinguished gentleman who was a member of Radcliffe's governing corporation not only of child abuse but also of wanting to profit financially from the separation. Had Gilman forgotten that the money she had collected was for the joint support of both Helen and Annie and "in the event of any separation of the two beneficiaries, the trustees, of course, have no other recourse than to return the entire sum raised to the various donors"?

One of Annie Sullivan's enemies once wrote that "Helen's intellect may develop under the guidance of Miss Sullivan and under her influence, but she can never be the true and noble woman she might be until she is emancipated from a thralldom worse than her father's slaves. The mother is almost as much a slave to Miss S. as her daughter."

This was an astute judgment regarding the three women, although the anonymous writer neglected to take into account Kate Keller's ambivalent feelings toward her daughter. Upon her arrival at the Chamberlins' farm, Kate had a swift change of heart, announcing to an overjoyed Helen that she had decided not to fire Annie Sullivan. Although Kate had her own doubts about Teacher, she knew that without her, Helen's care would fall on her own shoulders. It was a responsibility that she, as a struggling widow, was not prepared to handle. "I always think of Helen as partly your child and whilst in this I think first of her I think of you, too, and utter ruin to the life you have striven so patiently to develop and round out," she recently had written Annie with evident relief. As for the thoroughly bewildered Gilman, Mrs. Keller suddenly concluded that he had "made very cruel use of the authority I had given him to distress my children and Miss Sullivan after ten years of service. I certainly never dreamed of Miss Sullivan being forced away from Helen. I could not but feel on my arrival in Wrentham that I had been made to endure most unnecessary and uncalled for distress. Helen is in perfect physical condition, and if she shows any evidence of nervous prostration or overwork, I cannot discover it."

Had Helen been sickly or incapacitated, Mrs. Keller, despite her conflicted feelings, undoubtedly would have fired Annie Sullivan and taken Helen home to Alabama. There, she would have either languished in some lonely, shuttered back room or somehow achieved a more normal existence. But neither scenario was to be her destiny. Triumphant against their enemies, Helen Keller and Annie Sullivan were closer than ever.

CHAPTER 9

"Half-Rome"

AFTER STUDYING WITH a private tutor who helped her pass the final preparatory examinations, Helen entered Radcliffe College in the fall of 1900. It was the first time that anyone with her handicaps had ever enrolled in an institution of higher learning.

It was largely a lonely triumph. As the twenty-year-old Helen soon discovered, college was not the "romantic lyceum" that she had envisioned. At Radcliffe, which had been forced to accept her as a student, she was more profoundly aware than ever before of her blindness and deafness. Only one of her classmates knew the manual finger language. Another girl had learned to write Braille, copying as a present Elizabeth Barrett Browning's *Sonnets from the Portuguese*, but Helen never heard from her after graduation. The other students tried to be friendly whenever they saw her at a local lunchroom, and according to Helen, "Miss Sullivan spelled their bright chatter into my hand." But she was painfully aware of the gulf between them, even though her classmates tried to bridge the gap by such lavish, awkward gestures as buying her a Boston terrier, which she promptly named Phiz. Presumably the dog would compensate her for what they were either too timid or too busy to give and what she secretly longed for: "the warm, living touch of a friendly hand."

Helen with Phiz, a
Boston terrier that was
the gift of Helen's fellow
students at Radcliffe

Of Helen's professors, only one, William Allan Neilson, who later became the president of Smith College, took the time to master the manual finger language so he could communicate directly with her. As Arthur Gilman was closely associated with the college, she and Annie were politely ignored by the rest of the faculty and administration, including the autocratic Agnes Irwin, the dean of Radcliffe, and the august Dr. Charles W. Eliot, the head of Harvard.

The snub did not surprise Annie, who was still furious about the plot at the Cambridge School to separate her from Helen. "I would much prefer to have people despise me as they certainly would if they guessed how full of distrust and contempt my heart is towards my fellow beings," she wrote to Hitz. "I know it pains you to hear me speak in this way and doubtless it will hurt you still more to have me write it: but I want you to know just how detestable I am. I find people hateful and I hate them. Mr. Gilman seemed to me a fair specimen of our noble race. . . ."

"Radcliffe did not desire Helen Keller as a student," Dean Irwin later explained to an interviewer. "It was necessary that all instruction should reach her through Miss Sullivan, and this necessity presented difficulties. They were overcome and all went well if not easily."

Helen was wounded whenever her classmates passed her on the stairs and in the lecture halls without a sign of acknowledgment. Most of her teachers were "impersonal as Victrolas," she recollected years later, and "the professor is as remote as if he were talking through a telephone." And she despised the frenetic pace of college life because it deprived her of the time for meditation. "I used to have time to think, to reflect, my mind and I. We used to sit together of an evening and listen to the inner melodies of the spirit which one hears only in leisure moments. . . . But in college there is no time to commune with one's thoughts."

As she discovered to her dismay, college was for learning and not contemplation. She had to read Molière and Corneille in French, Goethe and Schiller in German, and Milton's poetry in English as well as study history, algebra, geometry, and physics. It was impossible to take notes in her large classes because her hands were "busy listening" to Annie's rapid-fire spelling of the important points in the lectures. Although William Wade did his best to supply her with embossed books, the majority of the books she had to read were not in Braille, so that Annie had to spell them into her hand word by word. When she returned home, she recorded on her Braille typewriter what she recalled of the lecture, relying on her prodigious memory. Despite her valiant efforts, she had trouble keeping up and blamed herself for being "a slow, halting" student. Her examinations, administered by two proctors, were nightmarish events. By Dean Irwin's directive, Annie was not permitted to give her tests.

As in the past, this elaborate system of proctors was to prove to the world that she was not a fraud. Still, there was campus gossip about which woman was the real student. Recalled one of Helen's proctors, a former teacher at the Perkins Institution, after Helen's death in 1968: "When the word became public that Helen was to enter Radcliffe there was much talk— 'Why don't they say outright that Miss Sullivan is entering Radcliffe instead of Helen Keller, a blind, deaf and dumb girl.' . . . The Dean at that time was anxious to prove in every way that Helen was the important one. She made certain rules: Miss Sullivan was to leave the building when the examinations started. . . . She, the Dean, would pay personally for two proctors, one to proctor Helen, and another to proctor Helen's proctor. She had her typewriter for work in answering the exam questions. I had my Braille typewriter to translate the questions. . . . All records for the four years were kept on file in the Dean's office and a surprising number asked to examine them."

As it turned out, the proctor had a handsome, brilliant brother around Helen's age who Annie Sullivan thought might make a suitable tutor for her. But when Mrs. Keller came to Boston and met the dashing young man who would be in close proximity to her daughter as she read his lips, she immediately squelched the idea. "Mr. S. is too attractive and being with a young man with his personality, Helen could easily fall in love and what would happen with the college course," the proctor quoted Helen's mother as saying.

Not that Helen desired a lover at this point. Her mother's revulsion at her having a suitor, coupled with Annie's possessiveness, had succeeded in momentarily dampening her interest in the opposite sex. At twenty, an age when most women of her generation were married with children, Helen Keller was forced to remain sexually immature. As this conversation with Alexander Graham Bell suggests, she was afraid of marriage and sexuality. Their intimate conversation took place at Bell's summer retreat in Nova Scotia, Beinn Bhreagh, where she and Annie had spent a vacation following the end of Helen's freshman year:

"It seems to me, Helen, a day must come when love, which is more than friendship, will knock at the door of your heart and demand to be let in."

"What made you think of that?" I asked.

"Oh, I often think of your future. To me you are a sweet, desirable young girl, and it is natural to think about love and happiness when we are young."

"I do think of love sometimes," I admitted, "but it is like a beautiful flower which I may not touch, but whose fragrance makes the garden a place of delight just the same."

He sat silent for a minute or two, thought-troubled, I fancied. Then his dear fingers touched my hand again like a tender breath, and he said, "Do not think that because you cannot see or hear, you are debarred from the supreme happiness of woman. Heredity is not involved in your case, as it is in so many others."

"Oh, but I am happy, very happy," I told him. "I have my teacher and my mother and you, and all kinds of interesting things to do. I really don't care a bit about being married."

"I know," he answered, "but life does strange things to us. You may not always have your mother, and in the nature of things Miss Sullivan will marry, and there may be a barren stretch in your life when you will be very lonely."

Annie Sullivan (seated) with John Hitz (top right), the first superintendent
of the Volta Bureau, who introduced Helen (center) to Swedenborgianism;
Alexander Melville Bell (the inventor's father); and Alexander Graham Bell
(kneeling), 1901. They are watching Dr. Bell's giant kites being flown on the
hillside of Beinn Bhreagh, Nova Scotia.

"I can't imagine a man wanting to marry me," I said. "I should think it would seem like marrying a statue."

"You are very young," he replied, patting my hand tenderly, "and it's natural that you shouldn't take what I have said seriously now: but I have long wanted to tell you how I felt about your marrying, should you ever wish to. If a good man should desire to make you his wife, don't let anyone persuade you to forego that happiness because of your peculiar handicap."

I was glad when Mrs. Bell and Miss Sullivan joined us, and the talk became less personal.

During those years, the only escape from Helen's melancholia seemed to be the rich world of her Braille books, where as her nimble fingers skimmed the raised letters, she was unencumbered by blindness and deafness and could explore the myriad wonders of the universe. "The noble men and women of history and poetry moved and breathed before me vividly on the picture screen of time," she wrote in her ornate style. "My imagination glowed as I beheld Socrates fearlessly teaching the youth of Athens the truth and drinking the fatal cup rather than surrender. Columbus's sublime perseverance as he sailed chartless seas with an unfriendly crew quickened my sense of adventure in exploring and perhaps mapping a dark, soundless world."

But of the books she read with her fingers, the philosophical treatises were the ones she most treasured. "I was so happily at home in philosophy, it alone would have rendered those four difficult years worth while. . . . Philosophy taught me how to keep on guard against the misconceptions which spring from the limited experience of one who lives in a world without color and without sound. . . . I was delighted to have my faith confirmed that I could go beyond the broken arc of my senses and behold the invisible in the fullness of the light, and hear divine symphonies in silence. I had a joyous certainty that deafness and blindness were not an essential part of my existence, since they were not in any way a part of my immortal mind."

Of the philosophers, Emanuel Swedenborg remained her favorite. The famous Swedish member of Parliament and scientist was fifty-five years old when he had a series of profound religious experiences and abandoned his brilliant work in paleontology, physics, and physiological science that anticipated many later discoveries. Before his illumination, he revealed that he had been instructed by dreams and experienced extraordinary visions. According to Swedenborg's own account, the Lord filled him with His spirit to teach the doctrines of the New Church by the word from Himself, and he was permitted into the spiritual world so he could talk with angels and spirits. After these revelations, he wrote extensively on the internal meaning of the Bible, heaven and hell, and divine love and wisdom.

Swedenborgianism, with its concepts of a universal spiritual reality and brotherhood, a loving God, and an afterlife in which no one would suffer from limitations and handicaps, appealed to Helen. She drew much inspiration and insight from the Swedish seer's writings and his enthralling presentation of morality as a battle between God and the devil, calling him "the light in my darkness, the voice in my silence." According to Swedenborg, death is simply a transition to a new world, a larger, nobler life beyond the grave, and she believed that in this spiritual world she would not only be able to see and hear, but also could marry and enjoy the "conjugal love" that had been denied her in life.

"I am always eager to learn more about the spiritual world," she wrote to Hitz, explaining why the religion to which he had introduced her at age sixteen had become one of the sources of her strength.

> Swedenborgianism is more satisfying to me than the creeds about which I have read. For the very reason that it is the most spiritual and idealistic religion, it best supplies my peculiar needs. It makes me feel as if I had been restored to equality with those who have all their faculties. . . . I feel weary of groping, always groping along the darkened path that seems endless. At such times the desire for the freedom and the larger life of those around me is almost agonizing. But when I remember the truths you have brought within my reach, I am strong again and full of joy. I am no longer deaf and blind; for with my spirit I see the glory of the all-perfect that lies beyond the physical sight and hear the triumphant song of love which transcends the tumult of this world. What appears to be my affliction is due to the obscurity, yea, the darkness, as Swedenborg says, occasioned by terrestrial things. I cannot help laughing sometimes at the arrogance of those who think they alone possess the earth because they have eyes and ears. In reality, they see only shadows and know only in part. They little dream that the soul is the only reality, the life, the power which makes harmony out of discord, completeness out of incompleteness.

HELEN'S DIFFICULTIES IN COLLEGE took their toll on Annie Sullivan. As a result of having to read and spell to Helen four to five hours daily, she was gradually losing her sight until one day, according to her alarmed pupil, she "could not see much farther than the end of her nose." No longer could she write in longhand, and Helen, who was a superb typist, had to copy "all her accounts, memoranda and letters. . . . Then her ideas bubbled out freely, and it consoled me to feel that I was of some small service to her."

The thought of Annie's losing her sight terrified Helen. She knew that Annie was openly telling other people that she would kill herself if she became blind. Certain that her tormented teacher was capable of suicide, Helen was relieved when an ophthalmologist finally convinced the stubborn Annie that she would indeed go blind if she did not rest her eyes and that her health was more important than Helen's education.

After their visit to the doctor, whenever Annie asked Helen if she wanted her to repeat a passage, Helen lied and told Annie that she could recall the words, when in reality "they had slipped from my mind." Suffering from headaches, anemia, and neuralgia, Helen refused to consult a doctor for fear that Annie would again be accused of overworking her.

Fortunately, for both Helen and Annie, Helen's second year at Radcliffe was somewhat easier, as her literary ability was recognized by one of the professors. He was Charles Townsend Copeland, a crusty English composition professor who was the first person to encourage her to write about the unique world in which she lived.

". . . I have always accepted other people's experiences and observations as a matter of course," she wrote him. "It never occurred to me that it might be worthwhile to make my own observations and describe the experiences peculiarly my own. . . . When I came to your class last October, I was trying with all my might to be like everybody else, to forget as entirely as possible my limitations' peculiar environment. Now, however, I see the folly of attempting to hitch one's wagon to a star with a harness that does not belong to it. . . .

"Henceforth I am resolved to be myself, to live my own life, and write my own thoughts when I have any. . . ."

Although Helen found writing "a burden," at times even "hating" it, she took Copeland's advice and began to write about her singular life. Copeland was impressed by the new direction of her work. "In some of her work she has shown that she can write better than any pupil I have ever had, man or woman," he observed. "She has an excellent 'ear' for the flow of sentences."

Helen's themes came to the attention of the editors of the *Ladies' Home Journal*, who contacted her about publishing the story of her life in five monthly installments for which she would be paid three thousand dollars. The money was tempting, so with Annie's encouragement she agreed to sign a contract but soon found that it was impossible to keep up with her

Playing chess with Annie Sullivan at Radcliffe College, 1900

studies and write a book. Adding to her sense of pressure was the fact that the editors had started publishing the articles before she had even completed the manuscript.

Aware of their plight, Lenore Smith, a good friend, introduced the two women to John Albert Macy, a tall, twenty-five-year-old instructor of English at Harvard and an editor of *Youth's Companion* who was both a gifted critic and a writer. Swiftly learning the manual alphabet to communicate directly with the twenty-two-year-old Helen, he helped edit her book, *The Story of My Life*, which was published by Doubleday, Page in late March 1903.

As Macy later recollected, "When she began work at her story, more than a year ago, she set up on the Braille machine about a hundred pages of what she called 'material,' consisting of detached episodes and notes put down as they came to her without coherent order or definite plan. Then she wrote on her typewriter two articles, the first of which is, with a very few minor changes which she made later, the opening chapter, which was published in the April number of the *Journal*."

The second article did not go as smoothly. It was unchronological and omitted vital information about Helen's early language training that she did not insert until it was almost time for the magazine to go to press. In addition to the unfinished article, there was an enormous amount of material still in Braille.

> This she transferred to typewritten copies for Miss Sullivan, whose eyes are in too delicate a condition to permit her reading the Braille points, which are intended to be felt, not seen. Then Miss Keller, who had little experience in handling large quantities of subject-matter, made a grave mistake. Thinking that when she had put her "material" into typewritten form there was no further need of her Braille transcript, she destroyed it, so that what she had written in preparation for the rest of her story was lost to her. Only the typewritten copies remained.
>
> Then came the task where one who has eyes to see must help her. Miss Sullivan and I read the disconnected passages, put them in chronological order, and counted the words to be sure the articles should be the right length. All this work we did with Miss Keller beside us, referring everything, especially matters of phrasing, to her for revision. We read to her the sentences on each side of a gap, and took down the connecting sentences that she supplied.

Like Bell and many others, Macy was struck by Helen's astonishing tactile memory.

> She remembered whole passages, some of which she had not seen for many weeks, and could tell, before Miss Sullivan had spelled into her hand a half-dozen words of the paragraphs under discussion, where they belonged and what sentences were necessary to make the connections clear.
>
> . . . One fault she has. Partly from temperament, partly from the conditions of her work, her mind runs to brilliant passages, and has not yet learned to conceive as a whole large quantities of material. Her articles fall into episodes. She knows that and is dissatisfied. So now, in preparing her manuscript for her book, she has had it all set up, as it appeared in the *Journal* in Braille, in order that she may have it under her fingers as a whole and rewrite it. That determination to do better is characteristic of her. She regards her successes merely as promises that she can win nearer to perfection.

Although careful to minimize his own role in Helen's writing, Macy did not shy away from the controversy surrounding Helen and Annie: namely, which woman was the real genius. Macy continued:

> The lives of teacher and pupil are inseparable, and to tell the truth about Helen Keller I must say a word about the good and sweet woman who has been with her for fifteen years. The only person who will not be glad to hear what I have to say is Miss Sullivan. She does not think it necessary for Miss Keller or me or any one else to tell the world what she is or what she has done. Independent and willful as her pupil, of vigorous personality, she has shut her door squarely against the world and says with characteristic frankness, "It is nobody's business who I am; I want Helen to stand on her own feet." . . . Miss Sullivan's self-effacement, however beautiful it is, has had one bad result. Deprived of valid information, the world has invented facts to suit its own whims. "Half-Rome" believes that Miss Sullivan is merely a companion to Miss Keller, using her eyes and fingers for her pupil's benefit; while the "Other Half-Rome" held for some time the absurd notion that Miss Sullivan was the author of all the sweet and clever speeches attributed to Miss Keller.

Shrewdly realizing that the *Journal* articles could be expanded into a book, John appointed himself as a literary agent for the two women and then, after skillfully playing off several publishers against one another, negotiated the best terms with Doubleday. The literary community, however, was not entirely convinced that he was acting only as their editor and agent. Because of his close association with them, there would now be a third group of skeptics who believed that the Helen Keller legend was largely being perpetuated by John Macy, who had written most of the deaf-blind woman's autobiography. Many of these scoffers were Macy's closest friends, to whom he retorted, "You are just the person who needs to read this book."

The Story of My Life, which was published in 1903, was dedicated to Alexander Graham Bell ("who had taught the deaf to speak and enabled the listening ear to hear speech from the Atlantic to the Rockies"). Besides Helen's own story and selections from her journals and letters, it included a supplementary account of her education that was composed of edited letters that Annie Sullivan had written Mrs. Hopkins from Tuscumbia. There was no mention of her early years in the poorhouse, a secret she had not yet divulged to Helen and John. Although critically well received, the book was not the best-seller that Helen, John, and the editors at Doubleday had envisioned. In the first two years it sold only ten thousand copies. In the intervening years, however, *The Story of My Life* has become a classic and is still in print. In 1996 it was named one of the hundred most important books of the twentieth century by the New York Public Library. In the same year, the editors of the *New York Times Book Review* reprinted the autobiography's original 1903 review in a special centennial issue that honored many authors whose writing had changed the world.

One of the book's most enthusiastic fans was Samuel Clemens. From his home at Riverdale-on-Hudson, he wrote Helen on St. Patrick's Day to tell her how "enchanted" he was with her work. "I suppose there is nothing like it in heaven; and not likely to be, until we get there and show off. I often think of it with longing, and how they'll say, 'There they come—sit down in front!' I am practicing with a tin halo. You do the same. . . ."

In 1904, shortly after the publication of her autobiography
The Story of My Life

In the book Helen, with the help of Macy, had dealt frankly with "The Frost King" episode, and Clemens was outraged that she had been subjected to such an ordeal. "Oh, dear me, how unspeakably funny and owlishly idiotic and grotesque was that plagiarism farce! As if there was much of anything in any human utterance, oral or written, *except* plagiarism! . . . For substantially all ideas are second-hand, consciously and unconsciously drawn from a million outside sources. . . .

"In 1866 I read Dr. Holmes's poems, in the Sandwich Islands. A year and a half later I stole his dictation, without knowing it, and used it to dedicate my 'Innocents Abroad' with. Then years afterwards I was talking with Dr. Holmes about it. He was not an ignorant ass—no, not he: he was not a collection of decayed human turnips, like your 'Plagiarism Court.' . . .

"To think of those solemn donkeys breaking a little child's heart with their ignorant rubbish about plagiarism! I couldn't sleep for blaspheming about it last night. . . . A gang of dull and hoary pirates piously setting themselves the task of disciplining and purifying a kitten that they think they caught filching a chop! Oh, dam——"

Less personally involved critics of *The Story of My Life* were for the most part highly impressed with the book, but there were a few dissenters, and their opinions are worth quoting because they raised legitimate questions about Annie and Helen's relationship. Noted a reviewer in the *New York Sun*:

It is perhaps worth reminding the readers that the wonderful feat of drawing Helen Keller out of her hopeless darkness was only accomplished by sacrificing for it another woman's whole life, and if ever the attempt is made in another similar case, it must be at the same cost.

A critic for *The Nation* was skeptical about Helen's experience of a visual-auditory world that she had never seen or heard, which included such detailed visual descriptions as "We bought a lily and set it in a sunny window. Very soon, the green, pointed buds showed signs of opening."

All her knowledge is hearsay knowledge, her very sensations are for the most part vicarious, and yet she writes of things beyond her power of perception with the assurance of one who has verified every word.

If it could be brought home to her that such likeness in her case could be attained only by the sacrifice of truth; if she could only realize that is better to be one's self, however limited and afflicted, than the best imitation of somebody else that could be achieved! . . . One resents the pages of second-

hand description of natural objects, when what one wants is a sincere
account of the attitude, the natural attitude towards life of one whose eyes
and ears are sealed.

This criticism revolved around the previously discussed word-mindedness, or verbalism, of the blind in which they were taught to communicate
with others about the world not as they relate to it, but as sighted people
know it, writing and speaking about things they have personally never seen.
As in the case of "The Frost King" scandal, it was an implied attack on
Annie Sullivan's teaching methods, which stressed literary expression and
visual respectability at the expense of Helen's own unique experiences.

On this occasion, an outraged John Macy rushed to Helen's defense. In
a blistering letter to a Boston newspaper, he accused the *Nation* critic of "a
kind of arrogance of his senses. He thinks that a blind person cannot know
what we know, or imagine what we know, through our ears and eyes. Worse
than that this critic thinks he knows what only a deaf-blind person can
know—that is, her attitude toward life." Also by way of rebuttal, John Hitz,
in an article in *American Anthropologist,* pointed out that the eminent psychologist Dr. John Dewey felt that when it came to imagination, the deaf-
blind excelled over all other human beings. In Hitz's opinion, Helen's case
was typical rather than abnormal, and he emphasized the "great danger of
laying too much stress upon sense perception" in the education of children,
adding that "The wonderful and varied imagery which these minds in
silence and darkness have created for themselves stands as a perpetual challenge to those teachers who are encouraging their pupils to revel in the endless panorama of sense perception. It is not necessary to make our pupils
blind-deaf, but it may be well sometimes to require them to shut their eyes
and ears, if need be, *and think.*"

ON JUNE 28, 1904, one day after her twenty-fourth birthday, a tall, serious young woman sat expectantly with a diminutive middle-aged woman
dressed in black in the auditorium of Sanders Theater in Cambridge, Massachusetts. With ninety-five classmates, Helen was waiting to receive her
diploma—it was the largest class Radcliffe had ever graduated at the time.
When Helen's name was called, she and Annie gracefully mounted the
steps of the stage together, and then Helen's eager fingers gripped something that no other deaf-blind person had ever held—a bachelor of arts
degree, coupled with the distinction cum laude. Additional words were

inscribed on her diploma in Latin: "Not only approved in the whole academic course, but excellent in English letters."

Some newspapers reported that an immense crowd of well-wishers had filled the auditorium to watch Helen graduate from college. In reality, only a few close friends attended the ceremony, including the faithful Hitz and John Macy. Mrs. Keller could not attend her daughter's graduation because of illness. Nor did Samuel Clemens see "his little child" receive her diploma. On that day, attired in mourning clothes, he was on board the *Prince Oscar* in Italy, accompanying the coffin of his beloved wife, Livy, home to the United States. Ironically, the same faithful servant who had

Helen Keller's graduation photograph from Radcliffe, 1904

been with Susy when she had died at their home in Hartford attended Livy in her final, agonized moments, while on a downstairs piano an unaware Clemens was playing the Negro spirituals that both his wife and daughter had loved.

But the person who had given life to Helen Keller stood lovingly beside her on that June day, as she had stood by her day and night ever since Helen was seven years old and a prisoner of her dark, quiet world. As she watched Helen receive her diploma and heard the standing ovation, Annie Sullivan felt a surge of pride and satisfaction. This lovely young woman—her pupil and creation—who only seventeen years before had been hurling plates at her relatives, was now a college graduate, one of the few intellectually daring women of her time to obtain a degree. Her only disappointments were that Helen had not achieved the coveted summa cum laude and that she herself had not received a degree from Radcliffe, as Helen and many other people thought she deserved. Yet Annie knew that without a Helen Keller, with her fame and her aristocratic old southern family, she never would have been exposed to an institution of higher learning. At the turn of the century, college was out of the question for working-class women, especially the children of Irish immigrants. But even without a degree, all her sacrifice—the endless hours of reading and spelling to Helen, even the threatened loss of her eyesight—had been worth it. Not only had Helen graduated with distinction, but also at Radcliffe Annie had found a very different kind of fulfillment.

The charming young Harvard instructor John Macy was now part of their circle, editing Helen's writing and suggesting studies for her last two years, as well as occasionally reading to her. His work, as well as his friendship, had not only spared Annie's eyes but also helped relieve her of the entire responsibility of Helen's care. More significantly, this witty and handsome young man had recently become Annie Sullivan's lover. That he was her first paramour is doubtful, but at thirty-eight, she was enjoying a passionate love affair with this youthful liberal and radical who was eleven years her junior and three years older than Helen.

CHAPTER 10

John

JOHN ALBERT MACY WAS a writer, literary critic, poet, and socialist who made a career out of attacking and scandalizing not only the establishment, but also other socialists in the hope of goading them on to loftier political goals. In 1928, when his friend and fellow socialist Upton Sinclair published *Boston*, his documentary novel on the Sacco-Vanzetti case that Macy felt misrepresented socialism, Macy wrote him a letter that began: "As you go hammer and tongs after writers who write better than you do, you will have to stand criticism from me who write worse than you do. *Boston* is unspeakable rubbish . . . bad art, bad story-writing, bad propaganda. . . . You are deficient in literary tact, in adroitness; and put your reader out of sympathy with you, which means complete failure. . . ."

A racy bohemian and a revolutionary who was a friend of the American Communist John Reed, John Macy was the kind of man, his friends said, who would have been insulted if his biographer did not thoroughly document his rascality and outspoken opinions, including, among others, a loathing for do-gooders. "Temperamentally, I hate reformers," he once said. "They mostly give me a pain in the arse. . . . There ought to be a reform school for reformers, which of course is itself a reform proposition!"

To be sure, John Macy was not always a renegade. Women disarmed him, especially if they were older, iron-willed, and resembled his own adored mother. A petite, beautiful woman whom people compared to an exquisite piece of Dresden china, she was a staunch Unitarian and a suffragist. Her son worshiped her, once describing her as "a midget of courage" who helped him endure his own disappointments. Yet as much as he venerated them, ambitious, dominating women irritated him, and he tired of them eventually.

John Macy, who came from a distinguished but poor Nantucket whaling family, was born in Detroit, Michigan, in 1877. His parents, Powell and Janet Foster (Patten) Macy, were of the middle class. One of five children raised in modest circumstances, John was admitted on a scholarship in 1895 to Harvard, where he achieved an outstanding academic and extracurricular record. Not only did he win the coveted Phi Beta Kappa key, but he was also editor in chief of the *Harvard Advocate* and an editor of the *Lampoon*, was elected to the best clubs, and was chosen class poet.

When John Macy was first introduced to Annie and Helen at Radcliffe, both famous women seemed in desperate need of his guardianship. Not only was Annie's physical health beginning to deteriorate — in addition to her failing eyesight, she had orthopedic problems — but her dark moods had become so unremitting that she suffered a nervous breakdown soon after Helen's graduation. Helen, too, was in danger of a mental collapse, admitting many years later that "a bad fairy of nerves chased me uphill and down dale for a long time" after she had received her diploma.

The cause of Annie's latest mental breakdown was unknown, although Helen herself provided a clue in *Teacher*, describing Annie during this period as being "rent with emotions and overwrought by my apparent lack of zeal in obtaining the summa." Whatever the cause of Annie's depression, upon her recovery she denigrated their hard-won mutual achievement. "For Helen Keller to have won a degree under such difficult conditions is worth something," she announced, "but from an educational viewpoint I consider our four years in college wasted, except for the genuine service rendered by Charles T. Copeland, her instructor in English. He helped her to self-expression. And that is what real education means."

Undoubtedly, Annie Sullivan's breakdown had more to do with her own conflicts than Helen's lack of ambition. At age thirty-eight, she was in the throes of a midlife crisis. Helen, whom she considered "her very life — her job and her child," was now an adult, and for Annie, much of the fun and challenge of "creating" her was gone. Helen may have graduated from Radcliffe, which proved to the world that she was not an impostor, but to Annie,

John Albert Macy

their mutual achievement seemed hollow. In an era that extolled motherhood as a woman's entire purpose in life, she considered herself a failure. As
one doctor of the period put it, only married women with children could
"reach the highest and most harmonious development of which they
are capable. Without [children], one of the most beautiful regions of
[a woman's] nature must forever remain without appropriate and direct
culture. . . ."

For a woman who had known some of the wealthiest, most powerful
men of her time—and undoubtedly hoped to marry one of them—the boy-
ish John Macy must have seemed at first an unlikely marital prospect. She
was thirty-eight and world-famous; he was twenty-seven and a nobody outside of Harvard circles, an impoverished assistant in English at Harvard

who lived at St. Botolph's Club in Boston and who seldom got a square meal except when he went to his mother's or was invited out. His only worldly possessions, as he admitted with some humor to a prospective landlord, included "two desks, desk chairs, five book cases, and a mess of books, most of which are no good but all of which I need in my business as pen pusher," adding that he was "rather fond of my own chairs because they have through long habit shaped themselves to the rear aspect of my anatomy. . . ."

But John Macy had attributes, Annie knew, that the doddering tycoons of industry lacked. He was young, brilliant, and virile, and according to Helen, who was aware of the couple's love affair, he also possessed "a pent-up genius" to match Annie's own superior intelligence. And, as Annie herself soon discovered, he was hot-blooded and passionate, a wonderful lover who, as she reminded him in an undated letter, made her forget about Helen when they were together.

Dearest Heart:

I was very sorry to say good-by to you yesterday after the *pleasant* hours we spent together. The sense of being at home comes to me so deeply when I am near you that I am always a little shivery when you leave me, as if the spirit of death shut his wings over me; but the next moment the thought of your love for me brings a rush of life back to my heart.

The house seemed very empty when I got home in spite of the fact that it held the dearest thing in all the world to me until a few months ago— dear, dear Helen. . . . Later after every one had gone to bed I went out on the porch to say good-night to the fragrant, beautiful world lying so quietly under the pines. . . . Somehow I felt out of sympathy with the calm loveliness of the night. My heart was hot and impatient—impatient because the repression and self-effacement of a life-time—and my life seems a century long as I look back upon it—have not stilled its passionate unrest. I sat a long time thinking of you and trying to find a reason for your love for me. How wonderful it is! And how impossible to understand! Love is the very essence of life itself. Reason has nothing to do with it! It is above all things and stronger! For one long moment I gave myself up to the supremest happiness—the certainty of a love so strong that fate had no dominion over it and in that moment all the shadows of life became beautiful realities.

Then I groped and stumbled my way back to earth again—the dreary flat earth where real things are seldom beautiful.

Dearest—this is the first letter I have written to you and I am afraid I have said things in it which you will not like. You will say that we have no right to test present happiness by harping on possible sorrow. It is because your love is so dear to me beyond all dreams of dearness that I rebel against the obstacles the years have built up between us. But you will not leave off loving me will you—not for a long time at least. . . .

I kiss you my own John and I love you, I love you, I love *you*.

This was the letter of a woman in the grip of sexual passion, yet when John Macy proposed marriage, Annie Sullivan hesitated. According to Helen, "She changed her mind continually for a year in regard to marrying John, and I quoted to myself, 'The course of true love never did run smooth.' . . . One evening after we had returned from a meeting in Boston, where I had spoken for the blind, and John had acted as my interpreter, and I was sitting in her room, she told me how pretty and graceful I had looked standing before the audience and announced that she would never marry. 'Oh, Teacher,' I exclaimed, 'if you love John, and let him go, I shall feel like a hideous accident.' "

Annie Sullivan's reluctance to marry the magnetic Harvard instructor was puzzling. Her revealing remarks to Helen suggest that on some level she was jealous of her youth and beauty and felt that Helen might make a more suitable bride for John than herself. Undoubtedly she was stung by the newspaper reports that, noting the eleven-year discrepancy in their ages, had assumed it was Helen to whom he was engaged. Then, too, she may have feared that John might be threatened by her unique relationship with Helen, a bond that was more enduring than many marriages. But John had promised her that he understood her complete commitment to her pupil. Helen, he assured her, would always come first.

Annie had told John that she would not even consider marrying him unless he first obtained Helen's approval. According to a sentimentalized but authentic newspaper account headlined "Helen Keller, ALMOST Married," which was based on an interview with Helen and the couple, Helen was moved to tears when John had reassured her that his marriage to Annie would not alter her relationship with her teacher:

> The lover sought Miss Keller in her study at their home in Wrentham and made a second proposal of marriage, this time to a gentle arbitrator. . . .
> "What did Miss Sullivan say?" she asked with the swift hand pressures that stand to her for speech.
> "She said—she spoke of you," was the answer of quick fingers.
> "Dear Miss Sullivan. Do you love her?"
> One hard hand clasp told the story.
> "Does she love you?"

Another unmistakable hand clasp.

"Then marry, of course, and I hope you will be very, very happy."

"We want you to be with us always. You will be as dear and as necessary to Miss Sullivan as you have always been. We would not marry unless your life and hers were to go on just as before."

A grateful mist covered the blind girl's eyes. The pulse in her white throat throbbed with emotion.

"Thank you, my dear friends. Now please go to Miss Sullivan and tell her that what you have told me has made me very happy and that I will be very unhappy unless she marries you."

Even after Helen had given her consent, Annie continued to vacillate, and John, instead of taking her misgivings seriously, reacted as if they were a joke. He threatened to print "Subject to change without notice" at the bottom of the wedding invitations.

The wedding was a peculiar affair when it at last occurred on an early May day in 1905 at the Wrentham, Massachusetts, farmhouse that Annie and Helen had bought some years before with shares of Spaulding's sugar stock. Most brides of the period were young women in their early twenties, taking their vows in beautiful white gowns with leg-of-mutton sleeves, a scalloped bertha collar, and a tight-fitting waistline. In contrast, the matronly Annie was somberly attired in a blue traveling dress and a white silk waist. At her own wedding, she was largely ignored. Instead, all eyes were focused on her protégée, radiant in a becoming moss-green gown, who stood beside her while Lenore Smith read into Helen's hand the words of the wedding ceremony as it was performed by Helen's eighty-five-year-old cousin, Dr. Edward Everett Hale. It was a small, intimate wedding, attended by only twenty guests, including Mrs. Keller, who approved of the match. Impressed by John Macy's intelligence, charm, and gentleness, Kate was of the opinion that "his wholesome presence" would enhance both Helen's and Annie's lives, as they had been "cut off from everything human and natural."

"It would have been too cruel," she had written to John before his marriage, "if you had not loved Helen."

Concerned as well for Helen's well-being, Dr. Hale wrote to her a few days after the ceremony, pointing out that there was nothing like her and Annie's relationship "in history or literature" and stressing the "possibilities for you which I see in the new marriage. . . . You have gained a brother and not lost a sister. . . ."

That afternoon the newlyweds left for New Orleans on their honeymoon. After they had departed, Helen went home with her mother to Tuscumbia. Despite her protestations of feeling happy about her teacher's marriage, she complained of being lonely and isolated, even though her mother knew the manual finger language. A few days later, she was overjoyed when John and Annie, lonely for her presence even on her honeymoon, dropped by for an unexpected visit. "My cup ran over! It seemed like a dream, having them with me, reveling in the beauty of early summer in the Southland," Helen remembered with pleasure many years later. "When we were all back in Wrentham, I heard that several people thought I was jealous and unhappy, and one letter of condolence was actually inflicted upon me!"

Rumors aside, no evidence exists that Helen was ever in love with John Macy, or he with her, although being attractive young people, they undoubtedly had passing sexual fantasies about one another. For John, in particular, the intriguing, physically attractive Helen Keller, with whom he had to be in continual close contact to communicate, must have been something of a temptation. Like many sophisticated members of his generation, he believed in free love; yet even if he had made an advance, it is doubtful that Helen would have responded. Any encouragement on her part would have meant betraying her beloved Annie.

Yet Helen now secretly yearned to fall in love and marry like her teacher. Ever since she was a child, she was more drawn to men than women, and by her own admission later in life, was possessed of a strong sex drive. But Annie and especially her puritanical, guilt-ridden mother had succeeded in convincing her that a romance with anyone was strictly forbidden. Disabled persons must refrain from sex. Although there were some handicapped men who enjoyed an active sex life, then, as now, disabled women continued to be the victims of a double standard, stemming from society's view of the female role as primarily one of a caregiver and nurturer, a role that a gravely handicapped woman such as Helen felt she could not fulfill.

That she was still pathetically aware of herself as an encumbrance became apparent when she and Annie went to Washington to tell Alexander Graham Bell about Annie's engagement, and the inventor reminded her of their conversation some years before at his summer retreat. " 'I told you, Helen, she would marry,' " Helen quoted him as saying. " 'Are you going to take my advice now and build your own nest?' "

" 'No,' I answered, 'I feel less inclined than ever to embark upon the great adventure. I have fully made up my mind that a man and a woman

Helen, Annie Macy (standing), John Macy with their dog Kaiser, and John Hitz at Wrentham, Massachusetts, 1907

must be equally equipped to weather successfully the vicissitudes of life. It would be a severe handicap to any man to saddle upon him the dead weight of my infirmities. I know I have nothing to give a man that would make up for such an unnatural burden.' "

Still, she could live vicariously through Annie's marriage, and the unaccustomed sensation of strong male fingers upon her palm, tapping in code new impressions and ways of dealing with a world she had never seen or heard, must have been a thrilling one.

Although Helen continued to maintain that John Macy was like "a brother" to her, a letter that John had written to her prior to his marriage to Annie Sullivan suggests that he did not entirely accept that role and that

Helen did not regard him in such a prim and proper light. His letter—salty, flirtatious, suggestive—was too roguish to be considered "brotherly" in the conventional sense of the term:

> Dearest little Billy—
>
> Phiz [Helen's Boston terrier] followed me to the train Friday and I sent him home. That night I stayed in town. When I came back next day, I found Teacher in distress, not because she missed me but because Phiz had not returned. We found later that he had gone into the school house to the great delight of the children. By the way, Teacher says that Phiz and the new Jap servant are more comfort to her than I am. Phiz came home on a halter looking very sheepish. Every time Teacher spoke to him, he hung his head and felt ashamed of his spree. That is a base humility for a good male animal to show. I never reveal such spirit when I have been on a spree. The Jap, whose name is Kawakami, which Mrs. Hopkins insists on calling Yokahama, is a joy to Teacher, no doubt because she has a man she can really boss.

Despite the letter's jocular tone, it was obvious that John, besides attempting to impress Helen with his maleness and sexual prowess, was already chafing at his future wife's dominating personality. He may have outwardly deferred to her by calling her "Teacher," but he also had a new, silly nickname for her, "Bill." Helen, the "offspring" of her mind—was "Billy." Clearly, by not giving Annie and Helen different nicknames, he had discovered another truth about his prospective marriage, that he was marrying not one, but two women. Whether they were in fact two separate personalities or the two disparate sides of Annie Sullivan's personality remained a tantalizing question.

As for Annie, the head-over-heels-in-love stage of her relationship with John was over, at least in her correspondence. She was reverting to character, and it was a smothering, maternal one. No longer was she addressing John in her love letters as "Dearest," but as "my own dear little Johnny," an endearment exactly like the one she used for Helen when she wrote to her—"my dear little girl"—even though Helen was now twenty-four years old.

As an old woman, Helen concluded that Annie's constantly shifting moods and eternal restlessness with her incessant need for self-renewal, rather than their unusual relationship, was the cause of her marital discord. "Annie never wholly acquiesced in the fact of her marriage," Helen wrote.

"She gained greater self-control—she held her darker moods well in hand like an animal trainer, but now and then she could hear them growling, and she said she needed me to keep her quiet and reasonable. . . ."

For a brilliant, unstable woman, a faithful deaf-blind female companion was a far more compatible "mate" than a bright, challenging male.

Yet for a very brief period Annie and John were happy together, and later Helen would observe that "the few years during which marriage yielded its satisfactions to her were in some respects the most fruitful part of our lives together." Still, Annie's black moods continued to periodically overwhelm her. There were times when her eyes tormented her, and periods of even deeper depression when she failed to become pregnant. Vainly hoping to find release from her troubles, she resumed her old habit of riding unruly horses. One morning, when Helen discovered that her teacher had been thrown from a horse and badly shaken, she was furious. In her mind, Annie deliberately courted danger. "She had tried my patience with her mad escapades, and now I was at my wits' end. 'I am sorry, Helen, I was trying to run away from the kitchen and everything that makes one old. Kiss me, and I will turn over a new leaf.' I never heard a complaint from her about house-keeping again, and it was only after many years that I discovered the real cause of Teacher's extraordinary behavior. But that is one of the tragic secrets that are locked up in the hearts of men and women who see deeply into life's mysteries."

What was the cause of Annie's self-destructiveness that Helen could never bring herself to mention? Had her brutal, drunken father abused her before he abandoned the family? Had she committed incest with her little brother in the almshouse? Or had Annie perhaps hastened his death to spare him further suffering? In an age in which women were expected to be chaste until marriage, was she sexually promiscuous with Michael Anagnos, Alexander Graham Bell, John Spaulding, or one of the deranged male inmates who fondled her at the poorhouse? Helen went to her grave without revealing Annie's dark secret, and letters that might have shed light on it were consumed in a fire that destroyed Arcan Ridge, her Westport, Connecticut, home, in 1946.

One by one, Anagnos, Gilman, and others had, in Annie's own words, "met their Waterloo." Although no evidence exists that she ever had a sexual attraction toward Helen, or vice versa, the "near-perfect" female she reportedly created and who was perhaps in part the embodiment of her pure, ideal self provided Annie with something no man ever could. Locked into her limited, controllable world, Helen could be counted on to remain ever faithful. As Annie had observed years earlier, she would never be capable of establishing an independent life for herself.

It was during those early years of her unconventional marriage that Annie Sullivan burned the diary she had begun keeping when Helen was nine years old. Smelling the smoke, Helen, who had never read the journal, was appalled, exclaiming to her teacher that she should not have destroyed it, as it must have contained "original thoughts" and Annie's own "ideas of education." According to Helen, Annie dismissed these concerns. "I saw so many scolding passages extending over page after page I flung the stuff into the flames. I couldn't have had a moment's peace if it had been read by you or John," she told her. Rationalizing Annie's odd behavior, Helen imagined that she had used the diary "as a kind of medieval self-mortification and come back to the world friendly, compassionate" and that it had contained details of Annie's horrific childhood that she wanted to spare her.

Despite their close relationship, Annie remained an enigma to Helen, a woman of secrets.

FOR A TIME this ménage à trois was a harmonious one, and later Helen would describe that deceptively halcyon period at Wrentham as "a sort of pre-existence—a dream of days when I wore another body and had a different consciousness."

For Helen, these were creative, fruitful years. John Macy may have been Annie's husband and sexual partner, but for Helen he functioned as the perfect editor and collaborator, criticizing her "severely" when her work was not up to par and praising her when she wrote something he liked. According to Nella Braddy Henney, Helen's next editor and something of a literary snob, "the best critic she ever had was Mr. Macy. He pruned her style of its wordiness, curbed her proneness to dogmatic preaching and generally pulled her down out of the clouds."

Helen was fortunate to have such a brilliant individual as her editor. A lively, original thinker, Macy was an intellectual pioneer in American letters. In 1906, in an article for the *Atlantic Monthly*, he had praised the little-known writing of Joseph Conrad. According to his biographer,

> For Macy early on became a Socialist, and saw literature always to some extent in that social and economic context so emphasized in literary criticism in the last two years. This was evident in *The Spirit of American Literature*, published in 1913, in which he reviled the leading historic figures in

our national letters both from a romantic and social standpoint. In dealing with a ruling god like William Dean Howells, Macy insisted that he did not know life because he would not know 'how to sit down and eat his grub with a bunch of workmen and find out what they think of things.' Macy's book helped to raise the current reputation of Whitman in particular; it was a pioneer volume in the attack, which H. L. Mencken was later to carry much further, against the genteel tradition dominant then not only in the universities but most current criticism. It ridiculed the pretensions of literature that did not draw 'the grand passions, sexual or other.' If it seems a very quiet and moderate book to most readers today, it is only because the point of view for which it argued has now been so widely accepted.

Prophesying the future era of realistic writing, Macy believed that only Edith Wharton's *Ethan Frome* and Theodore Dreiser's *Jennie Gerhardt* came "to grips with the problems of life."

John's literary genius augmented Helen's understanding of the outside world, and in his own way, he became almost as vital to her life as Annie. "Both had a magical way of breaking up the monotony for me with bright comments and rapid, frequent reports of what I could not see or hear,"

The house in Wrentham. Helen always maintained that the happiest days of her life were spent there with Annie and John Macy before the disintegration of their marriage.

Helen at Wrentham
with her "tree friend."
A mystic, Helen liked to
listen to "the lonely
murmur" of the trees.

Helen observed years later in *Midstream.* "And such a difference as there was in the way each talked! My teacher's comments on scenes and news and people were like nuggets of gold, lavishly spilled into my hands, while her husband put his words together carefully, almost as if he were writing a novel. He often said he wanted to write a novel, and certainly there was material for one in his brilliant conversation. . . . Next to my teacher, he was the friend who discovered most ways to give me pleasure and gratify my intellectual curiosity."

John could bring Helen out of a depressed mood with a joke or a wise-crack, which he communicated through their special code. A special delight for her was a stroll or a drive along the curving roads of Wrentham, where he would describe to her a pond "smiling like a babe on earth's breast, or a gorgeous bird on the wing. . . . There are no words to tell how dear he was to me or how much I loved him."

It was John who stretched a wire and ropes almost a quarter of a mile along a field so that Helen, a physically active woman, could take a walk without hurting herself—"the longest and most free walk" she had ever had alone—and who took her out for long walks in the morning or rides on her tandem bicycle. To his surprise, he discovered that the faster they rode, the more exhilarated she became.

Yet all the time they were together, John, who was now the perpetuator of her legend, was observing this singular woman—her seemingly over-wrought manner that often led people to mistakenly conclude she was having a nervous breakdown, her constantly moving hands, which seemed "a confusion of bird's wings," and her extraordinary tactile memory—so he could present a convincing portrait of her to the world:

> . . . Her memory of people is remarkable. She remembers the grasp of fin-gers she has held before, all the characteristic tightening of the muscles that makes one person's handshake different from another.
>
> If she does not know the answer to a question, she guesses with mischie-vous assurance. Ask her the color of your coat, she will feel it and say "black." If it happens to be blue, and you tell her so triumphantly, she is likely to answer, "Thank you. I am glad you know. Why did you ask me?" . . .
>
> Her whimsical and adventuresome spirit puts her so much on her met-tle that she makes a poor subject for the psychological experimenter. More-over, Miss Sullivan does not see why Miss Keller should be subjected to the investigation of a scientist, and has not herself made many experiments.
>
> Her enjoyment of music is genuine, for she has a tactile recognition of sound when the waves of air beat against her. When the organ was played for her in St. Bartholomew's, the whole building shook with the great pedal notes, but that does not altogether account for what she felt and enjoyed. The vibration of the air as the organ notes swelled made her sway in answer. Sometimes she puts her hand on a singer's throat to feel the muscular trill and contraction, and from this she gets genuine pleasure. . . .
>
> Most that she knows at first hand comes from her sense of touch. This sense is not, however, so finely developed as in some other blind people. She seems to have very little sense of direction. She gropes her way without much certainty in rooms where she is quite familiar. Most blind people are aided by the sense of sound, so that a fair comparison is hard to make, except with other deaf-blind persons. Her dexterity is not notable either in comparison with the normal person, or with other blind people. The only thing she does which requires skill with the hands is her work on the type-writer. Although she has used the typewriter since she was eleven years old, she is rather careful than rapid. She writes with fair speed and absolute sure-ness. Her manuscripts seldom contain typographical errors when she hands

them to Miss Sullivan to read. Her typewriter has no special attachments. She keeps the relative position of the keys by an occasional touch of the little fingers on the outer edge of the board.

Miss Keller puts her hand lightly over the hand of one who is talking to her and gets the words as rapidly as they can be spelled. As she explains, she is not conscious of the single letters or of separate words.

The time that one of Miss Keller's friends realizes most strongly that she is blind, is when he comes on her suddenly in the dark and hears the rustle of her fingers across the page. . . .

Like every deaf or blind person, Miss Keller depends on smell to an unusual degree. When she was a little girl she smelled everything and knew where she was by the distinctive odors. As her intellect grew she became less dependent on this sense. To what extent she now identifies objects by their odors is hard to determine. The sense of smell has fallen into disrepute and a deaf-blind person is reluctant to speak of it.

. . . Miss Keller is distinctly not a singular proof of occult and mysterious theories and any attempt to explain her in that way fails to reckon with her normality. She is no more mysterious and complex than any other person.

Of the real world she knows more of the good and less of the evil than most people seem to know. Her teacher does not harass her with the little unhappy things; but of the important difficulties they have been through, Miss Keller was fully informed, took her share of the suffering, and put her mind to the problems.

She has a large, generous sympathy and absolute fairness of temper. So far as she is noticeably different from other people she is less bound by convention. She has the courage of her metaphors and lets them take her skyward when we poor self-conscious folk would think them rather too bookish for ordinary conversation. She always says exactly what she thinks, without fear of the plain truth; yet no one is more tactful and adroit than she in turning an unpleasant truth so that it will do the least possible hurt to the feelings of others. Not all the attention that has been paid her since she was a child has made her take herself too seriously. Sometimes she gets started on a very solemn preachment. Then her teacher calls her an incorrigible little sermonizer and she laughs at herself.

In contrast to William Wade, who believed that any proficient teacher of the deaf-blind could have educated an intelligent child like Helen, John was convinced that only one woman in the world was equipped to teach her and "that the unanalyzable kinship between these two women is the foundation of Helen Keller's career." In a passage he had omitted from *The Story of My Life*, he pointed out that even though he was an expert in several subjects that Helen was studying in college and was also fluent in the manual alphabet, he was inept at teaching them to Helen. "Miss Sullivan's skill in presenting material, some of which she does not try to retain herself, but allows to pass through her to the busy fingers of her pupil; her instinct in striking out the inessential: her feeling, which is now a matter of long experience, for just the turn of thought that Miss Keller needs at the moment— all this is quite beyond me and, I believe beyond anybody else."

Clearly, John considered his wife to be the brilliant one. Elsewhere he wrote that Helen was "not even scholarly in her interests. Her mind is stout and energetic, of solid endurance. . . . I, for one, cannot see that she has the intellect of a genius, or much creative power, or great originality. . . . She writes well not by virtue of a facile gift, but by scrupulous revision, patient thinking, and diligent attention to the criticism of her instructors, and to the advice of Miss Sullivan. . . . Labor is the secret of her advancement."

FOR YEARS HELEN HAD relied on Annie, a talented writer, to edit her letters and speeches, but now it was primarily John who continued to assist her with her literary work. With his help she wrote *The World I Live In*, which had appeared previously as a series of essays in *Century* magazine under the title "Sense and Sensibility." Although she usually hated to write, finding it a laborious process, she found, to her surprise, that writing the book, which was published in 1908, was a pleasurable experience. "I do not remember writing anything in such a happy mood as *The World I Live In*," she later wrote. "I poured into it everything that interested me at one of the happiest periods of my life—my newly discovered wealth of philosophy and the feeling of the New England beauty which surrounded me."

Of all her books, *The World I Live In* would hold the most appeal for the public. In it, she at last revealed the real nature of the inner world that was her entire world.

CHAPTER 11

The World I Live In

The *World I Live In* remains the most fascinating of Helen Keller's works, as it offered a detailed account of her alternate reality and the ways in which she received her impressions of the world. Realizing that her life seemed unimaginable to a hearing-sighted person, she explained that it was a complete and sufficient one for her, a place in which she did not feel disabled or inadequate but had her own identity. "Patiently the [deaf-blind] child explores the dark, until he builds up a knowledge of the world he lives in, and his soul meets the beauty of the world, where the sun shines always, and the birds sing," she wrote. "To the blind child the dark is kindly. In it he finds nothing extraordinary or terrible. It is his familiar world; even the groping from place to place, the halting steps, the dependence upon others, do not seem strange to him. . . . Not until he weighs his life in the scale of others' experience does he realize what it is to live forever in the dark. . . ."

Made up of touch sensations that were devoid of color and sound, Helen's world nevertheless throbbed with interest and life. "Every object is associated in my mind with tactual qualities which, combined in countless ways, give me a sense of power, of beauty, or of incongruity," she added, "for

with my hands I can feel the comic as well as the beautiful in the outward appearance of things."

Through the sense of touch Helen was able to instantly recognize the faces of her friends, enjoy famous works of sculpture, and appreciate "the delicate shapes of flowers, the noble forms of trees, and the range of mighty winds."

From touching a person's hand, she could instantly deduce his or her character or mood. "Not only is the hand as easy to recognize as the face, but it reveals its secrets more openly and unconsciously," she observed. "People control their countenances, but the hand is under no such restraint. It relaxes and becomes listless when the spirit is low and dejected; the muscles tighten when the mind is excited or the heart glad; and permanent qualities stand written on it all the time."

Annie Sullivan's brilliant teaching methods and her keen appreciation of the natural world had enabled Helen to imagine that she lived in a world of color. "I have talked so much and read so much about colors that through no will of my own I attach meanings to them, just as all people attach certain meanings to abstract terms like hope, idealism, monotheism, intellect, which cannot be represented truly by visible objects, but which are understood from analogies between immaterial concepts and the ideas they awaken of external things," she noted. "The force of association drives me to say that white is exalted and pure, green is exuberant, red suggests love or shame or strength."

Vibrations were also a vital part of Helen's world. "Every atom of my body is a vibroscope," she commented. "I derive much knowledge of everyday matters from the jars and jolts which are to be felt everywhere in the house."

When Helen was in her study, she was able to know that it was mealtime when someone stamped on the floor in the dining room below. To some extent, she could distinguish different persons by their tread on the stairs or on the floor. "Footsteps, I discover, vary tactually according to the age, the sex, and the manner of the walker," she explained. "It is impossible to mistake a child's patter for the tread of a grown person. . . . I know when one kneels, kicks, shakes something, sits down, or gets up."

In her study, she was able to recognize the flight of airplanes passing in the vicinity of her house. She also could recognize the difference between the vibrations produced by implements used by a carpenter in the house nearby barn, such as sawing, planing, or hammering. "A slight flutter on rug tells me that a breeze has blown my papers off the table. . . . A rou

Helen and a model of Nike of Samothrace, c. 1903. The art that she appreciated the most was sculpture, which is palpable as well as visual.

thump is a signal that a pencil has rolled on the floor. If a book falls, it gives a flat thud. . . . Many of these vibrations are obliterated out of doors. On a lawn or the road, I can feel only running, stamping, and the rumble of wheels."

Although Helen could not distinguish one composition from another, it was through "attractive" vibrations that she was able to enjoy music, which, according to an authority on the subject, may be defined as pulsating air stimulating the organs in our ears. "I love the instrument by which all the diapasons of the ocean are caught and released in surging floods—the many-voiced organ," she enthused about her favorite instrument. "If music could be seen, I could point where the organ-notes go, as they rise and fall, climb up and up, rock and sway, now loud and deep, now high and stormy, anon soft and solemn, with lighter vibrations interspersed between and running across them. I should say that organ-music fills to an ecstasy the act of feeling."

The violin was another instrument that delighted Helen. It seemed to her "beautifully alive as it responds to the lightest wish of the master. The

distinction between its notes is more delicate than between the notes of the piano."

As for the piano itself, she enjoyed it the most when she touched the instrument. "If I keep my hand on the piano case, I detect tiny quavers, returns of melody, and the hush that follows. This explains to me how sound can die away to the listening ear."

In later life, by putting her hands on the radio to enjoy a musical concert, she was able to discern the difference between the cornet and strings, and by placing her hand on a person's throat and cheek, she could enjoy a song or a conversation itself through the changes of the voice. "I know when it is low or high, clear or muffled, sad or cheery," she said. "The thin, quavering sensation of an old voice differs in my touch from the sensation of a young voice. A Southerner's drawl is quite unlike the Yankee twang."

Highly sensitive to the interrelationships among the senses, Helen herself was unsure whether touch or smell conveyed the most knowledge about the world. Her sense of smell was so refined that she could distinguish different types of roses and wildflowers. She could also distinguish one mushroom from another, including the deadly amanita.

Another of Helen's amazing sensory abilities was that she knew when a storm was coming hours before its arrival. "I notice first a throb of expectancy, a slight quiver, a concentration in my nostrils. As the storm draws near, my nostrils dilate, the better to receive the flood of earth odors which seem to multiply and extend, until I feel the splash of rain against my cheek. As the tempest departs, receding farther and farther, the odors fade, become fainter and fainter, and die away beyond the bar of space."

Although Helen termed smell "a potent wizard that transports us across a thousand miles and all the years we have lived," she felt that "for some inexplicable reason the sense of smell does not hold the high position it deserves among its sisters. There is something of the fallen angel about it."*

Like Marcel Proust, whose entire life was brought into his conscious mind by the aroma of a tea-soaked madeleine in his mother's kitchen, Helen, whenever she smelled fruit, felt as though she were transported

---

* New studies into the nature of smell, which is considered the most primitive of the senses, have confirmed Helen's observations. According to a recent Associated Press report, scientists have discovered that "memories dredged up by flavors and odors feel more vivid and emotional than those brought on by sights, sounds and tastes; in the case of flavor, taste is actually less important than smell. . . . Modern research shows that the brain handles information from the nose in a unique way, sending it directly to parts of the brain [the limbic system, which includes the hippocampus, a brain area closely associated with memory, and the amygdala, which neuroscientists have recently identified as a center for emotions]. In contrast, sights, sounds and sensations are routed through the brain's analytical apparatus before reaching more primitive, emotional areas."

With Jascha Heifetz. Helen holds the neck of the violin to "hear" its vibrations, 1937. In later life she liked to listen to radio concerts, her fingers on a specially made loudspeaker; she could also distinguish among the oboe, piano, and harp. She disliked jazz. It had a bombarding sensation not pleasant to her touch, and it disturbed her emotions. "When it continues for some time," she admitted, "I have a wild impulse to flee."

In 1941 Helen attended a performance of Wagner's opera *Tristan and Isolde* at the Metropolitan Opera House in New York. She is seen here listening to Lauritz Melchior as he sings for her.

across the years to her southern home, "to my childhood frolics in the peach orchard. Other odors, instantaneous and fleeting, cause my heart to dilate joyously or contract with remembered grief. Even as I think of smells, my nose is full of scents that start awake sweet memories of summers gone and ripening fields far away."

From a person's odor, Helen often knew their line of work. "The odors of wood, iron, paint and drugs cling to the garments of those that work in them. Thus I can distinguish the carpenter from the iron-worker, the artist from the mason or the chemist. When a person passes quickly from one place to another, I get a scent impression of where he has been—the kitchen, the garden, or the sick-room. . . . Human odors are as varied and capable of recognition as hands and faces. The dear odors of those I love are so definite, so unmistakable, that nothing can quite obliterate them. If many years should elapse before I saw an intimate friend again, I know that I should recognize his odor instantly in the heart of Africa, as promptly as would my brother that barks."

Many years after Helen's death, Diane Ackerman, in her acclaimed *Natural History of the Senses*, would pay tribute to her as "the most famous prodigy of the nose." "Helen Keller had a miraculous gift for deciphering the fragrant palimpsest of life, all the 'layers' that most of us read as a blur," she observed. ". . . How someone blind and deaf . . . could understand so well the texture and appearance of life, let alone the way our eccentricities express themselves in the objects we enjoy, is one of the great mysteries. She found that babies didn't yet have a 'personality scent,' unique odors she could identify in adults. And her sensuality expressed itself in smell—and explained an age-old attraction. 'Masculine exhalations are, as a rule, stronger, more vivid, more widely differentiated than those of women. In the odor of young men there is something elemental, as of fire, storm, and salt sea. It pulsates with buoyancy and desire. It suggests all the things strong and beautiful and joyous and gives me a sense of physical happiness.'"

Ackerman described Helen as a "sensuist—a person who rejoices in sensory experiences" who beautifully described "the whelm of life's aromas, tastes, touches, feelings, which she explored with the voluptuousness of a courtesan. Despite her handicaps, she was more robustly alive than many people of her generation."

Although Helen's knowledge of the world was gained through touch, smell, and taste, it was her powerful imagination that made it a meaningful place. "Without imagination what a poor thing my world would be! My garden would be a silent patch of earth strewn with sticks of a variety of shapes and smells. But when the eye of my mind is opened to its beauty, the barge ground brightens beneath my feet, and the hedge-row bursts into leaf, and the rose-tree shakes its fragrance everywhere."

THE PUBLIC LIKED to imagine that Helen existed in a black pit, but in *The World I Live In*, she explained that she lived in a world of silence and "of tangible white darkness," a contradiction in terms, although her description does support the theory of several investigators that she lived in a neutral gray environment.* Others who have become deaf-blind in later life describe the condition as feeling as if they had stepped "into a London fog—one of the thick yellow variety . . . a dull, flesh-colored opacity. So much for literal 'darkness.' "

For Helen and other blind men and women, it was important that people realize that they do not inhabit a dark world. As Reverend Thomas Carroll, who worked extensively with the blind, pointed out, "the analogy which makes sight and light the same thing, or obversely blindness and darkness the same thing, is positively untrue, and moreover, *seriously harmful* to the blind, a barrier to their acceptance in society. It uses as symbols of sight and blindness two symbols which are basic to mankind, and in so doing gives blindness a symbolic meaning which it should not have."

KNOWING THAT the public was curious about the dreams of a deaf-blind person, Helen devoted two chapters in *The World I Live In* to a description of her dreams, including some recalled from early childhood:

> In my dreams I have sensations, odors, tastes and ideas which I do not remember to have had in reality. Perhaps they are glimpses which my mind

* According to two blind scientists who were sighted until adolescence, this "world of darkness" does not exist for either the blind or the sighted. Both cite the phenomenon known as "dark adaptation." For example, upon entering a lightless cave, at first a person will be startled by the complete darkness; then gradually, after becoming dark-adapted, the person will feel as if he or she can distinguish objects in the neutral gray surroundings. According to one of the researchers, "The dark world without any light will not remain a dark world; it will become a neutral gray world without either light or darkness in it. . . . The dark experiential world of the totally blind from birth consists of visual nothingness so far as its nature can be discovered. . . . In all those cases of partial blindness in which the retina is sensitive to light, the blind, like the seeing, can perceive darkness, and again like the seeing, they experience degrees of light and darkness in proportion to the intensity of physical stimulation. Those of the blind who lack functional retinas [like Helen Keller] perceive neither light nor darkness. They probably see exactly what the seeing do when they have become what is known as dark-adapted, a visual field filled with neutral 'gray.' Those blind individuals with retinas that are incapable of external stimulation but that support entoptic activity have their world of darkness made up of visual experience equivalent in color and movement to Fourth-of-July pyrotechnics."

Wrentham, 1907. Helen once wrote, "If you can enjoy the sun and flowers and music where there is nothing except darkness and silence you have proved the mystic sense."

catches through the veil of sleep of my earliest babyhood. I have heard the trampling of many waters. Sometimes a wonderful light visits me in my sleep. Such a flash and glory it is! I gaze and gaze until it vanishes.

Once in a dream I held in my hand a pearl. I have no memory vision of a real pearl. The only one I saw in my dreams must, therefore, have been a creation of my imagination. It was a smooth, exquisitely molded crystal. As I gazed into its shimmering deeps, my soul was flooded with an ecstasy of tenderness, and I was filled with wonder, as one who should for the first time look into the cool, sweet heart of a rose. My pearl was dew and fire, the velvety green of moss, the soft whiteness of lilies, and the distilled hues and sweetness of a thousand roses. It seemed to me the soul of beauty was dissolved in its crystal bosom. This beauteous vision strengthens my conviction that the world which the mind builds up out of countless subtle experiences and suggestions is fairer than the world of the senses. The splendor of the sunset my friends gaze at across the purpling hills is wonderful. But the sunset of the inner vision brings purer delight because it is the worshipful blending of all the beauty that we have known and desired.

In describing her dreams, Helen commented that they were like her experience when she was awake, an observation that was borne out by later studies of the deaf-blind in which it was found that the sensory composition of their dreams is identical with that of waking experience.

Helen's dreams were of interest to the medical profession, and in the early 1900s, Joseph Jastrow, an eminent psychologist, had analyzed them based on her written descriptions. Jastrow was one of the earliest investigators of dream imagery in the blind, and his studies, in conjunction with those of G. Heermann, who undertook similar studies a half century earlier, are still considered valid today, as subsequent research has reproduced their findings. In his book *The Psychology of Blindness*, Donald Kirtley, a psychologist, summarized their findings:

> Both researchers concluded that the congenitally blind, as well as individuals blinded before the age of five, do not experience dream vision—blindness prevents the stimulation of the immature visual cortex to maintain its integrity; people who lost their sight between the ages of five and seven may or may not retain such images, because by age seven the occipital region is sufficiently mature to sustain appreciable visual activity in the absence of environmental input, so that blinding at this time does not eradicate the visualizing power; most persons losing their vision after the seventh year continue to experience optical imagery, though its initial photographic clarity tends to fade markedly with the passage of time. One subject reported dream vision following thirty-five years of blindness; another after fifty-four years, after which it faded out.
>
> In terms of imaginal content, we found that the dream reports of persons blinded after age seven are scarcely distinguishable from those of the seeing. Likewise, the congenitally or early blind differ from the sighted only with respect to the absence of dream vision. In regard to thematic or narrative content, as well as personality factors affecting dreaming, individual differences in our blind subjects clearly predominated over group trends.

When Jastrow analyzed Helen's written descriptions of her dreams, he found that she often used visual and auditory images to record her sensations. Although Helen had speculated in *The World I Live In* that her new sensations in her dreams may have been memories retained from a hearing-sighted early childhood, Jastrow and other researchers have viewed the imagery as pure verbalism—that is, the result of linguistic associations and fantasy rather than from experiencing actual visual imagery. In Jastrow's opinion, Helen's dreams were sparse in sensory detail but "rich in affect and creative imagination."

There were several important differences between Helen's dreams and those of Laura Bridgman, who was studied by G. Stanley Hall in 1878, when Laura was forty-seven years old. According to Kirtley, Hall found that Laura's dreams, which were usually nightmares, did not contain any visual, auditory, smell, or taste imagery. When she was asleep, she often spelled with her fingers, as did the people who appeared to her in her dreams. "A typical dream was described by Laura simply as 'hard, heavy and thick,' " Kirtley noted. "Other dreams were described largely in terms of internal sensations such as 'blood rushing' and rapid heartbeat. Thus the sensory core of her dreams consisted of tactile-motor and visceral images that mirrored the sensations uppermost during her diurnal existence. In the words of Jastrow, who later reviewed Hall's study of Laura: 'She is perchance dreaming of an animal which to us would first make itself seen or heard, but to her is present only when it touches and startles her. She lacks the anticipatory sense.' "

In contrast to Laura, Helen's sense of touch seemed unimportant in her dreams; she seldom spelled with her fingers, nor did the characters in her dreams spell into her hand. She also claimed that in her dreams she would seldom grope and could walk freely without a companion, even through congested city streets.

Interestingly, Helen's dreams were often filled with rage and aggression against Annie Sullivan. One of her recurrent nightmares involving Teacher had to do with a spirit that visited her frequently, bringing "a sensation of cool dampness, such as one feels on a chill November night when the window is open. . . . My blood is chilled and seems to freeze in my veins. . . . After a while the spirit passes on, and I say to myself shudderingly, 'That was Death. I wonder if he has taken her.' The pronoun stands for my Teacher."

The following two dreams, which were unpublished during Helen's lifetime, indicate that the rage and rebellion Helen first displayed toward Teacher when she arrived in Tuscumbia had not been entirely transformed into hero worship. In some respects, the battle between the two women was an ongoing one, and Helen—in her dreams, at least—continued to resent Annie's control and dominance:

> When I am in Dreamland, I generally have the same thoughts, emotions and affections that I have in my waking hours. However, there are some unaccountable contradictions in my dreams. For instance, although I have the strongest, deepest affection for my teacher, yet when she appears to me in my sleep, we quarrel and fling the wildest reproaches at each other. She seizes me by the hand and drags me by main force towards I can never

decide what—an abyss, a perilous mountain pass or a rushing torrent, whatever in my terror I may imagine. One night we stood at the foot of a stairway
that seemed to rise to the very stars, and she commanded me to climb it. I
refused stubbornly, declaring that my feet would stumble, and I should be
hurled from the dizzying heights. At last, unable to make me yield, she
struck a match and flashing it in my face tried to make me swallow it. Still I
resisted and remonstrated, and at last I tore myself away from her firm grasp.
I rushed blindly in an opposite direction, pursued by my teacher and was
just letting myself down into a cellar by a trap-door when I awoke.

Sometimes my teacher changes her conduct strangely and smiles at me,
but then she is so far away, I cannot reach her. Once I dreamed that I saw
her all robed in white, standing on the brink of Niagara Falls. At first I did
not recognize her; but I thought she was an angel. Suddenly she was swept
out of sight, and I dashed forward; for I knew she had plunged into the
whirlpool. In another instant she rose on the crest of a huge wave, and with
superhuman strength I seized her and held her fast. In a flash I knew who
she was, and my efforts to save her were most frantic; but in vain I could not
draw her ashore. I could only prevent her from sinking below the water's
surface. It seemed as if some unseen power were trying to wrest her away
from me, and forgetting our past quarrels I thrust my love between her and
her destruction. At last, mustering all her strength, she threw herself on the
shore; but to my surprise she vanished without appearing to know who I
was, or what danger she had been in; I really thought she must indeed be an
angel, and therefore beyond all harm. Yet I was at a loss how to account for
her ignoring me—that was worse than all our quarrels put together.

The public yearned to learn more about Helen's world, but her next
work, *The Song of the Stone Wall*, which was published two years later, in
1910, was in a different genre. In this epic poem, Helen expressed her joy in
helping to build up an old stone wall around the Wrentham acres so she
could extend her walk. As she kept fingering the various shapes, textures,
and sizes of the stones, she found herself identifying with them—"O beautiful, blind stones, inarticulate and dumb!" They also evoked New England's
past and the ancestors—the courageous spirit of the Pilgrims who had built
the wall with "their hardened hands" and saw "the eternal spring," the
extermination of the "wronged, friendly, childlike, peaceable" Indian
tribes, and the "groaning" voices of the women who were condemned in
Salem to die as witches.

The Song of the Stone Wall is a problematic work, in that one wonders
why Helen chose to undertake such an ambitious project, since after "The
Frost King" scandal she had vowed to never again attempt fiction or poetry.
Several years later, her confidence apparently restored, she did write several
poems with mixed results, including a long poem, "The Chant of Dark-

ness," which concluded *The World I Live In*. To the dismay of her publishers, it contained many lines that appeared to have been lifted from the Book of Job. Helen later explained this and other borrowings by saying that her friends often spelled to her "paragraphs that strike them, and I do not always know the name of the book or the author. . . . Sometimes I think I ought to stop writing altogether, since I cannot tell surely which of my ideas are borrowed feathers, except for those which I gather from books in raised print."

In this instance, and perhaps others, John appears to have functioned as more than Helen's editor. A comparison of the text of *The Song of the Stone Wall* with both Helen's and John's previous writing reveals more similarities with his poetry than with her verse, and it seems likely that John was the principal author, fashioning a sensuous, polished poem that was based on Helen's poetic fragments expressing her yearning for romance, marriage, and motherhood:

> I see a young girl—the spirit of spring she seems,
> Sister of the winds that run through the rippling daisies.
> Sweet and clear her voice calls father and brother,
> And one whose name her shy lips will not utter.
> But a chorus of leaves and grasses speaks her heart
> And tells his name: the birches flutter by the wall;
> The wild cherry-tree shakes its plumy head
> And whispers his name; the maple
> Opens its rosy lips and murmurs his name;
> The marsh-marigold sends the rumor
> Down the winding stream, and the blue flag
> Spreads the gossip to the lilies in the lake:
> All Nature's eyes and tongues conspire
> In the unfolding of the tale
> That Adam and Eve beneath the blossoming rose-tree
> Told each other in the Garden of Eden.
> Once more the wind blows from the walls,
> And I behold a fair young mother;
> She stands at the lilac-shaded door
> With her baby at her breast;
> She looks across the twilit fields and smiles
> And whispers to her child: "Thy father comes!"

Despite the enthusiastic reviews and generally decent sales of her books, Helen was ambivalent about continuing her literary career. By this time, she had realized that the public wanted her to write only about herself and

the blind. She had written herself out on both subjects, and she soon discovered that whenever she wanted to write about anything else—for example, her political views that reflected her growing disenchantment with a
capitalistic system that encouraged the accumulation of wealth at the
expense of the poor, or her literary opinion that Francis Bacon was the true
author of Shakespeare's plays—editors politely turned down her articles.

"It is difficult for me to get a hearing on any subject not connected with
myself and my own experience," she wrote to a friend. "When I write seriously about the broader aspects of human life, people are apt to laugh and
tell me that I know nothing about the practical world. . . . " As the financial
pressures mounted and the Wrentham household fell into debt, her friends
privately went to the industrialist and philanthropist Andrew Carnegie in
1910, and he offered her a pension to supplement her income. His offer was
a generous one—five thousand dollars a year for the rest of her life.

The Scottish-born Pittsburgh steel magnate, who had retired from business after selling in 1901 the Homestead steel works, which were then incorporated into the U.S. Steel Corporation, was now gleefully disposing of
most of his vast fortune on whatever good cause he could think of. Among
these good works was the provision of the Carnegie Trusts, the second
largest and perhaps most remarkable group of charitable foundations in the
world, as well as the establishment of public libraries in the United States,
Great Britain, and other English-speaking countries.

Helen resisted becoming one of Carnegie's good causes. She would find
another way to earn a living besides writing, she informed the industrialist
proudly in a letter: "I hope to enlarge my life and work by my own efforts,
and you, sir, who have won prosperity from small beginnings, will uphold
me in my decision to fight my battles without further help than I am now
receiving from loyal friends and a generous world."

A mentor about whom she felt no such ambivalence was Samuel
Clemens, with whom she and the Macys had spent a few days in the winter
of 1909 at his newly built Italianate villa, Stormfield, in Redding, Connecticut. "More than anyone else I have ever known except Dr. Alexander Graham Bell and my teacher, he aroused in me the feeling of mingled
tenderness and awe," she wrote. "To one hampered and circumscribed as I
am it was a wonderful experience to have a friend like Mr. Clemens. . . . He
never made me feel that my opinions were worthless, as so many people do.
He knew that we do not think with eyes and ears, and that our capacity for
thought is not measured by five senses. He kept me always in mind while he
talked, and he treated me like a competent human being. That is why I
loved him. . . ."

Clemens was waiting for Helen on the veranda as her carriage approached the white villa, waving his hand when it rolled between the huge granite pillars. Helen could not see or hear him, of course, but John and Annie informed her that "he was all in white and that his beautiful white hair glistened in the afternoon sunshine like the snow spray on the gray stones."

After tea, Clemens escorted them through each room of his elegant new home, which was on top of a hill with a dazzling view of the cedar and pine forests below. When they entered his bedroom, with its ornately carved bed, where he did most of his writing in the morning, it was pointed out to Helen that hanging from a candlestick on the mantel was a card he had written to would-be robbers, explaining to them where valuable articles were kept in the room. The house had recently been robbed, the humorist explained, and when the burglars returned in the near future, he did not want his sleep interrupted.

After a dinner during which he dominated the conversation and ate practically nothing—"his talk fragrant with tobacco and flamboyant with profanity"—Clemens led Helen to her room, instructing her where she would find "cigars and a thermos bottle with Scotch whiskey, or Bourbon if she wished, in the bathroom."

Although charmed by her host's unusual thoughtfulness, Helen—and her intuitive fingers—had long ago discovered something about her famous host that was more profound than his delightful wit and eccentricities. She sensed that for Clemens, "humor was on the surface, but in the center of his nature was a passion for truth, harmony, beauty. . . ."

"Perhaps my strongest impression of him was that of sorrow," she later wrote in a touching portrait of him in *Midstream*. "There was about him the air of one who had suffered greatly. Whenever I touched his face, his expression was sad, even when he was telling a funny story. He smiled, not with the mouth but with his mind—a gesture of the soul rather than of the face. His voice was truly wonderful. To my touch, it was deep, resonant. Ah, how sweet and poignant the memory of his soft slow speech playing over my listening fingers."

On that visit Clemens spoke tenderly of his wife, Livy, to Helen and regretted that the two women had never met. "I am very lonely, sometimes, when I sit by the fire after my guests have departed," Helen quoted him as saying. "My thoughts trail away into the past. I think of Livy and Susy and I seem to be fumbling in the dark folds of confused dreams. . . ."

Aware of Clemens's faltering strength, Helen wondered as she left Stormfield if she would ever be in his company again. So many of her dear friends had died recently, including her beloved John Hitz. In late March 1908, when she and her mother had visited Washington, D.C., he had met them at the railroad station. He appeared in good health, putting his arm around her and spelling into her hand some affectionate German words of greeting—his custom upon meeting her. After walking with them a short distance, he became weak and had trouble breathing. An ambulance was summoned, but he died en route to a hospital. When Helen, who was following in a carriage with her mother, learned of her friend's death, her first reaction was that she must be taken to the hospital room where his body was lying. After passing her sensitive fingers over his face, which she had adored but never seen, she kissed him good-bye for the last time.

Helen's fears about Clemens's health were justified. The two friends were never to meet again. The following year he died at Stormfield, his last coherent conversation about "Jekyll and Hyde and dual personality." Some years later, when she returned to Stormfield, the house was in ruins. After Clemens's death the house had been sold and a year later caught fire. Only the charred chimney was standing. As she sat on the dilapidated step where they had once stood together and he had described to her the peaceful evergreen landscape that helped assuage his restlessness, she imagined that she felt someone coming toward her. "I reached out, and a red geranium blossom met my touch. The leaves of the plant were covered with ashes, and even the sturdy stalk had been partly broken off by a chip of falling plaster. But there was the bright flower smiling at me out of the ashes. I thought it said to me, 'Please don't grieve.' I brought the plant home and set it in a sunny corner of my garden, where always it seems to say the same thing to me, 'Please don't grieve.' But I grieve, nevertheless."

Although Helen had deeply loved Clemens and Hitz, she was able to accept their deaths with equanimity, possibly because John Macy had now assumed the role of her wise male protector. It was John who would show her a revolutionary way of viewing the world, one that led her not only to a new political and social vision but also to a startling personal rebellion.

CHAPTER 12

A Fiery Radical

ELEN WAS NOW an impassioned socialist, to the discomfort of her family as well as those who later sought to perpetuate her image as a handicapped wonder woman. Whether she would have been naturally drawn to this economic system had she not been exposed to John Macy, a fervid socialist himself, is a matter of debate. Along with his fellow socialists, John believed that the institution of producing private property should be discarded and transformed into public property and the resultant public income equally divided among the population. In 1916 he wrote *Socialism in America,* in which he defended socialism and the militant labor union the Industrial Workers of the World (IWW), which other, less enchanted socialists accused of dual unionism and sabotage. It would be this small volume that would cause John to be refused membership in the Harvard Club of New York. "The trouble with the generation which is now happily passing is that it did little else than strive for individual fortune. Its heroes, its representative products, typical though grotesquely exaggerated, are Morgan, Rockefeller and Carnegie," he wrote, glossing over the fact that the comfortable manner in which Annie, Helen, and he lived was chiefly due to the largesse of philanthropists such as H. H. Rogers and Mrs. William Thaw.

Aghast that Helen had shattered their divine image of her by becoming an impassioned radical, people accused her of being John's "puppet," and there was some truth to that accusation, but it was also true that it was Annie (at the time not a socialist), and not John, an enthusiastic Marxist propagandist, who introduced her to socialism. It was Annie who suggested that Helen read H. G. Wells's *New Worlds for Old*, a book that Annie admired because of its "imaginative quality and electric style" and that moved Helen deeply, as she concluded that the workers' struggles against their oppressive capitalist bosses mirrored her own battles against deafness and blindness.

Her emotions aroused, she asked John, who had been converted to socialism after reading in German Karl Marx and Friedrich Engels's *Communist Manifesto*, what else she might read, and he recommended some socialist tracts and that she read Marx and Engels in German Braille. Like him, she was moved by the ending of the *Manifesto*, which finishes with these words: "The Communists disdain to conceal their views and aims. They openly declare that their ends can be attained only by the forcible overthrow of all existing social conditions. Let the ruling classes tremble at a Communistic revolution. The proletarians have nothing to lose but their chains. They have a world to win. Workingmen of all countries unite!"

It was John who informed Helen by way of code about the aim of socialism, which was "to revolutionize work and the fruit of work and to substitute for a society in which part of the people do necessary work a society in which all people shall do necessary work." He also informed her about the program of the Socialist Party, whose aim was "to strengthen the working class in its fight for the realization of its ultimate aim, the Cooperative Commonwealth, and to increase the power of resistance against capitalist oppression." These included such demands as the collective ownership and democratic management of railroads, telegraphs and telephones, steamboat lines, and all other social means of transportation and communication; the extension of the public domain to include mines, quarries, oil wells, forests, and water power; the collective ownership of the land where practicable and in cases where the ownership is impracticable, the appropriation by taxation of the annual rental values of all land held in speculation; the collective ownership and democratic management of the banking and currency system; and unrestricted equal suffrage for men and women. Moreover, he told her that many of the great men of history—William Morris, William Dean Howells, Alfred Russel Wallace, Anatole France, and Maurice Maeterlinck, among others—had been socialists. And it was from John that she learned that "among the younger writers, whose names are not yet known, socialism of some color is as much the fashion as the flowing tie." But, as she was always careful to stress, John did not urge his books on her, nor did he instruct her about socialism.

Helen and John were hardly alone in their beliefs. In 1912 nearly a million Americans voted for Eugene Victor Debs, a socialist, for president, and more than a thousand American socialists held public office. As Irving Howe has pointed out in *Socialism and America*, "American socialism flourished a few decades after the time of the robber barons, the brutalities of Social Darwinism, rapid industrialization, shameless strike breaking, labor spying. Coarsely primitive in its accumulations, early industrial capitalism could easily be taken as the enemy by everyone within, and a good many outside the party. . . . Meanwhile, the glow of Progress shone on the native horizon, and socialists basked in this glow quite as much as other Americans, only they gave it a different name. If, somehow, you managed to blend faith in Progress with a Marxist, or vulgar-Marxist, notion about 'the inevitability of socialism,' then you could respond to the once-famous slogan of the *Appeal to Reason* [an influential socialist weekly]: 'Socialism is not just a theory—it is a destiny.' Today this may seem embarrassingly uncomplicated, but in 1912 intelligent and serious people held to it firmly."

Helen had been a member of the Socialist Party of Massachusetts for three years at the time of the infamous Lawrence textile strike that began on January 12, 1912. The American Woolen Company, in retaliation for the enactment of a Massachusetts law that reduced the number of hours that women and children might work in factories, cut their wages proportionally. The twenty-five thousand workers who walked away from their jobs petitioned the Industrial Workers of the World, or Wobblies, as they were also called. A picturesque group, the Wobblies were a singing union and had been so since their founding in 1905 by a group of revolutionary socialists who understood that these migratory workers, millhands, and unskilled laborers could grasp the union's message more quickly from songs than from tracts. By 1913 the Wobblies' songbooks had print runs of fifty thousand copies.

"It is the first strike I ever saw which sang," wrote an observer of the Lawrence strike. "I shall not soon forget the curious lift, the strange sudden fire of the mingled nationalities at the strike meetings when they broke into the universal language of song." This was no accident. The IWW's members were very different from labor leader Samuel Gompers's educated artisans of the American Federation of Labor. They were, in John Macy's words, "a dusty army of men, women, and children, speaking twenty languages, not very well dressed . . . there would be the textile workers, mostly from the Eastern States, then the forest and lumber workers, harvesters, 'blanket stiffs' from the South and West, marine and transport workers from both seacoasts. One would be struck by the youthful appearance of the marchers, for the IWW is young in fact and in spirit, and it has the virtues and defects of youth."

In response to the textile workers, the Wobblies sent in organizers. One was Joe Ettor, a young Italian who advised unity and peace. His chief lieutenant was Arturo Giovannitti, an Italian poet. Later that month, one of the female strikers was killed, and Ettor and Giovannitti were accused of her murder and sent to prison. Many people felt that the two leaders were innocent—why would they kill one of their own people?—and it was suspected that the police put them in prison in the hope that their arrest would break the strike. But William "Big Bill" Haywood, the pugnacious Wobbly leader who preached "direct action," which meant violence, and Elizabeth Gurley Flynn, who later, as a veteran Communist, would be removed by J. Edgar Hoover from the ACLU's board of directors, rose to the support of the workers, and the strike gained momentum as it went along. As the situation grew more grave, workers sent their children to live in other towns. Many went to New York City, where they marched down Fifth Avenue bearing placards that read "A Little Child Shall Lead Them" and "They Asked for Bread; They Received Bayonets," a reference to the Massachusetts governor's ordering out a bayonet-armed militia when the strike began. The demonstration so turned public opinion against the company that Lawrence officials refused to let any more children leave the city. One hundred fifty attempted to flee, only to be stopped by policemen, wielding clubs. It was a tactical blunder by management. The public was so outraged that from that moment on, almost everyone sided with the workers. Peace finally came on March 12, sixty days after the strike began, on the terms that the workers dictated, and eventually Ettor and Giovannitti were set free.

Like many other Americans, Helen followed every agonizing detail of the Lawrence strike. However, because of her intensely vivid imagination, which enabled her to believe at times that she was living in another era and another country, the harrowing events may have been more traumatic for Helen than for a hearing-sighted person. The songs of the Wobblies as they marched determinedly along . . . the description of oppressed children carrying placards in New York . . . the unwarranted imprisonment of men such as Ettor and Giovannitti . . . all these events sickened her as Annie or John described them to her in code. For the first time she tended to see herself not as a unique individual—a freak, so to speak—but as one who shared a common plight with all of suffering humanity. Then, too, socialism provided her with an acceptable outlet for the rage and anger that she seldom permitted herself to express about the fate that had left her disabled and helpless.

During this period in American history, Helen became personal friends with many anarchists and radical leaders. John Reed, the American journalist who soon would become an active supporter of the Bolsheviks; Emma Goldman, the anarchist and onetime lover of Alexander Berkman, the would-be assassin of industrialist Henry Clark Frick; and Giovannitti were all welcome at Wrentham. John had dedicated *Socialism in America* to Arturo Giovannitti and his wife, Carolina, and Helen was equally stirred by the poet, later writing a preface to *Arrows in the Gale,* Giovannitti's book of poems in which she stated that he symbolized "the struggle of a new world against the old world of customs blindly obeyed. . . . The seeds of the socialist movement are being scattered far and wide, and the power does not exist in the world which can prevent their germination."

Like other socialists, she was violently opposed to American entry into World War I, not because she was a pacifist, but because she, too, believed that the war was largely imperialistic and "a crime against the people," affecting the whole working class, which shed blood, suffered poverty, and got nothing in return. This antiwar, antipatriotic stand brought the entire Socialist Party to grief. After the declaration of war and the Espionage Act of 1917, almost every Socialist Party leader, including Eugene Victor Debs, the party's spokesman whom Irving Howe has called "an orator able to establish a rapport with the American people such as no other radical in this country has ever had," was prosecuted and jailed, their publications banned from the mails. Members of the IWW were treated even more harshly. Many of its supporters in the Southwest and West were tarred and feathered, and left to die in the desert. Also prosecuted and jailed were Goldman and Berkman, who, two years later, were deported to Russia in 1919 by a zealous young J. Edgar Hoover, then head of the Justice Department's General Intelligence Division. As one historian notes, "it is some index of Goldman's power that nearly twenty years later he still regarded her deportation as his salient achievement."

Closer to home, John was also being watched by the Justice Department. As he gleefully wrote his Harvard classmates, his views on the folly of war had earned him "the supreme honor of having been reported as a traitor to the fools in Washington, D.C., who were called with unconscious irony, the 'Intelligence' Department."

In 1913 Helen had published *Out of the Dark*, a series of essays in which she examined the forces that had impelled her to socialism and why the socialists' beliefs—universal brotherhood, peace, and education—stirred and influenced her. This little book, which seems so innocuous today, practically destroyed her angelic image. No longer was she viewed by the public as a virginal young woman with a Braille book on her lap as she savored the sweet smell of a rose, but as a fierce revolutionary who kept a large red flag in her study and who marched in suffrage parades, supporting the more militant suffragists such as the Briton Mrs. Pankhurst, who advocated such extreme measures as hunger strikes and window smashing. ". . . I am a militant suffragette because I believe suffrage will lead to socialism and to me socialism is the ideal cause," Helen told a *New York Times* reporter. Even her most devoted admirers were shocked by her viewpoint, and she found herself sharing the front page with baseball and Teddy Roosevelt's activities, a cause for celebration as far as she was concerned, as she despised Roosevelt's progressive politics. She seemed to revel in the notoriety, saying that it made people think about socialism, even though it was reported in the newspapers that she was being exploited by both the socialists and the "Bolsheviks," and that because of her deafness and blindness, she could have no knowledge of politics.

This last accusation hurt Helen deeply, as it implied that a deaf-blind person was naive about the world. As her friend the writer Van Wyck Brooks points out, "from the time she was twelve, politics had absorbed her. Puzzled by her interest, Michael Anagnos had asked her whether she was a Republican or a Democrat, and she had replied, 'I am on the fence. I must study civil government, political economy, and philosophy before I jump.' As an adult, she came to believe that socialism alone could solve the inequalities in society and the problems of the poor living in the city slums. As one of her friends pointed out, 'All her life she grieved over the catastrophes that filled the news . . . and she instinctively hated the unjust and the cruel. . . . She understood George Orwell's defense of the so-called 'materialism' of the working classes, their realization that the belly comes before the soul. . . .' "

For some people these were inflammatory ideas, and Helen Keller's books would be among those burned in a square on Unter den Linden opposite the University of Berlin on May 10, 1933, while Dr. Paul Goebbels, the new propaganda minister of Germany, addressed the thousands of exuberant students who had piled them up with other books by world-famous authors and were watching them being reduced to ashes. "The soul of the German people can again express itself," Goebbels told them. "These flames not only illuminate the final end of an old era; they also light up the new."

THE BLIND REMAINED Helen's primary mission, however, and it was during this period of intense activism, in which she openly advocated woman suffrage and opposed child labor, that she began her lifelong work on their behalf. In addition to serving on the Massachusetts Commission for the Blind, she wrote articles on the prevention of blindness, the education of blind children, and the need for the state to implement private philanthropy and provide manual training and jobs for the blind. She also made the public aware of the plight of the adult blind, which she felt was almost hopeless, as many had lost their vision when they were past the age of being educated and lacked a job or resources of any kind.

The two most vital needs, Helen felt, were for a central clearinghouse and improvement in the devices used by the blind. Not only were embossed books expensive, but there was no unified system of embossed printing, as various educators of the blind supported their own theory as to which type of print was best, and the blind themselves were not consulted. To read everything that had been printed for the blind, she herself had to master five different prints—New York Point, American Braille, European Braille, Moon type, and Boston Line Letter. "A plague upon all these prints!" she once exclaimed, wishing that only European Braille had been invented, for it could be easily adapted to many languages, and decrying the "American fever of invention" that had given rise to the four other kinds of raised print.

With characteristic determination, she persuaded the editors of both the *Kansas City Star* and the *Ladies' Home Journal* to publish her articles on a taboo subject: *ophthalmia neonatorum*, an easily preventable infection that mothers suffering from venereal disease passed to their infants and that was the major cause of blindness in the newborn.

Helen was constantly asked to write articles, attend meetings, speak to legislatures, or visit schools in other countries to awaken public awareness of the deaf or the blind. Dr. Bell and others urged her to bring the problems of the deaf before the public. She refused, later writing that "although I was as deeply interested in the cause of the deaf as I was in that of the blind and had always thought deafness before the acquisition of language a greater affliction than blindness, I found that it was not humanly possible to work for both the blind and the deaf at the same time."

Annie did not share Helen and John's optimistic vision of the future. Neither Marxist nor socialist, she argued loudly with her husband in public about the virtues of capitalism. When Helen bluntly told a startled reporter that she was both a socialist and a Bolshevik, Annie, who feared for their livelihood, tried to soften her words by lightly slapping her hand and saying, "Only red-handed workmen are admitted to the party of the Bolsheviki. You are poking your nose in where you are not wanted."

Unlike Mrs. Keller, Annie did not share Helen's belief in woman suffrage, but expected men to look after her and protect her. "She was not a woman suffragist, and I was. She was very conservative at the time," Helen recollected in *Teacher*. "She was never a standard-bearer. The more we talked, the less we thought alike, except in our desire of good and our intense longing for intelligence as a universal attribute of mankind. . . . Like Mark Twain, she was very pessimistic with regard to progress. Even the work for the blind was no exception . . . she was dubious about the capacity of the average blind person to achieve a full life."

Annie shrewdly realized that such doubts, if publicly expressed, would ruin their careers, and in October 1904 she had consented to visit the Louisiana Purchase Exposition, in St. Louis, with Helen and John. Helen was excited by the prospect of attending the event. She was convinced that her presence would create a wider interest in deaf-blind children among the educators who were present. As it turned out, the teachers were thrilled at the thought of meeting her. October 18 was set aside as Helen Keller Day, and as soon as the doors opened on Congress Hall, where the exercises were held, the hall was filled to capacity, and the guards had to turn away the hundreds of people clamoring to get in. According to a newspaper report, "the windows had to be guarded, for some enterprising individuals had secured step-ladders and climbed in, a number of very sedate old gentlemen and ladies coming by this entrance, while the window seats, at least eight feet above the floor, were all filled."

The crowds overwhelmed the guards and then the guest of honor. Helen's dress was ripped, the roses snatched from her hat for souvenirs. Somehow she managed to reach the platform and make a speech in which her articulation was so clear that the president of the exposition was able to repeat it after her without Annie's assistance. Then blind twin boys who played the violin were hoisted onto a table with their instruments. According to an observer, they were untalented musicians, playing several selections miserably. Many in the crowd began to sob as the children sawed away impassively.

As a disappointed Helen remembered sometime later, "in spite of this warmhearted reception, nothing constructive was done for the deaf-blind of America. And now . . . I still grieve that so few of these little unhappy ones have been led out of their imprisonment." (It would not be until many years later that Helen would feel that she had partially achieved her goal, when, in 1946, with her assistance, the American Foundation for the Blind formed its special service for deaf-blind persons. Of her work for the foundation, she considered it her proudest achievement.)

What she did not elucidate in her speech was that liberation for a deaf-blind person often led to a different type of isolation. Helen's world fame, her superior intelligence, as well as her celebrated relationship with one teacher had always set her apart from the deaf-blind and the blind, many of whom were jealous of her. Nauseated by the hoopla surrounding the "luminous" Helen Keller, one deaf-blind person who was equally accomplished but unknown to the public was moved to surreptitiously displace a statue of her from the library where he was working at a menial job. The envy of the deaf-blind and the blind distressed Helen deeply, but she felt that there was little she could do to remedy the situation other than to make the hearing-sighted public aware of their plight.

CHAPTER 13

"More of an Institution Than a Woman"

H ELEN'S VOICE —tinny, robotic, and grotesque—was always her nemesis. It was her true handicap, she felt, this lack of a comprehensible speaking voice and not blindness or deafness. Always susceptible to people who proposed a way to enable her to speak normally, in 1909 she met Charles White, a singing teacher at the Boston Conservatory of Music who felt that he could help her, as he had invented a special sort of singing lesson for the deaf, dumb, and blind to increase the flexibility of their voices. Late in 1910 she started voice lessons with him, not to learn to sing, but to strengthen her vocal cords so she could be heard in a lecture hall. She wanted to give lectures on the education of women afflicted like herself, she told him, and then about women in general, whom she believed should become involved in the world's education, which would prove to men that they were not the weaker sex. But there was another, more practical reason for her wanting to go on the lecture circuit. She needed money for them all to live on, as John, even though he was now in charge of her literary career, appeared to possess even less talent for business than she and Annie did.

But first Helen had to do something about her appearance. For years she had always been carefully photographed in right profile to hide her left eye, which was protruding and obviously blind. Aware that she would now be exposed to the merciless gaze of the public, she had both eyes surgically removed and replaced with glass ones. Aside from the medical benefits of replacing nonfunctioning eyes with prosthetic ones, the operation drastically improved her appearance. No longer did Helen Keller have to be photographed in profile, and from then on, most photographs would show her gazing straight ahead. She was often described in newspaper interviews as having "big, wide, open, blue eyes," few reporters realizing that such a luminous countenance came out of a box.

In the midst of Helen's voice lessons, Annie and John began to quarrel frequently over what John perceived to be his wife's overinvolvement with Helen at the expense of their relationship. Their constant wrangling, coupled with financial worries, in part caused by her and John's extravagances, and her never-ending responsibilities toward Helen undermined Annie's fragile health. She began to suffer from a female ailment that contributed to her debilitated state. The nature of her condition remains a matter of speculation, as Nella Braddy Henney only primly alluded to it in her 1933 biography of Annie, and other sources who might have shed light on it are dead. However, in view of Annie's subsequent hysterectomy, which was performed a few months later, she may have experienced profuse and uncontrolled menstrual bleeding that was caused by uterine fibroid tumors. In any event, her symptoms were serious enough to alarm not only Helen but also the wealthy, powerful people Annie had taken pains to cultivate.

One of those friends was Mrs. William Thaw, heiress to the Pennsylvania Railroad fortune and mother of Harry K. Thaw, who had shot to death Stanford White in June 1906 as the famed forty-seven-year-old architect sat on the Madison Square Garden roof listening to a tenor sing "I Could Love a Million Girls." Thaw was driven to this desperate act after discovering that his girlish sixteen-year-old wife, Evelyn Nesbit, a dancer in the enormously popular Floradora Sextette, had been cavorting au naturel on a red velvet swing in White's apartment. "Sometimes he would set me stark naked on the red swing and laugh aloud with delight as he sent me soaring toward the ceiling," Evelyn later divulged to tabloid readers.

Following two sensational but inconclusive murder trials, Harry Thaw was declared insane and confined to Matteawan State Hospital, a New York mental hospital. Although Mrs. Thaw was obsessed with freeing her son, she was sufficiently distressed by Annie's fragile condition to insist that she and Helen, as well as Charles White and his wife, use one of her cottages at

Cresson, in the Alleghenies, near Pittsburgh. After Annie's years of hard work and devotion to Helen, Mrs. Thaw felt that she was sorely in need of rest and relaxation.

But no sooner were Helen and Annie and the Whites ensconced at Cresson than White was called back to Boston on business. Annie and Helen returned to Wrentham, where the voice lessons continued until September, when Annie had a hysterectomy at St. Vincent's Hospital in Brookline, Massachusetts. By this time she and John were separated, and John was living alone in Schenectady, New York, where he was working as the secretary to Rev. George Richard Lunn, the first Socialist Party mayor ever elected in the state of New York. John had obtained the secretarial position because he was a friend of Lunn's first executive secretary, Walter Lippmann, who, after resigning to pursue other interests, had recommended him for the job. "I am sure you will find him an asset to the city, a power to your administration and a delightful person to have as a friend," Lippmann told the mayor. Lunn, who had earlier announced that he was "as red as Debs," had wanted Helen to serve on the Board of Welfare, and the headlines in the local paper that announced John's appointment read "Noted Blind Girl Coming with Macy." Although at the time the three of them had talked about moving from Wrentham to New York and Helen had even given a newspaper interview wherein she declared that her first act upon being appointed to the board of public welfare would be "to wipe out the slums," they decided against moving. The Macy marriage was foundering and Annie was in poor health, so Macy had gone alone to Schenectady.

Upon learning of his estranged wife's hysterectomy, John immediately resigned his position in Schenectady and returned to Wrentham, while a terrified Helen was sent to Lenore Smith's home in Washington. Before she left for Washington, Helen had visited Annie in the hospital, and the memory of Annie's feeble fingers, which for the first time in their long relationship were too weak to form words, made Helen almost ill every time she thought about it. Although well-meaning friends tried to keep it from her, she knew that Annie had suffered from complications following the surgery and was close to death.

Lenore did her best to make her feel at home, but Helen felt lonely and confused in a strange house, more conscious of herself as a burden than ever. In one of the few letters she ever wrote where she did not attempt to be courageous about her limitations, she blamed herself for getting "in people's way. I am a perpetual stumbling block, a handicap, a hindrance, a hanger-on . . . a disturber of peace, an upsetter of plans, 'a tremendous burden.' . . ."

To Helen's considerable relief, Annie recovered from her illness, although her doctors informed her that she must guard her health for at least a year. Although still barely able to get out of bed, she insisted that she and Helen resume their voice training, and four months later, in 1913, they both appeared on the lecture stage for the first time, in Montclair, New Jersey.

Helen's first appearance went badly. She was seized with stage fright as she began her speech, titled "The Heart and the Hand or the Right Use of Our Senses," becoming so rattled by the experience that she forgot all of White's rules and felt "my voice soaring, and I knew that meant falsetto; frantically I dragged it down until my words fell about me like loose bricks." She fled the stage in tears. But, to her surprise, the audience was sympathetic, and she felt sufficiently buoyed by their enthusiastic reception to make a number of other engagements that spring.

Clearly, at thirty-three, she had lost none of her power to amaze and inspire. Although men would always be more fascinated by her than women — perhaps because the tactile world in which she lived was, for many males, intimately linked with their own eroticism — her curious existence also had special appeal for beautiful, narcissistic women, many of whom were fascinated that she had never seen her own reflection in a mirror.

One day in the winter of 1912, Georgette Leblanc, the companion of Nobel Prize–winning Belgian poet, dramatist, and essayist Maurice Maeterlinck, spent two days with Helen and Annie at Wrentham. Maeterlinck was one of many artists and writers who were fascinated by Helen Keller — she was his *belle au bois dormant*, the sleeping beauty who had once been imprisoned in the castle. And so when Georgette arrived at Wrentham, she brought love and good wishes to Helen from a man who shared her belief in the spiritual life of all living things, the author of such symbolic dramas as *L'Oiseau Bleu* (The Bluebird).

Georgette was a singer and an actress. Her portrait of Helen, which was published the following year and appropriately titled *The Girl Who Found the Bluebird*, was the work of a woman who reveled in the theatrical. From beginning to end, her book is sheer melodrama, from its lush prose to its two photographs, a study in vivid contrasts as the first is of Helen, the epitome of piety in her Radcliffe graduation robes, and the second, of the author, obviously a very different type of woman, judging from her sultry appearance. Yet, for all its theatrics, *The Girl Who Found the Bluebird* is an extraordinary document in that it is the first study of Helen Keller written by a woman other than her teacher that dared to suggest that for all her courage in overcoming her disability, there was something eerily "incomplete" about her.

As is obvious from Georgette's reaction to Helen, meeting the deaf-blind woman for the first time could be far from a serene experience:

> From the moment, therefore, when I first set eyes on Helen Keller, I was excited, anguish-stricken, shuddering, tossed incessantly between enthusiasm and horror. . . .

After she had gotten a grip on herself, Georgette, like many other observers, was struck by Helen's beauty and vitality:

> Helen is tall and well-developed. She has a finely-shaped head and well-cut, regular features: the nose almost classically straight; the rather full mouth nobly curved; the chin small but firm; the eyes set in their deep sockets, alas, to screen a too-penetrating glance. . . . Encircling her brow is a black-velvet ribbon, its edges prettily worked with very dainty steel beads. Her chestnut hair, dressed low down in the neck, is devoid of wave or parting and drawn back into a tight knot behind . . . and yet this severe style suits her and, when we study her profile and her rather masculine throat, straight and pure as a column, we are reminded of the Athenian youths on some bas-relief.
>
> You have but to observe the girl for a moment to feel in her an impetuous force, captive passions that at first knock impatiently at closed doors and then escape by unsuspected outlets. Very few people give so powerful an impression of vitality. In a drawing-room full of visitors, in a volatile atmosphere of glances, smiles and chatter, Helen, quivering as the forest quivers in the night wind, changeful, impetuous, eloquent as nature itself, or suddenly terrifying in her adamantine immobility, Helen would proclaim the victory of the inner life and would stand there, in the midst of pleasure, like a sublime and eternal interrogation! . . .

But it was Helen's unique world—of eternal darkness and silence, touch, smells, and vibrations—that fascinated Georgette, as it intrigued everyone:

> At moments of direct communication . . . her grave expression first denotes attention; next a joyous convulsion of her whole body takes us by surprise. It is a movement brilliant as a lightning-flash which tells us that her darkness is suddenly riven. Thus her erect and formal bearing is constantly broken by shivers which are caused by nothing that is apparent to those who watch her. To her, they correspond with so many vibrations and with a whole little world of sensations which we do not perceive. Those faint thrills and violent convulsions, which make her start exactly as though she had received

an electric shock, are the revelation of a life that has its own laws and its own conventions.

Then Annie, wearing a white veil to protect her weak eyes from the sun, moved suddenly away from Helen, and Georgette was confronted with "Helen's silence . . . I look at Helen, immured upright, enigmatic in her tomb. . . . She dwells in a solitude where my imagination loses itself. Where is she? Where is she? The gulf that opens before me is too deep. . . ."

Helen had been speaking with her lips for a long time, while holding her friend's hand and pressing it nervously to the rhythm of her sentences. She did not seem tired; and, whenever the strain was apparent, her bright smile was always there to soften an impression that might have otherwise been painful; but I felt relieved each time that Mrs. Macy's fingers met her

Georgette Leblanc, 1913

thought half way. How could I accustom myself to that barbarous voice repeating words, dictated by the most exquisite of souls, mechanically and with no feeling for their beauty? For everything is disconnected in this curious woman. Her means of expression, created by her will, are scattered materials which her intelligence is continually striving to bring together and which, for that very reason, make the blundering of a body that is not adapted to our conditions of life appear still stranger. . . .

But for all Helen's beauty and intelligence, Georgette felt that there was something absent in her. Her lovely face was essentially unformed, a beautiful blank, the face of a person who had never experienced life:

I rise absent-mindedly and catch sight of Helen in the glass. A strange vision! With her back turned to the window and to the bright snow-clad landscape, the blind girl is seated stiff and straight in a chair which happens to be opposite a mirror. Her set, unconscious face looks like a portrait in its frame. Her broad, finely-shaped head stands out against the vast wilderness of snow; and the sun draws a glittering halo round her head. . . . Absolutely absorbed in thought, dominated by a definite, obvious intelligence, she nevertheless suggests something unfinished. . . . Many times I have asked myself what Helen lacks; the mirror tells me: it has not instructed her; it has never told her charms and her defects; it has never revealed her image to her. That image lives and dies in the mirror, whereas with us it is the revealer, teaching us, correcting us and becoming the eternal companion of a grace which it unceasingly abandons and directs by turns. . . . But, though we have need to see ourselves in order to find fulfillment, it is not in the glass of the docile and faithful mirror that we really know ourselves. It is by the looks of others; for the eyes of others seem to pour out the beauty that fills them.

Then, in conclusion, Georgette Leblanc summed up Helen's appeal for the Victorians, with their adoration of heroes, heroines, and, especially, sages.

Helen is the example necessary to our day, the glorification of effort, intelligence and strength, the sanctification of continuous and hidden heroism. She is a primitive saint and a saint of tomorrow! She is the archangel of the victories that are eternal and of the virtues that do not change with moral systems or with people. . . . Be happy, Helen, and be free, for you have proved that there is no real prison save in mediocrity, that the darkness which has no ending is the darkness of the mind and that mortal silence reigns only in loveless hearts. . . . Tell us the secret of your wisdom and your light. By the science of touch and smell, you have revealed to us a kingdom which we knew imperfectly; there is another, Helen, which we do not know at all: it is the world of eternal darkness and silence. . . . Tell us what voices charmed your tomb, what stars lighted it. Analyze for us the springs of a power, which we cannot conceive. . . . Helen, wonderful Helen, you have surpassed us in strength and wisdom, tell us by what golden gate we may join you in our turn!

FOR ALL HER PERCEPTIVENESS about Helen, Georgette appeared to have no inkling of her unhappiness about the disintegrating Macy marriage. Annie and John were quarreling almost nightly, and after their violent arguments Annie retreated to her room in tears—which perhaps explains another reason for the white veil—and John consoled himself with liquor. Perhaps only a deaf-blind person could have endured such an incompatible, wretched couple, and undoubtedly there were times when they sent Helen back to her "tomb," deliberately shut her out so they could have the privacy to scream at one another as loudly as they pleased. Still, through vibrations, she must have been aware of the anger filling the room, John's pounding gestures, a door slamming in the night. But Georgette was oblivious to this unhappy household, describing John as "a young American with a smile full of sympathy and understanding," while Annie was viewed as Helen's savior and guardian angel. "Except for Anne Sullivan's intelligence and goodness, Helen would still be what she was at first, a living nullity."

"Is she not there, in the house, as a safeguard of beautiful living?" Georgette enthused. "She is protected, it is true, but see how she herself protects others! Can we doubt the quality of the bonds which unite that admirable trio at Wrentham? To the husband and wife, Helen's presence has the sweetness of a starry night. . . ."

By this time John Macy was finding Helen's presence anything but "sweet." He was snidely referring to her as "more of an institution than a woman," blaming her as well as Annie for the deterioration of his marriage. In his view, although Helen was the president of this enterprise, Annie had neglected her responsibilities as his wife "to serve as chairman of the board, vice-president, secretary, treasurer, janitor, matron, and office boy."

Disillusioned with both women, and perhaps in search of another female who would adore him as completely as Helen and Annie worshiped each other, John sailed to Europe alone in May 1913. He was gone four and a half months, spending most of his time in Italy. That he was able to afford the luxury of an extended vacation was the result of Helen and Annie's earnings on the lecture circuit, and also because Helen had changed her mind about accepting a pension from Andrew Carnegie. Sometime earlier, at a tea with the philanthropist and his wife, she had continued to decline his offer of financial support, telling him that she "hadn't been beaten yet," and countering him bravely when he humiliated her by threatening to take her over his knees and spank her for her socialist beliefs. Then, that spring, when she and Annie were lecturing in Bath, Maine, Annie had come down with a severe case of the flu. Unable to call a doctor or summon help, Helen was terrified. Fortunately, Annie gathered the strength to call a doctor herself, and several days later, with the help of the hotel manager, they boarded a train and went home to Wrentham. A week later Helen wrote Carnegie that she was ready to accept his financial help. For a dedicated socialist to be driven to accept an industrialist's tainted money was an opprobrious prospect, even if that industrialist was as enlightened about his social responsibilities as Andrew Carnegie. Characteristically, with stiff upper lip, she never wrote about her feelings at having to accept the Carnegie pension.

But money—Andrew Carnegie's or her own earned income—could not save the Macy marriage. Things were no better when John returned from abroad. He was still drinking heavily, and he and Annie quarreled continuously about Annie's fixation on Helen at the expense of their relationship, and their mutual spending sprees, which were depleting their bank accounts. In an attempt to put some distance between himself and the two women, John rented an apartment in Boston. Although Annie and Helen sometimes stayed there, Annie despised the pied-à-terre—in her mind, it was one more proof that her young husband found his obese, middle-aged wife sexually undesirable, for after her hysterectomy Annie had put on a great deal of weight. One night, after a particularly violent quarrel, she stormed out of the apartment, vowing never to stay there again. In retaliation, John consulted a lawyer, who advised him to have papers drawn up in which he charged Annie with desiring a divorce.

In early January, Helen, Annie, and Mrs. Keller embarked on a Canadian lecture tour, leaving John alone at Wrentham. Flowers, compliments, honors, and salvos were showered on them wherever they appeared, and it was a welcome change from their depressing home situation. Obviously trying to downplay the graveness of their domestic problems, Helen wrote

Kate Keller, Annie Sullivan, and Helen, 1914

John a lighthearted letter from the road: "I thought we were going on a lecture tour. But now we seem bound for Vanity Fair. While we were in
Canada, every one said we were 'wonderful, fascinating, charming and
beautiful women.'"

But John was not to be swayed by other people's glowing assessments of
them. In a letter written to Mrs. Keller, who was instructed to spell it into
Helen's hand, he accused his wife of interfering with his own relationship
with Helen, as well as needling her unnecessarily about her crippled voice.
His exact words may only be surmised by reading Helen's replies, as with
the exception of the one letter of John to Helen about Annie's bossiness that
was previously quoted, all of John's correspondence to Annie and Helen
was destroyed in a fire that in the mid-1940s consumed Arcan Ridge,
Helen's home in Connecticut. This loss was an incalculable one for scholars, as John undoubtedly had many interesting observations about Helen
and Annie, as well as about his own role in this unusual ménage à trois.
Nevertheless, by reading between the lines of the following letter that
Helen wrote to John in late January from Appleton, Wisconsin, it becomes
apparent that John believed the two women were conspiring against him:

Dear John,

You are wrong, John, in thinking that Teacher has tried to influence me against you. She never has. . . . She has impressed it upon me that very few men would have endured my foolish tears, my fussy and exacting ways as you have all these years, and I love you for it. . . .

As for my voice, you know, John, and every one else knows that for twenty years we worked hard together to make it better. . . . No, there has not been any "unintelligent nagging" or nagging of any kind about my voice. Please, please be fair, be just.

You say you can "never explain to me what your life with Teacher has been." I remember that in spite of many hard trials in the past we have had happy days, many of them, when we three seemed to feel in each other's handclasp a bit of heaven. Have you forgotten it all, that you should say such bitter things about my teacher, about her who has made my darkness beautiful and rent asunder the iron gates of silence. . . .

I know how imperious, changeable and quick-tempered Teacher is. I have suffered just as much from those failings as you have: but my love for her has never wavered. . . .

You say that she "has never been a wife to you, or done any of the things that a woman might be expected to do." You know, we have shared everything we had with you. You have helped us in all our literary work, and all that has come from it has belonged to you as much as to us. . . .

Again; Teacher does not like the lecturing: but she was glad to do it last year when she thought that some money would take you to Italy and give you the change you desired. I copied all the letters she wrote to you last summer, often with her tears running over my hand. . . . And now you say that "she has played a game" — that she has been untrue to you!

I know that in the past year Teacher has changed in some essential respects. By talking with her daily I have learned that you have helped her to see the world, the workers and economic, social and moral conditions as she never saw them before. Living so close to her as I do, I can prove, absolutely prove, that she has new aims, a new conviction, a new vision of life. . . .

Now, dear, you have every one of Teacher's failings, as I can show you from my experience with you: and your letter has proved that you have more grievous ones than she has, and I still cherish you. . . . You and I are comrades journeying hand in hand to the end. When the way is dark, and the shadows fall, we draw closer. . . .

> Affectionately,
> "Billy"

John's reply, by way of Mrs. Keller, made Helen even more wretched. She had hoped for a "gentler, more magnanimous answer," but John used the occasion of his second letter to make "sweeping charges against Teacher," saying that "she had not played fair" and, to Helen's outrage, implying that she was "a living lie."

> You, her husband, my brother, dare to say such things about your wife, my teacher! And further, you declare that you can "abundantly prove" what you say. This you cannot do because it is a lie, and when you come to your senses, John, you will know this. . . .
>
> Next, you write; "It is Teacher's act which involves separation from me." But she did not tell mother or me that she would not return to the apartment. In fact, mother did not know that she had asked you to consult a lawyer until the lawyer's letter reached Teacher in Detroit. Of course we understand that a divorce involves separation. But that is a very different matter from what you say. You tell me that "she left my house with the express and final decision never to return." She did not say so to mother or to me or to any other person that we know of, unless she said it to you, and we do not know about that. But even if she did say so to you how could you believe that we would never come back to the apartment? Where else could we go? The apartment is full of our things, and we think of it as our home — not a happy home, to be sure, but all the home we have in the world.
>
> As to the money question, mother knows, and every one of our friends knows that Teacher is generous to a fault. You speak of her making "a disgraceful row on two occasions" when you proposed to send some money to your mother. You say nothing about the many times that money was sent to your family when Teacher did not "make a disgraceful row!" . . .
>
> Teacher's difficulty now is not that you no longer love her, but that your whole attitude towards her is one of distrust and suspicion. Yet her love for you has survived all this wreck and misery and confusion, and I must say I am surprised. She never talks unkindly to me or, I believe, to anyone else about you.
>
> I love you both, I always shall, and I did think that you both loved me well enough to hold my hands and support my weakness through all the years allotted to me. Every word of your two bitter letters about Teacher is cruelly stamped upon my mind, and will darken every day of my life as my physical blindness has never done. You, and you alone can lift this burden of sorrow from my heart. My love for you makes me confident that somehow, somewhere, sometime you will again be the dear brother and generous friend that I have known for twelve years.
>
> Affectionately your sister,
> HELEN

The reason that the once-enamored John had come to believe his wife a fraud becomes apparent upon an examination of letters that are in the

Nella Braddy Henney Collection at the Perkins School for the Blind in
Watertown, Massachusetts. Like almost all of her letters, Helen's correspondence with John was flawlessly typed, which meant that Annie had read
them before they were mailed, as it was her habit to make Helen endlessly
retype her letters until both the style and typing met with her approval. Not
only is it likely that she scrutinized every word of this correspondence, but
there is also a distinct possibility that she had a hand in its composition, perhaps dictating portions of the letters to Helen, especially since they offered
her a perfect forum for listing her husband's shortcomings. In general, their
style is more typical of her writing than of Helen's biblical-sounding prose.
Furthermore, in the second letter, there is a telltale sign of her collaboration, a correction to the word "physical," which Helen typed as "pysical." A
small handwritten "h" was inserted to correct the error, and so it is not surprising that John was outraged when he read the letter. The handwriting
was unmistakably his wife's. On recognizing it, he must have realized
instantly that Annie had used Helen. No wonder that he accused Annie of
"not playing fair" and untrustworthiness.

Infuriated by Helen/Annie's last letter, John replied with what Helen
termed an "unkind and altogether unbrotherly note in St. Louis," the contents of which have been unfortunately lost. Not to be outdone, Helen, with
Annie's help, rebutted his accusations, replying on March 4, 1914, from Salt
Lake City:

> You know, John, that you took that apartment in Boston because YOU
> wanted it, not because we did. . . .
> You had no business to call me "a fook" [*sic*] as you did in your last letter
> to mother. You know I am not a fool, and that it was directly in answer to
> what you said about Teacher's being ungenerous that I brought up the sub-
> ject of money. You know me well enough to realize that I do not value
> money any more than you say you do. I have always been willing, glad to
> share with you, evenly or any way that pleased you, all I had. But do you
> think it is fair or generous or consistent to say you "hate our money," and in
> the very same letter to tell us that you deposited a thousand dollars of that
> "hated" money for yourself? It is all right for you to have the money. But it is
> mean thus to insult me.
> You say "it was Annie, and not I, that wrecked us." If it was she, you
> DROVE her to it. Your first letter to mother showed that you did and when
> the facts are known, everyone else will see it.
> As to your helping me in the future, how do you think we could work
> together with advantage when you keep saying that Teacher is dishonest,
> that you cannot be harassed by a woman whom you cannot trust, that she

has lied and deceived you? Cannot you see, John, that it was you who wrecked us. . . .

While they were still on their lecture tour, John left a cigarette burning and set the Boston apartment on fire. All of Helen and Annie's "things were ruined." According to Helen, there was no insurance. Confronted by the two women on their return home, John claimed it was an accident.

In what she vowed would be her last letter to John about his relationship with Annie, Helen wrote:

> I understand that you have taken Mr. Fagan as your secretary to attend to some of my correspondence. Well, if you do not want to write yourself, why not let him write the home news, and so help me straighten out the many details which always come up when I return home? I love to be of use to others, but I do not let any one spare me in my tasks, and I never shall.

John had recently taken a job as literary editor on the *Boston Herald*, and Peter Fagan was his associate, a young socialist who also worked at the newspaper. As she mentioned Fagan's name in passing, Helen had no notion of the part he was soon to play in her life. If she thought about him at all, it was probably with the expectation that he was going to be like the other men to whom she had been introduced. She was never permitted to date them, but they served a purpose for Annie and others who sought to perpetuate her image as the model handicapped person. A carefully set-up photograph of the radiant deaf-blind woman who looked neither blind nor deaf as she performed the turkey trot with a male partner could reassure a sentimental public that disability was not to be feared, that it was not inevitably accompanied by deformity, suffering, and limitation, as well as sacrifice and a loss of freedom for family members. Despite her handicaps, Helen Keller was like any other normal woman who enjoyed pretty clothes and dancing.

For years she appears to have been resigned to her monastic lifestyle and to have taken refuge in the image she helped create of a deaf-blind woman as a sightless high priestess, a messianic figure who was both a social reformer and a seer who had penetrated the mysteries of the universe in her dark silence. But then the ailing, despondent Annie became ill again, and Helen seized the opportunity.

CHAPTER 14

"A Little Island of Joy"

HELEN'S SECOND CHAUTAUQUA TOUR in 1916 was a dismal failure. As the United States geared up to enter World War I, battle-ready Americans were in no mood to listen to the antiwar views of a socialist deaf-blind woman. On this particular tour, she was accompanied by Annie and her new twenty-nine-year-old secretary, Peter Fagan, who, like herself, was a "violent" socialist and a firm advocate of disarmament. Polly Thomson, a slim, self-effacing young woman who had joined the household as a secretary and assistant in 1914, had gone home to Scotland for a vacation, and Fagan, who had swiftly mastered the manual finger language and Braille, interpreted for Helen in her absence. For Helen, the summer was a "disappointing and exhausting" one, and when they returned to Wrentham in the autumn, her despair deepened as John Macy was not there to greet them. After the Boston apartment had been gutted by the fire, he had reconciled with Annie and moved back to Wrentham in the fall, but the couple soon quarreled, and he moved out again, this time to the St. Botolph Club in Boston. In the hope of cheering up herself and Annie, Helen invited her mother to come to Wrentham, "and in a few days her presence sweetened our loneliness."

No sooner had they returned to Wrentham, when Annie developed a hacking cough and a darting pain in her side. She consulted a doctor, who, after performing a sputum test, told her she had tuberculosis.

Annie's latest illness was exacerbated by her separation from John Macy. Although she would never grant him a divorce, the marriage had essentially ended by 1914. When war had broken out that same year, he wanted to join an American volunteer ambulance unit, but as he later admitted to a friend, "the armchair patriots at the club were not able to find money for my passage and expenses."

Prevented from remarrying, John would soon form a happy companionship with a deaf-mute named Myla, whom that same friend described as being "a woman of talent and charm, a sculptor by profession," and with whom he had a daughter. Few details of this relationship have survived, but it is known that Myla died after they had lived together for five years.

According to one of Annie and John's mutual friends, it was "degenerate, careless" John who was to blame for the failure of the marriage. "It was all John's fault," this woman said, "and as for his saying afterwards that he had married an institution, he knew that in the beginning. Helen came first. He was willing to have it so. The relationship between Teacher and John was always rather more that of a mother and son than that of husband and wife which makes many things that he did more understandable."

For Annie, the loss of her brilliant, charismatic husband in midlife was almost as crushing a blow as the death of her little brother in the almshouse. Predictably, she turned to Helen for solace. "She kept demanding my love in a way that was heartbreaking," Helen reported in *Teacher*. "For days she shut herself up almost stunned, trying to think of a plan that would bring John back or weeping as only women who are no longer cherished weep. . . . To no one, except myself in the silence of the night, did she speak of her anguish or the terrible dreams that pursued her. Her health was not good. She had once exercised vigorously, but one of her chief difficulties, overweight, was causing her immeasurable discomfort. Her sight was worse, and she could no longer console herself by even short periods of independent reading. . . . At that time the melancholy which had now and then seized Teacher overwhelmed her with a despair that made it misery for her to exist. Actually she feared insanity for a while, but her judgment was not impaired and she never ceased to work with her brain or her hands. It was her imagination, not her reason, that was disturbed. Occasionally she would lay her head on my shoulder saying, 'How I shrink from this day!' Then she would straighten herself exclaiming, 'Our audiences have nothing to do with what has happened to me. At least I have your story to tell, and you may encourage some people to bear burdens that would otherwise crush them.' "

To recover her health, Annie's doctor had advised her to spend the winter at Lake Placid. As she was too unwell to travel alone, Polly was to accompany her, while Helen would go with her mother to the home of her sister Mildred in Montgomery. After Mildred had married Warren Tyson, Mrs. Keller divided her time between Mildred and her family and Helen and Annie.

As it always did, any separation from Annie unnerved Helen. "I saw more clearly than ever before how inseparably our lives were bound together," she wrote. "How lonely and bleak the world would be without her. Once more I was overwhelmed by a sense of my isolation."

Morose and fearful of a life without Annie, she was alone in her study one evening when Peter Fagan, who could communicate with her directly, entered the room. According to Helen, he "sat down and held my hand in silence, then began talking to me tenderly. I was surprised that he cared so much about me. There was sweet comfort in his loving words. I listened all a-tremble. He was full of plans for my happiness. He said if I would marry him, he would always be near to help me in the difficulties of life. . . . His love was a bright sun that shone upon my helplessness and isolation. The sweetness of being loved enchanted me, and I yielded to an imperious longing to be a part of a man's life."

Helen wanted to share her joy with her mother and Annie, but Fagan, who knew that Mrs. Keller disliked him, advised secrecy. Thinking themselves unobserved, the lovers walked in "the autumn splendor of the woods," and he often read to her. Soon the happy couple traveled to the city registrar's office in Boston, where they applied for a marriage license. Still, Helen was troubled by the clandestine relationship. "The thought of not sharing my happiness with my mother and her who had been all things to me for thirty years seemed abject, and little by little it destroyed the joy of being loved."

She had made up her mind to tell her mother about Fagan, when, according to Helen, an overwrought Mrs. Keller burst into her room.

" 'What have you been doing with that creature?' " Helen quoted her mother as saying. 'The papers are full of a dreadful story about you and him. What does it mean? Tell me!' I sensed such hostility towards my lover in her manner and words that in a panic I pretended not to know what she was talking about. 'Are you engaged to him? Did you apply for a marriage license?' Terribly frightened, and not knowing just what had happened, I denied everything. I even lied to Mrs. Macy, fearing the consequences that would result from the revelation coming to her in this shocking way."

In the hope of defusing her mother's anger, Helen feigned nonchalance, calmly combing her hair by the window. Her cool demeanor did not fool Mrs. Keller, whom Annie had asked to Massachusetts after she had learned of Helen's affair from their Russian houseboy, who had spied the couple kissing. When Helen was brought to her teacher's sickbed, she continued to deny the relationship. Unlike Mrs. Keller, Annie was convinced there was nothing in the story. In her mind, Fagan was an "insignificant" person, and, incredibly, she never thought of him as an attractive and sensual young man who could woo Helen away from her.

On that same day, Mrs. Keller banished Fagan from the house. Helen was not permitted to say good-bye to him, although he managed to sneak her a note in Braille, informing her of his whereabouts. Helen was forced to deny their engagement publicly, and at her mother's insistence, even issued a written statement of denial through the family lawyer. Nevertheless, she and Fagan continued to search for a way to see each other.

An elopement was the only answer. One wonders who dreamed up the scheme, Helen or Fagan, although considering its Byzantine nature, it is likely that Helen was the instigator, copying the plan from one of the potboilers of the period that she somehow managed to read against Annie's wishes. Peter Fagan would abduct her as she and her mother were returning home to Alabama on a boat that stopped at Savannah, where they would then board a train that would take them to Montgomery. After kidnapping Helen as she made her way from the boat to the train, Peter would flee with her to Florida. There, a minister who was Peter's friend would marry them.

Unfortunately for the lovers, Mrs. Keller discovered that Fagan had booked passage on the same boat. At the last minute, in November 1916, she changed plans, returning home with Helen by train while Fagan sailed alone.

Fagan was not an easy man to get rid of. In her journal, Helen's editor, Nella Braddy Henney, described the couple's attempt to find happiness:

It was after she got to Montgomery that Mildred saw her one morning talking to a strange man on the porch. He was spelling away into her hand at a great rate. Before going out to see her she went upstairs to her mother who had a presentiment which proved correct that this was Fagan. She told Warren [Mildred's husband] who got his gun and then they all went on the porch. Fagan stood up before the gun and said that he loved her and wanted to marry her but they ran him away and again thought the matter ended. Again it was not.

One night some time afterwards Mildred was wakened by the sound of someone on the porch. She waked her husband who did not share her fright at all but said at once that it was Sister Helen. Sure enough it was. How she had managed to keep up communication with Fagan no one was ever able to say but she had. She was expecting him this night and had packed her bag and gone down on the porch to wait for him. He never came, or, if he did, he realized before he got very close that there was trouble afoot and there was no use getting mixed up in it. It is a terrible picture to me of the blind deaf-mute girl waiting on the porch all night for a lover who never came.

Her hopes for love and marriage dashed, Helen had no choice but to resume her cloistered lifestyle, where she was guarded, as well as protected, by two women who for their own reasons had a vested interest in ending her romance. Rather than rage against them both for denying her a husband and motherhood, she blamed herself for having been foolish enough to fall in love. It was she who had acted wrongly and hurt her family by telling them that she "could not bear to live with them."

"The memory of her [Mrs. Keller's] sorrow burns me to the soul," she wrote many years later. "She begged me not to write Mrs. Macy anything about it until we knew that she was stronger. 'The shock would kill her, I am sure,' she said. It was months later when my teacher learned the truth.

"I cannot account for my behavior. As I look back and try to understand, I am completely bewildered. I seem to have acted exactly opposite to my nature."

But what was her nature? Writing in *Midstream* about her romance, Helen strongly suggested that she was no longer naive about love and sex. "The brief love will remain in my life, a little island of joy surrounded by dark waters," she confided. "I am glad that I have had the experience of being loved and desired. The fault was not in the loving, but in the circumstances."

By "loving," Helen, who was unusually frank in her writing about many aspects of her life, did not mean a few chaste kisses. As a militant socialist, she would not have hesitated to consummate her love for Peter Fagan. The circles in which she and her young lover moved were in rebellion against the sexual mores of the Victorian age. Many of their friends—John Macy, John Reed and his bohemian wife, Louise Byrant, as well as Emma Goldman—were ardent champions of free love.

But what about Annie Sullivan, herself a highly sexual woman? If she had been present, would she have encouraged Helen's love affair? In an effort to rationalize her only documented attempt to break free of both her mother and Teacher, Helen wrote in *Midstream* that she "was sure that if Mrs. Macy had been there, she would have understood and sympathized with us both. The most cruel sorrows in life are not its losses and misfortunes, but its frustrations and betrayals."

It is doubtful that Annie Sullivan would have blithely let Helen marry Peter Fagan. Not only was Helen her creation, but she derived her identity, as well as her own celebrity and livelihood, from their association. Over the years she had systematically destroyed men's relationships with Helen when they tried to usurp her role in Helen's life. Michael Anagnos, Arthur Gilman, even her own husband, John Macy, had all been thwarted in their attempts to come between her and Helen.

But many of Annie's concerns for Helen's welfare were legitimate. As her longtime teacher and companion, she was keenly aware of the responsibilities facing any man who chose to marry Helen Keller. Would he, like herself, possess the dedication and stamina to satisfy her almost insatiable need for a steady stream of information about the outside world? Even Annie found constantly being with Helen a nerve-racking experience, and after spelling to her for several hours, she often suffered from a headache and nausea.

Peter Fagan's hasty departure from Helen's life suggests that he had second thoughts about marrying a woman who would be completely dependent on him. Fearing for his own independence, he had no choice but to leave her reaching for him, yearning, in the familiar quiet darkness.

CHAPTER 15

Separation

W HILE HELEN WAS experiencing a sexual awakening, Annie
Sullivan was luxuriating on her own "joy isle." It was Puerto
Rico, an island she likened to "a great ship afloat in violet
waters" and where she had retreated with Polly after Annie had discovered
that she loathed Lake Placid, with its "frozen face," "forlorn people," and
dictatorial doctors. Succumbing to a travel advertisement in a Sunday
paper that promised palm-fringed beaches, romance, and escape, she and
Polly had sailed on the S.S. *Carolina* against the wishes of Mrs. Keller and
of Annie's doctor, who warned her that she was courting certain death.
With her usual perversity, she proved them wrong. Almost immediately, the
sight of two half-clothed natives fighting fiercely under the dim light of a
golden moon piqued her curiosity. As she confided to Helen, "the primitive
life interests and rests me."

In Puerto Rico, this unhappy woman who had taken to clothing her
obese body in black as a symbol of her husband's defection became, temporarily, an almost carefree person. With the exception of sending for her
car and chauffeur, she rejected her extravagant ways, renting for a small sum
a shack in the hills in the midst of an orange and grapefruit grove. There,
with lizards engaged in a nightly death struggle and with fantastic, colorful

bugs swarming around the lamps like glowing gems, she wrote poetic letters to Helen in Braille. She had not used it for more than twenty years, pricking out the words with a stiletto that was "so awkward in my hand, it feels like trying to punch a hole in the universe with a toe!" The following extracts from her undated letters are remarkable in that they were among the very few letters she wrote during the course of her life. More important, they reveal their author at age fifty to be sensual, uninhibited, and daring, a woman whose course in life might have been completely different had her destiny not been linked with a willful, unformed deaf-blind mute. As she would later confess to her startled biographer, she and the adult Helen had such fundamentally different conceptions of life that they would have loathed each other had they met under ordinary circumstances.

The letters Helen and Annie exchanged during this five-month separation on the eve of America's entry into World War I make clear their differences. Helen was sentimental, malleable to the point of being naive, intensely spiritual and religious, and by nature an optimist and "impassioned reformer." Essentially she saw the universe as a contest between good and evil forces, while Annie, who was exquisitely sensitive to the subtleties of life to the point of suffering frequent severe depressions, was a tough negotiator and survivor. Perhaps not surprisingly, when free of the burden of her pupil, she was transformed into another person, becoming both poet and sybarite. In yet another stunning shift of mood, she had not been on the island for very long before she convinced herself that had her life not consisted of Helen, she might have lived only for pleasure and new sensations. Even more startling, as she lay on the warm sand in her widow's weeds, her thoughts began to mellow about her estranged husband, the man whom she would never bring herself to divorce.

She wrote Helen:

I'm glad I didn't inherit the New England conscience. If I did, I should be worrying about the state of sin I am now enjoying in Puerto Rico. One can't help being happy here, Helen — happy and idle and aimless and pagan — all the sins we were warned against. I go to bed every night soaked with sunshine and orange blossoms, and fall to sleep to the soporific sound of oxen munching banana leaves.

We sit on the porch every evening and watch the sunset melt from one vivid colour to another — rose, asphodel (Do you know what colour that is? I thought it was blue, but I have learned that it is golden yellow, the colour of Scotch broom) to violet, then deep purple. Polly and I hold our breath as the stars come out in the sky — they hang low in the heavens like lamps of many colours—and myriads of fireflies come out on the grass and twinkle in the dark trees!

In another undated letter, she confided to Helen the sense of déjà vu that had haunted her ever since she had arrived on the island:

> ...I am having a very strange experience here. I constantly seem to remember things, sometimes in a shadowy way, again vividly, of having been here before, or in a similar tropical place. The feel of the sudden hot sun after a downpour of rain stirs and excites me. The green of the sugar-cane on the hills is disturbingly familiar, and the blue shadows cast by the shoulder of a mountain where there is a sharp curve on the road make me—well, make me turn my head aside quickly, as if I expected to see some one I know. Isn't it queer? The bayonet-plant makes me want to run. I'm sure I feel the sting of its long, sharp fingers in my flesh! The impression is so strong that I find myself feeling the spot.

A mystic, Helen ordinarily would have been intrigued by Annie's super-natural experiences, but in her reply, she did not allude to them. She was too absorbed in her own misery now that her romance with Peter Fagan had been brought to an ignominious end to dwell on Annie's peculiar feelings. Obviously fearful of upsetting her teacher during her recuperation, she did not tell her about her doomed attempt at elopement. Instead she bitterly complained about the people she met at her sister Mildred's house in Montgomery, many of whom—it seemed to her—lacked "individuality," and whose only topics of conversation seemed to be "parties, dresses, babies, weddings, and obesity."

More ominously, death seemed to be stalking her while she was in the dark, soundless South unprotected by Annie. One evening, as she was lying on her bed in her room, she smelled tar and burning wood. Jumping out of bed, she threw open a window and then rushed to her mother's room. After the firemen arrived at the house and evacuated the family, they discovered that the fire, which had started under Helen's bed, was caused by a defective flue. In five more minutes, the house would have burned to the ground.

"It distresses me to think that my lack of sight might have proved fatal to my loved ones," she later wrote Annie, characteristically blaming herself for the accident. "It seems as if I could never sleep quietly here again without putting my face down close to the floor and hunting all over for an odor or a hidden spark.

"When are you coming back to America, Teacher? I hate to have you so far away while we're on the verge of war, and those dread submarines are scouring the ocean for whatever they can destroy. . . ."

Far away in Puerto Rico, Teacher felt exultant as she read those plaintive words from her thirty-seven-year-old protégée. "Dear, I do want to get well for your sake. You do need me still. Your letters make me realize it more and more. This separation is teaching us both a number of things, is it not? What experiences you are having! The fire must have been a terrible shock to the nerves of the family! You poor child! It was awful, waiting in the dark and feeling those frantic sounds and not knowing what was going on. It's a wonder you aren't all in sanatoria."

But if anything were to propel Helen's conventional southern family into a rest home, it would be her radicalism, to which they were adamantly opposed. Their Helen, sweet and manageable since Annie Sullivan's arrival, was now a changed woman, a militant crusader for a new society and an uncompromising rebel whom the New York *Call*, a daily socialist newspaper, was addressing in their articles as "our Comrade," going on to say that "her liberal views and wide sympathies ought to shame those who have physical eyes, yet do not open them to the sorrows that compass the mass of men." Seeming to thrive on controversy, she staunchly defended the militant IWW, becoming a Wobbly herself because she felt that the Socialist Party was "too slow and sinking into a political bog." She also championed the Russian Revolution in November 1917, passionately declaring her admiration of Soviet Russia three years later, in an emotional speech at New York's Madison Square Garden: "In the East a new star is risen! With pain and anguish the Old Order has given birth to the New. . . . Onward, comrades, all together! Onward to the campfires of Russia! Onward to the Coming Dawn!"

When IWW organizer Joseph Hillstrom, better known as Joe Hill, was convicted of killing a Salt Lake City grocery owner in a trial that many Americans considered a travesty of justice, Helen wrote Woodrow Wilson, urging a new trial. Although Wilson did urge the Utah governor for "a thorough reconsideration of the case of Joseph Hillstrom," an appeal was rejected, and Hill was executed in November 1915.

But the Wobblies and protests against capital punishment were not the only unpopular causes with which Helen became involved. When William Sanger, Margaret Sanger's husband, was imprisoned that same summer for giving out a single copy of his wife's pamphlet *Family Limitation*, an irate Helen dashed off an article for the *Call* that was in support of birth control:

"Already countless mothers are obliged to work outside their homes and leave their little ones without the proper care. Unwatched, exposed to all the influences of evil, these children of the poor grow or waste away. . . . And the incalculable mischief of an uncontrolled birth rate sucks up the vitality of the human race. This is the real suicide we must combat. . . . Once it was necessary that the people should multiply and be fruitful, if the race was to survive. But now, to preserve the race, it is necessary that people hold back the power of propagation."

To her family, this new, crusading Helen was almost as remote and unreachable as the barbaric child who had pinched them until they bled. Recently she had confessed to a reporter with an exalted look in her sightless blue eyes that she felt "like Joan of Arc at times. My whole being becomes uplifted. I, too hear the voices that say 'come,' and I will follow no matter what the cost, no matter what trials I am placed under. Jail, poverty, calumny—they matter not."

Her relatives failed to realize that her monumental childhood rage had not been dampened—it had simply been channeled into a political and social activism they found equally incomprehensible. As far as the perplexed Keller family was concerned, her unorthodox social views brought shame, not glory, to the family. In 1916 their Alabama-born relative, who confessed publicly that "ever since childhood, my feelings have been with the slaves" that her family owned had done the unthinkable when she had sent a check for one hundred dollars to Oswald Garrison Villard, the vice president of the National Association for the Advancement of Colored People. Never one to mince words, she sent Villard a letter with the check that made clear her views on segregation:

> . . . The outrages against the colored people are a denial of Christ. The central fire of his teaching is equality. His gospel proclaims in unequivocal words that the souls of all men are alike before God. Yet there are persons calling themselves Christians who profit from the economic degradation of their colored fellow-countrymen. Ashamed in my very soul I behold in my own beloved south-land the tears of those who are oppressed, those who must bring up their sons and daughters in bondage to be servants, because others have their fields and vineyards, and on the side of the oppressor is power.

W. E. B. DuBois had printed the letter in a NAACP publication, and when an infuriated Southerner got wind of it, he arranged to have the article reprinted in a Selma, Alabama, newspaper and then accused Helen of advocating social equality between whites and Negroes, and of disloyalty to her fellow white Southerners. In his view, it was obvious that Helen was only parroting the sentiments of her northern teacher. "The people who did such wonderful work in training Miss Keller must have belonged to the old Abolition Gang for they seemed to have thoroughly poisoned her mind against her own people."

Embarrassed that Helen had disgraced the family by publicly airing such sentiments, Mrs. Keller pleaded with her to issue a statement that would explain her views. Although Helen did not change her thoughts about segregation, she deferred to her mother's wishes in this instance by writing a letter to the Alabama newspaper, in which she said that nowhere, in her letter to Villard, did she use "a phrase that justifies the editors' assertion that I advocate the social equality of white people and Negroes, so repugnant to all. The equality I advocated in my letter is the equality of all men before the law. . . ."

Adding to the Kellers' distress was Helen's embarrassing involvement in the war issue. Although in fact neutral, she gave the impression of siding with the Germans when she wrote such statements as "I haven't taken sides, as you know; but I get hot because almost everybody is down upon Germany. Not a word is said about the centuries in which 'perfidious Albion' [England] has pushed her conquests to the ends of the earth, strewing her path with blood, tears and untold crimes" and "I am neutral, yes, but I consider my second country the land of Beethoven, Goethe, Kant and Karl Marx."

When she unwittingly turned over the royalties from the German edition of *The Story of My Life* to German soldiers who had lost their sight in battle, a professor at a French school wrote her indignantly that blind French soldiers were more deserving of her charity. Soon the French were declaring that Helen was pro-German, overlooking the lectures she had given on the behalf of British, French, and Belgian blinded soldiers. As one of her defenders pointed out, the only reason why she had not given the French blind the royalties of the French edition of her autobiography was that there was no French edition.

Perhaps because she felt lonely in Montgomery, misunderstood not only by her relatives but also by a world that had once worshiped her, she counted the days until her teacher's return. Her first long separation from Annie had been a "bitter" one. Although the slower pace of life in Montgomery made feel her less nervous and tense, and as she wrote Annie, seemed to diminish her "storming tendency," their time apart had not given her confidence in her independence. Predictably, with Peter Fagan banned from her life, she resumed her fixation on Teacher. What would she do if anything happened to her? Polly had written her and her mother that Annie was still not well, reporting that Annie often complained of feeling "old and tired." Who would take care of her affairs when Annie died?

Dearest Teacher:

. . . I have one or two plain questions to ask you. If anything should happen to you suddenly, to whom would you wish me to turn for help in business matters? How could I best protect myself against anyone who might not be honest or reliable? Mother loves me with a deep, silent love; but in all probability she will not be with me constantly.

Another thing, if you should be taken from me, or be unable to attend to our affairs, what shall I do with all our papers? Whom could I trust to go over them with me? I hate to worry you with these questions; but I know enough to realize my dependence upon others, and I try to think, plan and consult you so that I might find the right person or persons to depend upon. Oh Teacher, how alone and unprepared I often feel, especially when I wake in the night!. . . .

Given her turbulent feelings for her estranged husband, Annie's reply was surprising:

Dearest:

You are never out of my thoughts. They keep me awake at night, and daylight brings no satisfactory answers to them. When I married John I thought I had solved the greatest of them. He promised me that in case of my death, which in the natural course would come before his, he would be a brother to you, look after your happiness, and take charge of your affairs. For years my mind was at rest on this—to you and me—most important of matters. But ever since he left us, I have worried. He seemed, and still seems, the only one to take care of you when I go. Perhaps, dear, it would be best all round to let him do what he can to make things a little easier for you when I am gone. He understands your business better than any one else. And would it not be better in every way to let the suffering, the unhappiness, that has come to all three of us die with me? You still love John. I am sure you do love him. Such love as we have felt for John never dies altogether. For my own part, I think of him constantly, and since I have been ill much of the bitterness has gone from my thoughts of him. I wish you could forgive and forget too. You would be much happier if you could, Helen. If that cannot be, why I suppose you will have to depend upon lawyers to advise you on business matters. . . . I have often wished that you knew Phillips better. If you would write to him oftener you would soon get to feel nearer to him. I think he is a very fine boy and if you give him a chance he may prove a good friend as well as a kind brother.

Helen's reply is lost, although we do know that she never subsequently sought John's advice about her business affairs, and in her later correspondence with other people, often referred to him as a deadbeat and a sponger. "From the year 1905, when Teacher was married, until 1920, when I rose up in my wrath and said John should not have another penny of my earnings, we were constantly paying considerable sums for him—for his family, for his tailors, his books, and a trip of four months and a half in Europe, and for any one he wished to assist," she wrote to Mildred in 1933. Only when she was a senile, elderly woman would she revise her opinion of John, in her ramblings remembering him kindly. In asking Helen to forgive John, as she herself claimed to have pardoned his behavior, Annie had hit upon an essential truth about her character. Helen might convince herself that she loved all of mankind, but in truth she had no compassion for anyone who dared to hurt the only person she had ever loved—Teacher.

Now that John was gone, it was Annie, and Annie alone on whom she relied to inspire her to accomplishment. But with Annie far away in Puerto Rico, she became indolent and unambitious, a stereotypical southern belle. Unlike her teacher, who was highly literary, Helen continued to find writing a tedious process. Without Annie to stand behind her, she wrote her that she was unable to finish a commissioned article on woman suffrage, a cause to which she remained deeply committed. Annie's reply was revealing:

The game of words is the only game you can play on equal terms with the best of them. Don't get impatient because the game is slow. Remember, the great writers often practice for days before the right phrase or image comes to them.

I am sorry, dear, that you find it so difficult to write the suffrage article. I should think it would be rather good fun. It is too bad that writing should come so hard with you, especially when it is your only medium of self-expression. I sympathize with you, writing is "a lonely, dreary business" if you don't love to play with words. But is there any other way that you can reach the mind and heart of the public? You are interested in the questions of the day and the handicapped. You desire to serve mankind. How can you do that, except by writing?

That Helen, as she approached forty, still venerated Annie as her creator and deliverer was obvious from a letter that she wrote to her in early March 1917 from Montgomery:

Dearest Teacher:

Just think, last Friday was my soul-birthday, and I had to spend that day of days away from you! Do you realize it? Thirty years ago you came to a quiet village, you, a young girl all alone in the world, handicapped by imperfect vision and want of experience—you came and opened life's shut portals and let in joy, hope, knowledge and friendship. My brain is as a disc upon which the finger of God has traced the record of the waking, the resurrection, the glory, the eternal blessedness of the day I was born again. I play this wondrous record over and over, and my soul exults, trembles, aspires under the holy influence of its living strain. I pray that "this doomed time may build up in me a thousand graces which shall thus be thine," and repay you for that mighty deliverance. God bless you, my teacher, from everlasting to everlasting.

Still in a mood of spiritual exultation, she wrote Annie a few days later about "a wonderful dream" she had that morning about them standing

on the ghastly battle-fields of Europe. The living were all retreating with a tumult that stunned our senses. The dead lay piled around us—pillowed upon each other, and Oh my God, they were all young. One instant we gazed upon their marred, broken bodies, and our hearts seemed about to burst. Then they changed, and the fury, the agony, the cruelties of war vanished. Angels were bending over those young forms and touching their foreheads. Beauty and light stole back into the marred faces, the shattered limbs became straight and whole. . . . Truly I want to shake myself out of this war and hear again the whispered messages from a happier world. Dreams are my only refuge from a life in which I have no part or lot.

But Annie, an agnostic who had never shared Helen's spiritual beliefs and thought Swedenborg a scientific genius who had descended into madness, did not encourage her belief in immortality:

It pains me deeply, Helen, not to be able to believe as you do. It hurts not to share the religious part of your life. To me, as you well know, this life is the most important thing. What we do Now and Here matters much because our acts affect other human beings.

I am fond of the Bible as poetry. I find beauty and delight in it, but I do not believe that it was any more inspired by God than all fine writing is — inspired. The future is dark to me. I believe that love is eternal, and that it will eternally manifest itself in life. I use the word eternal in the sense that it is as far as my imagination can reach.

With you the belief in a future where crooked places will be made straight is instinctive. Faith in conscious immortality helps you to find life worth living despite your limitations and difficulties. The idea of living forever in some place called Heaven does not appeal to me. I am content that death should be final, except as we live in the memory of others.

Three days after the United States had officially declared war on Germany on April 6, 1917, Helen wrote Annie: "There is little to tell — little that is bright or good. All happiness has left us with the departure of peace from our land." But for Helen, the awesome conflict had a silver lining. Annie, who was in no hurry to leave her indolent, sun-drenched life in Puerto Rico, had no choice but to return home by the next boat.

Immediately Annie, Helen, Polly, and Mrs. Keller returned to Massachusetts, but not to take up residence. Wrentham, with its costly upkeep, was depleting their small resources and would have to be sold. In June, the twenty-one-acre property, where Helen had spent the happiest thirteen years of her life, "thrilling to the beauty of so many golden seasons" and communing with her "tree-friends," was purchased by the Jordan Marsh Company, a Boston department store. Perhaps fittingly, given the febrile natures of its inhabitants, Wrentham was to be used as a rest home for its female workers. As they drove away from the house, Helen reflected that Wrentham had "so endeared to me by all intimate joys and sorrows that no matter who lives in it and no matter where I go, I shall always think of it as home."

At the end of the summer they returned to Lake Placid, where Annie was reexamined and then told by her physician that the initial diagnosis had been in error. In studying her records, he suddenly realized that her original test results had been mixed up with another patient's. She had never had consumption. This news came as a surprise to them all, especially Annie, although there is something odd about a woman feeling that she was near death for five months from a disease she never had. Still, a potentially fatal disease, even if one doesn't have it, serves a purpose. It provided her with the only means of escape from her chosen life of dedication, responsibility, and service. For if Annie was one of Helen's jailers, Helen was one of hers, their strange bond making it impossible for each of them to lead independent lives.

For Annie Sullivan at age fifty, illness had become a retreat, a way of not having to remember the unchosen life and her bright, improvident husband who was producing a child—the child she was now physically unable to bear for him—with a woman who in her beauty and affliction of deaf-mutism was disturbingly like Helen. Not surprisingly, even after the doctor's good news, Annie still complained of feeling ill. Hoping to aid her recovery, they rented a cottage for the summer on a Vermont lake, where she rested her failing eyes, a forlorn, overstuffed woman in funereal clothing who was unable to sleep, unable to read, while Helen took daily walks with Polly and, with her, even climbed two thirds up Whiteface Mountain near Lake Placid. At least one observer could not help noting that as Annie grew wearier, sicker, and more perverse in her behavior, Helen retained her youthful beauty—if anything, appearing even more radiant and perfect.

CHAPTER 16

Hollywood

HELEN KELLER STOOD on a movie set, unrecognizable in a blond wig and white makeup, waiting for the director's signal taps. As a dresser adjusted the collar of her pale pink dress, Polly spelled the director's instructions into her hand. After Polly had finished, Helen anticipated the vibrations of the "tap, tap, tap" of his foot that would tell her to walk toward a bird's cage, express surprise, then feel for the bird and express more surprise.

In Hollywood to film the story of her life, Helen was discovering that moviemaking was a far from glamorous process. The mercury-vapor tube lights, with their greenish glare, were so close that she felt as though she were melting. Also through vibrations she could sense the roar of their motors, which "glowered" at her like "a monster."

It was 1918, the golden era of the silent film and a time when actors had to wear gold hairpieces, dead white makeup, and pastel colors to look natural onscreen, and when audiences liked their films to be chock-full of orgies and other sinful pursuits before delivering a moral. In keeping with the spirit of the times, Hollywood envisioned Helen's story as the ultimate virtuous lesson, making up in spiritual oomph for what it lacked in sex, pageantry, and battles. If a Helen Keller could find "joy and light" in life, why not ordinary people, bewildered and bereft in a war-torn world? And, as Helen reminded her admiring public, was not her own amazing liberation from a cruel fate a sign that mankind could be saved from "strife and social injustice, spiritual deafness and blindness"?

"It will help me carry farther the message that has so long burned in my heart—a message of courage, a message of a brighter, happier future for all men . . ." she wrote with characteristic messianic fervor about the film, which she had decided to call *Deliverance.* "As the dungeon of sense in which I once lay was broken by love and faith, so I desire to open wide all the prison-doors of the world."

Ironically, Helen's real motive for making *Deliverance* was not an idealistic one. She and Annie, who had still not recovered from her mysterious illness, were almost broke, the result of Annie's being too weak to lecture for more than a year. But even if Annie had been well enough for the rigors of the lecture circuit, there was a dwindling demand for their presentation.

A film advertisement for *Deliverance,* 1919

Many communities, seeking to economize during wartime, were doing without their usual chautauquas.

As she lay awake at night, Helen was haunted by the thought of her teacher's future in the event that Annie outlived her. For some time, she had been aware that the trust funds provided by her rich friends would immediately cease upon her death, and Annie would be left almost penniless.

A box office smash, on the order of D. W. Griffith's *The Birth of a Nation*, which was released in 1915 as "the greatest motion picture of all time," would solve all their financial problems and provide for Annie's future.

The idea for a film based on Helen's life began with a popular historian named Francis Trevelyan Miller, who was in the midst of writing an eighteen-volume history of the world when he decided that a movie based on Helen's life would be even more of a moneymaker than Griffith's eye-popping, controversial spectacle, which, among other scenes sympathetic to the cause of the South in the Civil War and the carpetbagging era, featured a ride of the Ku Klux Klan.

Miller was shortly to doubt his decision when Helen made a fiery plea in *The New Republic* in support of the Wobblies, who, following the Espionage Act, were being jailed, and, in some cases, lynched by lawless mobs. Along with other prominent American intellectuals, Helen urged that they receive a fair trial, a statement so alarming to the Department of Justice that it warned the editors not to reprint it. A confirmed Republican, Miller was alarmed by Helen's impassioned defense of a Bolshevik organization that most Americans despised. Through Annie, it was immediately impressed upon Helen that the only "humanitarian effort" in which she was to be involved was the film about her life. Although her sympathies remained with the Wobblies, she had no choice but to conform to her screenwriter's wishes.

Helen's controversial article was soon forgotten by her worshipful public, but Miller and Hollywood still had to figure out how her almost singular life should be portrayed on film. From the beginning, there were conflicts about its slant and development. A 1918 Hollywood story conference, it appears, was every bit a hair-tearing experience as it is today. Purists such as Annie, Helen, and Miller wanted the picture to be an accurate record, while the multimillionaire who put up the money pushed for a commercial "thriller." Tempers flared, and several times Annie stalked out of meetings in a fury. Privately, she was filled with self-doubt after a top female theatrical agent pointed out that Helen's life, though amazing and admirable, was not motion picture material. She had no lovers, no exotic adventures, except in her extraordinarily vivid imagination. In this agent's opinion, after Helen's release from silence and darkness, nothing dramatic happened to her.

In *Deliverance*, the very real melodrama of Helen Keller's life, people's power struggles over her, her thwarted love affair with her socialist secretary, her complicated relationship with her teacher, and the downside of being viewed by the world as "the perfect symbol" of a handicapped person are ignored. The picture focuses on "the miracle," or as Miller put it in an opening title in case anyone missed the point, "THE MIRACLE OF MIRACLES." A sequence of tableaux deals with incidents in Helen's early life and Annie's arrival in Tuscumbia that playwright William Gibson more than forty years later would present so compellingly in *The Miracle Worker*. After a savage Helen is made to stop biting her relatives, her fate is enshrinement. A typical scene title reads "HELEN KELLER: *Deaf-Dumb-Blind, The Most Wonderful Girl in the World.*"

However, on some level, Miller and the producers were uncomfortable with their subject's seemingly sexless existence. Unlike the Victorians, they were not content to send her to a cloister, in ecstasy only when she sniffed a rose. As far as they knew, she never had a lover, but they also knew that if they presented her as an asexual woman, their audience would soon start shuffling toward the nearest exit. They had to give her a boyfriend. The question was: Who?

Helen's love of Homer was well known. She even had a large plaster medallion of the blind Ionian poet in her studio with which she communed daily. Possessing an uncanny ability to separate her consciousness from space and time, she was the first experimenter with what we call today "virtual reality." In her case, however, she didn't require any special visual apparatus to transport her to another world. As a young girl, she had been in the library with Annie Sullivan, reading a book in Braille, when suddenly she had a vivid sensation of being in ancient Greece:

> "Such a strange thing had happened! I have been far away all this time and I haven't left the room." "What do you mean, Helen?" She [Annie] asked surprised. "Why," I cried, "I have been in Athens." Scarcely were the words out of my mouth when a bright amazing realization seemed to catch my mind and set it ablaze. I perceived the realness of my soul and its sheer independence of all conditions of place and body. It was clear to me that it was because I was a spirit that I had so vividly "seen" and felt a place thousands of miles away. Space was nothing to spirit!

Capitalizing on Helen's well-known ability to divorce herself from the external environment, Miller decided that her lover should be none other than the mythical Ulysses. Scenes were filmed that depict this unlikely couple's romance, which takes place only in Helen's mind. Helen has graduated from Radcliffe College, when in the next shot she is clothed in a revealing tunic and seated outside a Greek temple, where she is wooed by the bare-chested Ulysses, the survivor of a shipwreck on the isle of Circe (actually the island of Balboa off the California coast). Their love for each other is demonstrated by a lusty kiss, and then there's the requisite discreet fade-out.

Like many people confronted by the phenomenon known as Hollywood, Helen found filmmaking a crazy business. She laughed every time Annie described to her the Ulysses scene (where an actress impersonated her), as well as a sequence filmed in the Hollywood hills where "Knowledge" (played by a stuntwoman) and "Ignorance" (played by a male giant) had a fistfight for her mind as an infant at the entrance of the "Cave of Father Time." There was also a bedroom scene in which she revealed to the prurient public that like other people, she could do her own hair. In the final scene of the picture, which she also found hilarious, she was required to ride a white charger and blow on a trumpet as she represented a sort of Joan of Arc leading the peoples of the world to freedom. Unfortunately, as the sequence was being filmed, her horse reared, and if it hadn't been for the quick intervention of a cameraman, she might have been seriously injured. This unsettling episode temporarily dampened Helen's missionary zeal, and as she later recalled, "I was glad when it was all over, and my quaint fancy of leading the people of the world to victory has never been so ardent since."

For Helen, the most ludicrous scene was the one in which she had to appear at a formal banquet that was attended by all her friends, both living and dead:

I felt as if I had died without knowing it, and passed on to the other world, and here were my friends who had gone before coming to greet me. But when I grasped their hands, they seemed more substantial than I had imagined spirit hands would be. Moreover, they did not resemble the hands of the friends they were impersonating. . . . It gave me a little shock every time one of them interjected a remark into the conversation, and when Mark Twain made a witty or complimentary speech, I did not know whether to laugh or cry. The climax of incongruities came when, after all the music, banqueting and talk, the scenario required that I say words to this effect: "Eighty thousand blind people are unhappy and unhelped, and in the present state of society it is impossible to give them the opportunities they should have. . . . Millions of human beings live and die without knowing the joy of living. . . . Let us resolve now and here to build a saner, kindlier world for everybody."

As a film, *Deliverance* was a hodgepodge, an early docudrama that combines actual footage of Helen, symbolism, and a fanciful plot line (as a child, Helen has a hearing-sighted friend named Nadja who is not only insanely jealous of her, but also so dumb that she cannot believe the world is round; fittingly, Nadja recognizes Helen's worth only after her own son becomes blinded in the war).

In a scene that revealed her powerful hypnotic hold on the public, Helen as the "Mother of Sorrows" appeared to the afflicted and deformed, bearing a torch of hope. On the day it was being filmed, the actors, many of whom were handicapped, began to spontaneously scream and fall to their knees at the sight of her unseeing eyes and swaying motion, which was caused by her lack of balance. Unfortunately, this compelling sequence wound up on the cutting room floor, although Helen provided an account

A still from the motion picture *Deliverance*: (left to right) Helen's brother Phillips Brooks Keller, with Helen and their mother, Kate, 1918

in *Midstream* in which she acknowledged that at that moment she thoroughly identified with her role, believing she was mankind's savior. "I thought my heart would burst, so overcharged was it with longing to lift the weary load of misery beneath my hands. Scarcely knowing what I said, I prayed as I had never prayed in my life before."

Deliverance remains an important historical document, capturing on film a still beautiful and luminous Helen—dancing, reading Braille, answering her correspondence, strolling serenely in the garden with her hovering, ambivalent mother, and taking a ride in a fragile biplane, despite the protests of her family. There are also some intriguing shots of Annie Sullivan looking like a doughty Boston terrier in her ill-fitting black evening gown as she accompanies her beguiling pupil to a party. (In a revealing scene, Helen gratefully rests her head against Annie's bosom even though both women are well into middle age.)

But Helen, despite her immaturity in these moments, comes across on the screen as an immensely attractive figure. Despite her limitations, she seems fearless and unquenchable and displays no hesitation whatsoever when a pilot offers her the chance to experience the new sensation of flight:

> Was I afraid? How could fear hold back my spirit, long accustomed to soar? Up, up, up the machine bore me until I lost the odors of the flying dust, the ripening vineyards and the pungent eucalyptus! Up, up, up I climbed the aerial mountains until I felt rain-clouds spilling their pearls upon me. . . . Then the machine went through a series of amazing dips! I felt in them, as it were, organ music and the sweep of the ocean, winds from off mountains and illimitable plains. As the machine rose and fell, my brain throbbed with ecstatic thoughts that whirled on tiptoe, and I seemed to sense the Dance of the Gods. I had never had such a satisfying sense of physical liberty.

She had hoped that Hollywood's casual atmosphere, like Puerto Rico, would "bring out more revelations" of Teacher's real self, but to her disappointment, Annie was reserved and distant when she was introduced to Hollywood's reigning couple, Mary Pickford and Douglas Fairbanks. Although they were friendly, Helen sensed that in their effusive compliments to her, they were snubbing Annie and that Annie was miffed, as she was always annoyed when people brushed her aside to meet Helen. As Helen commented in her florid style, "Few, if any, spoke of Teacher as one who deserved special praise for having ploughed furrows through my limitations and given me the precious harvest of my human heritage."

However, Helen was pleased that Charlie Chaplin, who let her feel his famous tramp costume, seemed to pay Annie the proper respect. With him, she was "her exuberant, charming self," and Helen sensed that the reason Annie had gravitated toward the world-famous comedian was because "they had both endured poverty and the deformations it creates in body and soul. . . . Both were shy and unspoiled by their victories over fate. So it was natural that they should understand each other and form one of the friendships that afford solace to great artists in a world too often unfaithful to the children of genius."

As might be expected, Helen was not part of the Hollywood scene, which ranged from Doug and Mary, who entertained royalty at their palatial estate, Pickfair, to scandals and wild parties where aspiring extras were raped in drunken brawls and where cocaine was passed out like candy. The only pleasure she found in Hollywood was in horseback riding with Polly every day at dawn. As Helen later recalled, "Nothing refreshed me as did the cool breeze, scented with sage, thyme, and eucalyptus. Some of the happiest hours of my life were spent on the trails of Beverly Hills."

In December, after the picture was finished, Helen, Annie, and Polly returned to Forest Hills, New York, where they had bought a small, ugly, odd-looking house that had so many peaks and angles they facetiously called it their "Castle on the Marsh." That summer a friend drove them to see John Macy, who was living in Boston. Although only forty-one, he was in poor health, a feeble old man complaining of back trouble and heat exhaustion. At least that was how Annie described him to Helen in their special code. From Boston they drove out to Wrentham, but feeling her way through the rooms of her comfortable former home was an upsetting experience for Helen. "I thought I could visit the old Wrentham place with some equanimity, but alas! — as we came away, I just sobbed aloud, greatly to my own mortification."

They came back to New York for the opening of *Deliverance*, only to discover that it was to coincide with the Actors' Equity strike on August 18. Most of the theaters were dark on Broadway. When Helen realized that her picture was being used as a strikebreaker, she refused to attend the opening and joined a protest march with the striking actors and actresses. Siding with the theatrical community provided her with an additional excuse not to see the picture, which she had recently disavowed. When she and Annie had been shown a rough cut in Hollywood, they had threatened to block the film's exhibition after viewing a scene in which Helen, attired in an outlandish medieval costume, appeared at a peace conference in which the

Helen reading Charlie Chaplin's lips, 1918

In Hollywood: (left to right) Annie Sullivan Macy, Helen Keller, Mary Pickford, Polly Thomson, Charles B. Hayes of the American Foundation for the Blind, Douglas Fairbanks, and an unidentified man

Helen, c. 1918

four major powers were deciding the fate of the world, and proclaimed the Rights of Man. A few cuts were hastily made, but when Annie saw the revised film and spelled a description of it into her hand, Helen realized that it was far from the noble triumph she envisioned. The public thought so, too. Despite some glowing reviews, *Deliverance* was a box office failure. Helen was dead broke and had no choice but to accept the offer of which they had a lifelong horror.

CHAPTER 17

"The Star of Happiness"

T HE CURTAIN RISES on the set of a handsomely appointed drawing room, complete with a fire crackling on the hearth. On the
right side of the stage there are French windows overlooking a
painted garden; on the left is a grand piano on which rests a large vase of
fresh American Beauty roses. After her introduction, Anne Sullivan Macy,
who is wearing a dark-colored evening gown, enters briskly from stage left.
She tries not to squint as the full spotlight shines on her watery, bloodshot
eyes. In a resonant, cultured voice, she tells the audience, which is composed mostly of working-class people and foreigners who know no English,
about Helen's history and accomplishments. She is fifty-four years old, and
offstage she can barely walk without assistance, but her voice becomes ani-
mated as she tells Helen's story:

> ANNIE: All the world knows and loves Helen Keller, the girl with the
> unconquerable spirit. She has fought her way uncomplaining against
> the greatest obstacles that ever confronted a human being. . . . Today
> she is the Star of Happiness to all struggling humanity.
>
> *(Piano with orchestra, playing Helen's theme song, "The Star of Happiness,"
> which was composed especially in her honor.)*

ANNIE: Helen can feel the music not only with her fingertips but with her whole body.

(Velvet curtains part at the back of the stage. As Annie disappears into the shadows, Helen enters, a tall, slender woman who is smiling radiantly. She walks toward the piano with an unsteady gait until she touches it.)

HELEN: It is very beautiful.

(Annie emerges from the shadows to take Helen's hand and lead her down to the footlights.)

ANNIE: Can you tell when the audience applauds?

HELEN: Oh, yes, I hear it with my feet.

Annie tells the audience how she taught Helen how to speak. Helen demonstrates this accomplishment, saying in her odd, barely comprehensible voice, "I am not dumb now." At one point during the act, she will stop and sniff, and with her hands outstretched, walk toward the piano, where she will pick up the bouquet of American Beauty roses, burying her face in the flowers as she joyfully smells their fragrance.

HELEN: What I have to say is very simple. My teacher has told you how a word from her hand touched the darkness of my mind and I awoke to the gladness of life. I was dumb; now I speak. I owe this to the hands and hearts of others. Through their love I found my soul and God and happiness. Don't you see what it means? We live by each other and for each other. Alone we can do so little. Together we can do so much. Only love can break down the walls that stand between us and our happiness. . . . I lift up my voice and thank the Lord for love and joy and the promise of life to come.

Voice Offstage Reciting a Refrain from "The Star of Happiness":

> Wonderful star of light!
> Out from the darkness of night,
> Sending down a silver ray
> Turning nighttime into day.
> Wonderful star of light,
> Forever shining bright,
> Always send your ray to me,
> Even to eternity.

HELEN *(raising right hand)*: This is my message of hope and inspiration to all mankind.

                                        CURTAIN.

This was the act, with variations, that Helen would perform twice daily on the vaudeville stage from February 1920, when she opened to a full house in Mount Vernon, New York, to the spring of 1924. She loved being in the theater, with its "rush, glare, and noise" as well as the "life vibrations" of the friendly and sympathetic audiences whose "breath" she could feel on her face. In vaudeville she could deck herself out in sequined evening gowns with chiffon trains and wear theatrical makeup, which she quickly learned to put on herself after a few lessons from Annie and—it was said—the legendary Sophie Tucker. More important, vaudeville, which paid better than writing or lecturing, was the answer to her financial problems. She and Annie were among the highest-paid performers on the vaudeville stage, headlining for two thousand dollars a week at the Palace and other theaters. Helen had at last succeeded in acquiring the modest trust fund for Annie that she had dreamed of ever since she was a girl.

In vaudeville they could stay in one place for a week, instead of traveling from town to town, as they had to do on the lecture circuit, and their presentation, which was essentially the same as their lecture, was shorter. They were onstage only twenty minutes in the afternoon and evening. To earn their three-hundred-dollar fee for a lecture, they had to entertain their audiences for an hour and a half.

Helen later wrote:

> I found the world of vaudeville much more amusing than the world I had always lived in, and I liked it. I liked to feel the warm tide of human life pulsing round and round me. . . . I enjoyed watching the actors in the workshop of faces and costumes. . . . The thought often occurred to me that the parts the actors played was their real life, and all the rest was make believe. I still think so, and hope it is true, for the sake of many to whom fate is unkind in the real world. . . . I can conceive that in time the spectacle might have grown stale. But I shall always be glad I went into vaudeville, not only for the excitement of it, but also for the opportunities it gave me to study life.

Besides the usual dancers, comedians, singers, performing animals, and acrobats, vaudeville shows sometimes featured what was known in the business as "freak and odd acts." A freak act was someone who had been on the front page of the newspapers, preferably a person of notoriety. Headliners included Peaches Browning, the sixteen-year-old whose May-December romance with the aging Edward "Daddy" Browning, an eccentric millionaire, was aired in court and the tabloids; the black world heavyweight champion, Jack Johnson, who displayed photographs of the recent funeral of his white wife, Etta Duryea, who had committed suicide; a Dr. W. B. Thompson, who claimed that a person's illness could be cured by placing his fingertips together, touching fingernails; and "The Human Tank," who swallowed

Helen and Annie in
vaudeville, c. 1920

live frogs and threw them up alive until he was stopped by the ASPCA,
which as one wag put it, "claimed cruelty to animals and to audiences."

"Prison talent" was also highly popular. An audience favorite was a man
named Snodgrass, who had sung on the radio from a penitentiary where he
was serving time as an accomplice to murder. He was such a hit that he was
pardoned and booked on the Orpheum circuit for a thousand dollars a
week. Another hugely popular performer was a man acquitted of murder,
Freddie Thomson, who had led a bizarre double life as the wife of a man
and the husband of a woman. Billed as "the Man-Woman," he appeared at
a Chicago vaudeville theater for five hundred dollars a week until the act
was stopped by the police.

In contrast to the freak act, which lasted only a short time, an odd act,
which was unconventional in style and presentation, was booked for many
seasons. Odd acts ranged from the great Wagnerian opera singer Madame
Schumann-Heink to the prize-winning poet Carl Sandburg to Edna Wallace Hopper, whose specialty was giving matinee performances for women
only in which she imparted her antiaging secrets. During her act she
revealed that she practiced what she preached by stripping naked and

bathing in full view of the audience, unaware that at one performance four of the "feminine" spectators who were ogling her were college boys in drag.

Helen was considered an "odd act," and in the opinion of Joe Laurie, Jr., a vaudeville historian and performer, "the greatest of all the odd and interesting acts we have ever seen or worked with was Helen Keller. . . . We spoke to her like you would speak to anybody, and she touched our lips with her hand to 'hear' us. Miss Sullivan, the great lady who taught her, was her constant companion. Miss Keller's act was a great lesson in courage, faith, and patience to everyone in the audience and to everybody backstage. She headlined in vaudeville for a number of years. A great lady."

A more revealing glimpse of Helen backstage was supplied by another vaudevillian, Will Cressy, who like the other performers marveled at her ability to make her way unaided from her second-floor dressing room to the stage twice daily. She was apparently guided by the scent of the two dozen American Beauty roses supplied fresh daily for the act:

> I have sat in her room and watched her waiting so patiently and yet so eagerly to be told what is going on; what is being said and done. Her hands are continually seeking Miss Sullivan's lips to know if she is speaking. Or her hands are flying to Miss Sullivan's hands to spell out some question. A thousand different expressions are chasing each other over her face. Her head is perched to one side as if she was listening; and yet she cannot hear. Her great big wide-open beautiful eyes are continually shifting around as if she was looking for something; and yet she cannot see. But yet, in some mysterious way, she senses many things. Let anyone walk by that she has grown to know, and she learns them as quickly as she does anything else, and she will look up and smile. She recognizes the vibrations of their footsteps.

Helen's friends were scandalized by what they called her "deplorable theatrical exhibition." When she performed in Pittsburgh, the regal Mrs. Thaw filled the boxes with her friends. But her delight turned to disgust when she glanced at the program and realized that Helen and Annie's fellow vaudevillians included strong men, stunt performers on stilts, as well as "a large company of lavishly clad, and Luscious Looking Girls of Rare Joyousness and Bewitchment." Calling for the manager, she imperiously demanded that these tawdry acts be replaced at once with more cultured fare.

Undoubtedly Mrs. Thaw's dismay had something to do with her daughter-in-law's success as a vaudeville dancer. Refusing to be billed as Mrs. Harry Thaw, Evelyn Nesbit had gone on the vaudeville stage in 1910 under her maiden name, becoming even more of a box-office draw after Mad Harry, as the press dubbed him, had escaped from Matteawan, and she told an avid press that she feared for her life, as Thaw had often beaten her before murdering her lover Stanford White. As a publicity stunt, uniformed guards who were hired by the theater's management watched her day and night.

Unlike Helen, who was proud to earn a living by what she termed "a dignified act," Annie, who still aspired to high society, was mortified by Mrs. Thaw's disdain. Sharing her patron's low opinion of vaudeville, which catered to the lower classes, she winced every time she had to pass the signs backstage at the Palace that read "Vulgarity will not be tolerated. Check with manager before using any material you have any doubt about. Don't use words 'hell,' 'damn,' 'devil,' 'cockroach,' 'spit,' etc." As for the vaudevillians themselves, she felt that they were far from the vibrant, interesting people Helen imagined, but degenerates who went straight from their silly stage performances to wild parties.

For Annie Sullivan, every performance was a physical and mental ordeal. Her eyes hurt her every time she had to appear in front of the footlights. Although possessed of a beautiful stage voice, she still suffered from shyness and hated public speaking. As Helen noted, "Her life seemed always to turn and turn in circles of futility as a fish in an aquarium, and her fits of melancholy did not help her. . . . It causes me remorse as well as admiration to reflect that Teacher went on her vaudeville tours at an age when she should have rested. It also saddens me to remember how I troubled her with my propensity to answer awkward questions with little or no reserve."

By "awkward questions" Helen was referring to the question-and-answer period that followed their act. Many of her responses, having to do with her opinions on social and political issues, were frank and outspoken. Although Annie did not share Helen's extreme liberalism, she believed it was her duty to translate her radical point of view to the public. It was an uncomfortable position for a shrewd, practical woman who knew that many of Helen's stands were unpopular and that she would be attacked in the press for not confining herself to issues such as the blind and social service.

What is Miss Keller's age?
There is no age on the vaudeville stage.

Does Miss Keller think of marriage?
Yes. Are you proposing to me?

Does talking tire you?
Did you ever hear of a woman who tired of talking?

Do you close your eyes when you sleep?
I guess I do, but I never stayed awake to see.

What do you think of President Harding?
I have a fellow feeling for him. He seems as blind as I am.

Who is your favorite hero in real life?
Eugene V. Debs. He dared to do what other men were afraid to do.

What do you think of the Ku Klux Klan?
I like them about as much as I do a hornet's nest.

What do you think of Harvard College's discrimination against the Jews?
I think when any institution of learning applies any test other than scholarship, it has ceased to be a public service institution. Harvard, in discrimi-
nating against the Jew and the Negro on grounds other than intellectual
qualifications, has proved unworthy of its traditions and covered itself with
shame.

Can you enjoy trees?
Yes, they speak to me of the silent works of God.

Do you think women should go into politics?
Yes, if they want to.

Do you think women should hold office?
Yes, if they can get enough of their fellow citizens to vote for them.

Who are the three greatest men of our time?
Lenin, Edison, and Charlie Chaplin.

What do you think of Soviet Russia?
Soviet Russia is the first organized attempt of the workers to establish an
order of society in which human life and happiness shall be of first
importance, and not the conservation of property for a privileged class.

Who are your best pals?
Books.

What is your definition of a reformer?
One who tries to abolish everything his neighbor enjoys.

What is your conception of light?
It is like thought in the mind, a bright, amazing thing.

What do you think of capitalism?
I think it has outlived its usefulness.

What do you think of the League of Nations?
It looks like a league of bandits to me.

What did America gain by the war?
The "American Legion" and a bunch of other troubles.

Do you believe with Arthur Conan Doyle that spiritualism is the cure for the world's troubles?
No. I think the world's troubles are caused chiefly by wrong economic conditions, and the only cure for them is social reorganization.

Helen's replies were not as spontaneous as they appeared. Some months before, she and Annie had compiled a seventeen-page list of questions that she might possibly be asked, and they had rehearsed the answers. Other topics included whether America had been true to her ideals ("I am afraid to answer that; the Ku Klux Klan might give me a ducking"), her opinion of ex-president Wilson ("I think he is the greatest individual disappointment the world has ever known"), her idea of unhappiness ("Having nothing to do"), and could she really perceive colors ("Sometimes I feel blue and sometimes I see red"). As a student of her vaudeville performances points out, "On the vaudeville stage, she was free to address any subject brought to her capable mind. . . . Playing to hundreds of thousands of vaudeville patrons, Keller and Macy brought a simple and timeless message to common people. It was their desire to bring good will to a world recovering from war and a world undergoing rapidly changing technology."

Helen was a trouper, and not even the death of her mother from unknown causes in 1921, when she and Annie were appearing on the Orpheum circuit in Los Angeles, could prevent her from going onstage. "Every fiber of my being cried out at the thought of facing the audience, but it had to be done," she recalled, noting that she had received the news of the death of her mother, whom she had not even known was seriously ill, two hours before a performance.

The death of Kate Keller, a lonely, unhappy woman with few friends, rekindled Helen's old conflicts about her family. Although she and her mother had grown closer during her visit to Montgomery while Annie was

Polly Thomson (left) and Helen dance in front of a studio backdrop, c. 1920

recuperating in Puerto Rico, she knew that her mother had never accepted her handicaps and regarded her as a tragedy that had wrecked the Keller family. Although Kate had never said so to Helen, her dream of a happy family life was satisfied only through her two younger children, Mildred and Phillips. Helen remembered that her mother used to tell her wistfully, "Yes, life was good to us both for a few brief months," and wrote that after Helen's illness her mother's "life was never the same to her. It was as if a white winter had swept over the June of her youth."

Helen's politics had also become a wedge between them. "My mother talked intelligently, brilliantly, about current events, and she had a Southerner's interest in politics," she observed with sadness. "But after my mind had taken a radical turn she could never get over the feeling that we had drifted apart. It grieves me that I should have added to the sadness that weighed upon her."

Although Helen did not discuss her mother's medical condition in her autobiographies, there is some indication that Kate Keller was ill for several months before her death and wished to prepare her daughter for her demise. After their mother's death, Helen reminded Mildred in a letter of Kate's visit to New York the previous summer. Their mother was recovering from an undisclosed illness, and as Helen wrote Mildred, "just as she was leaving me at the station in New York, she said suddenly, 'Helen, you will not see me again, but whatever happens, I shall wait for you.' Afterwards she wrote, 'Do not let your feelings spoil your work, always do the best you can, and think of mother watching until you come.' "

The aloof Kate had a lifelong dread of a prolonged terminal illness, and Helen took solace in the thought that her mother's death before she became completely incapacitated was what she had wished. But it was her own firm belief in Swedenborgianism and immortality that made it possible for her to bear her mother's loss. "I had absolute faith that we should meet again in the Land of Eternal Beauty; but oh, the dreary blank her going left in my life! . . . She seemed to have died a second time when I visited my sister in Montgomery the following April. The only thought that upheld me was that in the Great Beyond where all truth shines revealed she would find in my limitations a satisfying sense of God's purpose of good which runs like a thread of gold through all things."

With her mother dead, she now had only Annie, but in 1921, while they were performing in Toronto, Annie collapsed with a severe case of the flu. Polly Thomson, their secretary who also served as her understudy, went onstage in her place. Annie recovered and resumed her performances. The following year, severe bronchitis prevented her from appearing with Helen. She could not speak above a whisper. It was clear that her stage days were over.

From then on, it was Polly—seemingly humble and chic in an elegantly understated little black dress—who explained Helen to the public.

CHAPTER 18

"The Dreadful Drama
Is Finished"

NNIE SULLIVAN WAS slowly going blind. Ever since her fifth
birthday, when she had suffered a virulent case of trachoma, she
was terrified of permanently losing her vision. Although a series
of operations had restored her sight when she was a student at the Perkins
Institution, she suffered recurrent attacks of granular conjunctivitis and
other eye disorders throughout her life. In middle age her eyesight deteriorated to the point where flickering candles, unshaded lamps, even the
expanse of a white tablecloth caused excruciating pain. She could read
only by wearing double-lensed telescopic glasses that weighed heavily on
her face.

In 1929 Annie's right eye, which had developed a cataract, became so
painful that the eye itself had to be removed. Then her left eye developed a
cataract, and her vision became very dim. The only way she could see was
to use powerful drops to expand her pupils. By 1934 her sight had almost
completely failed. Against the advice of Dr. Conrad Berens, an eminent
New York eye surgeon, she had an operation on her left eye in May 1935. It
was unsuccessful. As the doctor had warned her, she rapidly lost the little
sight she had left, distinguishing only light and color. Toward the end of her
life she could perceive only gray shadows.

Annie was becoming dependent on Polly to nurse and read to her, and on Helen for spiritual support. Refusing to admit to anyone that she could no longer see, Annie often stumbled. Of the two women, Helen was the far more surefooted.

Their roles had become reversed. Annie was now the pupil, and Helen the teacher, as she attempted vainly to ease her teacher's fear of blindness. Like many people who lose their sight in later life, Annie could not reconcile herself to her disability. It was much harder for her to accept blindness than it was for Helen, who never remembered seeing. "All my life I have lived in a dark and silent world. I seldom think of my limitations, and they never make me sad, but to see the light failing in another's eye is terrible, especially when one is unable to do anything about the tragedy," Helen noted sadly, concluding that Annie was "one of the sensitive spirits that feel shamed by blindness. It humiliates them like a stupid blunder or a deformed limb."

During the period when she could still see, Annie refused to rest her eyes despite her doctor's advice. Always suspicious of her fellow human beings, she became a semirecluse. She would not answer the phone or doorbell when Polly was out of the house. Instead Annie retreated to her bed with her books and her dogs, a mammoth woman in a black dressing gown who read until she suffered nauseating pain and headaches.

Books were as important to Annie as they were to Helen. As Annie herself admitted toward the end of her life, she was "afraid of people in the flesh," and the people she liked best "are in biographies and autobiographies because there is less danger of disillusionment in book-friendships."

Helen tried to teach Annie to read Braille. But the Braille system had changed since Annie had taught it to Helen, and she found it difficult to learn. "Helen is and always has been thoroughly well behaved in her blindness as well as her deafness, but I'm making a futile fight of it, like a bucking bronco," Annie confessed to a friend. "It's not the big things in life that one misses through loss of sight, but such little things as being able to read. And I have no patience, like Helen, for the Braille system, because I can't read fast enough."

Besides her books, their dogs, on whom she doted, were among her few remaining pleasures. Over the years she and Helen had owned Great Danes, terriers, and Shetland collies, but the old and sickly Sieglinde, a reddish-gold Great Dane whom friends swore that Annie had taught to say "Ma-ma" and "wah-ter," was her favorite. Sieglinde seemed to read Annie's moods, and whenever anyone came to the house who bored her mistress — and there were many such persons — Sieglinde tried to push the visitor away.

Annie (top center) and Helen with Mrs. Leslie Fulenwider (right), her son Howard, and Sieglinde at Helen and Annie's house in Forest Hills, New York, 1920

When Sieglinde died, Annie was devastated. Next to children, whom she loved, possessing endless patience for them, she loved animals, particularly dogs and horses. In her mind the death of Sieglinde was as tragic as the loss of a child. She informed Helen that "she would make friends with all dogs if she could."

Sieglinde's death was a reminder of her own mortality. "She loved perfection and nonsense—two entities that seem quite opposite but which often meet in artistic natures," Helen noted. "But once back in Forest Hills, she said to me, 'Oh, Helen, what a sad experience it is to feel one's decline! Every power that leaves me is a foretaste of the decay that is worse than death. To climb down again in the scale of being, isn't that awful?'"

In contrast, Helen still felt young and vital. Although her chestnut hair was graying and her figure was no longer slim, her profile had a chiseled, Grecian elegance. Her blue eyes, which seemed expressive, continued to magnetize almost everyone who met her. They had "none of the lack-luster look usual to the blind. When she talks, they take on animation; and they gaze at you with what seems a seeing glance," wrote a man who met her around this time and had no inkling they were artificial.

That she was still an attractive woman was apparent from the hordes of men who continued to flock to her public appearances and to write to her.

Less than a year after her mother's death, in September 1922, she had received in the mail a marriage proposal from a widower in Kansas City with five children. Although Helen had no intention of marrying him, she entered into a lengthy correspondence with him that was remarkable for its frankness. For the first time she revealed her true feelings about the impact of her disabilities on her sexuality:

... All the primitive instincts and desires of the heart, which neither physical disabilities nor suppression can subdue, leap up within me to meet your wishes. Since my youth I have desired the love of a man. Sometimes I have wondered rebelliously why Fate has trifled with me so strangely, why I was tantalized with bodily capabilities I could not fulfill. But Time, the great discipliner, has done his work well, so that I have learned not to reach out for the moon, and not to cry aloud for the spilled treasures of womanhood. I have come to feel that it was intended for me to live and die unmated, and I have become reconciled to my fate.

You have knowledge of human nature. You understand the workings of the normal mind. But I wonder if you know the consequences of the triple affliction of blindness, deafness and imperfect speech. You have read my books. Perhaps you have received the wrong impression from them. One does not grumble in print, or hold up one's broken wings for the thoughtless and indifferent to gaze at. One hides as much as possible one's awkwardness and helplessness under a fine philosophy and a smiling face. What I have printed gives no knowledge of my actual life. You see and hear, therefore you cannot easily imagine how complicated life is when one has to be led everywhere and assisted to do the simplest things. Somehow your letter has made me acutely aware of my situation and the discomforts of it. I realize, as perhaps you cannot, the almost unthinkable difference between your life and mine.

You seemed to have lived a full, normal man's life. I have lived inwardly. They say that all women partake of the nature of children. I am absurdly childish in many ways. My nearest friends tell me I know nothing about the real world. In some respects my life has been a very lonely one. Books have been my most intimate companions. My part in domestic affairs is usually that of a wistful looker on. . . . your willingness to marry me under the circumstances fills me with amazement. I tremble to think what an inescapable burden I should be to a husband.

. . . I told you that time had done its work well, and that I no longer cried for the spilled treasures of womanhood. I did not mean to imply by this observation a forced and melancholy resignation. Through the wise, loving ministrations of my teacher, Mrs. Macy, who since my earliest childhood has been a light to me in all dark places, I faced consciously the strong sex-urge of my nature and turned that life-energy into channels of satisfying sympathy and work. I never dreamed of suppressing that God-given creative impulse. I simply directed the whole force of my heart-energy to the accomplishment of difficult tasks and the service of others less fortunate than myself. Consequently, I have led a happy, and I hope, a useful life.

Perhaps her mother's death the previous year had liberated the forty-two-year-old Helen to the point where she could correspond frankly with a man about her limitations. From her point of view, it was a safe relationship even though his marriage proposal stirred up old fantasies and desires. As she was well aware, it had come too late. Long ago she had absorbed her mother's—and society's—taboo against marriage and motherhood for a severely handicapped woman. She consented to meet the widower once, briefly, in New York, and then abruptly, to his disappointment, ended their correspondence.

IF SHE WAS NOT PERMITTED—and did not permit herself—a woman's traditional life, she would find another way to fulfill herself. It was in middle age, after a motley career as a handicapped whiz kid, writer, lecturer, movie actress, vaudevillian, and radical activist, not to mention secular saint, that Helen Adams Keller found the work that would absorb her for the rest of her life.

It was as the national and international counselor for the American Foundation for the Blind, the central clearinghouse that was started in 1921 for the agencies that were helping the blind. When they were in vaudeville, Helen and Annie had been offered jobs as fund-raisers, but it wasn't until 1923 that they began speaking at occasional meetings. By that time they again needed money. Neither woman possessed any sense about finance, and they had squandered their earnings in vaudeville on expensive apparel for their public appearances, vacations, pedigreed dogs, and renovations to their Forest Hills home, as well as generous gifts for friends and the needy. "I never think about money until I haven't any," Teacher admitted, adding that although she loathed the upper class for exploiting the poor, John Macy was right when he accused her of "resembling the rich in the vulgarity of your tastes." Yet the two women were not entirely to blame for their impoverished circumstances. After two years on the Keith Orpheum circuit, the public was no longer flocking to see their act. As a social historian of the blind has pointed out, "They had only one story to tell, and few audiences were interested in hearing it a second time. There was no way for them to create fresh material equal in impact to that initial drama."

Fund-raising was not a new role for Helen. At the Perkins Institution,

Michael Anagnos had shrewdly let her make the appeal herself for the Kindergarten for the Blind, and she had raised astonishing sums of money. In middle age she had not lost her old touch, even though she was privately ashamed of her extraordinary ability to extract money from wealthy people. Philanthropy went against the grain of her socialist beliefs. "At the same time Teacher and I felt real shame to appear as mendicants at the doors of plenty, even though we were laboring with all our might to raise the blind from beggary," she wrote. "There was always a volcano of resentment within her because, despite all praise and high-sounding professions of philanthropy, the fact remained that the blind were looked down upon as they had been through the ages."

Encouraging manufacturers to donate radios at minimal cost was one of Helen's first projects for the foundation. Such was the magic of her name that one manufacturer donated 250 radios after receiving one letter from her.

Obviously fearful of jeopardizing their livelihood, she was careful not to mention her socialist views in her campaign speeches for the foundation. Her activism in the socialist movement diminished as well. She rarely spoke publicly about socialism after 1922, revealing her enthusiasm for Soviet Russia only in letters to friends whom she knew shared her views. Yet in her autobiography *Midstream: My Later Life*, which was published in 1929, she stated that socialism was the answer to creating a world without war and poverty and that she continued to support and identify with working-class people.

As Frances A. Koestler points out in *The Unseen Minority: A Social History of Blindness in the United States*, Helen's campaign speeches for the foundation "did not reflect such views. Basically all alike, their major themes may be sampled in excerpts from the address she made in June 1925 to the International Convention of Lions Clubs, the world's largest fraternal organization, in which she challenged its members to become "knights for the blind in the battle against darkness."*

Try to imagine how you would feel if you were suddenly stricken blind today. Picture yourself stumbling and groping at noonday as in the night, your work, your independence gone. In that dark world wouldn't you be

* The Lions Club, a nationwide organization founded in 1917 to promote civic welfare, had already dedicated itself to the cause of the blind. After Helen's moving pleas, it made its sponsorship permanent. Over the years the Lions established numerous sight-saving programs, eye clinics, and other medical services for the blind; raised money for the Brailling and sound recording of books; supplied blind persons with canes, radios, typewriters, and other useful appliances; and, as Koestler points out, "fulfilled in innumerable other ways the crusading role that Helen Keller had urged them to adopt." In 1990 the Lions rededicated themselves to "Sight First."

glad if a friend took you by the hand and said, "Come with me and I will teach you how to do some of the things you used to do when you could see"? That is just the kind of friend the American Foundation is going to be to all the blind in this country if seeing people will give it the support it must have.

. . . It is because my teacher learned about me and broke through imprisonment which held me that I am able to work for myself and for others. . . . The gift without sympathy and interest of the giver is empty. If you care, if we can make the people of this great country care, the blind will indeed triumph over blindness.*

For a fledging organization like the foundation that needed the public's support to advance its cause, Helen Keller was, as Koestler points out, "the perfect symbol" of a handicapped person. Who could better convince people that the "great need of the blind is not charity, but opportunity" than this shining woman, whose well-known triumph over tragedy moved them to tears? Spiritually as well as physically beautiful, intelligent, with an unquenchable zest for life, Helen delivered a message that the public, afraid for its own health and normalcy, desperately wanted to hear: being disabled was not synonymous with despair and physical ugliness, but an opportunity for heroism and spiritual transcendence.

People flocked to the meetings at which she mounted her appeals for the blind. These were at first held in the homes of wealthy society people and then, to accommodate the many hundreds of people who wanted to hear her speak, in churches and larger meeting places. The appeals were a repeat of Helen and Annie's vaudeville act, which in turn had been based on their lectures. After a performance by one or more blind artists, including the versatile Edwin Grasse, who played both the violin and the piano, and a brief talk by someone representing the foundation, Helen and Annie made their long-awaited appearance. As she had done hundreds of times before, Annie told the rapt potential donors about Helen's education, and then Helen fielded questions and made a short speech in which she asked people to give money on behalf of the blind to the foundation. The meeting concluded with another musical interlude as ushers collected cash donations and distributed memberships blanks.

Helen Keller may have been the ideal, unthreatening image of a handicapped person, but Annie Sullivan, with her volcanic rages and possessive

---

* For a full account of Helen Keller's and Annie Sullivan's work for the American Foundation for the Blind, see Frances Koestler's *The Unseen Minority: A Social History of Blindness in the United States* (New York: David McKay, 1976).

attitude toward Helen, was hardly the ideal image of a standard-bearer for the blind. Not that Annie desired to be one. At sixty, she still harbored an ambition to become a writer. One of her favorite books was William James's *Talks to Teachers*, which John Macy had once read to her. She was rereading it, with the hope that soon she might be able to write a similar book. "If Teacher had been left free to choose her destiny, she would never have limited herself to the cause of the blind," Helen observed in *Teacher*. "It was only because she saw a chance of usefulness to them that she joined her wealth of mind and heart to my endeavors."

Nella, who as Annie's biographer was observing her subject as closely as Annie Sullivan had once studied the child Helen Keller, was blunter in stating the reasons why Annie had become involved with the foundation. "Left to herself, Mrs. Macy would never have chosen this field as the object of her life's work. She would have elected larger issues. There is something terrifying about the sweep of her energies, terrifying in the thought of what she might have done with them if she had not submerged them in Helen."

Predictably, this thwarted woman's relationship with the American Foundation for the Blind was a stormy one, as she clashed with Moses Charles Migel, an equally quick-tempered retired silk manufacturer who was the executive director, over what she regarded as their meager salary and traveling expenses. Another area of contention was the Helen Keller Endowment Fund—Annie and Helen wanted the money for it to come from small donations by ordinary citizens, while "Major Migel," as he preferred to be called, and the trustees wanted the fund raised from large gifts from wealthy individuals. In addition, there were squabbles about the endowment fund itself—Annie and Helen wanted to obtain contributions to it first, while the trustees wanted them to solicit memberships in the foundation and raise money for current program needs. When the foundation announced the invention of the Talking Book for the adult blind and asked Helen to join in the campaign for funds to manufacture machines for this new method of "reading," which would be easier for older blind people who did not read Braille, Helen balked, saying that she was disappointed that nothing was being done for the deaf-blind. As Koestler points out, strangely she would be the person who "fought hardest of all against involvement in the drive to launch the Talking Book, one of the landmark achievements in services to blind people."

Annie and Helen's association with both the Perkins Institution and the Cambridge School had come to abrupt and disastrous ends. Their relationship with the American Foundation for the Blind might have ended in the same tempestuous manner, only by this time Annie was too infirm and worried about Helen's future to sever ties with the organization that was providing them with their livelihood. Annie needed the trustees of the foundation even more than they depended on her and Helen to enhance its image and raise money. Besides, the flamboyant Migel, who was described by one observer as "a bon vivant . . . a man who played cards for high stakes, bet heavily on horses and even owned a few," proved to be a genuine friend who understood both women's complex natures. According to Frances Koestler, it was Migel's courtly attitude toward women that prevented him from taking Annie Sullivan's personal attacks too seriously. ". . . He felt great compassion for her deteriorating health," Koestler wrote. "He and she were the same age, but he was hale and hearty while she was not only fast approaching total blindness but was also plagued with numerous other ailments."

In 1927 Helen took a leave of absence to write *Midstream*, an account of her later life that Doubleday, her publishers, had been pressing her for and that she had been postponing because she still found writing laborious. No sooner had she started work on the book than a minister of the New Church in Washington, D.C., asked her to write a book about Emanuel Swedenborg and what his teachings meant to her.

Annie prodded Helen to resume work on her memoir after her deeply felt book about Swedenborgianism, titled *My Religion*, was published by Doubleday in 1927. Although she had urged Helen to write frankly about her life since her sophomore year at Radcliffe College, she wanted a sanitized version of her own life. Helen was not to mention her humble birth, the years at the almshouse, and especially her tumultuous marriage to John Macy.

Annie had reason to conceal her private life. Although they had not lived together for fourteen years, she refused to grant her husband a divorce. Even a visit from John's resolute mother, pleading with her to release her son from the marriage, had not persuaded her to give him up. Annie had promised his mother that she would grant a divorce, but then procrastinated about starting the proceedings.

It is surprising that a man of John's stature did not confront his wife directly about terminating their marriage. By then regarded as one of America's foremost literary critics as well as a brilliant editor and writer, John had succeeded Carl van Doren as literary editor of *The Nation*, a job he held for one year, from 1922 to 1923. In 1926 he became literary adviser to the recently formed publishing firm of William Morrow & Company.

By this time, too, John was an alcoholic. The disease had ravaged his handsome John Barrymore–type looks, and he looked brittle and prematurely old, a white-haired man with a flushed, mottled complexion. When he was working at *The Nation* he often brought his illegitimate daughter to the office, where she aroused the curiosity and pity of the staff. His friends regarded him as a delightful man, recalling that they were "invariably struck by the humanness of his nature. There was nothing pretentious about him, nothing austere or bookish, but rather a debonair air which reflected his enjoyment of life."

John's mother blamed Annie's refusal to consent to a divorce for her son's alcoholism, but Annie told her that the reason she had postponed getting a divorce was that she was afraid of the publicity. Her real motive, however, was that she was still in love with John and hoped that he would come back to her. He haunted her dreams and thoughts, and, as she confided to Helen (who later told Nella), one of her frequent psychic experiences involved their reconciliation:

> Last night you came to me, John. I do not know if it was a dream or your spirit presence. I felt your step so near and you were the very same—your manner and the smell of your clothes. I held your hand so tight and you called me Bill, but I felt the same glad thrill I always felt when you put my hand on your lips and said Hello Bill. Oh I was so happy because you had come back to me. . . . We walked in the hill wood and we hunted toadstools and got a basket full that was good to eat. . . . I can't tell if it was a dream or a vision. I only know I have been happier today because you called me Bill in the dear old way.

Helen's reaction to Annie's continuing obsession with John is unknown, although Helen made it clear that she was upset about having to lie in her book about her teacher's life. "Actually I felt humiliated, as if I had almost lied to God Himself, and I never spoke of *Midstream* to her after an experience that caused aversion to myself. For I loved Teacher and not myself in her."

By this time Annie had finally confided to Helen about her dismal years in Tewksbury, which she blamed for her "self-indulgent" and "changeable" nature. She had talked to Helen as a child about her youth in the village of Feeding Hills and the death of her little brother Jimmie, but Helen had never known the sordid facts of her childhood until Annie, Helen, Polly, and Nella, who was now functioning as Helen's editor, had visited Feeding Hills in 1927. The purpose of the trip was to refresh both Annie's and

Helen's memories of their early years in Massachusetts, which they felt would enhance not only Helen's autobiographical *Midstream* but also a biography of Annie that Nella was writing.

If Helen felt resentful that Annie had not taken her into her confidence many years before, she never publicly expressed it but characteristically glossed over Annie's secretiveness, writing in *Teacher* that "Annie never cast the shadow of her years in the almshouse at Tewksbury upon the joyous mind of a child growing up in normal surroundings."

Helen's love for Annie remained unquenchable. For years tactless people had asked her what she would do without her teacher, to which Helen had always made a cheery response that God's love would somehow fill the void if Annie died. In *Midstream*, however, she confessed that "it terrifies me to face the thought that this question brings to my mind. I peer with a heavy heart into the years to come. Hope's face is veiled, troubling fears awake and bruise me as they wing through the dark. I left a tremulous prayer to God, for I should be blind and deaf in very truth if she were gone away."

Midstream, even with Nella's editorial help, was a tremendous strain on Helen. Composing and revising mainly in Braille, she rewrote the book at least four times, and Annie, Polly, and Nella were constantly spelling back to her pages, paragraphs, and chapters. To the end she was revising and rewriting and was only able to get a sense of what she had written when the Braille edition was printed. According to Nella, after *Midstream* was finished, Helen interrupted washing dishes to inform her and Annie, " 'I just want to say this,' and she pronounced the words carefully so that there could be no mistaking her meaning. 'I just want to say this: There will be no more books. I put the best years of my childhood and youth into *The Story of My Life*. I have put the best years of my womanhood into *Midstream*. There will be no more books.' "

HELEN'S SINGULAR WORLD had always fascinated the medical profession, and although as a young woman Annie had vowed that she would never let her pupil become the object of scientific experimentation like Laura Bridgman, Annie later changed her mind and allowed Helen to be studied by a number of physicians. In 1929 Dr. Frederick Tilney, a famous professor of neurology at Columbia University and the doctor of Helen's publisher, F. N. "Effendi" Doubleday, wanted to test her sense organs to discover if they were more sensitive than the average person's. A personal

At Saranac Lake, 1929: (left to right) Annie, Helen, Herbert Haas, their
helper, and one of Helen and Annie's many canine friends

friend of Helen, he had been amazed by her ever since they had taken a
drive from her home in Forest Hills to Garden City, a distance of about
twenty miles. The windows of the car were rolled down, and Tilney had
asked Helen if she could tell him anything about the surrounding country-
side. Her first observation was that they were making their way through
open fields, which was the case, as the road ran through a golf course. She
then told him that they had just passed a house with an open fire, and looking back, the doctor saw a cottage with smoke pouring out of its chimney.
She recognized at once when they entered a major highway, and as they
drove along it, she told Tilney that they were passing several large buildings.
Looking behind him, Tilney saw that they had just passed Creedmore State
Hospital for the Insane.

Tilney was curious to learn more about Helen's extraordinary olfactory
sense, which he believed had played an important part in her intellectual
development. A short time later he was delighted to receive a letter from
her that not only answered his questions but also revealed "the remarkable
content of Miss Keller's mind, her literary appreciation, her phenomenal
memory, and her mastery of literature."

In her letter to Tilney, Helen reiterated that the sense of smell was associated with "poignant memories, deep emotions and the glories of poetry." She also confided that because she could smell at a great distance, she identified with the Indians who could detect a distant campfire while a white man could not perceive it. "The sense of smell is the esthetic sense, I think, even more than sight," she wrote the doctor, confiding that she was "very sensitive to unpleasant odors. They have a depressing influence upon me; for they suggest all manner of dread things—disease, accidents, coming evil and unhappy lives. Sometimes, when such an odor comes between me and a beloved object, a nervous tremor seizes me, and I find it difficult to control myself."

Helen's letter ended with an erudite discussion of odors in literature and in the Bible, but on testing Helen subsequently with six aromatic substances, Tilney was disappointed to discover that her olfactory sense showed nothing above the normal average person's. Similar tests were conducted on her sense of taste and touch and vibratory sense. In all three cases her test results were the same as the normal average adult's. Puzzled, Tilney was forced to conclude that the secret of Helen's sensory superiority lay in her concentration and patience. Similarly, experiments with blind people have demonstrated that their acuteness of hearing and sensitivity to touch are not compensatory gifts but the result of hard work and training. They learn to pay attention to sounds that a sighted person would customarily ignore.

In the recognition of objects by palpation, the sensory process known as stereognosis, however, Helen's ability far exceeded that of any normal person whom Tilney had ever tested. "Not only is she able to recognize all familiar objects about her, to tell the form and size of many articles with which she has not had previous contact, but she also has the ability to identify by touch the difference between a great variety of flowers and plants," he observed. "This is a feat far above the capacity of most average persons even when aided by all of the senses."

At one point during the testing, Tilney placed a coin in Helen's hand, telling her that "this was the one touch of nature which made all men kin." "Pessimist," she instantly replied.

Tilney also noted that painful stimuli seemed to cause Helen less distress than was experienced by the normal average adult. Sometime earlier he had been surprised to observe her composure when she had fallen and seriously injured her knee. He speculated that her stoicism, as well as her religious convictions and philosophy of life, had grown out of her long meditations. "One feature concerning this philosophy is the almost complete displacement of physical fear, particularly the fear of death. . . . Perhaps Miss Keller is different from other persons in her lack of fear concerning disease and death, because she firmly believes that with the passing of this life she will enter another in which all of those senses whose privileges she has here been denied will be restored to her in full, and she will then be able to hear, and to see, and to extol the glories of a new world then revealed to her."

Laura Bridgman had a remarkable sense of direction, but Helen revealed on rotation that she possessed a complete lack of it. Tilney speculated that this was because Laura had retained her eyes until the end of her life, while Helen had her eyes removed as a young woman. Unlike Laura, Helen did not have retinas, "and this, in conjunction with the fact that she is devoid of any sense of direction, may have an important bearing on certain but little understood sensory pathways connected with the eye."

In his study Tilney made a comparative sensory analysis of Laura Bridgman and Helen Keller, noting that there were important differences between the two deaf-blind women. Laura had made her adjustment to life with only one of the principal contact senses, the sense of touch. On the other hand, Helen had the advantage of olfactory sensation and the sense of taste.

Toward the end of her life Annie Sullivan had told their startled friends that she had always believed Laura Bridgman to be intellectually superior to Helen. Tilney, however, did not support her conclusion.

But, however brilliant this mind may have been, it had little of the richness of Miss Keller's. . . . There would be no doubt that Miss Keller has led a fuller life, one characterized by a greater variety of interests, more extensive contacts, greater depth of mental content and more impressive influence on her time.

The fact that Laura's life was less full than Helen's must in large measure be attributed to the fact that her education ceased when she was 20 years of age, and that her discipline depended on fixed times and set exercises. The method of Mrs. Macy in developing Helen Keller was totally different. From the very beginning of her instruction this ingenious teacher has arranged every experience so that it might have real pedagogic value, whether in play, in work or in rest, as well as in all other social activities. Helen Keller has been taught to capitalize every opportunity for learning from each impression entering her sensorium. This began when she was seven years old and continues to the present day.

In fact, if she were compared with those who have enjoyed a full college education, there is no question that her rating would far surpass the average of those trained in this way. Indeed, it is my opinion that there are few intellectual men and women living today who could develop a higher intelligence quotient than Helen Keller, with properly adjusted tests. There are many features in her intellectual development which must justify her inclusion in the class of genius.

Laura Bridgman and Helen Keller, with a small portion of their brains in active commission, have made an intellectual and social adjustment to life which, at the very least, is equal to the average. This must mean that the average brain with all of its parts working develops only a small fraction of its potential power.

These findings, based on Helen's history and achievements, led Tilney to conclude that the human race had not as yet developed more than a fifth of its potential brainpower.

Tilney carried out his experiments on Helen in Nella and Keith Henney's living room. According to Nella, "four long afternoons were spent at it and Dr. Tilney was shocked. Keith's hands were more sensitive than Helen's. As an engineer, his had been accustomed to small bits of wire and tiny pieces of electronic apparatus. Helen's were superbly trained for larger objects, and that was that."

Helen was disappointed by Tilney's results, feeling that she had failed to live up to his expectations. In a letter written several weeks later to F. N. Doubleday, she expressed the fear that the reason she had not seen the doctor recently was that he "found out there was nothing extraordinary about me. When you see him, please tell him that I have forgotten everything, except his not taking me fishing last summer. I suppose the tests showed that I couldn't tell a fish from a thumb-screw. That's a stab at my vanity—something a woman can't forgive."

HELEN WAS GOOD-HUMORED about being studied by medical doctors and psychologists, but there was one controversy that deeply upset her. It was the persistent criticism by many scholars and psychologists, several of whom were blind themselves, that her literary efforts, like the plagiarized "The Frost King" story of her youth, were without merit, as they contained an abundance of visual and auditory images. They accused her of verbalism, or word-mindedness—that is, that she used words for which she had no firsthand sensory basis.

Helen's most voracious critic was an iconoclastic psychologist named Dr. Thomas Cutsforth, himself blind since age eleven. In 1932 he published a book called *The Blind in School and Society*, in which he described the tendency of blind children to use words for which they had no experiential reality. As the following extracts from Cutsforth's blunt criticism make clear, Helen was the prime offender. In his opinion, what happened at the water pump in Tuscumbia was not a miracle but a tragedy:

> Was or was not Helen Keller better adjusted to her simple life prior to the advent of Miss Sullivan? The child Helen appears, from all accounts, to have had the situation well in hand, from the paternal Captain down to the family dog. She was markedly egocentric in her social behavior. The adult Helen is still so, but along lines which are more in accord with the practices of the majority. With all her education in visual verbal concepts, there is far less experiential reality and situational insight in the adult Helen than there was in the untutored child. The important question is, where in the process of education and personality-building should natural growth be sacrificed to artificialities?

In support of his thesis that Helen expressed herself with imagery that she could not possibly have experienced, Cutsforth quoted one of her poetic descriptions:

> We followed a tributary of the Tamar, which we glimpsed through a mist of green. The trees were just budding. The willows were already in leaf, and I could smell the virgin grass and reeds—a tide of green advancing upon the silver-grey stream. It was misting, and soft clouds were tumbling over each other in the sky which, Teacher said, had the effect of intensifying the greenness until the land seemed a great emerald. . . .

Cutsforth then pointed out:

> The paragraph conveys the conventional meaning to the average reader. The words and sentences are intelligently structured so that the average reader will recognize meanings and situations that are common to him and his fellows, but relations and situations from which the writer is excluded. . . . The implied chicanery in this unfortunate situation does not reflect upon the writer personally, but rather upon her teacher and the aims of the educational system in which she has been confined during her whole life. Literary expression has been the goal of her formal education. Her own experience and her own world were neglected whenever possible, or, when this could not be done, they were metamorphosed into auditory and visual respectability.
> . . . In this case the process was a lifetime, and the capitulation took place on an infantile level, when the personal affection and confidence of

the child Helen were given completely to her teacher. From that time on, Helen's world contracted by expanding into that of her teacher. Her teacher's ideals became her ideals, her teacher's likes became her likes, and whatever emotional activity her teacher experienced, she experienced. . . . It is a birthright sold for a mess of verbiage.

In *The World I Live In* and her other writings, Helen had defended herself against her opponents, presenting her argument in support of the right of a blind or deaf person to comment on a world they had never seen or heard:

> Critics . . . assume that blindness and deafness sever us completely from the things which the seeing and the hearing enjoy, and hence they assert we have no moral right to talk about beauty, the skies, the mountains, the songs of birds, and colors. . . .
> . . . The bulk of the world's knowledge is an imaginary construction. History is but a mode of imagining, of making us see civilizations that no longer appear upon the earth. . . .
> . . . Suppose I omitted all words of seeing, hearing, color, light, landscape. . . . I should suffer a great diminution of the wonder and delight in attaining knowledge; also—more dreadful loss—my emotions would be blunted, so that I could not be touched by things unseen.

Although Helen never publicly mentioned Cutsforth's attacks, her feelings about his criticisms were expressed in a letter to Nella shortly after his book's publication, in which she referred to him snidely as "Dr. Cutsforth, who declares that Teacher's method destroyed the real Helen and substituted one of her own design."* Some years later, after Annie's death, she avenged Teacher by vetoing Cutsforth's nomination for the Migel Medal that the American Foundation for the Blind awarded yearly for "outstanding service to the blind."

LIKE HELEN, Annie Sullivan chose not to publicly rebut Cutsforth's criticism of her teaching methods. By this time she was too frail to enter yet

---

* In 1951 Cutsforth would publish another report in which he maintained that verbalism led to "incoherent and loose thinking" by the blind child. As a result, many educational programs for the blind were restructured to avoid the use of words and concepts that a child could not possibly experience. Recently, however, several researchers have expressed criticism of Cutsforth's beliefs and the educational practices they fostered. Their arguments mirror the ones Helen expressed in 1908 about the right of blind and deaf people to use visual and auditory imagery. In the researchers' opinion, sighted people use many words for which they have no direct experience, and there is no evidence that "the concepts based on these words are meaningless or involve loose thinking."

another battle that she knew would exhaust her mentally as well as physically, even if she were the victor. As her vision failed, she had become even more petulant and unpredictable. Helen had always prided herself on understanding Annie's whims and caprices, and whenever her teacher got into one of her contrary moods, she liked to quote John Macy's remark that "if Annie was drowned, they must look upstream for her body." But even Helen was nonplussed when Annie had refused to budge from the house several hours before they were to board a ship that would take them on their first trip abroad, in the spring of 1930. The trip was canceled. Then Annie, in a puzzling change of heart, insisted that they book passage on the next ship. She spent most of the voyage in her cabin terrified by the rough seas, while Helen, who was exhilarated by the gale, insisted that Polly take her up to the deck, where she could feel the cold spray of the ocean on her face.

In April Helen, Polly, and the sickly Annie spent six months in Scotland, England, and Ireland, where Annie attempted unsuccessfully to learn about her doomed parents. Her genealogical quest was perhaps triggered by the earlier expedition that the three women and Nella had made in 1927 to Feeding Hills. It was in a working-class section that Annie had learned the fate of her father, who had abandoned her and her brother to the poorhouse. According to relatives who were reluctant to discuss him, Thomas Sullivan had never gotten to Chicago, the city where he dreamed of making his fortune as a ditch digger, but had committed suicide. "All the bitterness and anger in his daughter's heart were burned away," Nella wrote of Annie, "and she has remembered him since as she loved him, laughing and singing and telling stories of Ireland."

Helen had looked forward to visiting the country that had given her Teacher, but Annie, who acknowledged that she had inherited the Irish melancholy and mysticism, as well as "their waywardness, their fitful tempers and erratic desires" did not share her enthusiasm for Ireland. She loathed the hopeless poverty, grim rocks, and bogs, informing Helen that Ireland made her feel as if she "was held fast as if in a nightmare."

Her misgivings aside, she was determined that Helen enjoy the country. Later, Helen shared Teacher's vivid descriptions with Nella in a letter:

You must see Killarney, Nella. . . . Can you imagine mountains of rhododendrons rising and massive into the bluest sky you have ever been under— white, crimson, scarlet, pink, buff, yellow and every shade God has painted on leaf and flower! . . . As if this was not beauty enough, you come out of a mountain pass and gaze, breathless and trembling, upon "purple peaks that out of ancient woods arise," and there, in the gorge below, are silver lakes, reflecting as in a row of mirrors all the glory that surrounds them!

Annie may have spent the trip mourning the loss of her youth—"the thought of age is repugnant to me," she once wrote, "only youth and life at full tide are beautiful"—but Helen was feeling in her prime. On her fiftieth birthday, she spent the day "drinking a bottle of liquid sunshine" and taking a long walk on Bray Head, a rocky spur of the Wicklow Mountains.

In the summer of 1931, after they had participated in the first World Council for the Blind, which was held in April in New York and attended by foreign delegates from thirty-two nations, Annie, Helen, and Polly went to Concarneau, Brittany, for a vacation. They felt they had reason to celebrate, as thanks to Helen's pleas for standardization, Braille had been accepted as the world's standard alphabet for the blind. And as a result of her first appearance before the U.S. Congress, the Pratt-Smoots Bill had become law; it provided for a national system of libraries for the blind under the direction of the Library of Congress.

From Brittany they traveled to Yugoslavia, where they were the guests of King Alexander, and raised funds for the rehabilitation of the blind. Upon their return to Brittany in late September, Annie was in worse health.

It was during their first trip to Brittany, in late August, that Annie, despising "the dreadfulness of age" and believing that she had not long to live, made her last will and testament. She gave the Forest Hills house, their furniture, and all articles of personal property to "my beloved friend and pupil Helen Keller, to have and enjoy for her own personal use and benefit." This included her bar pin with diamonds, a long string of pearls, and a Russian silver inlaid cup.

All of her manuscripts, letters, photographs, scrapbooks, and other documents relating to Helen Keller and to her own life were to be given to Nella Braddy Henney, with the understanding that she was willing to assist Helen Keller in her literary work.

"An engagement may be entered into by Mrs. Henney with any person or persons she considers qualified to assist Helen Keller in the preparation and publication of any material that it seems advisable to publish," Annie stipulated. "But after the material is used, sorted and catalogued, I suggest that all manuscripts, letters, photographs, etc. be given over to the American Foundation for the Blind to be preserved for future reference."

Annie's share of the twenty-three-thousand-dollar Eleanor Hutton trust fund, of which she and Helen were joint owners, was to pass to Polly Thomson, "in consideration of her great services to Helen Keller and myself during many years." In addition, Polly, who shared Annie's love of luxury and expensive clothing, was to receive Annie's short string of pearls, her red china fox coat and Chinese shawl, and lest she be tempted to neglect her overwhelming responsibilities, a small portrait of Annie as well as a larger, tinted portrait of Helen Keller and her teacher.

Although they had frequently clashed, the executor of Annie's estate was Major Migel.

Christmas was gloomy that year. As the country was in the depths of the Depression, Helen was unable to raise funds for the foundation to meet its current expenses. Polly, on whom they both depended, was in the hospital most of December, recovering from an operation for appendicitis. Their two new dogs, Darky, a black Scottish terrier, and Helga, a Great Dane, had disappeared. But even their sudden reappearance did not lift Annie's mood. Almost totally blind and sensitive about meeting strangers, she was not able to read or shop or do anything festive, even if they had felt inclined to celebrate. Usually in robust health, Helen herself was ill and had to cancel all her engagements for several months.

Within a few months, both women had recovered their health sufficiently to make a third trip abroad, in the summer of 1932. They were returning to Scotland, where on June 15, at its commencement exercises, the University of Glasgow was to confer on Helen an honorary degree of Doctor of Law.

In her speech Helen paid tribute to Teacher: "When I think of what one loving human being has done for me, I realize what will someday happen to mankind when hearts and brains work together. That is why there is such a glow in my thoughts as I accept the declaration of Glasgow University that darkness and silence need not bar the progress of the immortal spirit."

On this trip, Helen and Annie were both presented with honorary fellowships from the Educational Institute of Scotland. It was unusual for Teacher to accept such honors. For her entire life she had been ambivalent about receiving awards and public acclaim—on the one hand, refusing them, and on the other hand, complaining that the public was interested only in Helen.

"Honors which would have transported us with joy if they had come earlier have no thrill in them, especially when they are forty years overdue," she wrote during this period. "Then one is old, sated, bored. In youth I would have gone round the world for a compliment. Now I am indifferent."

Recently the trustees of Temple University in Philadelphia had wished to honor both women with honorary degrees. Helen had gladly accepted her degree in February 1931, but Annie refused the honor, writing in a letter to the president of the university that she did not deserve it. Despite his protestations, she continued to decline the degree, although in the end, after much flattery, he persuaded her to change her mind. A year later, when she traveled to Philadelphia to accept it and the reporters clustered around Helen, Annie said, "Even at my coronation Helen is queen."

In Scotland Annie permitted herself to enjoy being honored, even though publicly she behaved with an undue modesty that was perhaps disingenuous. In her acceptance speech, in which she downplayed her own role in Helen's achievements, she referred to Ariel, a sprite in Shakespeare's *The Tempest* who was imprisoned in a pine rift by an evil witch until Prospero "made gape the pine and let him out":

"I have never thought I deserved more praise than other teachers who give the best they have to their pupils," Annie said. "If their earnest efforts have not released an Ariel from the imprisoning oak, it is no doubt because there has not been an Ariel to release."

In early July they visited London, where Helen opened a school of massage for the blind under the auspices of the National Institute, and they were invited to dine at the House of Commons. During her stay Helen visited schools for the blind and deaf, often making five speeches a day, which were short in length, as she was still incapable of a sustained speaking effort. She also was introduced to Lady Nancy Astor, the American expatriate and first female member of Parliament who within a few years would be suspected of being pro-Nazi. Deceived by Lady Astor's charm, as described to her by Polly, Helen became one of her boosters, wondering why she received such bad press. "She is most emphatically not a shrew. . . . She has a sweet, friendly way of taking your hand and telling you she has always loved you because you are a Southerner. She is as charged with energy as an electric battery. . . . She agreed reluctantly when I said publicity must be accepted along with the rest of the evil we moderns have fallen heir to. . . ."

It was at Lady Astor's that they met George Bernard Shaw, to whom Helen, as she shook his hand, had a very different reaction. "Bernard Shaw was as bristling with egotism as a porcupine with quills. His handshake was quizzical and prickly, not unlike a thistle. Lady Astor tried to interest him in me. 'You know, Mr. Shaw,' she said, 'that Miss Keller is deaf and blind.'

" 'Why, of course!' he replied, 'all Americans are blind and deaf and dumb.' "

Although Shaw later insisted that he made the remark "to make her feel

as much as possible that she was a highly distinguished visitor at no disadvantage whatsoever with us," Helen disagreed. When Lady Astor wrote to
convince her that Shaw, "one of the kindest men that ever lived," had made
the remark to disregard her handicap, Helen replied that she believed Shaw
to be one of the greatest of men, but certainly not one of the kindest and
that he had not been "particularly gracious" to her that afternoon.

They were to receive a far more cordial reception at Buckingham Palace
later in the month when they met King George and Queen Mary at a royal
garden party. The king asked Polly if she could understand everything that
Helen said, and when she replied that she could, he was curious to see how
people communicated with Helen. Although Annie was too old and too ill
to spell extensively to Helen, she rose to the occasion and gave a lipreading
and spelling demonstration. According to Helen, "Their Majesties were
both deeply interested in everything we did. The queen turned to the king
and said, 'It is wonderful,' and he replied, 'And it is all done through vibrations—how extraordinary.' "

The hoopla surrounding Helen's honorary degree from the University
of Glasgow had fatigued Annie and Polly. With the hope of finding some
rest, the three women rented a picturesque Elizabethan cottage in Kent for
the summer. But Memory Cottage, as it was called, proved too small, dark,
and antiquated, and when it rained, "a green twilight" filled the place.
Annie could not read at all, and Polly and Helen felt "imprisoned and
smothered in roses." While in Kent, Annie contracted a severe bronchial
cough. A doctor thought that she would benefit from a higher altitude, so
they returned to the Scottish highlands. To their disappointment, it was
crowded with hunters and fishermen. Then a friend of Polly arranged for
his brother to let them have his old farmhouse in South Arcan, not far from
Inverness.

In Scotland, Annie was tired, nervous, and ill, but Helen felt in wonderful health. She loved the highlands, enthusing about the "soothing quiet of
deep heather or walking through lanes lovely with ferns and silvery
birches." Her pleasure in Scotland was intensified by a new dog—a bow-
legged Scottie named Ben-Sith, which was Gaelic for "mountain fairy."
Describing her vacation as one of the most "glorious" experiences in her
life, she wrote in one of her disturbingly elaborate visual descriptions, "I
love it all—the moorland peace and hills of beauty. I love the mountains
when they are cloud-capped or when soft veils of mist, spun of wind and
dew and flame, are drawn around their shoulders. . . . If I am ever born
again, I know I shall be a Scot. . . ."

Annie, Helen, and Polly with their dogs at Arcan Ridge in the Scottish highlands. They had returned to Scotland in 1932 in an attempt to restore Annie's health.

In late August, while they were still in Scotland, they received news that John Macy had died of a heart attack at a hospital in Stroudsburg, Pennsylvania. He had been rushed to the hospital from Unity House, where he had been stricken in the midst of delivering a speech to the members of the International Ladies' Garment Workers' Union. It was the third of a scheduled series of five lectures, titled "Revolution and Rebellion in Classical American Literature." He was fifty-five years old, and despite his literary fame, impoverished. He died on August 26, 1932.

John's premature death deeply affected Annie, who paid for his funeral. Shortly before her own death she recorded her passion for her estranged husband in a curious document titled "Teacher Whimsically Sketches Her Life and Philosophy, Calling Them 'Foolish Remarks of a Foolish Woman' ":

August 23? 1934

As we drove up in front of the Arcan Farm-house, we saw a gull close to the door. It lifted wide wings and flew away over the corn-fields. As I entered a telegram was put into my hand telling of John's death. Now my heart is full of withered emotions. My eyes are blinded with unshed tears. Today only the dead seems to be traveling. I wish I was going his way. The House of Life is shattered with the wounds he inflicted, the broken walls are of his forgetting.

Three thousand miles away his body, once so dear, lies cold and still. The dreadful drama is finished, the fierce struggle that won only despair is ended.

The essence of him was old. I will not retell the things he did. I am not his historian. Much will be hid of what was deeply, intimately mine. Some may tell how we did thus and so, but who can know what we refrained from doing, the paths we did not take, the secret separate ways down which we looked and longed for, but took another journey after bright, strange things we dreamed? Deep in the grave our dust will stir at what is written in our biographies. . . .

Now I wait for death—not sad, not heroically but just a little bit tired. To love and succeed is a fine thing, to love and fail is the next best, and the best of all is to fail and yet keep on loving.

John's death and her own blindness broke Annie's unyielding spirit. By the following year she was an invalid, a frail, emaciated woman suffering from pain in her left eye that had recently been operated on in a doomed attempt to save her vision, gastric pains, and "a ghastly siege of carbuncles," which were caused by septicemia.

As her sight failed, she penciled the following words. They were the last ones she would ever see:

Why did you not ask your questions before my heart was cold, my hair gray? What does it matter now who my father was? Or my mother? How my childhood was nurtured? Your meed [sic] of praise or blame or sympathy or scorn cannot touch me. I am as indifferent as a stone. Love has betrayed me; friendship is a broken reed; life has pierced me in a thousand ways; but the wounds are all dry. I think I have forgotten how they used to bleed. You have kept aloof, proud world, too long. The time for confidence is passed. The most safe abode for my secret is where the darkness shelters all.

She was dying by inches of heart disease and senility, yet as Helen observed, "a new lamp had been lighted within her" when Annie heard about a neglected deaf and blind baby girl named Patricia in Louisville, Kentucky. Immediately she wanted to adopt the baby, and it took all of Helen's and their friends' power of persuasion to induce her to abandon the idea.

In the spring of 1935 Annie Sullivan entered Doctor's Hospital in New York for treatment. Helen was allowed only a few minutes with her occasionally, as her presence overexcited her teacher. "I have behaved like a naughty child, and cried for the moon and disobeyed all my own injunctions to treat a handicap as an opportunity for courage," she told Helen on one of her visits, adding that her brain was crowded with all sorts of ideas, and Helen must write them down for her. Then she could not remember them.

That summer Helen and Polly took her to the Catskills, and according to Helen, "There she sought solace in the shadows of the hills, trees and lakes." But Annie could not stop talking about her "joy isle," and in October 1935 they traveled with her to Jamaica. For the dying woman, the mountainous island, with its palm trees and tropical gardens, which she could perceive only as indistinct forms, lacked the fascination of Puerto Rico. The only topic that interested her was her failing health.

In August they returned to New York and then rented a cottage by the ocean at Greenport, Long Island. Helen later reported:

> That was our desperate last effort to strengthen her so that her life might be tolerable. One day she surprised me by walking down and wading into the water, thinking, I suppose, that its salt buoyancy would support her. Suddenly she became dizzy and collapsed. We half carried and half led her to the cottage and put her to bed. "I am trying so hard to live for you" she said sobbing. . . . The next day she was taken to the hospital in an ambulance. Before she left she said to me tenderly, "I have wasted time grieving over my eyes. I am very, very sorry, but what is done is done."
>
> When she returned from the hospital, she shifted from mood to mood. She would yield to despair and much of the time did not care that Polly and I were full of anguish. When someone tidied her room, she kept talking to me about the Angel of Death coming for her, and we should have everything in order at his arrival.
>
> My last memory of Teacher as I knew her was an October evening when she was fully awake, sitting in an armchair with us around her. She was laughing while Herbert [a Forest Hills neighbor who was working for them] told her about the rodeo he had just seen. She spelled to me all he said, and how tenderly she fondled my hand! . . . Afterwards she drifted into a coma from which she never awoke on earth.

With Helen Keller at her bedside, holding her hand, Anne Sullivan Macy died on October 20, 1936, at seven-thirty in the morning. On her death certificate, the cause of death was listed as chronic myocarditis and arteriosclerosis of three years' duration. She was seventy years old. Her occupation was listed as "teacher."

SCORES OF BLIND MEN and women were among the twelve hundred persons who attended Annie's funeral on October 22 at the Park Avenue Presbyterian Church on Eighty-fifth Street in New York. The pastor, Rev. Edmund M. Wylie, read the thirteenth chapter of First Corinthians, which had been Annie's favorite passage from Scripture. "Though I speak with the tongues of men and of angels and have not love, I am become as sounding brass or a tinkling cymbal." At Helen's request, Dr. Wylie had substituted the word "love" for "charity." In a note, she explained that "Teacher and I have always felt that love was meant when the word charity was used." Among other musical works, the choir sang Dvořák's "Going Home," one of Annie's favorite selections. Rev. Dr. Harry Emerson Fosdick of Riverside Church delivered the eulogy. He compared Annie to an aviator whose plane takes off against a fierce wind yet uses its power to achieve a perfect flight. He told the mourners that Helen and Annie were like twin stars in the heavens that required the efforts of an expert astronomer with a powerful telescope to observe that they were not one human being.

After the service the funeral procession passed down the middle aisle of the church. Behind the black-robed ministers came twelve honorary pallbearers preceding the coffin, which was banked with pink roses and ferns. They were followed by Helen and Polly, who was weeping.

Alexander Woollcott, an admirer of Annie Sullivan who had sent her a daily bouquet of flowers and read to her while she was in the hospital for an eye operation, attended the funeral and was moved by the pathos of the occasion:

> At Annie Sullivan's funeral there could have been no one who was not quick with a sense of the unimaginable parting which, after nearly fifty years, had just taken place. While I live I shall remember those services. Not for the great of the land who turned out for that occasion, not for the flowers that filled the church with an incomparable incense, nor for the wise and good things which Harry Emerson Fosdick said from the pulpit. No, what I shall remember longest was something I witnessed when the services were over and the procession was filing down the aisle, Helen walking with Polly Thomson at her side. As they passed the pew where I was standing, I saw the tears streaming down Polly's cheeks. And something else I saw. It was a gesture from Helen—a quick flutter of her birdlike hands. She was trying to *comfort* Polly.

Then, according to her wishes, Annie Sullivan's body was taken to Long Island for cremation.

During the last week of her life, Annie had drifted in and out of consciousness, and Polly recorded her final lucid thoughts:

> Good-bye John Macy, I'll soon be with you, good-bye, I loved you.
>
> I wanted to be loved. I was lonesome—then Helen came into my life. I wanted her to love me and I loved her. Then later Polly came and I loved Polly and we were always so happy together—my Polly, my Helen. Dear children, may we all meet together in harmony.
>
> My Jimmie, I'll lay these flowers by your face—don't take him away from me. I loved him so, he's all I've got. She took the bed clothes and threw [?] [the] bucket of flowers out of there.
>
> Teacher was complimenting nurse and nurse said, "Oh, you are playing to the gallery." Teacher threw her head back smiling and said, "I've play acted all my life and I shall play up till I die!"
>
> Polly will take care of Helen. As the years go on her speeches won't be so brilliant as what people will think [sic] but my guiding hand won't be there to take out what should be taken out.
>
> Thank God I gave up my life that Helen might live. God help her to live without me when I go.

As they watched Helen comfort the sobbing Polly, many of their friends whispered the same prayer. Like Rev. Fosdick, they were unsure of whether Helen Keller and Annie Sullivan were two distinct personalities. In 1931, when Helen had been chosen by *Good Housekeeping* as one of the twelve greatest living American women, the magazine writer observed that perhaps Helen Keller and Annie Sullivan should have been named as one of the twelve greatest American women. The Russian artist who painted Helen's portrait that accompanied the article went even further. Like Helen's other detractors, including the two women's intimate friend Nella Braddy Henney, he believed that Teacher was by far the greater of the two women. If only one of the women had to be selected, it should have been Annie Sullivan. As an artist, he recognized her as a sculptress whose clay was Helen.

A short time before Annie died, a friend, meaning it as a compliment, had told her, "Helen would be nothing without you." "Then, my life has been wasted," Annie said.

CHAPTER 19

Helen Without Annie

"I ACHE ALL OVER as I remember how she grew thinner and thinner," Helen later recorded in the journal that she had started keeping after Annie's death to discipline her mind back to regular work. "I was glad she could not see my swimming eyes as I massaged her and noticed skin and bones where I had once felt the firm softness of her chest and shoulders.

"I live over the last few minutes of her earth life: the death rattle after an eight-hour struggle for breath . . . her darling hand growing cold in mine . . . the smell of opiates heavy in the room . . . sorrowing friends who drew me away so that her body might be prepared for the funeral . . . the Gethsemane I passed through an hour later when I touched, not Teacher's blessed face, but fixed features from which expression had fled. I feel again the recoil, the cry that escaped me, 'It is not Teacher, it is not Teacher!' . . .

"When she breathed no more, somehow the faith she had wished she could hold with me rose up stronger than ever and, leaning over, I said, 'You know, dearest, don't you, that life is beginning over again, glorious with light and peace.' Then it came over me that she was thinking of the joy of being reunited with her little brother, and I talked about him, feeling his nearness vividly. I wonder if her mind answered mine from afar. There was such a surge of memories sweeping over me, and I remembered the first joyous days of release when we spelled winged words to each other, and life was a continuous great discovery. . . . As I murmured to her I still felt the indefinable response of the spirit in her face. The change I sensed afterwards was more than I could bear. Everything was blurred. It seemed as if I should henceforth tread paths that led nowhere, climb steps that would lead to nothing because they could not bring me to her."

As Helen was communing with Annie's soul among the books that she had cherished, her grief gave way to ecstasy. "The body," she was convinced, "was only a shadow of the soul," and she knew that Teacher would never be far away.

On November 3 Helen traveled to Washington, where, at the National Cathedral, Annie's ashes were placed in the columbarium in the Chapel of St. Joseph of Arimathea. At the time of Annie's death Helen had received word that the bishop of the cathedral "will consider it a privilege to offer the right of sepulcher in the cathedral for Mrs. Anne Sullivan Macy . . . and that the privilege of sepulcher at the cathedral should also be offered to Miss Keller."

Annie Sullivan was the first female offered this distinction for her own achievements. "Among the great teachers of all time," the bishop of Washington referred to her in his address, "she occupies a commanding and conspicuous place."

At the committal service Helen spoke a few words that were recorded by a friend: "Blessings upon the receptacle of the precious dust which my heaven-sent Teacher wore as a garment as she wrought her miracle of liberation through Him who is the Lord of Life and Love."

In the hope of adjusting herself to her loss as well as escaping from the interference of well-meaning friends, she decided to visit Polly's family in Scotland. Two days after Annie's service, she and Polly, who had immediately applied for citizenship, sailed on a German ship, the S.S. *Deutschland*, for England. On the first night of the voyage Helen was plagued by dark thoughts and insomnia. Although Polly tried to break her mood of melancholy by reading to her with her fingers, as she used to do with the blind Annie, Helen could not concentrate. She regarded herself as a "somnambulist, impelled only by an intense faith." The following day was "a day dreadful beyond words" as she began to emerge from "the stupor of grief, and every nerve is aquiver. It does not seem possible that the pain flooding through my heart can ever be stilled but I know it is a sign of returning spiritual health."

Helen's despondency lifted when Polly, on their walks up and down the deck, described the gulls circling the ship and the white sea swallows that were capable of flying several thousand miles. The next day, however, she was again plunged into a deep depression. "What earthly consolation is there for one like me, whom fate has denied a husband and the joy of motherhood?" she mourned. "At the moment my loneliness seems a void that will always be immense." But then she remembered her work for the blind and the deaf-blind, as well as her unshakable belief in immortality and an afterlife in which she would be able to both see and hear, and her faith sustained her.

By the ninth day at sea, after a hearty lunch of frankfurters and sauerkraut, one of her favorite dishes, she noted, with pleasure, that her interest in philosophy, poetry, and travel was returning. Although she was deeply concerned about "the demoniac forces like Hitlerism" in Europe, her loathing of the Nazis did not prevent her from appreciating the "homelike atmosphere" of the *Deutschland* and "the German love of beauty that greets my fingers." She was especially delighted by the bouquets of small and large chrysanthemums that seemed to be omnipresent, and her cabin, which even though it was small and "cozy," boasted every modern convenience.

Still, Annie's presence seemed omnipresent. On the tender to Southampton, she strongly felt her spirit, "tantalizing almost beyond endurance." Several nights before, on shipboard, she had a wonderfully comforting dream in which Teacher had kissed her, and "literally her face against mine breathed youth, sunshine and flower-sweet air. Since then I have had a sense of following, following, following her, and I keep expecting to find her somewhere—in London or up in the Scottish highlands that her Celtic soul loved."

On the train from England to Scotland, Helen had difficulty believing that it was just she and Polly who were in the compartment. Teacher had accompanied them on their previous trips to England, and Helen fancied that she was merely asleep; otherwise, she would be spelling into her hand "the charm of light or color of flying cloud." She consoled herself by the thought that Annie, for whom teaching had been "her work and her glory," was instructing "the sensorially crippled" in heaven. "My soul was so conscious of her presence I could not—I would not—say she was dead, and I do not now."

As the days went by, fresh life pulsed through her. She began reading André Maurois's *Life of Disraeli*, which, as a biography written in French by a Frenchman about one of Britain's most distinguished political leaders, appealed to her as an internationalist. Closing the book, she marveled for "the millionth time" at the freedom that literature had given her.

Politics and world affairs again began to deeply absorb her. Although she believed that world peace would triumph over the insuperable evil that was Hitler, her heart sank when she learned that forty million gas masks were being prepared for use in Britain and Scotland alone.

Her hatred of Hitler, "a Mephistopheles," intensified in late December when she received a letter from her German publisher informing her that he was going to delete her admiring views of Bolshevism and Lenin from the German edition of *Midstream*. The publisher, Otto Schramm, wrote, "I must today emphasize that I hope you meantime have become convinced of your error of judgment, and therefore feel obliged to let me know that your attitude now towards Russian Bolshevism has entirely altered since you have learned about the evil and monstrous destruction to which this world doctrine tends."

But Helen's views of Soviet Russia had not changed. Although she was becoming increasingly disturbed by the totalitarian government of the Soviets, she refused to believe, as Schramm asserted, in the Soviet purges and that millions of Russian people had been slaughtered; otherwise "that country would not now be emerging, as we know it is, stronger than ever from its age-long fight against hunger and ignorance. . . . No doubt Russia has committed blunders, grave ones; but so has National-Socialist Germany, and now it has reverted to the darkest of the Dark Ages. . . ."

She wrote Schramm an angry, impassioned letter, saying that she had no intention of deleting her views, as she knew about "Germany's anti-Semitic atrocities, fear-clamping state control over lives and homes, and imprisonment of thousands without trial," and that she planned to withdraw her book from publication in Germany.

Other world events also aroused a fiery response. When King Edward VIII abdicated to marry the American divorcée Mrs. Wallis Warfield Simpson, she had no sympathy with his plight. "I doubt whether His Majesty will reap from his decision the happiness he anticipates," she wrote in her journal. "There is a love of the people surpassing the love of a woman. . . . Many persons have a wrong idea of what constitutes true happiness. It is not attained through self-gratification but through fidelity to a worthy purpose. . . ."

Clearly the king's decision to give up his throne to marry Mrs. Simpson rankled Helen, perhaps because she herself had never been permitted to relinquish her public image as a handicapped icon for personal happiness. "Only through experiences of trial and suffering can the soul be strength-

ened, vision cleared, ambition inspired and success achieved," she continued. "Most of the men and women honored in history for their services to
mankind were acquainted with 'the uses of adversity.' They triumphed
because they refused to be turned aside by difficulties or opposition."

In Bothwell they stayed at the manse of Polly's brother Bert, who was a
minister, and his wife and children. Although Helen intended her visit to
be a quiet one, free of the constant interruptions that plagued her at home,
it proved stimulating. Visiting a mine, she felt thrilled as she was placed in a
cage and then lowered nine hundred feet down a shaft. Swaying from side
to side and feeling the drippings from a well as she descended were almost
as powerful tactile sensations as flying, which she loved, because it released
her from the physical restraints that constrained her in her house and on
the street. As she traveled through tunnels that she was told were lighted
only by safety lamps, Helen was reminded of her own condition. "Airmen
flying blind in a fog and miners quarrying in a deep pit are among the few
who can imagine what blindness means," she noted.

A far different type of delight was provided by the minister's children,
who knew the manual finger language. They watched with curiosity as
Helen typed her correspondence—it was her habit to write at least eleven
letters a day—and their presence made her feel less weary and restless. Like
Annie Sullivan, she loved all children, comparing them to "sunshine"—
their companionship made her feel young again.

Although Helen was an adept typist, she could not keep up with her
recent correspondence. There were hundreds of sympathy letters to answer,
and she was beginning to worry about her hands. She felt that she was using
them too constantly for writing, reading, and listening to conversation, as
well as reading people's lips. If they became injured or crippled with arthri-
tis, she would become truly helpless, completely isolated and shut off from
human society. Quickly she reminded herself that she had to keep on using
her hands, as "work is the only sure bulwark against despair."

The strain of having to reply to the sympathy notes of concerned friends
and relatives, as well as strangers, became so overwhelming that she considered renting a room at a quiet hotel where she could live like a recluse. This
was impossible, and on a single afternoon, for three hours, Polly was forced
to spell letters of condolence into her hand. Exhausted, Helen inadvertently said something thoughtless. As high-strung as Annie and Helen, Polly
reacted emotionally, and a bitter exchange occurred between the two
women. For several minutes they sat in stony silence, with tears in their
eyes, biting their lips in frustration. Then they broke down and embraced

each other, as they remembered the last wishes of Annie Sullivan that someday they all might be reunited in harmony.

Another time, as they were looking through a pile of letters and business papers, Helen realized what she had been spared when Annie sorted the mail and conveyed the necessary information to her with expert brevity.

They departed for the United States on board the S.S. *Champlain* on February 2, 1936. A fellow passenger was the English author Hilaire Belloc, who was planning to lecture in America. It was a rough voyage. Helen spent most of her time reading and thinking deeply about the soullessness of modern life and its impact on present and future generations whose imaginations, she feared, unlike her own, intensely vivid one, were becoming stunted.

> This repels me—a future civilization likely to be hard, practical, monotonous. I feel fortunate indeed that it has been possible for me to be a barbarian, to enjoy sculpture, the flow of graceful lines on surfaces, poetry, happy make-believe in bleak corners of my limitations. It also seems to me more urgent than ever to foster in the present young generation a spiritual philosophy and imagination that shall keep the morning dew in their souls when an age arrives that knows not the muses or the graces.
>
> The present generation is losing the capacity of enjoying life from within. They are sacrificing the delight in handicrafts born with every child to machine products. They want machines to sing, play, talk and read to them. They demand to be amused instead of amusing themselves.

Although Helen knew that people were surprised that a deaf-blind person could get any pleasure from the cinema, she liked to attend films and the theater regularly, perhaps because it made her feel like other people. One evening on shipboard, she attended the film *Camille*, with Greta Garbo starring as Marguerite. But as Polly's facile fingers described the dialogue as well as Garbo's cool beauty and her magnificent costumes, Helen regretted exposing herself to this tragic tale only three months after Annie's death. She saw similarities between Teacher and Marguerite—like Annie, Dumas's courtesan was an unconquerable spirit who rose from her sickbed and put on her sunniest face for the lover who refused to give her up. Helen began to weep as she recalled the small party Teacher had planned at their Long Island cottage during her final illness. Before the guests arrived, she struggled to put on her shoes with Polly's help; then, suddenly, she was seized with a violent pain. A doctor was immediately summoned and put her into the hospital the next day. As she dressed herself in street clothes for the last time, she silently gripped Helen's hand, and Helen sensed her imminent death when she spelled, "Dear, there is the ambulance," and Polly supported her downstairs.

Although she cheered up the following day when the captain invited them to tea in his cabin, her grief intensified as their ship approached New York. Friends sent her radiograms aboard the ship, but there was none from Teacher, and "this finality about our earthly separation seemed more than I could bear."

Her homecoming was not as sad as she had imagined. On her arrival, the dogs greeted her, wagging their tails against her and kissing her face. As she walked through the rooms, her hands lovingly felt Teacher's desk and the chair where Annie used to sit when she could see enough to read to her. To her relief, her teacher's bed, on which she had endured months of darkness and anguish, had been taken away. But when Helen touched Annie's books, she was again overcome with grief. "I had watched the darkness descending upon the eyes she had used during half a century to assist me and enrich my happiness. Only by the hardest work could I shut out that mournful memory and the heart-stabbing loneliness that pursued me every moment."

Hoping to console Helen, a friend who was a sculptress presented her with a cast of Annie's hand that she had made before Annie's death. It took all of Helen's composure to touch its delicate, familiar outline, with the thumb and index finger forming the letter L, which suggested love. But as Helen traced each line in the palm, "a likeness snatched, as it were, from death's relentless waves," she succumbed, in spite of herself, "to the old heartbreak . . . my tears fell; and I could not speak."

She was not alone in the world, of course. She still had Polly, on whom she could rely to communicate the beauty of a flower or a sunset, even though her new companion's descriptions ran to such clichés as "Pink! . . . Blue! . . . Mauve! . . . Green! . . . Gold! . . . Lavender! . . . Oh, Helen! The water is one sheet of burnished gold! . . ." But, one morning, as Polly's hands coolly informed her that her favorite coat from Scotland was now "too shabby" to wear into town, Helen lost her temper. It was clear that this fashion-conscious, thoroughly unimaginative Scotswoman could never take her beloved Teacher's place.

WITH THE DEATH OF Annie Sullivan, Helen Keller had met her severest crisis with immense courage and fortitude. Although after *Midstream* she had vowed that her literary career was over, in the years following Annie's death she would write three more books and numerous magazine articles. When the first one, *Helen Keller's Journal*, was published in 1938, she demonstrated to an admiring public that she was capable of a fine literary effort without Teacher at her side.

In death Annie Sullivan had answered her critics. Despite her dominating, irrational, and impulsive personality, she had enabled Helen to function without her. Far from creating a dependent, helpless woman, she had made a strong, resilient one who was more than capable of dealing with life's inevitable traumas and losses.

Although it was clear that Helen Keller could live without Annie Sullivan, her disability prevented her from living on her own. Even though she was now fifty-eight years old, she was forced to rely on Polly and other people for her needs. That she was able to adapt quickly to different people and situations was to her credit. Many of her blind contemporaries, particularly those who attended some schools for the blind where they were oversupervised, were haunted by the persistent feeling that they were being watched even in the privacy of their own rooms. Amazingly, Helen never became wary and suspicious of those around her. This woman, who had lived perhaps one of the most observed and documented feminine lives in history, continued to greet the world with characteristic sincerity and optimism.

CHAPTER 20

Polly and Nella

T HE FIRST THING people noticed about Polly Thomson was that her hands and wrists were of a completely different size and shape. One hand was small and delicate. The other—the one that she used to spell to Helen—was sinewy and overdeveloped, like a prizefighter's.

At the time of Annie's death in 1936, Polly Thomson, who was five years younger than Helen, had been with the household for twenty-two years as a secretary and a general factotum. Polly, whose real name was Mary Agnes Thomson, was born in Glasgow, Scotland, on February 20, 1885. Her father was a draftsman in an engineering firm; her mother, Isabella Fraser of Inverness, was a member of the Fraser clan.

In 1913 the brown-haired spinster came to the United States to visit an uncle, a well-to-do shoe manufacturer in Swampscott, Massachusetts, and to look for a job. Polly's formal education had ended when she had finished the public schools in Glasgow. Her father had died when she was twelve years old, leaving her mother with four children: two boys and two girls. Like Polly, her sister, Margaret, never married. Her brother David later became an ear, nose, and throat specialist in Blackpool, England. The other brother, Robert, or Bert, was the minister of the Church of St. Bride's in Bothwell. The family was close. According to one source, "the devoted sisters never grudged the opportunities that had gone to their brothers, but Polly was left with a sense of inferiority from which she never recovered."

Polly quickly got a job as a governess. The job was pleasant, but she found it unchallenging and wanted to find another line of work. One day in the autumn of 1914, a Boston hairdresser told her that another of her clients, a Mrs. Macy, was looking for someone to travel around the country with her and Helen Keller on a lecture tour.

"And who," asked Polly, "is Mrs. Macy? And who is Helen Keller?" She had never heard of either of them.

Polly confounded her friends and relatives. Dr. William Allen Neilson, who was the president of Smith College, said he could usually place a Scot, but with Polly he had no idea what kind of person she was. She seemed like a character in a novel. Her motives were not apparent, and there was an air of detachment about her. Neilson sensed that she looked after Helen and Annie not from a feeling of affection but from a sense of duty. Whatever capacity she had for emotional reaction had not yet been touched.

Another friend noted: "Polly was a complex person to begin with and she was in a situation which became increasingly complex. She never felt adequate to the demands that were made upon her. She was lonely and frightened and always hard on herself. . . . An intimate, yet not intimate, member of the household, Polly's admiration of Teacher was limitless; but she was not welded into the unity that was formed of Helen Keller and Annie Sullivan. She was a lonely figure in the background, deft in service and devoted, usually silent, always busy."

According to her brother, "Her early life was of an ordinary character and had no incidents in it that held any promise of great usefulness, so far as I can think of at the moment."

In 1921 in Toronto, when Annie was confined to her bed with the flu, Polly had made her first appearance on the platform alone with Helen and did so well that from that time forward it was she more often than Annie who stood beside Helen to interpret her broken speech to the audience.

After secretly attending several of Helen's lectures where she was aided by Polly, Annie was convinced that the two women made an attractive platform appearance. Possessing a strong sense of style, Polly would see that Helen was groomed and smartly but simply dressed, better turned out than she had been during Annie's years of blindness. She also liked Polly's manner, which was quiet, self-possessed, and deferential, and her Scottish burr, which would sound appealing on the radio. According to a friend, Annie immediately saw that "Polly was a lady. She was a strong, handsome young woman with brown eyes and soft brown hair, a little prim, a little drab. One of the first things Annie did for her was to replace the muted tweeds with bright colors. 'Color, Polly,' she cried, 'and life.' "

Still, Annie had reservations about Polly. For one thing, she was not a literary person, and Annie wanted Helen's writings to be the most enduring part of her work. She also mistrusted Polly's ability to withstand the pressures from people and organizations who wanted to use Helen for their own special purposes and glory. One night toward the end of her life, when Annie could not sleep, her nurse reportedly said, "Dear Teacher, you must not worry about Helen. She will be taken care of." "I know that," Teacher answered. "It is my dear Polly that I am worried about. I know how many people will fight not to stand back of Helen but to stand beside her. I don't know if Polly will be strong enough."

Helen's friends did not share Annie's faith in this dour, practical Scotswoman who never told a joke and never saw the point of one. They wanted Helen to give up public life, go home to Alabama, and live quietly with her sister Mildred. Polly herself was plagued with self-doubt. She knew that no one could ever replace Annie, and she was also aware that she had enemies, but she also had friends of Helen who believed in her. One was Lenore Smith, and it was largely because of Lenore's support that objections to her subsided.

Polly Thomson was not the only woman on whom Helen relied after Annie's death. The other was Nella Braddy Henney, a serious, bookish young woman from a small town in Georgia who had written a well-received biography of Annie Sullivan that was published in 1933 and who, as an editor at Doubleday, Doran, Helen's publisher, had been engaged by Annie to help Helen with her literary work. Later, Nella, to whom Helen granted a power of attorney, would act as her agent in literary matters.

Nella was married to Keith Henney, an editor for *Electronics* magazine. Like Helen, Annie, and Polly, she had no children.

For almost forty years, until their bitter breakup in 1963, Nella was Helen Keller's most intimate friend. Impressed by Annie's firm belief that "it is not a teacher that the deaf-blind want, it is another self," Nella dedicated her life to becoming one of Helen's "other selves." Quickly mastering the manual finger language, she became, as one friend noted, a "lifeline in keeping Helen in touch with the world. For all her devotion Polly would never have been able to interpret the political, literary and scientific events of the world which Helen found so stimulating."

A keen observer of people and a talented writer, Nella was intrigued by Polly Thomson. Nella hoped to write her biography. It would be similar to the one she had written of Annie Sullivan wherein she had painted a hagio-graphic portrait of Teacher as a true heroine and master teacher. As much as Nella admired Polly for her commitment to Helen, she nevertheless regarded herself as Teacher's intellectual heir apparent, taking it upon her-self to continue Annie's mission of conveying to Helen an outer world where intelligence, morality, and high standards prevailed and where Helen, as the world's most famous handicapped person, had to conduct herself in an uplifting manner.

Nella's book about Polly was never written, but Nella, on her death in 1973, left behind hundreds of pages of notes recording her impressions of Helen Keller, Annie Sullivan, and Polly Thomson, and in particular her dismay over what she perceived as Polly's mounting obsession with Helen.

Nella had met Helen and Annie in 1924. Like John Macy's some years earlier, Nella's initial impression of Helen's intelligence was not a flattering one. "Helen not original—not a genius—good mental equipment—perse-verance—no aptitude for emotional expression—Annie used to tell her to hug her mother and then would tell her how pleased her mother was," Nella noted in her journal.

Nella Braddy Henney (left), Helen, and Polly Thomson, New York, c. 1937

She also observed that "the Helen I know is the one the world knows. . . . The closer one comes to her, the deeper the miracle, the greater the love. A saintly woman who dislikes being called a saint. A great world symbol of faith and hope. A simple, hardworking woman whose daily sacrifice is her own humble and contrite heart. One comes awed into her presence; in a little while is calling her 'Helen' and laughing with her. She is 'terrific,' she is fun, she is wonderful, she is human."

More astutely, she observed that Helen, despite her reputation as a humanitarian, was far more interested in abstract or political and philosophical ideas than she was in individual people, whether blind or seeing. "For all her love of mankind, she could be harsh toward the individual man or woman," Nella recorded in her notes, at the time little dreaming that she, too, would one day become the target of Helen's wrath.

Nella was not an unbiased observer. As Annie Sullivan's biographer, she clearly felt that her subject was the more talented and intelligent of the two women and often underestimated Helen, citing what she perceived as her sentimental, pliant nature and penchant for radical or unpopular causes. On the contrary, when anyone said something negative about her idol Annie—for example, several persons suggested that she drank and ate herself to death—she immediately pooh-poohed the rumor. Maddeningly, for future scholars, she did not probe Helen about Annie's "deep, dark secret" when Helen told her that she knew what made Annie so self-destructive and reckless. Nella was far too well bred to mention the subject again.

Polly, Nella, and Herbert Haas, a former Forest Hills neighbor who before Annie's death had come to live with them and perform general household chores, provided for Helen's physical, emotional, and intellectual needs. As for her financial ones, before her death, Annie, who realized that Helen would require help in business details as long as she lived, had asked Migel, as the president of the American Foundation for the Blind, to watch over her finances. Migel suggested that two other trustees be added: Harvey Gibson, then president of Manufacturer's Trust, and William Ziegler, a director of Standard Brands, Inc., who administered the trust fund that his mother had set up for *Ziegler Magazine for the Blind*. Such a financial arrangement was not new to Helen. An advisory committee of six had been selected to look after her business affairs while she was at Radcliffe in 1900, but the Migel Committee was to endure as long as Helen lived.

Ultimately, Annie Sullivan had done everything in her power to ensure Helen a meaningful, productive life after she was gone.

"LIFE IS A DARING ADVENTURE or nothing," Helen once said, and a little more than a year after Teacher's death, she set out to prove it when she sailed for Japan, at the request of the Japanese government, to raise money for the blind and deaf. This trip, the first of three tours in which she would establish a close relationship with the Japanese people, whose culture reveres the triumph of spirit over physical infirmity, was also important for sentimental reasons. One of Annie's last requests had been for Helen to help the 100,000 deaf and 160,000 blind in Japan. Through their good friend Takeo Iwahashi, the director of the Lighthouse at Osaka, they had learned to their dismay that only 4,000 blind and deaf people were being educated.

In San Francisco, in late March 1937, before Helen departed in a flurry of newspaper interviews and photograph sessions, she received a letter from President Franklin Delano Roosevelt from Warm Springs, Georgia, about her lecture tour. "I feel confident that your presence will prove a lasting inspiration to those Japanese laboring under physical handicap," Roosevelt wrote her, "and that your association, brief as it may be, with Japanese individuals and groups interested in humanitarian endeavor will contribute to promoting that spirit of friendship and good will between our people and the people of Japan upon which good international relations must rest."

Helen thanked Roosevelt for his letter and could not resist adding, "It would be wonderful if a host of men and women might bear good-will messages from America to a world still groping its way through fear and anger. Then all the militarists and dictators united could not drive it into another war and the frightful increase of handicapped human beings which war inevitably creates."

Helen had long been a champion of Roosevelt, who was a zealous supporter of the disabled. Their relationship had begun in 1929, when he became governor of New York, and she sent him a fund-raising letter in which she asked him to become a member of the American Foundation for the Blind. Roosevelt declined her request, but when she received his letter of refusal, someone pointed out to her that he had not signed it. Immediately she returned his letter, with a note written in her square printed script on the back of the paper:

PLEASE, DEAR MR. ROOSEVELT SIGN YOUR FULL NAME. SOMETHING TELLS ME
YOU ARE GOING TO BE THE NEXT PRESIDENT OF THE "LAND OF THE FREE AND

THE HOME OF THE BRAVE," AND THIS SEEMS A GOOD TIME TO GET YOUR
AUTOGRAPH. IT MAY INTEREST YOU TO KNOW I HAVE NEVER ASKED FOR ANY-
ONE'S AUTOGRAPH BEFORE. WITH ALL GOOD WISHES.

I AM, CORDIALLY YOURS,
HELEN KELLER

An enchanted Roosevelt complied with her request, and Helen was
delighted when her prophesy became reality, and he was inaugurated president on March 4, 1933, and then reelected for a second term. She had read
every speech of a newly elected president ever since she was twenty-one
years old. None, with the exception of Woodrow Wilson's, had inspired her
with as much hope for the future as Roosevelt's second inaugural speech,
on January 20, 1937. She was moved by his determination to make the welfare of every American, including the disabled, his concern. "More than
any other president, I believe, since Lincoln, has he stressed the need to
find in government a means to promote the economic security and well-
being of all the people. If only Congress and the people would stand solidly
behind Roosevelt, new vitality would quicken our democracy, and 'the new
materials of social justice' would strengthen the oft-shaken republic our
forefathers founded."

Roosevelt's concern for the handicapped grew out of his own disability.
In August 1921, at age thirty-nine, after a vigorous jog and a swim in the
pond with his children at the family summer home on Campobello Island
in New Brunswick, Canada, the athletic Roosevelt had been stricken with a
mysterious fever that turned out to be polio. The muscles of his legs and
lower abdomen became paralyzed. Through careful exercises and winter
treatments at Warm Springs, Georgia, he gradually recovered, but after
seven years of excruciating effort, he was still permanently crippled. He was
able to walk only short distances supported by canes, heavy metal leg
braces, and the strong arms of his sons and friends. According to one of his
biographers, his illness completely transformed the aristocratic Roosevelt's
life. "No longer belonging to his old world in the same way, he came to
empathize with the poor and underprivileged, with people to whom fate
has dealt a difficult hand."

It was not surprising, then, that FDR, who once remarked of Helen,
"Anything Helen Keller is for, I am for," provided her with more national
support for the blind than any other president. Although Helen had refused
to raise funds for the Talking Book program because she felt it would not
benefit the deaf-blind, she later changed her mind and did publicize it,

meeting with Roosevelt in 1935 to plead for government support of the project. It was Helen's charisma and persuasiveness that induced Roosevelt to personally endorse the Talking Book machines, which were manufactured as a work relief project.*

By 1937 she had been repaid for some of her struggle to interest people in the handicapped: Thirty states had established commissions for the blind since the day she had served on the first one in Massachusetts, and more than half of the Helen Keller Endowment Fund had been raised. Still, she continued to give unreservedly of her time to complete this fund, helping the cause by appearing before legislatures, by giving lectures, and by her own luminous example of what a severely handicapped person could accomplish.

This support soon became international, as Helen began her ambassadorial tours on behalf of the blind of other countries. These tours were sometimes sponsored by a foreign government, sometimes by the U.S. government, and sometimes by the American Foundation for the Overseas Blind, a sister organization to the American Foundation for the Blind. In her later years, Helen, who was an insatiable traveler as well as crusader on behalf of the blind, would make nine globe-circling tours, which would take her to thirty-four countries all over the world.

As for Eleanor Roosevelt, Helen admired her feminism and her constructive efforts on behalf of the underprivileged. Before Franklin Roosevelt's first inauguration as president, in 1933, Helen sent Eleanor a bouquet of flowers, with a note expressing the hope that the First Lady would wear it at some point during the ceremonies as proof of her awareness of the needs of the blind.

Like Helen, Eleanor Roosevelt viewed disability as an opportunity for an individual to develop latent abilities and to achieve a higher spiritual plane. According to Blanche Wiesen Cook, author of a recent biography of Mrs. Roosevelt, "Eleanor considered Franklin's triumph over his disability 'a blessing in disguise.' Although many believe that his strength of character predated his bout with polio, and served to help him transcend his cruel circumstances, ER believed that his struggle 'gave him strength and courage he had not had before. He had to think out the fundamentals of living and learn the greatest of all lessons—infinite patience and never-ending persistence.' She believed that during these grueling months and years of recov-

* Ironically, Annie Sullivan, who had lost most of her vision by the early 1930s, was one of the first users of Talking Books.

Eleanor Roosevelt applauding Helen at her seventy-fifth-birthday luncheon, 1955. Polly Thomson is at left.

ery he developed a new seriousness about himself, and a deeper empathy for other people."

In her newspaper column "My Day," Eleanor later wrote, "I thought how wonderfully both Miss Keller and my husband typified the triumph over physical handicap."

The rapport that Eleanor Roosevelt felt with Helen Keller may also have resulted from the series of devastating losses that the First Lady had suffered as a child. Her beautiful mother, Anna, a cool and distant woman, died of diphtheria when she was eight; the following year her younger brother Ellie, four years old, died of the same disease; and a year later, when she was ten, her adored father, Elliott, who had been estranged from the family for years, died of alcoholism at age thirty-four. Shy, unattractive, and forced to wear a heavy brace for several years to correct a spinal curvature, Eleanor felt herself a bitter disappointment to her glamorous mother, just as Helen sensed that Mrs. Keller had always regretted her birth.

Eleanor's childhood tragedies, coupled with her feeling of being a perpetual outsider, resulted in recurring depressions and irrational fears when she became an adult. Although she would have been loath to admit it, her fascination with Helen Keller may have had something to do with her lifelong dread of being buried alive. Like the Victorians whose awe of an educated deaf-blind person was associated with their terror of being mistakenly declared dead, Eleanor had a horror of waking up six feet under. In her last will and testament, which was made public after her death in 1962, she stipulated that instead of being embalmed, her major veins be severed so there could be no chance of her waking in her coffin.

LIKE HER MANY OTHER ADMIRERS, the Roosevelts could not help speculating about Helen's reaction had she suddenly been granted the gift of sight. Would she be able to recognize the objects that she knew solely through touch? They had been intrigued by her article "Three Days to See," which was published in the *Atlantic Monthly* in January 1933, during the depths of the Depression. In this poignant piece, which made people realize the beauties of life despite their desperate economic straits, Helen described her fantasies about seeing for the first time the mysterious world that others had described to her. She also expressed her deep conviction that hearing-sighted people could add joy and meaning to their lives if they took the time to observe their surroundings:

> I who am blind can give one hint to those who see—one admonition to those who would make full use of the gift of sight: Use your eyes as if tomorrow you would be stricken blind. Hear the music of voices, the song of a bird, the mighty strains of an orchestra, as if you would be stricken deaf tomorrow. Touch each object you want to touch as if tomorrow your tactile sense would fail. . . .

At this point Annie Sullivan was alive, and to illustrate her point, Helen wrote that she would tell her readers what she would most like to see if she were given her sight for three days. "And while I am imagining, suppose you, too, set your mind to work on the problem of how you would use your own eyes if you had only three more days to see."

On the first day Helen wrote that she would like "to see the people whose kindness and gentleness and companionship have made my life worth living. First I should like to gaze long upon the face of my dear teacher, Mrs. Anne Sullivan Macy. . . ." On that first day, she would also like to see "the face of a baby, so I could catch a vision of the eager, innocent beauty which precedes the individual's consciousness of the conflicts which life develops" and "the loyal, trusting eyes of my dogs," as well as "the printed books which seeing people can read, for during the long night of my life, the books I have read and those which have been read to me have built themselves into a great shining lighthouse, revealing to me the deepest channels of human life and the human spirit." In the afternoon of that first seeing day, she would "take a long walk in the woods and intoxicate my eyes on the beauties of the world of Nature, trying desperately to absorb the vast splendor which is constantly unfolding itself to those who can see."

On the second day of sight, she would "arise with the dawn and see the thrilling miracle by which night is transformed into day" and devote herself "to a hasty glimpse of the world, past and present, by visiting the great museums of New York," where she would see for herself the scientific exhibits and great works of art that she had explored with her hands, and in the evening, attend one of Shakespeare's plays or a movie. On the third—and last—day of sight she would walk by herself through the city to see for herself "the workaday world of the present," going to the top of the Empire State Building, mingling with the crowds on Fifth Avenue, and visiting factories and the people in the slums to compare "her fancy with reality."

At the end of the third day, as blindness closed in on her once more, she "would realize how much I had left unseen. But my mind would be so crowded with glorious memories that I should have little time for regrets. Thereafter the touch of every object would bring a glowing memory of how that object looked."

Had Helen suddenly been able to see, however, she would have found the world quite different from the dazzlingly beautiful place she envisioned in her article.

Neurologists and ophthalmologists have long observed that people who are congenitally blind or, like Helen, blinded in early childhood, are completely bewildered by their first visual encounters with the world. People and objects that Helen could instantly recognize by touch—her beloved Annie Sullivan, her cherished dogs—would have been unrecognizable to her visually. She would have been unable to make sense of what she saw.

This phenomenon was first observed in 1728, when an English surgeon named William Cheselden removed the cataracts of a teenage boy who was congenitally blind. After the operation was performed, the boy had no idea of space, form, distance, and size. He had to learn to see. Later operations on cataract patients who were either congenitally blind or blind from an early age confirmed Cheselden's findings. Almost all had severe difficulties with visual perception. One patient confused roundness with depth. Others who in their blindness had named correctly a cube and a sphere by feeling or tonguing it had no idea of what they were looking at.

Reportedly, these cases have not numbered more than twenty over the past ten centuries. But for all these newly sighted people, vision was painful. The dark world in which they had been formerly comfortable was now a dazzle of patches of color that they could not make sense of. One person could not distinguish objects and saw the world as "an extensive field of light, in which everything appeared dull, confused, and in motion," while another patient saw "nothing but a confusion of forms and colors." Many were bewildered by the immense size of the world, which in their blindness they had previously thought was easily encompassed. They were often distressed by things that had seemed beautiful and appealing when they were touched, but now proved hideous visually. In some cases they were appalled by their own appearances and the faces of their loved ones. Many of them chose not to adapt to a seeing world. They preferred their old world of blindness, where they could identify objects with their hands and their tongues, and became deeply depressed to the point of contemplating suicide. Some people did die shortly after their vision was restored, and doctors have speculated that perhaps their fatal illness was brought on by depression and overwhelming stress.*

Some young people did learn how to see, but in many cases, the psychological adjustment was a tremendous one. One doctor commented on "the rapid and complete loss of that striking and wonderful serenity which is characteristic only of those who have never yet seen." A very few others,

---

* In *An Anthropologist on Mars*, neurologist Oliver Sacks describes the case of "Virgil," a fifty-year-old man who had been virtually blind since early childhood and whose sight was restored with catastrophic results. Like Cheselden's patient and other, similar cases, he had tremendous difficulty in adapting to a new sense. "In the newly sighted, learning to see demands a radical change in neurological functioning and, with it, a radical change in psychological functioning, in self, in identity," Sacks explained. "The change may be experienced in literally life-and-death terms. Valvo [Alberto Valvo, an ophthalmologist and author of *Sight Restoration after Long-Term Blindness*, 1971] quotes a patient of his as saying, 'One must die as a sighted person to be born again as a blind person,' and the opposite is equally true; one must die as a blind person to be born again as a seeing person. It is the interim, the limbo—'between two worlds, one dead/The other powerless to be born'—that is so terrible. Though blindness may at first be a terrible privation and loss, it may become less so with the passage of time, for a deep adaptation, or reorientation, occurs, by which one reconstitutes, reappropriates, the world in nonvisual terms. It then becomes a *different* condition, a different form of being, one with its own sensibilities and coherence and feeling."
 Sacks then points out the trauma of many congenitally deaf, or early deafened people who have received cochlear implants that have restored their hearing. "Sound, for them, at first has no associations, no meaning—so they find themselves, at least initially, in a world of auditory chaos, or agnosia. But in addition to these cognitive problems there are identity problems, too; in a sense, they must die as deaf people to be born as hearing ones. This, potentially, is much more serious and has ramifying social and cultural implications; for deafness may be not just a personal identity, but a shared linguistic, communal, and cultural one."
 Other researchers are of the opinion that a period of early vision may provide a person with an integrative basis for spatial relations that continues even after sight is lost, providing a person who becomes blind later in childhood with a substantial advantage over a person who has been blind from birth.

once they had mastered visual patterns, seemed, in the words of one doctor, "to experience great joy in visual learning. . . . They start thinking about wholly new areas of experience."

Helen herself was aware of this phenomenon when she wrote "Three Days to See," which she intended more as a moral lesson for the hearing-sighted than a wistful fantasy. She knew that her vision could never be restored and had long ago resigned herself to the permanence of her condition. Many years before, she had reminded her readers, "Remember that when a blind man recovers his sight, he does not recognize the commonest thing that has been familiar to his touch, the dearest face intimate to his fingers, and it does not help him at all that things and people have been described to him again and again."

IN HER WORLD, which seemed a mystery to the hearing-sighted, Helen continued to function efficiently. On the ship to Honolulu, she worked all day long on her dozen different short speeches that she would give in Japan on behalf of the blind and deaf. Each one had to be written, memorized, and practiced. Most days she was up before dawn, attempting to improve her enunciation with Polly's help, while the sailors were scrubbing the decks. For relaxation, Helen read the twelve Braille volumes of Margaret Mitchell's *Gone with the Wind*. Had she been alive, it is doubtful that Annie Sullivan would have approved of her taste in reading matter. But Helen found the book delightful, although repetitious. She liked Mammy, but disapproved of Scarlett, an "utterly selfish creature like Regan in King Lear or Empress Catherine" and felt relieved when she reached the part where Scarlett, temporarily, was "being transformed from a spoiled belle into a courageous, responsible worker." As for Rhett Butler, the heartthrob of millions of female readers, she dismissed him with contempt. "He is one of the sensible people without heart whom I shun as heartily as any fool—he is supremely selfish, sarcastic and bitter. I hate his truths conveyed with a sneer no less than falsehood."

Margaret Mitchell's descriptions of the old South made her nostalgic for Tuscumbia in the summer, and she remembered the fragrant smell of her mother's prized roses, as well as the heavy scent of tangled honeysuckle and paulownia blossoms in the afternoon heat. With fondness she recalled the large spring in town where young and old blacks came with buckets to fetch water and how good-naturedly the young ones had played with her, disregarding her disability. Swiftly this happy memory turned to a sad one as she recalled her later realization of "the degrading poverty, the ignorance and superstition into which those little ones were born and the bitterness of the Negro problem through which many of them are still living."

During the long ocean voyage she reflected on her condition, which she continued to believe was only a temporary state. "The spirit, like the sea, is greater than any island or continent of sense-experience within its waters. . . . My deep-rooted feeling that I am not deaf or blind is like the feeling that I am *in* the body but not *of* it. Of course I know that outwardly I am a 'deaf and blind' Helen Keller. That is a transitory ego, and the few dark, silent years I shall be here do not matter. I use my limitations as tools, not as my real self. If others are helped through them that is the seventh heaven of happiness for me."

In Japan, after giving ninety-seven lectures in thirty-nine cities, Helen raised thirty-five million yen for the blind and deaf, as she successfully implored the people to reject their old myths and superstitions about blindness and to start a nationwide movement on behalf of their own blind. As a people, the Japanese fascinated her, and on the ship, she had noted that they seemed conflicted between the old and the modern. On one hand, they were loyal to their emperor and intensely patriotic. On the other hand, they seemed more internationally minded than most Americans. Even at their most aggressive, they displayed a courtesy that Helen felt "conquers more surely than force. Even if a fanatical militarism should drive them further in empire building, I am sure they will never lose their catholicity or their benevolent neighborliness."

The Japanese had never seen anyone like Helen Keller. They venerated her like their own royalty, who, in turn, were mesmerized by her. The empress's sister traveled with her for a good part of the tour, and Helen and Polly were coddled by three servants to the extent that they were not allowed to put on their own shoes. Everywhere Helen appeared, schoolchildren, many of whom did not know the names of their own leaders, lined flower-strewn paths and shouted out her name. "No foreign visitor had ever been accorded such an enthusiastic reception," reported the *Akita Journal*.

In Japan Helen was taken to many historic sites. In Daibutsu she was the first woman permitted to touch the great bronze Amita Buddha seated on lotus leaves. In Tosa Province, wearing an embroidered silk kimono, she held in her lap and petted a famed white bird with an eighteen-foot tail, the result of two hundred years of cross-breeding. Normally this sole specimen

Helen (center) and Polly (right) in Japan. Helen is holding an exotic white
bird whose tail was eighteen feet long.

was perched high in a tree so its dazzling tail could fall without encumbrance and evoke awe in the viewer. The helpless creature could not fly or
even walk on its own until a page boy came and held its tail so it would not
trail on the ground.

But unlike the bird, she was far from defenseless despite her physical
reliance on others. Upon her return to the United States, she had her dis-
eased gallbladder removed at the Mayo Clinic in Rochester, Minnesota,
where she and Polly went annually for checkups. Polly was permitted to
watch the surgery and reported to Nella that it was "a wonderful experience." As for Helen, she approached the operation with her usual fearless-
ness. "The doctors advise me to have it removed," she wrote a friend, "and I
am determined to do it while I am strong."

CHAPTER 21

"A Source of Embarrassment"

O HELEN'S ANNOYANCE, people kept on calling her a saint.
And yet, paradoxically, she fostered the image, as she had since
childhood, playing the part of a sightless angel so convincingly that
many of the more average disabled men and women ceased to relate to her
and began referring to her disparagingly as "a plaster saint." In reality,
Helen was not attempting to be superior, but instead had been cast into the
role, as one observer has pointed out, of "a hero of adjustment, the handicapped person who lives up to the standards of the culture and therefore in
some sense reassures everyone else that a fixed game is fair . . . as a kind of
secular saint, she reassured normal people that the blind compensate, that
they are gentle and kind and that they bear no hard feelings."

But Helen did feel sadness and rage about her limitations. These negative emotions, which she never permitted herself to express publicly, fearing that people would ignore her or feel pity or disgust for her if she
expressed hopelessness or anger, were channeled into her radical politics
and activism. Here again, she was thwarted by a society that admires the
courage of disabled people from a distance but refuses to empower them if
their message threatens the establishment or is less than inspirational. Not
surprisingly, Helen's political views were hushed up by both her family and
the American Foundation for the Blind, an organization that was headed

mainly by conventional businessmen who adamantly opposed Roosevelt and the New Deal. "Helen Keller's habit of playing around with Communists or near-Communists has long been a source of embarrassment to her conservative friends. Please advise me," Robert Irwin, the executive director of the foundation, wrote to one of Helen's trustees.

Irwin's fears were not unfounded. Helen allied herself with many causes and organizations that were suspected of being Communist fronts, thereby threatening the work of the foundation, which depended on contributions from wealthy Republicans for its existence. One of the Communist groups with which Helen became involved was allied with the American Rescue Ship Mission, which planned to liberate Spanish Republican refugees from concentration camps in France. In 1940 Helen became honorary national chairman, relinquishing her position the following year when she learned, along with Eleanor Roosevelt, who had also lent her support, that the initiating group, the United American Spanish Aid Committee, was Communist-controlled.

Helen's FBI report, obtained under the Freedom of Information Act, also notes that in 1943 she signed a petition along with other prominent individuals, including Albert Einstein, demanding that the Dies Committee be discontinued—an act that brought her to the attention of the Department of Justice. She was also one of the original sponsors of the drive that the Committee of One Thousand (allegedly a Communist-front organization) mounted against the House Un-American Activities Committee. According to her FBI file, in her later years she was in the habit of sending good wishes or birthday greetings to prominent female Communists, including Mother Ella Reeve Bloor, and in 1955, the imprisoned Elizabeth Gurley Flynn.

Following Franklin Roosevelt's death, Helen became an enthusiastic sponsor of the Independent Citizens' Committee for the Arts and Sciences, which the House Un-American Activities Committee alleged to be a Communist-front organization. Headed by her friend Jo Davidson, the committee's aim was to ensure the presidential election of left-wing democrat Henry A. Wallace, Roosevelt's former vice president who had formed the Progressive Party. (Eventually Helen's friends, fearing that she would become the target of a witch-hunt, persuaded her to drop her support for the campaign.)

Her FBI file also notes that in 1946 she sent a letter of greeting to the participants of a meeting of the Veterans of the Abraham Lincoln Brigade, cited by the U.S. attorney general as a Communist organization. And in

November 1945 she had attended a reception at the Soviet consulate in New York that commemorated the twenty-eighth anniversary of the Russian Revolution, reportedly exulting as she entered the consulate, "Finally, I am on Soviet soil!"

The trustees of the foundation, who lived in fear that Helen's activities would result in an FBI probe of their organization, were understandably alarmed when the conservative columnist Westbrook Pegler attacked Helen in print: "At the Larry Adler opening, at Café Society, famous Helen Keller was able to follow the harmonic rhythms this way. A friend finger-coded the tempo into the palm of Miss Keller's hand. Sitting at the same table, Jo Davidson alternately cried 'Bravo!' and caricatured Larry on a nap-kin. . . . She [Helen] knowingly chose her political company a long time ago. No news here," and then Pegler went on to note that Helen "had been cited eleven times down to 1943 by the Dies Committee on Un-American Activities."

The trustees tried to excuse Helen's politics to their uneasy contributors by citing her belief in "universal brotherhood" and stressing that "naturally some of the Socialistic and Communistic leaders have taken advantage of her interest in the humanitarian side of their professings."

This was only partially the truth. Although there is no evidence that Helen was ever a card-carrying Communist, she was a fervent admirer of Marx and Lenin and felt that Russia, despite its problems, was advancing as a nation. In her opinion, Communism, even under the ruthless dictatorship of Joseph Stalin, was far preferable to Nazi tyranny.

In an era of rising anti-Communist hysteria that would soon culminate in McCarthyism, what saved Helen Keller from being the target of a witch-hunt was her handicap. Anyone who accused such a helpless, radiant woman of being a subversive would be in danger of losing his or her credibility with the public. The FBI kept close tabs on people suspected of being Communists, but, interestingly, it never conducted an investigation of Helen Keller, although her name did appear in records pertaining to other individuals. In J. Edgar Hoover's opinion, a deaf-blind woman, even if she was a Communist sympathizer, was no threat to national security. Then, too, the bureau may have realized that Helen Keller would pose unique problems if placed under surveillance. Her conversations were conducted in code with only a few chosen friends who knew the manual finger language; most people, including the admiring Eleanor Roosevelt, could not understand a word she said; and she rarely used a telephone, so a wiretap was useless.

As for Helen, she seemed unaware of the FBI's scrutiny. She continued to send J. Edgar Hoover her form fund-raising letters that pleaded the cause of the blind and the deaf-blind—sometimes he was addressed as "Miss Hoover." Many years later it would be revealed that America's leading policeman used illegal wiretaps and hidden microphones to destroy anyone who opposed him, but Helen, for one, was unaware of his sinister nature. She was perhaps the only person ever to send J. Edgar Hoover a letter that ended "Trustingly yours."

In part, Helen's leftist politics sprang from her continuing hunger to feel connected to the masses of people with whom she had little personal contact but with whom she felt a common bond. Although she had touched the face of practically every famous person of her time, the people she longed to know were ordinary working-class men and women. All too often this opportunity was denied her by her protective friends, who felt that she should hobnob only with the wealthy and distinguished. Still, whenever she could, she traveled from Forest Hills into Manhattan on the subway that had recently been built. "I was glad of the subway ride," she once wrote, "and I shall take one as often as possible coming home. I like any mode of transit—subway, elevated, or bus—that brings me in close contact with people. Polly describes their faces or their talk. Through the sense of smell, impressions tell me much—powder, perfume, tobacco, shoe polish . . . In an automobile, I miss these intimate revelations of how my fellow creatures live."

SOON THIS SIMPLE PLEASURE would become infrequent. Following Annie's death, the home they had shared together in Forest Hills seemed a depressing place. After selling it for nine thousand dollars, she and Polly were happy to accept the offer of Dr. Robert Pfeiffer, a biblical scholar at Harvard Divinity School, to live in a home he owned in Westport, Connecticut. Then, in 1939, his uncle, Gustavus Pfeiffer, a trustee of the American Foundation for the Blind, donated money to help build for Helen and Polly a new colonial home nearby that was surrounded by meadows, woods, brooks, and old stone walls. A white house with green shutters that boasted a large living room and a sunny, book-lined study for Helen, it was called Arcan Ridge, after the old Scottish farmhouse where Helen had been able to walk alone with a shepherd's crook to guide her and where she had known as much liberty as she had ever known in her life.

At the new Arcan Ridge, Helen was seldom guided around. As she had done for years, she could take a bath alone, pick out the clothes she wanted to wear, dress herself, and fix her own hair. In the kitchen she could help out by washing and drying the dishes. At mealtimes a bell was rung to summon her. If she was moving around or in the bathroom, she could not sense it, but if she was sitting at her desk or on the floor of her study, one of her favorite places to work, she was instantly aware of its vibration and pounded the floor to indicate that she had experienced it.

Every morning in the summer she got up at five o'clock to tend the flower beds. By her touch, she was able to distinguish the flowers from the weeds. In the summer she picked blueberries, knowing instantly by her fingers when they were ripe.

She spent the greater part of her day alone, either meditating or working in her study, or tramping around the Communion Walk that Herbert had built for her that twisted its way through the woods and then curved back to the house.

Although a Seeing Eye dog was of no use to someone with Helen's condition, she was as much of a dog lover as Annie, delighting in writing notes to her pets and then dreaming up their imaginary answers. On one occasion she even composed a poem in honor of "the baptism" of Ben-Sith, the Scottie she had acquired in Scotland. Of dogs in general, Helen wrote:

Arcan Ridge, Helen Keller's colonial home in Connecticut

"... The charming relations I have had with a long succession of dogs results from their happy spontaneity. Usually they are quick to discover that I cannot see or hear. Considerately they rise as I come near, so that I may not stumble."

In 1937 Helen and Polly owned eight dogs, including Helga, a lame Great Dane; Djealis (pronounced Jeelis), a dainty male Shetland collie that had been doted on by Annie in her last years; Et-Tu, a German shepherd that had been trained as a Seeing Eye dog but had flunked her examinations because of car sickness; and Big Black Boy, of which Helen was inordinately fond even though the dog was actually owned by a neighbor.

Soon Helen would become the proud owner of the first Akita in the United States. When she had visited Japan in 1939, the Japanese State Department presented her with one of the dogs, which historically had been used as temple guard dogs and in mythology were often credited with saving the lives of their masters. Ironically, in the light of future world events, Helen named her brown "barkless" Akita Kamikaze-Go, meaning "golden wind." (In Japanese, "Go" is a suffix that is added to the names of pets.) Unfortunately, Kamikaze-Go soon died of distemper after it reached the United States, and even though after the Munich pact she vowed to "buy nothing that is made in Japan, or Germany, or Italy," she accepted from the Japanese Foreign Office a second dog, Kenzan-Go, whose coat was a beautiful golden red. She rationalized her acceptance of the dog by telling people that it was a gift from the Japanese people, who had been generous to her during her tour of their country two years before, and not the Japanese government.

At Arcan Ridge, dogfights were common. Often Herbert and Polly were bitten as they tried to break them up. To no avail, friends pleaded with Helen to get rid of some of her animals. Eventually all the canines succumbed to old age or other natural causes. Whenever one of her dogs died, Helen never failed to write heartfelt letters of gratitude to the veterinarians who had offered their services free of charge, as did all of her own doctors and dentists.

In Westport, her new circle of friends included Jo Davidson, a genial sculptor who was known for his realistic bronze busts of famous people and for his leftist sympathies; Nella; the Pfeiffers; and the writer Van Wyck Brooks and his wife, Gladys. Her other new friends were the actress Katharine Cornell, who was married to the producer Guthrie McClintic, and her manager, lyricist Nancy Hamilton, a witty, fun-loving woman. Both Katharine Cornell and Jo Davidson knew the manual finger language, and this skill, in addition to their devoted friendship, enlivened Helen's later years.

But not everyone in her inner circle liked one another as much as they loved Helen. Katharine Cornell, who had captivated Broadway audiences in such plays as *The Barretts of Wimpole Street, St. Joan,* and *Antony and Cleopatra,* privately dismissed Davidson as an artist, considering his super-realistic portrait busts superficial. More important, she feared that he was an evil influence on Helen and that his radicalism encouraged her "red-ness." As much as she adored Helen, she was upset every time she heard her discuss politics, as was her husband, Guthrie McClintic, who was politically conservative and who went wild every time he heard Helen extol the virtues of Russia and denigrate the United States for allowing slavery, unbridled industrialism, and child labor. At a gathering at Arcan Ridge, Katharine, who was an admirer of the pope, had been offended when Helen derisively described a recent audience with the pontiff in Rome in which he had passed his hands over Polly, mistaking her for the famous deaf-blind woman. She later told Nella that she was convinced that Helen and Polly told the anecdote to delight the Davidsons, who hated the Catholic Church, branding it a reactionary institution. "Polly and Helen are not far behind them," Nella reported in her journal, adding that she thought that the reason Katharine put up with Helen's leftist views and less than laudatory opinion of the church was because she deeply admired her as a handicapped woman whose optimism and fortitude had inspired the world.

SINCE CHILDHOOD, Helen had dedicated her life to helping other handicapped people, and during World War II she became a symbol of hope to the thousands of blinded, deaf, and crippled soldiers. Although she had been a convinced pacifist during World War I, "atrocious happenings in Europe, the life-and-death quality of Nazi aggression, and the unique-ness of this conflict" made her feel that "it is better for all of us who uphold freedom, though often sinned against, to be impoverished by war, yes, and physical death than to submit to politico-social doctrines which . . . murder the soul and destroy human rights. . . ."

According to one historian, "Pearl Harbor extinguished, at least tem-porarily, whatever sentiments of friendship for the Japanese still lingered in her heart. Her response to the attack was the outrage that almost all Ameri-cans felt. She praised the President's leadership in the crisis. . . . Churchill

A still from the motion picture *The Unconquered*, showing Helen, Polly, and Herbert Haas at Helen's house in Westport, Connecticut. Polly finger-spells into Helen's hand.

was in Washington to concert Anglo-American strategy in the new situation, and his address to Congress appealed to her. . . . Her enthusiasm for Churchill and Anglo-American unity did not keep her from urging collaboration with Russia, which was then handing the Nazi Panzers their first major setback. Russian resistance seemed to vindicate her old hope, never fully relinquished, in communism's promises."

As she had in the first conflict, Helen promoted services for blinded victims of war. At first, many of the wounded men she visited at seventy army and navy hospitals during a six-month period thought she was like the others who had been sent to cheer them up, people who mouthed platitudes or gave them false hope. But as they listened to her words through Polly, they quickly became aware that this shining, beautifully dressed older woman who stood beside their wheelchairs and held their hands was encouraging them to deal realistically with their disability. They would never enjoy their old freedom, she told them, but there would still be the satisfying world of friends and family, books and accomplishment.

Inwardly Helen was quaking as she danced with the blind soldiers and lovingly stroked their hair as she told them they would soon discover that

Braille dots no longer felt like sandpaper. "Never have I felt as diffident as I did before I spoke at Walter Reed Hospital and Bethesda Naval Hospital," she wrote to a friend. "What message did I have, I wondered, for men who had borne the cruelest war ordeal on record and who must lie still in bed day after day!"

Yet as one hospital staff member noted, "She was her own best walking testimonial that happiness was possible. . . . One wounded soldier offered her one of his eyes if it would make her see." And another staff member, a brigadier general in charge of a southern army hospital, wrote her, "You are the most impressive and stimulating visitor we have had at our hospital and that puts you ahead of the Hollywood blondes, brunettes and playboys."

For Helen, it was "the crowning experience of my life. A drop of sweetness stole into my grief over the paralyzed as they tried to put their wasted arms around me, not always successfully, but their wish was a benediction I shall treasure forever."

She was at a naval hospital in Charleston when she learned of President Roosevelt's death. "The company went mute and limp," she wrote to a

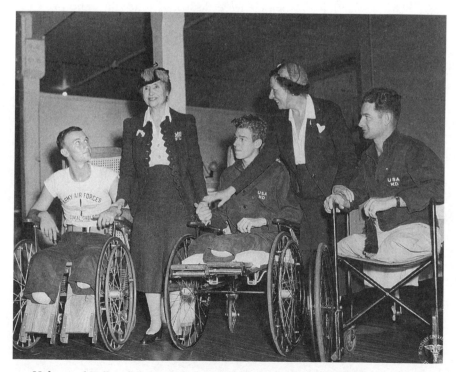

Helen and Polly talk with soldiers at McCloskey General Hospital, Temple, Texas, 1944.

friend. "It is an irreplaceable void we workers for the handicapped feel now that the tangible tokens of his sympathy and counsel are withdrawn. My hospital visits have lost an indefinable something which buoyed me up while he was among us."

IN 1946 HELEN MADE the first of her world tours for the American Foundation for the Overseas Blind, a sister organization to the American Foundation for the Blind. Within the next eleven years she would visit thirty-five countries on five continents on behalf of the disabled. Many of her visits resulted in schools being started for the blind and deaf. On this particular junket she and Polly visited the Acropolis at dawn. As Helen ran her hands over one of the fallen columns, she communicated to Polly that no other country uplifted her spiritually as much as Greece and made her feel as tranquil.

A raging fire destroyed Arcan Ridge in Westport when Helen and Polly were in Rome in late November. A malfunctioning oil furnace that had once singed off Herbert's eyebrows and eyelashes was the cause of the blaze. Almost all their possessions were destroyed, including the priceless oriental vases that Polly cherished. A far worse loss was the memoir Helen had been writing about Annie Sullivan, to be titled *Teacher*, which was almost three-fourths completed. Nella managed to salvage some of her Braille notes, but everything else, with the exception of the silver that had been removed from the house for safekeeping prior to their absence, was charred beyond recognition.

When their friends first heard the news, they feared for Polly's life. The house, with its elegant traditional furnishings and mementos from their visit to Japan, had helped compensate her for the strain and drudgery that were involved in being Helen's constant companion. Finally, Amelia Bond, Migel's secretary, worked up the courage to call Polly in Paris to tell her the news. When she did not reply for several minutes, Amelia feared that she had suffered a stroke. Her dangerously high blood pressure, as her friends were aware, was an ever-present danger, "a panther ready to spring out and destroy everything." Amelia felt relieved when Polly was finally able to recover her equanimity and speak and then, a few days later, when Amelia and the rest of their circle received telegrams saying that Polly and Helen would rebuild the house and that this was a minor tragedy compared to the horror and suffering they had seen in Europe.

Some of their friends wanted to raise fifty thousand dollars from the public for the project, but when Nella got wind of the idea, she was horri-

Helen with Djealis at
Arcan Ridge, 1946,
shortly before a fire
destroyed the house

fied, knowing how Helen had never asked anything for herself, only for the
blind and the deaf-blind. Helen had always found it humiliating to beg,
even for them. In her opinion, if the public gave her money for her own
personal use, she would never be able to raise funds for the blind again. She
was relieved when the idea was dropped.

Helen was serene about the tragedy.

"That murderous furnace," she told Nella when she and Polly came
home in late December. "I am glad we are rid of it. It almost cost Herbert
his eyes."

According to Nella,

> Something broke in Polly when the house burned. "I will never get over it,"
> she said, and she never did. Through Amelia Bond, money was quietly
> obtained to rebuild. The house, which was a replica of the first one, had
> various improvements and securities, but there was money enough for only
> ordinary department store furniture and all the life-time treasures except
> the silver and other valuables that had been in safety vaults were destroyed.
> Nearly everything about it, from the paper on the walls to the chairs on the

floor, offended Polly. Some of the furniture she sent back at once and slowly began making the house her own, a setting for Helen. Within a few years friends were saying that it was more beautiful than it was before. There were gifts from Japan, museum pieces among them, nutcrackers from Mrs. Roosevelt. There was nothing they did not need.

As for Helen, perhaps in a strange way she was glad that Arcan Ridge was gone. It was a house that held the answers to her and Teacher's secrets, including her love letters from Peter Fagan and John Macy's correspondence to Annie Sullivan, as well as the reason for Teacher's recklessness and self-destructiveness.

As Nella observed, "The undercurrent of distress and worry, kept under tight control, belonged to Polly. The whole business had struck her much harder than anyone else. The only comfort that she and I could find was that many decisions, which we had never felt ourselves qualified to make, had been taken from us. Some of these—the destruction of letters and papers—Teacher herself had not been equal to. We made a new start."

When her house and all her possessions were destroyed, Helen was sixty-six years old, an age when it is not easy to lose almost everything. But then Helen was no ordinary person. From the beginning, she had faced tragedies that would have crushed a less spiritual, less courageous woman. With her customary resilience, she looked forward to the challenge of the coming days.

CHAPTER 22

"In a Black, Silent Hole"

A MID THE ASH-COVERED RUBBLE of Hiroshima, Helen Keller felt sickened as Polly spelled into her hand a vivid description of the Japanese city that three years earlier, on August 6, 1945, had been leveled by an atomic bomb. In that enormous flash of light, bringing mass death and destruction, 90,000 men, women, and children had instantly perished. An additional 150,000 were injured and hideously burned, including many people who also lost both their sight and their hearing.

"Not one tall building is left and what has been rebuilt is temporary and put up in haste," Helen wrote Nella after visiting the decimated city in the fall of 1948. "Instead of the fair, flourishing city we saw eleven years ago, there is only life struggling daily, hourly against a bare environment, unsoftened by nature's wizardry. . . . Polly saw burns on the face of the welfare officer—a shocking sight. He let me touch his face, and the rest is silence— the people struggle on and say nothing about their lifelong hurts."

As Polly conveyed the sadness and horror in the eyes of the people they passed on the street, Helen was filled with indignation. "Hiroshima's fate carries with it the burden of deliberate wrong-doing . . . that inexorably summons our democracies to the Bar of Judgment," she wrote Nella.

She and Polly then traveled to Nagasaki, which also "scorched a deep scar" in her soul. In comparison to Hiroshima, only one third of the city had been demolished by a second atomic bomb, three days later, but, as Helen wrote Nella, "the testimony to the atrocities of atomic combat is equally damning." She was filled with sadness as she walked through "the mangled corpses" of the medical college and the clinic. "I felt the walls bending like a reed in the wind. . . . I felt sure that I smelt the dust from the burning of Nagasaki—the smoke of death. In that graveyard of a splendid establishment twenty-four professors lost their lives. Surgeons were operating at the time, and they and their patients perished together."

In Nagasaki they met a young scientist who was slowly dying from atomic radiation and who was not expected to be alive after Christmas. Normally self-contained in public, Polly was so moved by the dying man that she was almost unable to speak or spell to Helen. Deeply stirred by his plight, Helen said to him, "How you inspire us, lifting your soul up above the miseries of the flesh." She was close to tears when he replied, "My body is consuming away, but I am free spiritually, and today, besides being happy, I am fairly well because the sun is warm and pleasant."

Helen and Polly
in Hiroshima, Japan,
1948, three years after an
atomic bomb had been
dropped on the city

As she departed from the crippled city with which she identified in her deaf-blindness, Helen was more determined than ever to fight against "the demons of atomic warfare . . . and for peace."

The decade following the war was a time of intense activity for Helen Keller: She was constantly on the move, visiting Japan and Australia, as well as South American and African countries on behalf of the blind and the war-stricken blind. Next to Eleanor Roosevelt, she was considered by the State Department as the United States' most persuasive goodwill ambassador. Wherever she visited and lectured, she brought new hope to millions of blind people and improved their conditions. Vehemently opposed to segregating blind people from the rest of the community, she persuaded the Israeli government to disband a village for the blind. "They should be trained for membership in normal society and not as a society of handicapped persons," she insisted.

It was in Japan, during their twelve-month tour of the Far East, that Polly began to feel unwell. A local doctor examined her and concluded that she had suffered a minor stroke. The remainder of their tour—which included visits to Korea, China, and India—had to be canceled. Immediately on their return to the United States, the two women checked into the Mayo Clinic, where doctors pronounced Helen in excellent health, but Polly was advised "to give up the old hectic life, live quietly and normally, which means no more lecture tours."

Still, Polly recovered sufficiently for them to return to Europe in the spring of 1950. On her way to Florence, where the Italian government had erected a scaffold specially for her to climb and touch Michelangelo's *David*, Helen visited her cousin Contessa Margot Besozzi, who lived in Portofino, high on a cliff overlooking the blue harbor. The contessa's neighbors who lived on the "downstairs plateau" were the British actor Rex Harrison and his wife, the German-born actress Lilli Palmer. A jeep was the only vehicle that could negotiate the hairpin turns up to both the contessa's and Lilli Palmer's mountaintop residences. One morning Lilli Palmer was startled to pick up the phone and hear the contessa asking, since her own jeep had broken down, would the actress mind going into town in her jeep and picking up her cousin Miss Helen Keller and her companion at a local hotel?

Like most people, Lilli Palmer had grown up hearing about the miraculous achievements of the deaf-blind Helen Keller. Neither a sycophant nor a skeptic, she couldn't wait to meet the legendary figure she had read so much about in her youth. Later she recalled their encounter in her perceptive memoir *Change Lobsters and Dance*:

Helen Keller, then in her seventies, was a slight, white-haired woman with wide-open blue eyes and a shy smile. "How do you do?" she said slowly and a little gutturally. I took her hand, which she was holding too high because she didn't know how tall I was. She was bound to make this mistake with people she was meeting for the first time, but she never made it twice. Later, when we said good-bye, she put her hand firmly into mine at exactly the right level.

As the hotel porter lifted Helen into the seat beside her, Lilli Palmer realized that her passenger might be in jeopardy on the drive up the mountain. "The jeep was open; there was nothing you could hold on to properly. How was I to keep a blind old lady from falling out of the rickety old thing?

"Helen was the first passenger who was oblivious to the danger; she was enchanted by the violent jumps and only laughed when she was thrown against my shoulder. 'This is fun,' she warbled happily, bouncing up and down. . . . Her thin white hair had come undone and fluttered about her face, and she was enjoying the crazy ride like a child riding up and down on a wooden horse on a merry-go-round."

Margot Besozzi invited Lilli Palmer to lunch. While Helen and Polly were being shown their rooms, she told the actress about her famous cousin's extraordinary life: that "heads of state, scholars and artists vied to receive her, and she had traveled all over the world to satisfy her burning curiosity. But don't forget," said Margot, "all she really notices is a change of smell. Whether she's here or in New York or in India, she sits in a black, silent hole."

Then lunch was served on the terrace.

Helen was led to her chair, and I watched her "see" her place setting. Quick as lightning, her hands moved over the objects on the table—plate, glass, silverware—memorizing where they were. Never once during the meal did she grope about, but reached out casually and firmly like the rest of us.

Conversation during the meal was difficult. Since she didn't know when anyone else was speaking, Helen would suddenly ask a question in the middle of somebody else's sentence, bringing the conversation to a halt. Miss Thomson, next to her, would stop eating and translate the answer into Helen's hand.

After lunch we stayed on the shady terrace, surrounded by trailing clusters of wisteria like a thick mauve curtain, the sun below us glittering on the sea. Helen sat in the usual way, head raised slightly as though listening to something, her sightless blue eyes wide open.

Like Georgette Leblanc, another famous actress half a century earlier, Lilli Palmer was struck by the incompleteness of Helen Keller's countenance.

> Her face, although an old lady's face, had something of a schoolgirl's innocence. It was a face that had not experienced, had not been exposed, had not lived. What suffering must have tormented her—and might still torment her, for all I knew—her face showed no trace of it. It was an isolated face, a saintly face.
> "There's still so much I'd like to see," she said, "so much to learn. And death is just around the corner. Not that that worries me. On the contrary."
> "Do you believe in life after death?" I asked.
> "Most certainly," she said emphatically. "It is no more than passing from one room into another."
> Suddenly, Helen spoke again. Slowly and very distinctly she said, "But there's a difference for me, you know. Because in that other—room—I shall be able to see."

ALTHOUGH SHE SEEMED to welcome death, ironically, Helen grew stronger with every passing year. In contrast, Polly, like her predecessor, Annie Sullivan, was aging prematurely. Though she loved travel almost as much as Helen did, their exhausting expeditions continued to take their toll. Despite frequent checkups, Polly continued to suffer from hypertension, a condition perhaps induced by the stress of having almost complete responsibility for Helen and their household, as well as having to fend off people who were attempting to use the prominent deaf-blind woman to further their own ambitions.

As she had her entire life, the luminous Helen inspired intrigues and power struggles, as her acquaintances and advisers fought with one another to gain possession of her. The trustees at the foundation distrusted Nella's influence over Helen, while "a vast hurt" was Nella's description of Migel; his secretary, Amelia; and Robert Irwin, one of Migel's colleagues who was blind since childhood. In Nella's opinion, the multimillionaire Migel was a money-mad social climber. As for Robert Irwin, he was "insanely jealous" of Helen, a man who sought to "manage her." "He is not the first to learn that Helen is unmanageable," Nella observed. "This began with her mother and has continued to this day. In many ways even Teacher did not manage her, and yet Teacher had to take the brunt, just as Polly does now. Anyone close to Helen is supposed to 'feed' her wrong ideas. No one ever blames Helen, only, in the old days, Teacher, and now Polly."

A blind father hands his
sighted son to Helen in
Durban, South Africa, 1950.

It was true that many people at the foundation disliked Polly. Her inability to suppress Helen's liberalism aside, they thought she had "a frightful"
disposition and was a dictatorial woman who was such a perfectionist that
she couldn't keep help. Although she continually fretted about expenses,
she was nonetheless a spendthrift, presenting an embarrassed Nella with a
one-hundred-dollar alligator purse from Saks Fifth Avenue for Christmas
and ordering shad roe ahead of season at the expensive lunches she hosted
for friends at Sardi's. As with Annie Sullivan, there were rumors that she
had a drinking problem.

But Nella liked Polly, despite her faults. She knew how devoted this
insecure woman was to Helen and the pride she took in Helen's beauty. It
was always incredible to Polly that anyone could be revolted by Helen. She
never forgave the tenor John McCormack for rushing from the room as he
was about to sing for her, or the actor Edwin Booth, who would not even
meet her, or Robert Barnett, the new blind executive director of the foundation, who was repelled the first time he met her.

Nella sensed the loneliness and insecurity behind Polly's anger. Even though, as Helen's companion, she had met the famous people of her time, she returned to a silent home after these glittering occasions. Most of the time Polly's life was drab and monotonous. Day and night, she was alone with Helen, a woman who could express herself in writing, but who due to the nature of her disability, was dismal at conversation. One evening, when they were taking their usual walk at dusk, the thought crossed Polly's mind that she and Helen were two old maids out with the dog.

Still, Nella had to concede that Polly Thomson was no Annie Sullivan. While Annie had judged people on their own merits and occasionally invited deaf-blind people to stay with them in Forest Hills, Polly wanted Helen to be surrounded by hearing-sighted people of wealth and distinction. The dinner parties at Arcan Ridge were never the democratic mixtures of people characteristic of Annie's soirees. Polly possessed neither Teacher's flair for making the average man or woman interesting to Helen nor her charisma.

But the two women were alike in one important aspect, and it distressed Nella deeply. Neither was grateful for the financial help she received from either the foundation or affluent friends. "Annie and Polly's careless attitude towards money, coupled with their extravagance has bothered Lenore and me—and many, many other people," Nella recorded. "The denunciations of the capitalists on one hand, the acceptance from them on the other."

Nella sensed that people at the foundation also disapproved of Herbert Haas, Helen and Polly's middle-aged male helper who lived with them at Arcan Ridge. "Migel and Amelia do not like Herbert. . . . Part of it may come from knowing that Herbert is much closer to the girls than they are, much deeper into the secret of their lives, and resentment of it. . . . Part of it may also be because Herbert doesn't like them. . . . But Herbert is more temperate than the girls are in his emotions towards them. He fully realizes that they cannot do without the Foundation and that the wild hopes of going to Japan to live quietly are but disordered fancies of the moment."

Given the chaotic nature of their domestic life at Arcan Ridge, it was understandable why Helen longed for a peaceful life. Perhaps in love with Herbert herself, Polly bickered continually with him over her attempts to make him presentable to her and Helen's circle of sophisticated friends. They also fought over his reluctance to drive them places. As he explained to Polly, he had not been hired as a chauffeur and disliked driving, which made him uneasy.

Like Annie Sullivan, Herbert had spent his early years in an orphanage. He never knew his father, a German-born musician. Herbert had married once and had a daughter, but his wife divorced him to marry his brother. Quickly realizing that she had made a mistake, she divorced the brother and attempted a reconciliation with her former husband. But Herbert wasn't interested in patching things up with his estranged wife. He was enjoying a love affair with one of the maids until Polly found out about it and fired the woman.

As both an employee and intimate of the two women, Herbert was in a strange position in that he was not accepted by either the servants in the neighborhood or by Helen and Polly's friends. "I think there is no one who does not feel some degree of embarrassment with Herbert and I include myself . . . ," Nella admitted. "The measure of the ridiculousness of this entire situation is the difficulty that any one of us would have in explaining it to Helen. These small social distinctions have no meaning for her. She loves Herbert, loves him specifically and not merely as she loves all mankind. She does love all mankind, which makes it hard for her to love individuals. Her love for Herbert is probably purer than the feeling she has for Polly."

This appears to have been true. When Herbert died suddenly at Arcan Ridge of a cerebral hemorrhage in 1950, Helen was devastated. To her friend and trustee Katharine Cornell, she described her grief: "Oh, Katharine, how swiftly Herbert was taken from us! Had breakfast with him, and the next thing I knew, Polly, speechless with sorrow, was taking me into his room, and I touched a lifeless body lying on the floor. Not once did it seem to me that Herbert was dead, but I was stunned. . . ."

The two women were equally upset when they learned Herbert had never told them that he had reconciled with his wife two years earlier. "His wife and daughter had come that morning," Nella recorded. 'The trouble is, Miss Thomson,' his wife said, 'that Herbert loved all of us.' He had tried to reconcile his loyalties and had not reached a conclusion when he died."

Polly and Helen were now two old women living together, one who was deaf-blind, the other, frail and unwilling to train anyone to be her replacement. When Nella broached the question to Polly about what would happen to Helen if she died, Polly simply said that Helen would go to live with her brother Phillips in Dallas or with Mildred's daughter, Katharine, a newspaperwoman. But when Nella pointed out that Phillips had a serious heart condition and that Katharine was involved with her career, Polly again dismissed the subject by saying that Helen's family appreciated her fame and would find the right person.

Whether Helen would have been happy living with Mildred is debatable. A visit with her sister, after she and Polly had returned from a triumphant tour of South Africa in 1951, had been an unhappy one. In South Africa, which was suffering under apartheid, the Zulus had called Helen *Homvuselelo*, a name that meant "You have aroused the consciousness of many." She also had received an honorary degree from the University of the Witwatersrand, which at the time was the only unsegregated educational institution in South Africa. During her visit, although she dared not speak out publicly against segregation for fear of hurting the people she had come to help, she did much to raise support "for the colored blind, who, owing to their handicap are more subject to the arbitrary will of white society than their seeing fellows."

According to Nella, Mildred and her family were "rock-bound, old-fashioned Southerners" who did not share the "unquenchable shame" that Helen felt about the situation of blacks, not only in Alabama but also around the world.

> This revolt has slumbered within me since I began to notice for myself how they are degraded, and with what cold-blooded deliberation the keys of knowledge, self-reliance and well-paid employment are taken from them, so that they may not enter the gate of social competence," Helen had written Nella in 1946, adding that she had never gotten over "my humiliation when a colored teacher of high culture and noble dignity who called on me at a hotel in a Southern city was ordered into a freight elevator. . . . The continued lynchings and other crimes against Negroes, whether in New England or the South, and the unspeakable political exponents of white supremacy, according to all recorded history, augur ill for America's future.

An article about Helen had appeared in the *Ladies' Home Journal*, but her family's only comment was that Helen looked so ancient and decrepit in the photographs that they tossed it in the trash. Some weeks later, Nella confided to Polly in a letter, "It saddens me to think of Helen and her family and absolutely terrifies me when I reflect upon the possibility that she may have to spend her last years with them." Three years later, in 1954, Mildred would make a similar comment when she received photographs of her sister made by the *New York Times*. Helen, she said querulously, looked old and haggard, perhaps because she was being overworked. Immediately Polly took it to mean that she was neglecting Helen.

Herbert had observed that it would be a greater blow to Helen when she lost Polly than it was when she lost Annie. When Teacher died, Helen still had Polly. When Polly died, she would have nobody. She would have to relinquish everything she had spent her life for. Nella agreed. She had heard Helen say many times that she was glad she and Polly were traveling together on the same planes and trains, because if they met with a fatal accident, they would "take off for the spirit world together." And she knew that in Australia, when Helen had been made aware of Polly's failing health, she had asked Polly, when the time came that she knew she was dying, to give her a deadly dose of prescription pills.

This posed a harrowing question for Nella. "Suppose Polly did become very ill, should Herbert hide the tablets which Helen ordinarily takes, reaching by herself into the cabinet in her bathroom? Some of them, taken in quantity, would give lethal doses. I too have a responsibility here. Shall we hide them or not hide them? My inclination is to let nature take its course, but this brings up such horrors in the way of half-doses and suffering that my chief hope is that the decision will never have to be made."

Unlike most human beings, Helen welcomed old age and death. In her view, modern medicine had made the last years of life bearable, while Swedenborgianism made heaven a delightful place where all human beings would be given a second chance and she would be able to see and hear, as well as be reunited with Annie Sullivan. "The belief in immortality is in her bloodstream, as much a part of her as the red corpuscles," noted a friend with some puzzlement after Helen had fervidly informed her that "Teacher will never die and that is one reason why I feel that I shall live. Teacher rises above us. Many of us have not yet reached the human level."

Friends hoped that the seventy-four-year-old Helen would die before Polly. "I can never think of Helen without Polly without shivering," Nella wrote grimly in her journal, and one day in 1954, she and Polly made out a list of pallbearers for Helen's funeral. They planned every detail, down to the music and flower arrangements.

CHAPTER 23

"A Witness of God"

HELEN TWIRLED GRACEFULLY as she was encircled by the legendary Martha Graham and her lithe female dancers in black leotards. In a smart dark dress and high-heeled sandals, she was "feeling" a dance that Graham had choreographed especially for her. The unusual ballet was to be part of *The Unconquered*, a documentary film about Helen's life that was being produced and directed by their mutual friend Nancy Hamilton.

Dressed in a dark blue Chinese robe and wearing full stage makeup, Martha Graham herself had greeted Helen, Polly, and Nella at the door of her studio. They were all surprised by Graham's petiteness; onstage she gave the impression of tallness and tremendous strength. After greeting them warmly, Graham disappeared, returning moments later in a vibrant red gown with tight sleeves and bodice, which was her costume for one of her famous dances, "Joan of Arc."

It had been arranged that Martha Graham was to supervise Helen during her contact with the dancers, and spectators could not help noting that every time Graham touched Helen, Polly became nervous. She was so used to "handling" Helen herself that she lacked confidence in anyone else who attempted it. Reportedly, Katharine Cornell was the only person with whom she would leave Helen alone. She was especially fidgety when Martha Graham and Helen were waiting near the dancers. But when Graham helped Helen join the dance, they observed that Polly lost her uneasiness.

Helen loved Martha Graham the minute she had met her in December 1952. Instantly Helen sensed that Graham possessed a creative spirit like that of Annie Sullivan, someone who was able to induce boldness of thought and action in others.

As for Graham's thoughts about Helen, she told a friend, "She allows no ego block—lets nothing stand in the way; becomes a completely receptive instrument, a witness of God." Later she communicated to Helen through Polly that she was a great actress because she had love. In Graham's opinion, no one could be an inspired actress without it.

Helen and Polly were pleased with the documentary, but Nella, who had watched the filming and contributed to the script, was disturbed by its content. In her view, Helen's handicaps were minimized, thereby misleading the public about the life of a severely disabled person. Helen still required help to do the simplest things. "Main point (or a main point),"

A still from the motion picture *The Unconquered*, showing Helen with Martha Graham and her dancers at Martha Graham's studio, 1954

Nella noted in her journal. "Documentary thus far shows the triumphant end, not the continuing struggle—the long, long hours spent over the mail, the long, long hours composing speeches, memorizing them (H & P both have to memorize them), practicing them."

At this point, Nella's main concern was not the documentary, but Polly Thomson, whose health remained precarious. The previous month she had received a call from a doctor at the Mayo Clinic, where Helen and Polly had gone for their annual checkup. Helen was still in excellent health, the doctor said, but Polly, who had complained of feeling dizzy and "funny" in the head, received a poor report. Her blood pressure was lower, but she was anemic. Though Polly was not in immediate danger, the doctor informed an alarmed Nella that he felt that others should start learning the manual alphabet.

Helen seemed oblivious of the possibility that Polly's life might be in jeopardy. Although Helen had promised to settle down into a more relaxed lifestyle, she and Polly were planning a trip to South America and India. That fall they had returned from another exhausting tour, of Egypt, Lebanon, Syria, Jordan, and Israel, where they met Golda Meir, the minister of labor who was then known as Goldie Meyerson, and David Ben-Gurion, with whom Helen discussed religion and philosophy.

It was clear to Helen's friends that she had no intention of slowing down. In 1953, after completing the filming of *The Unconquered*, she resumed work on her reminiscences of Annie Sullivan. For seven years, ever since the first draft was destroyed in the fire at Arcan Ridge, she had promised herself that she would rewrite it.

When she again set to work on this tribute to her teacher, she was seventy-three years old, a visibly aged woman whose hands had become far less sensitive than they were when she was younger. Recently Nella had given her a child's plastic toy to feel and was startled when Helen didn't know what it was.

Later Nella worked up the courage to ask Helen about it directly. She was not reassured when Helen told her that her hands were indeed less sensitive and she had to warm them before she could read her Braille books. Although she did not mention it to Helen, Nella also believed that her other senses were becoming less keen, especially her sense of smell. The last time Nella was at Arcan Ridge, Helen had identified a spike of stock as hyacinth.

Writing about her beloved Annie Sullivan was an emotional trauma for Helen. She began to suffer from insomnia and often had to ask Polly for sleeping pills. Another nervous symptom was an itchy rash, later diagnosed as eczema, that was unresponsive to treatment and made her life miserable. But the book absorbed her completely. She had dreams in which she felt the heat of the immense fire that had consumed the original Arcan Ridge. "How the flames pursue me," she confided to Nella, "as memories return which have slumbered so long."

Nella worried about the toll that the book was taking on Helen. After a trip to Arcan Ridge, she recorded in her journal,

> Helen's face was dead. She looked deaf-blind and seemed tired. Of her own initiative she talked very little and I did not urge her. She brightened some-what when we went out on the lawn after lunch and when I joined her said, "Come, the trees want to welcome you."
>
> She spoke of Teacher's eyes and the suffering they had caused her, as well as Teacher's grief when she knew John Macy was leaving her. "I thought she would go out of her mind." . . . Then suddenly Helen's face crumpled and she began to weep. I had seen her shed tears before in ten-derness or sorrow, but this was the first time I had ever seen her break down in anguish. "How can I bear the burden of this sacrifice!" It was like watch-ing the beginning of the end of the world and I comforted her as best I could, reminding her how much she had given to Teacher and to us all. She regained control quickly, but her suffering is intense in recalling the past. She made a comparison between herself and Isaac and wondered how Isaac felt the rest of his life knowing that he had been offered as a sacrifice. What she had in mind was not altogether clear and I did not prod her, but she feels what while Teacher was a sacrifice, she, too, because of Teacher was also a sacrifice.

Helen's anguish had to do with her awareness that many people thought that both Annie Sullivan and Polly Thomson had sacrificed their lives for her. She had never gotten over the words of an anonymous reviewer who had written in the *New York Sun* when *The Story of My Life* was published in 1903 that "the wonderful feat of drawing Helen Keller out of her hopeless darkness was only accomplished by sacrificing for it another woman's whole life, and if ever the attempt is made in another similar case, it must be at the same cost."

Intimate friends such as Nella were rankled by these pronouncements. After years of observing Helen and her two companions, she concluded that what Annie had with Helen was fulfillment and opportunity, not sacrifice and immolation, while Polly, too, was offered "development and fulfillment beyond her wildest dreams" when she was hired as a secretary in the Macy-Keller household in 1914.

In Nella's opinion, "If anyone was sacrificed, and I am not certain that anyone was, it was Helen herself. I am certain of this: Whatever AS or PT or anyone else gave to Helen was returned to them in brimming measure as individuals and given out beyond them to the world at large. Helen has enriched whomever and whatever she has touched."

Once Helen had broken the barrier of writing about her adored Annie, she began to find her literary work pleasurable. She later said that she enjoyed writing *Teacher* more than any other work she had written, with the exception of her epic poem "The Song of the Stone Wall" and *The World I Live In*. She confided to friends that she was glad that the original manuscript was burned, for it was not good, and she had not yet developed the right perspective about her teacher.

Still, *Teacher* brought back painful memories of what she perceived as injustices. In it, she wrote "the sin I cannot forgive" was the accusation made at the time of "The Frost King" episode that Teacher had warped her mind; the incident had happened more than sixty years before. Frank Sanborn, the head investigator of the State Board of Charities, to whom Annie had appealed to send her to school when she was living at the almshouse, had written a snide letter about Annie to the Perkins' trustees. In it he had brought up her sordid background and her "ingratitude" to Perkins. Helen bristled as she remembered his comments. She wrote, "To this day I cannot excuse his mean-spirited behavior. Little did he remember that, however impatient we may be with our fellow men, we are all bound together and live for and by one another." To her friends it was obvious that while Annie's anger had mellowed as she grew older, Helen's festered. She never forgave an injustice.

Helen had returned to Perkins briefly in 1952. Michael Anagnos was long dead, and the school by then had moved from South Boston to Watertown, Massachusetts. According to the school's director, Edward Waterhouse, it was the first time that Helen had set foot in Perkins since she left in a huff with Annie in 1892, sixty years before.

Four years later, in November 1956, when Helen was seventy-six years old, she would make her peace with the school where she had learned French and music and had met children like herself who could communicate with her in her own way. Accepting the invitation of the director and trustees to attend the dedication of the Keller-Macy cottage, she greeted enthusiastically the twelve deaf-blind children who were housed there.

When Nella read the manuscript of *Teacher*, she conceded that Helen had "dug in to herself and learned many things that no one could have taught her, not even Teacher. I have been greatly impressed by the profundity of this manuscript. Up to the time of reading it I myself had not had much confidence in Helen's ability to write about Teacher, but I have now."

Teacher was published by Doubleday in 1955. Although it sold well, the book was not a best-seller. Many readers thought it more like a book of poetry than a biography, and some were embarrassed by Helen's emotional intensity toward her subject. Others felt that Helen glossed over Annie's troubled personality and her obsessive control over her only pupil.

IN 1955, THE SAME YEAR that *Teacher* was published, when she was seventy-five, Helen embarked on one of her longest and most arduous trips, a forty-thousand-mile, five-month tour to survey the condition of the physically handicapped in the Far East. "Retiring?" she replied to a question when she returned. "I dislike the word." In India she met with Prime Minister Nehru several times. For Helen, Nehru's face, which he permitted her to touch, had "real nobility and a high-domed brow one needs the gift of a Poet to describe. It looked like what I had always seen in my mind, a personality that elevates human ideals and goals and shoves the world nearer to true Civilization."

After finishing *Teacher*, Helen told her friends that she wanted to study foreign languages and read history, archaeology, and philosophy, especially the works of Plato, Kant, and Swedenborg. As she grew older, she lost her taste for novels, although she still read a great deal of poetry. "I have grown to love life more than fiction," she said. But it was the extraordinary world of nature that fascinated her, and she devoured books on the subject, among them *One Day in Teton Marsh* and *Almanac for Moderns*. Secretly, she wished to practice exercises in parapsychology, in which she and Annie had become fascinated when they were living in Forest Hills. At age seventy-seven she told her amazed friends, "I shall devote my old age to study."

BY 1954 POLLY'S HEALTH HAD further deteriorated. Her perpetual rages—at Nixon and Eisenhower, the Catholic Church, Wallis Simpson, and Senator Joseph McCarthy—had given way to sadness and lassitude, perhaps induced by the tranquilizers and other medication that had been prescribed for her. In 1954 she had a tumor removed from her head.

The operation disfigured her face slightly, and she became morose and distraught.

All her life, Polly Thomson had been interested in politics and world affairs. Like Helen, she was an ardent Democrat and liberal, and the McCarthy hearings, which were being televised that year, made her so upset that friends began to fear for her health. Helen herself seemed far less passionate about the hearings. She, too, was slowing down. Her chronic eczema became so bad that she had to be hospitalized.

Her niece Katharine Tyson came to spend most of the week with the two women to learn about taking care of Helen. Helen's comment at the end of the time was, "I think Katharine will not do," which revealed to their friends that there was "a Helen-problem as well as a Polly-problem" about finding someone to help Polly.

After Helen was released from the hospital, a district nurse came two or three times a day to dress her skin condition. The doctor asked Polly if Helen was under any special stress, and Polly said no. When they learned of Polly's response, their friends were upset. Even though they had known her for years, Helen was an enigma to them, and it "frightened" them to speculate about what went on in the depths of her mind.

In the meantime, Helen continued with her public life. She made appearances and speeches, met with presidents and other heads of state, and received numerous honors and awards, including the Americas Award for Inter-American Unity, the Gold Medal Award from the National Institute of Social Sciences, the National Humanitarian Award from Variety Clubs International, and many others.

After Franklin Roosevelt's death she was received by President Harry Truman at the White House (it was reported that she found Truman to possess an open hand—"there were no crooks in his fingers"—and that he was moved to tears when she spoke to him). And in November 1953, wearing a blue hat and dress a shade lighter than her clear blue plastic eyes, which a reporter noted "glowed as radiantly as a girl of twenty," she met Dwight D. Eisenhower. Putting her hand on his face, she told him, "You have a wonderful smile." "But not much hair," Eisenhower replied.

Her White House visits were, of course, not new experiences. Ever since she was eight years old, she had met every president of the United States: Presidents Cleveland, McKinley, Theodore Roosevelt, Taft, Wilson, Harding, Coolidge, Hoover, and her favorite, FDR.

In June 1955, a week before her seventy-fifth birthday, Helen received an honorary degree from Harvard University, the first woman to be so honored. When her name was called, the entire audience rose for a standing ovation. She had never looked more beautiful — she was dressed entirely in white, with a white hat with small green flowers. Pinned to her dress was a corsage of white gardenias that the Swedenborgians had sent her.

She was similarly praised by her alma mater, Radcliffe College, which presented her with its Alumnae Achievement Award, dedicating the Helen Keller Garden in her honor and naming a fountain in the garden for Anne Sullivan Macy.

Yet another honor came to Helen in 1954, when her birthplace, Ivy Green, in Tuscumbia, Alabama, was made into a permanent local shrine and placed on the National Register of Historic Places. In conjunction with this event, the premiere of her film biography, *The Unconquered*, produced by Nancy Hamilton and narrated by Katharine Cornell, was held in the nearby city of Birmingham. Some years later, the documentary film was renamed *Helen Keller in Her Story* and was introduced by Patty Duke, who had portrayed a young Helen onstage and onscreen in *The Miracle Worker*. Like the earlier film about her, *Deliverance*, it made no mention of Helen's complicated relationship with Annie Sullivan, "The Frost King" scandal, the endless power struggles over her, her thwarted relationship with Peter Fagan, or her radical politics. It did feature, however, many vintage still photographs of Helen and Annie, as well as rare film footage of Annie explaining how Helen was taught speech and of Helen learning the art of the dance from Martha Graham and the acclaimed dancer and choreographer Robert Helpmann. Though not a commercial success, *The Unconquered* won an Academy Award as the best feature-length documentary film of 1955.

By the 1950s, many people in the world considered Helen Keller the greatest living American woman, a person who had overcome blindness and deafness to become a triumphant symbol of human resilience and courage. Such was the power of her name that several years after Helen's death, when veteran Hearst reporter Adela Rogers St. Johns told friends that she did not plan to include Helen in a book she was writing about America's most famous women, she was met with a horrified response. "They put her forth as THE great American woman and when I said I hadn't included her in my book at all they stared at me with incredulity and censure. But why? they said in unison.

"She will of course be in the Hall of Fame," St. Johns reassured them, backing down swiftly. "The Women's Hall of Fame. On a high pedestal surrounded by blue-birds and angels with her Seeing Eye dog at her feet. But it seems to me that she is a case so exceptional, her gallant spirit is one so dif-

Left to right: Nancy Hamilton, Katharine Cornell, Helen, and Polly with the Academy Award–winning film *The Unconquered*, which was produced by Hamilton and narrated by Cornell

ferent from any average normal woman that she must have a place all her own."

Adela Rogers St. Johns was not only mistaken about a deaf-blind person such as Helen using a Seeing Eye dog, but she was also in error about Helen Keller and other disabled people. Like the female theatrical agent in 1918 who had thought Helen's life was not screen material because it lacked drama, the reporter failed to comprehend that Helen Keller and the handicapped were no different from other people. That had been Helen's severest challenge, not against her own limitations, but to make the public aware that a handicapped person had the same need for social acceptance and financial stability as a nonhandicapped person. The disabled did not want to be put on a "high pedestal" any more than they wished to be ignored or ridiculed. But Helen, in her struggle to achieve equal rights for the blind, had not been entirely successful in transforming the public's attitude. Too many capable blind people were still unemployed and segregated from the rest of society. Lonely outcasts unless they were physically attractive and intellectually gifted like herself, they remained victims not only of their affliction but also of prejudice and fear.

BY THE MID-1950S it had become obvious to their friends that Polly's behavior toward Helen was "bordering on madness." For years it had been Polly who dressed Helen, a long and tedious job because Polly was such a perfectionist about Helen's public image. Lately, Polly had become even more fanatical about Helen's appearance. Because she insisted that Helen look her best, even with her closest friends, it was now a burden for them to have company. Spur-of-the-moment visitors, whom Helen might have enjoyed seeing, were told that Polly and Helen could not see them. As a result, Helen was even more isolated. Not that this was entirely Polly's fault. Even though she had never seen her own face in a mirror, Helen was as concerned about her appearance as any teenage girl. She once told Nella, "I want all the handicapped to look nice so that they won't repel people and maybe this picture will encourage them."

What deeply disturbed members of their intimate circle, however, was that even though Nella, Katharine Cornell, Nancy Hamilton, and Lenore Smith all knew the manual finger language, Polly would not let them spell to Helen when anyone else was present. Still a prisoner in her old age, Helen was cut off from contact with anyone but her senile, possessive companion.

CHAPTER 24

"I Am in Agony"

ON THE MORNING OF September 26, 1957, Helen and Polly were upstairs in Helen's book-lined study, practicing Helen's speeches for several upcoming events. The two women were tired. They had returned recently from yet another exhausting tour, to Iceland and Scandinavia. On their return to the United States, Helen discovered what she thought was a callus on the bottom of her foot. It turned out to be a bone tumor. Although the growth proved nonmalignant, doctors advised removing her toe. With her customary sangfroid, Helen sailed through the operation. The only things she disliked about her stay at Memorial Hospital in New York were the side rails that were required to be up at night for every patient more than sixty-five years old. While she was in the hospital, one of her doctors commented that he had never known a woman who was so well adjusted to life.

At about eleven o'clock, Polly suggested they go downstairs and have an early lunch so they could spend most of the afternoon working on Helen's speeches. As Helen later told Nella, "We started downstairs, and when we reached the kitchen door, Polly suddenly stood like one transfixed, as if she saw someone at the other end of the room, and called out 'John!' Polly was not steady on her feet; she had trouble breathing, and said she wanted to go out on the terrace. I could not do anything else with her and so I unlatched the kitchen door and we went out. It was cold and I got her back in as soon as I could. I forgot to latch the door.

"Then Polly insisted upon going back to the stove and getting lunch. Polly kept turning knobs on the stove and kept saying to me, 'Put it on the stove,' and I kept asking 'What am I to put on the stove, Polly?' I kept turning off the burners as fast as Polly turned them on."

Several times Polly came near to falling, and Helen had to support her. Then she told Helen that she had to urinate, and Helen led her toward the bathroom in the maid's room. But before they could reach it, Polly decided that she didn't need the bathroom after all. Helen tried to make her lie down, but Polly insisted on returning to the kitchen and making lunch. Then, according to Helen, Polly announced "I want to do number one," and the women returned to the bathroom, where Helen had to find the toilet paper for her. Again Helen begged her to lie down, and again Polly refused, once more returning to the kitchen and the stove. As Polly's legs began to splay, Helen had to support her to keep her from falling. Finally, Polly could no longer keep her balance, and Helen eased her to the floor. But Polly managed to scramble to her feet and returned to the stove. After a while Helen persuaded her to sit down in a kitchen chair. "I stood there, holding her shoulders," Helen demonstrated to Nella. "I stood a long time."

"She knew she did not have to tell me why she could not leave Polly to set off the emergency call to the police that she and Polly had installed," Nella recorded in her journal, referring to a special device called the Telerapid, which enabled Helen to get help in case anything happened to Polly. "A deaf-blind person cannot lose physical contact with another person, or the contact may be broken forever. Polly need not have moved far away to make it impossible for Helen to find her again."

When Polly fell a second time, Helen again supported her to break the fall. As her fingers felt the terrible throbbing of Polly's pulse, she knew instantly that her companion had suffered a stroke. "And oh Nella, the blood! the blood! Polly's temple."

For two and a half hours the two women remained huddled on the floor until the postman, finding the kitchen door ajar, walked in to deliver the mail. "Henry, I am in agony," Helen told him.

"There has been only one other day in my life like it," Helen later told Nella, "and that was the day Teacher knew that John was leaving her."

From the time she was eight years old, Helen Keller had enjoyed many public triumphs, but this was her finest hour. Her intervention had saved Polly from all external injury, except for burning her hand on the stove.

A SHORT TIME LATER, Nella visited Polly, who was recovering at home. "She was very thin and though her eyes had not changed in appearance it was obvious that she could not see very well. She knew that some catastrophe had taken place, that something dreadful had happened to her, but she did not know what. 'I'm so bewildered,' she kept saying. 'I'm so bewildered.' "

After Polly's stroke, the nurse who was treating Helen's eczema moved into the house, but Helen felt that she was too domineering with Polly. She was fired. Other nurses were brought in to care for Polly, but their friends sensed that it was a temporary solution.

Despite treatment, Helen's skin condition grew worse, perhaps exacerbated by the stress of Polly's illness. In recent years her own hair had grown very sparse, and she wore an obvious and ill-fitting wig in public, which aggravated the eczema around her ears. Knowing the discomfort it caused her, friends persuaded her not to wear it, and at first she was a bit embarrassed about not having it on when company came. But her friends thought she looked perfectly beguiling with her soft white hair brushed up and pinned into a tiny knot at the top of her head. At night she would curl the front on hairpins. "I have my little vanities," she informed one of her nurses. After she had stopped wearing the wig for a week, Helen said to Nella, "I am getting unexpected pleasure from my hair. I never thought I would. I never liked the transformation, but in public life one must do things and wear things that one would rather not." She told Nella that from then on she would leave the wig off while she was at home and don it only when she and Polly went to the theater in New York. Polly insisted that Helen continue wearing the wig even in the privacy of her own home, but she was still too weak to mount an effective protest. In mid-January Polly had suffered a convulsion that lasted about fifteen minutes. Doctors determined that the seizure, coupled with her previous strokes, had damaged her eyes and she now also suffered from a loss of association. She would never handle a heavy volume of correspondence or travel as she had in the past.

Still, she was tender with Helen and spelled to her rationally. A nurse commented that this may have been the one area in which Polly always felt herself adequate. When she repeated a phrase or a story, Nella reported that Helen said to her, "You just said that and when she says 'Oh Lord how long?' Helen says 'You ought to say How soon Oh Lord how soon?' and she gives Polly other bits of her spiritual philosophy without getting a response."

Even so, friends marveled that Polly seemed to be drawing strength from Helen.

Every morning Helen came to Polly's bed to kiss her and ask how she felt. Invariably Polly gave a discouraging answer. But Helen believed that she was getting better. After visiting with her companion, she spent most of the day at her desk, reading a psychiatric book in Braille.

"It does give her some ease of mind to know that Helen is there, but Helen's philosophy (the very breath of life to Helen and potent enough to see her through every crisis and the crises have been grim) has no personal meaning for Polly anymore than it had for Teacher or has for me," Nella recorded in her diary.

"Ever since Teacher's death Polly has been urged with reason, with prayers, with love, with terror, to provide a substitute for herself for Helen. All in vain. 'When the time comes,' she has said to me, 'I will train somebody.' The time is here and nothing is farther from her mind. She is so immersed in herself that she gives small thought to Helen. The old pitiful jealousy is still active, 'that last infirmity of a noble mind,' and fame the spur, the unquenchable thirst for applause. . . . If she gets better, she is going to object to everything about the household arrangements."

Helen's bed became Polly's new place to take her afternoon nap. Their friends feared that she had chosen it to block anyone else gaining access to Helen, who customarily took her afternoon nap on the window seat in her study. Polly became unreasonably angry when Winifred Corbally, a practical nurse who had been brought in to care for Polly, took Helen for a walk alone. Polly was suspicious of everyone and allowed no one to go near Helen, not even the good-natured nurse, whom everyone called "Winnie." Sometimes Evelyn Seide, a secretary at the foundation who was now staying at the house to help out, would slip upstairs while Polly was asleep and spell to Helen, but then Polly found out about it and exploded in anger. Nella believed that "Polly is in a hell of her own and has dragged Helen in with her and shut her into a prison, herself on guard at the door. Our major job will be to get Helen out of prison—but how?"

Fearful that Helen had become a virtual prisoner in her own home but not knowing how to help her, Nella warned Helen about writing despondent letters because everything that she wrote was read to Polly before it was mailed.

Friends began to feel that they would grieve less over Helen's death than they would over her current situation. She was now so cut off from the world, and "Polly's raging jealousy a madness."

Polly's paranoia made it almost impossible to see Helen alone, but one day Nella managed to corner Helen in her study, where she was straightening her books.

N. Polly does not like to have anyone but herself do things for you.

H. Isn't it pathetic!

N. Polly grows tired of people.

H. Alas!

N. I hope she is not growing tired of Mrs. Corbally.

H. I am afraid she is. I am sorry, she is a sweet girl.

N. If Mrs. Corbally goes, you will have to find someone else to take her place.

On another occasion, Nella reported that Helen was more revealing about her true feelings toward Polly: " 'It is a pity,' Helen said, 'that I have never been able to feel towards Polly as I did towards Teacher.' We spoke of Polly's possessiveness. 'Too much so,' Helen said, 'but I have always had my work and have been able to manage.' She also said that Annie had 'great intellectual powers' which Polly lacked."

Compounding Nella's problems was her own feud with Helen's new senior trustee at the foundation, Jimmy Adams, a general partner at Lazard Frères & Company who was one of the four richest men in the world (much richer than Migel, Nella noted with glee). Nella sensed that Adams was trying to wrest away control of Helen from herself, Katharine Cornell, and Nancy Hamilton. When Helen had needed foot surgery, he had suggested a doctor, becoming furious when they questioned his decision. In Nella's view, Jimmy Adams was a clone of Migel and his secretary, Amelia, both of whom had been jealous of anyone who tried to interfere with their plans to manage Helen and Polly.

IN DECEMBER 1958, Polly was rushed to the hospital after suffering from another series of convulsions at the hairdresser's. Helen, too, was in frail health. Physically sluggish, she rarely took a walk. More ominously, she had difficulty communicating through spelling, and people had to spell things twice to her.

The two women needed help, but when Evelyn Seide and her husband moved into Arcan Ridge, Nella was aghast. "It won't do. Evelyn lacks presence, with her mascaraed eyes, her dyed hair, and her awful makeup, and she lacks intelligence, and her husband is an oaf. . . ." Still, she had to grudgingly admit that the "vulgar" Evelyn possessed some virtues. "But I hope that Evelyn will always be with Helen as she is now—her like is not easy to find."

Although critical of Evelyn and Winnie, Nella herself was not prepared to help share the burden of Helen's care. Some years before, after realizing that Polly needed assistance, the trustees of the foundation had approached Nella about moving into Arcan Ridge with her husband, Keith. Quickly she had declined the offer, citing their advanced age and poor health, and privately confided to her journal that she hoped that Helen died before Polly.

On March 3, 1959, the seventy-second anniversary of Annie Sullivan's arrival in Tuscumbia, they had champagne at dinner, and Helen offered her usual toast to Teacher, ending with "We'll soon be with you." Without spelling her comment to Helen, Polly said to a guest, "That was very nice, but Teacher could be hard," and echoing Nella's sentiment, added, "I hope Helen goes first." Nella sensed that Polly's primary feeling toward Helen was still one of jealousy toward anyone who tried to do anything for her, even though Polly herself was now powerless to help her.

"Helen's aloneness hardly bears thinking about," Nella noted in her journal. "Her heart, if it breaks, will break in silence, and most of the people around her will not know that it is breaking."

Helen herself seemed to have given up. No longer did she like to ride in the car. Without Polly to spell to her, it was one monotonous bump after another. "I am old and tired," she told her friends, "and I want to be left alone."

For most of the day she stayed at her desk, reading the books she wanted to read before her death. Noting that Helen had never made much distinction between this world and the next, her friends sensed that she was ready for death, not particularly longing for it and certainly not dreading it, but waiting for a natural event that she would welcome.

Polly Thomson died on March 21, 1960. She was seventy-six years old and had served Helen for forty-six years. A few days before she died, a nurse at the hospital had asked her if she would like to see Helen Keller. "Who is she?" Polly wanted to know. Her response was reminiscent of Annie Sullivan's answer to the same question shortly before her death. "I never heard of Helen Keller," she had said.

Polly left her estate of $116,000 to her family in Scotland. Her jewelry, valued at $15,000, was given to her relatives, friends, and hairdresser. She left nothing to Helen. After her funeral services were held in Bridgeport, Connecticut, her ashes were deposited next to Annie Sullivan's at the National Cathedral in Washington, D.C. But Helen, who was upset about Polly's cutting her out of her will, refused to attend the committal service. As Nella noted, "It may not take place any time soon. Helen balky. Says Polly has already had a service in Bridgeport and that's enough." A member of the foundation had to deliver Polly's ashes to Washington.

Shortly after Polly's demise, Helen could be seen at parties wearing her former companion's $8,000 mink coat. She seemed happy and content. The fur was Polly's last extravagant purchase. She had always craved a mink and was paying for it "on time" before her fatal stroke.

CHAPTER 25

_____

The End of a Friendship

A FTER POLLY'S DEATH, in the spring of 1960, a talented child actress named Patty Duke visited Arcan Ridge. She was accompanied by Katharine Cornell, who had gone backstage one night to ask Patty, who was playing Helen as a violent, unkempt child in William Gibson's hit Broadway play *The Miracle Worker*, if she would like to meet the legendary woman on whom her character was based. Entranced by Patty, Helen gave her one of the beautiful Japanese dolls from the glass case in her bedroom. After their arrival, Katharine Cornell stayed in the background, while Patty spelled into Helen's hand. Then Patty asked Helen if she would show her the garden, and they visited it, Winnie Corbally trailing a discreet distance behind, to make sure that Helen did not fall.

Despite her advanced age, Helen had lost none of her intense vitality and interest in everything. Patty Duke later recalled:

When I first saw Helen walking down the stairs, she looked almost regal. She was wearing a blue dress, pearls, and what I found out were her favorite red shoes. She was close to eighty years old by then, but she carried herself very straight. She had alabaster skin, very thin white hair, almost like an angel's hair, and was very buxom with small hips and great-looking legs. And a ter-

320

rific smile. And she was so jolly, like a jolly grandma. I'd expected serious or sweet, but not jolly. . . . Not someone who loved to laugh, and about everything, even the fact that we'd come before she'd had a chance to take her bras—rather large bras, I might add—in off the laundry line. . . .

Occasionally she would spell to me, just to be gracious and indulge me because I wanted her to, but mostly she would talk out loud. Her voice was very hard to understand . . . she said she'd never been happy with the way it sounded. To understand me, she would put her thumb on my lips and her fingers on different vibration points. She didn't miss a thing.

We went for a walk in her gardens. They were fairly extensive, with railings all around, but very nicely done; nothing screamed, "A blind person lives here!" She told me the name of every tree and bush and flower and talked about how at one she felt with nature. And she told me about her martinis. The doctor had told her that she shouldn't have her martinis anymore, and she told the doctor that at her age, if she enjoyed a martini, she was going to have one.

The Miracle Worker, a drama that portrayed Annie Sullivan's first success in communicating with Helen as a child, was based on Nella's 1933 biography of Annie Sullivan and Helen's *The Story of My Life*. First broadcast live on the CBS dramatic anthology *Playhouse 90* in 1957, with Teresa Wright as Anne Sullivan, Burl Ives as Captain Keller, and Patty McCormack as Helen Keller, it won its author the Sylvania Prize "for outstanding contribution to creative television technique." Although the teleplay was successful, Gibson was unhappy with its sketchiness and rewrote it for the stage. Starring Anne Bancroft as Annie Sullivan and the twelve-year-old Patty Duke as Helen Keller (and Patricia Neal as Kate Keller and Torin Thatcher as Captain Keller), *The Miracle Worker* opened to rave reviews at the Playhouse on Broadway in 1959. Hailed by the critics as a contemporary classic, it was described as "harrowing and explosive" theater that was also "stirring." A Broadway smash, the play ran for almost two years for a total of seven hundred performances. Then Gibson wrote *The Miracle Worker* for a third time as a movie, which was produced by United Artists in 1962—Anne Bancroft and Patty Duke reprised their stage roles and received Academy Awards for their performances. At the time, Duke was the youngest actor to win an Oscar. When the play was produced on television for a second time, in the fall of 1979, Patty Duke, who by this time was a mature woman, reversed roles, playing Annie Sullivan to Melissa Gilbert's Helen Keller.

Gibson later wrote *Monday After the Miracle*, a sequel to *The Miracle Worker* that dealt with the intriguing ménage à trois that resulted when Annie married John Macy. Directed by Arthur Penn, with Jane Alexander

With Patty Duke, who played Helen as a young girl in *The Miracle Worker*,
at Helen's eightieth-birthday celebration on June 26, 1960, at the Gotham
Hotel, New York

as Annie, Karen Allen as Helen, and William Converse-Roberts as Macy,
the play closed soon after it opened on Broadway in 1982. Possibly the public, prepared for another work with the joyful optimism of *The Miracle
Worker*, was put off by the play's pessimism, as well as Gibson's speculation
that the dissolute Macy was sexually attracted to Helen.

For the actors in the 1959 play, *The Miracle Worker* was both emotionally and physically taxing. Duke, who had practiced her part with her eyes
closed, was told that she would have to act the part of Helen with her eyes
wide open and a fixed stare. The climax was the unforgettable fight scene
in the second act, when Annie Sullivan refused to be intimidated by one of
the manipulative Helen's dinnertime temper tantrums. The melee, in
which teacher and pupil pulled each other's hair and threw chairs and
water at one another, lasted for a full ten minutes and was intricately choreographed. Special techniques had to be used to protect the actors from
injury—the prepubescent Patty Duke wore shin guards, knee guards, and
hip guards, as well as a chest protector to shield her developing breasts. To
prevent them from slipping, Duke and Bancroft wore special rubber soles
on their shoes. Despite these precautions, Patty Duke developed blood blis-
ters from the spoons that Annie kept shoving into her hand to teach her

table manners, and suffered from painful bruises on the back of her legs from slamming them into a chair. Bancroft, too, became injured during the production: She suffered from a serious injury to her foot when she ran into a chair during rehearsal. According to Duke, the one part of "the fights that always had to be done for real, and was always horrible, was the slapping. From the acting point of view the most difficult thing for both of us was concentrating hard enough so we didn't flinch even though we knew we were going to take a whack right in the face. That never got any easier, and neither did the actual fact of getting hit."

Another hard moment for Duke was having to say "wah-wah, the otherworldly sound Helen makes to signify the miracle." According to Duke, she could not say it convincingly until Arthur Penn, the director, whispered to her, "I want you to make this sound as if you're very constipated and you've been constipated for a long time." Although Duke later said it was "the single most embarrassing direction" she had ever received during her career, she had to concede that Penn's advice worked. For many people in the audience, Helen's transformation at the water pump from an animal-like creature into a human being was the play's most affecting moment.

Duke, whose every action was monitored by tyrannical theatrical managers and who would subsequently be diagnosed as a manic-depressive, recalled some years later that her role as Helen Keller was the one bright spot in a horrendous childhood. "My emotional identification with Helen Keller was strong. In retrospect, I believe that I could identify with Helen, this blind, deaf child who was trapped physically, while I was trapped emotionally. Without knowing what I was doing, I used Helen as a vehicle to temporarily break out of my prison eight times a week. She was a life jacket for me."

As for Anne Bancroft, she discovered to her dismay that audiences reacted to her performance as Annie Sullivan in precisely the same manner as Helen's adoring public had treated the real Annie Sullivan. At lunch with Nella, Bancroft confided that it was Patty Duke as Helen who enthralled theatergoers. "What had troubled her was her own curtain call, after hers and Patty's together," Nella noted in her journal. "The applause was thunderous for the first, barely a polite trickle for the second. Anne felt naked standing there. And I told her that it had always been like that with Teacher, that people would trample her so as to get to Helen. . . . It says much for Anne's basic personality that she speaks well of Patty, 'a lovely little girl,' so good that at times she tends to loaf through the part and Annie has to drag it out of her on the stage . . . exactly as Teacher often had to do with Helen."

WHEN HELEN HEARD that a teleplay had been written about her early life, she was amazed. "Never did I dream a drama could be devised out of the story of my life," she said. Although she expressed interest in the project, she did not ask to read the script, although later it was Brailled for her. Nella, who thought the script had "great literary merit and dramatic power," was convinced that Helen would share her opinion, but to her surprise, Helen's response was less than glowing, and Nella was relieved when she changed her mind after it was shown on *Playhouse 90*. The reasons for Helen's initial reservations are unknown, although Nella offered a clue when she noted in her journal "there is nothing that Helen contemplates with more weariness than the reiteration of the story of her life." Perhaps Helen also felt that no fictional account of her relationship with Teacher could convey the depth of her own experience.

Polly's attitude toward *The Miracle Worker* was a hostile one. William Gibson had written it as a love letter to Teacher, and she was not a part of it.

The Miracle Worker was the occasion of the bitter breakup of Helen and Nella's forty-year-old friendship. In mid-December 1959, as Helen left for the hospital where Polly lay dying, she told her new companion, Winnie Corbally, "If Mrs. Henney telephones, tell her not to come up, I am too upset to see anybody."

Soon Nella was shocked to receive a coldly written letter revoking the power of attorney that Helen had given her in 1948:

Dear Nella:

Due to Polly's illness I have decided that all of my business affairs should be handled by my personal trustees, James S. Adams, Richard H. Migel and Jansen Noyes, Jr.

I therefore desire to cancel the power of attorney granted by me to you on March 5, 1948.

I am deeply grateful to you for all you have done to help me with my books and articles.

Sincerely yours,
HELEN KELLER

In a will written in 1958, Helen had named Nella as her literary executrix. In another communication, a month later, she informed Nella, "Since then, I have reconsidered the matter, and I have expressed my views in the new Will which will be ready to be executed by me within the next few days. . . . As I now desire that all my manuscripts, articles, letters, etc. be left to my three Trustees, i.e. Mr. James S. Adams, Mr. Jansen Noyes, Jr., and Mr. Richard H. Migel, for disposition in their absolute discretion, I would appreciate your being good enough to request Nella Henney to deliver to the American Foundation for the Blind for safekeeping in my name, all such material which may be in her possession."

Nella believed that Polly's possessiveness, and to a lesser extent, Jimmy Adams's determination to usurp her role as Helen's literary adviser, were responsible for Helen's flare-up. "I think he [Adams] had his part in it and that he played it with glee, but I still think Polly's jealousy was the primary cause," she recorded, adding that "it was unbearable to Polly to have anything important connected with Helen going on without her. In her half-mad mind she began to feed Helen with just what sort of half-mad lies I do not know. At any rate, her final gift to me was the destruction of Helen's confidence in me."

Was Polly Thomson responsible for the end of the friendship? Since Polly was a senile, dying woman, it seems unlikely that Helen would have listened to her "half-mad lies" about Nella, who had been such a devoted friend to them both. Over the years Nella and Polly had been particularly close—it was Nella whom Polly called whenever she felt lonely.

In his dual biography of Helen and Annie, Joseph Lash believed that money had been the issue and that Helen became convinced that Nella had been exploiting her all those years. He wrote: "Back in 1934 when the contract for *Anne Sullivan Macy* was negotiated, Teacher had resented Nella's offer to split the profits from the book with her only during Teacher's lifetime and had refused to sign the contract, saying the book was Nella's."

This theory doesn't seem probable, either. All her life Helen had little concept of money, and it seems strange that she would have begrudged Nella her share of the royalties from *The Miracle Worker* when the work was based partially on her biography of Annie Sullivan.

More likely, the answer had to do with Helen Keller in her old age. All her life she had been a hostage of one person or group who sought to use her for their own special purposes. She was "a luxurious captive," as one person characterized her. Although since childhood she had had no choice but to willingly participate in the creation of her public image, at times she rebelled against the people who had made her into an icon. Her anger at some officials at the foundation, which she expressed periodically, complaining that they were "trying to run my affairs," may have stemmed from

Helen (left) and Polly in the only photograph of Helen in which she looks tense, 1955

her awareness that they were controlling her to the point where she could never appear as less than superhuman. Seeking to present a positive image of the blind to the public, they had given strict instructions to outside photographers not to publish any photographs of her without first obtaining their approval. Over the years, the foundation had accumulated at least two thousand photographs of her, and in each one, which she would never see, she was beautifully dressed and smiling her beatific smile. Looking at those photographs, no one, if they had not known who she was, would have guessed that she was blind and deaf, wore artificial eyes, and in later life, a wig and false teeth. On each photograph the deception of physical normality was preserved, as was the illusion of emotional tranquillity in the face of impairment and loss. In only one of those two thousand photographs, which was taken in a car with Polly Thomson, did Helen look tearful and upset. On the back was scribbled the following note by an anonymous official: "Too tense. Just throw it away."

Despite her sincere interest in Helen and the blind, Nella was one of Helen's keepers, as much her jailer as Annie, Polly, Anagnos, her conflicted family, and the well-meaning officials at the foundation. A prim elitist, Nella spent her life in constant dread that someone would say or do something to sully Helen's virtuous public image. Over the years Nella had fretted unduly. Some years before, Dr. Conrad Berens, Helen and Annie's eye doctor, had taken Nella aside and asked her frankly whether Helen, Annie, and Polly were lesbians. When Nella said that they were "women who liked men," he had seemed relieved. Still, she feared that he would spread false rumors about the women's sexual orientation, something the doctor never did. When a new children's book about Helen and Annie by Eleanor Roosevelt's close friend Lorena Hickok was to be published, Nella was positive it would convey the impression that Helen was not nearly as brilliant as people imagined, even though Nella herself believed this to be the case. It turned out to be perfectly innocuous, the usual sentimentalized biography of the gifted deaf-blind woman who triumphed over her handicaps with the help of her dedicated teacher.

Another work that Nella felt could ruin Helen's reputation was Nicholas Monsarrat's lurid novel *The Story of Esther Costello*, which was published in 1953 and centered around a famous—and beautiful—deaf-blind woman whose sight and hearing are restored when she is raped by her benefactor's husband, a voyeur who for years has been peeping at her while she is bathing. Nella lived in dread that the public would believe the book was a roman à clef about Helen and John Macy, whose proximity to the helpless deaf-blind woman inspired speculation about his motives by at least two male authors—Monsarrat and then later William Gibson—despite a lack of evidence that Macy was ever romantically interested in her. In Monsarrat's case, Nella also worried needlessly. Books reviewers, as well as readers, did not even make the connection.

More important, Nella feared that Helen herself would do something inadvertently that would make people doubt her saintliness. It was one thing for her friends to know that Helen, who never knew the cost of anything, had asked Kit Cornell to buy her an expensive Labrador retriever, but what if she had asked somebody to buy her a dog who could not have afforded it? And it was Nella who had disapproved of Helen's wearing a lovely sapphire ring, which was a symbol "of her love for the Indian people." She thought it "utterly out of place on Helen's finger. Those unadorned hands have always been so eloquent, and the ring is a distraction, a gewgaw." She felt relieved when Helen consented to wear it only in private.

Helen never revealed to anyone why she was angry with Nella. It seems obvious, however, by her guarded response when Nella cornered her in her study and quizzed her about Polly's jealousy, that she did not like Nella either, but had merely suffered her over the years, as she had Polly. For years she must have known that Nella was studying her every move, recording her incomprehensible sentences for posterity, and analyzing her coldly. "I have always low-rated Helen Keller," Nella once wrote in her diary. Surely, Helen must have been aware of her poor opinion.

At the time of her breakup with Nella, Helen was eighty years old. Polly, who had enslaved her for twenty-four years, was dying. In the short time left to her, Helen must have longed to shed the trappings of her saintlike image. She wanted to wear mink coats and red high heels, to throw away her itchy, uncomfortable wig, and drink martinis.

IN HER OLD AGE, for a brief year or so before she lapsed into invalidism and senility, Helen Keller at last enjoyed some freedom. For the first time in her life, she was surrounded by ordinary people who demanded nothing of her. Although her two new companions, Winnie Corbally and Evelyn Seide, lacked, in the words of one of Helen's friends, "taste and education," they dutifully read to her every evening. Mrs. Corbally even spelled Lampedusa's *The Leopard* to Helen, reading her twenty-two pages a day, which delighted her as the number of pages were what Annie Sullivan used to read to her. Evelyn, too, rose to the occasion, making an effort to dress in a more understated fashion whenever she appeared with Helen on the lecture platform. Unlike the prodigal Polly, Evelyn was an economical woman; under her management, Arcan Ridge was a far less expensive house to maintain. Even Nella, who was saddened by "the dancing over Polly's grave," had to admit that "Helen is enjoying a sense of freedom as she had never known before."

Unlike Polly Thomson, Winnie Corbally did not share Helen's politics. On the contrary, she was a conservative who suspected every liberal of being "a parlor pink," but she was also a bright, warmhearted woman with a sense of humor who was determined that Helen in her old age was going to have a good time. "Those were the fun years," she later recalled. "It was a time of her life when she could have fun. Miss Helen was a rogue. . . . We had oodles of fun. We would go to a hot-dog stand. Polly Thomson would turn over in her grave. She would never allow hot dogs in the house. But Miss Helen loved them. 'Don't forget the mustard,' she would say."

People tried to patch things up between Helen and Nella, but for a long time, whenever Nella's name was spelled to her, Helen swiftly took her hand away. Although eventually Helen called Nella on the phone and asked her how she and her husband, Keith, were doing, things were never the same between them. Possibly Helen sensed that Nella was convinced that without her editorial help, Helen's speeches were no longer any good, and that without Polly to appear with her on the platform, her career as a public figure was over. "Problems: Who will dress Helen now? Not E [Evelyn Seide], she hasn't the taste and the dressmakers at Saks and Bendel's cannot be trusted, they are as willing to take Helen for a ride as anyone else," Nella noted in her journal. "Who will rehearse her speeches with her and stand beside her on the platform as interpreter? I think there will probably be no more major speeches. Who to watch her letters to make sure she is not tricked into support of communism or some ism?"

Although Nella had always portrayed Mildred in an unflattering light, she now identified with her. In her journal she mentioned that Mildred sympathized with her feelings of bewilderment and sadness after the breakup of her friendship with Helen, as she was "cut off for many years by Polly." After Annie Sullivan's death, Mildred had brushed up on her Braille at the Red Cross so as to write directly to Helen. She soon discovered that Polly thought that Mildred was writing Helen things that she didn't want Polly to know. After an argument, Mildred agreed to continue writing Helen letters that Polly would be able to spell to her.

With Evelyn Seide, 1960. Helen was eighty years old.

Ever the arbiter of what constituted the proper image of a handicapped person, Nella was startled to come across a full-page ad in *The Saturday Evening Post* featuring a color photograph of Helen reading the magazine in her living room at Arcan Ridge. It was accompanied by her endorsement of the *Post,* a magazine that Nella ruefully noted that Helen instructed Polly to throw in the trash, along with other magazines she felt sentimentalized her life. Aghast that Helen should endorse a publication she disliked, Nella became convinced that "Polly would never have allowed this and I should have advised against it—a little chipping away of Helen's dignity, another stroke of the new image of her that is emerging." Spitefully, Nella observed that, judging from the photograph, Helen seemed to have put on weight.

Yet Nella was genuinely distressed by their estrangement. For years she had been plagued by nightmares about Helen being by herself, and now she suffered from even more torturing ones. The worst had to do with Helen descending a circular stairway alone. Oblivious of the danger, she walked out the doorway onto a busy street, where a car was speeding toward her.

But Nella could not reconcile herself to the new Helen Keller, a woman who liked to eat hot dogs and get paid for her celebrity endorsements. The passage of time did not soften her opinion of Helen's less-than-spiritual lifestyle. Some years later, in 1962, Nella felt disgusted as she read an article that Helen had written for a Boston newspaper. In Nella's opinion it was a completely undistinguished piece, an exploitation of Helen by the foundation, to which, Nella noted with some horror, Helen had recently bequeathed all her private papers, including her personal correspondence with Mark Twain, Alexander Graham Bell, Albert Einstein, and many other distinguished people. During the years of their friendship, Nella had tried to persuade Helen to leave her papers to the Library of Congress, and Nella was convinced that Helen's recent decision was an ill-considered one. In Nella's mind, the foundation, which was her enemy, would destroy anything libelous or revealing about Helen and her inner circle. But Nella's fears proved unfounded. The foundation treated Helen's legacy respectfully, cataloging her papers and making them available in their unexpurgated entirety to researchers and scholars, as well as preserving the several thousand photographs of her, including the few that were unflattering.

During the 1960s, Nella continued to write Helen. Her letters were simply written, in the hope that Helen, who was now unable to make a decision, could comprehend them. One day, on her way to her country home at Foss Mountain, New Hampshire, Nella dropped by Arcan Ridge to see her former friend. But Helen did not recognize her. Ironically, Nella herself was developing arteriosclerosis and would eventually suffer the same fate as Helen. In December 1973, the woman who prided herself on her gift for words died at home after "going downhill for a long time," according to her husband, Keith, who confided to a friend, "We can no longer communicate because our words do not mean the same things to us, and so we can only guess what she is trying to tell us."

As she grew older, Nella worried about the disposition of her own papers and journals, which included her invaluable interviews with Annie Sullivan during the final years of her life. Convinced that she could not leave them to the foundation because they contained "libelous" observations of many people associated with the organization, she bequeathed them to the Perkins School, which Annie Sullivan, her idol as a hearing-sighted person, had attended.

IN HER LAST YEARS, Helen did little work for the American Foundation for the Blind. She spent more time with her relatives in Montgomery and, for the first time in many years, seemed to relish the experience. Hearing about Helen's relaxed work schedule and her newfound delight in her family made her friends wonder if they had misjudged her. Perhaps she had never been cut out for the career of service that Annie Sullivan had pushed her to follow. If she had not become deaf-blind, possibly she would have led the kind of life of her mother, living out her unremarkable days as a bright but frustrated housewife and mother in a small southern town.

CHAPTER 26

"A Fragile Porcelain Lady"

I N OCTOBER 1961, Helen Keller had finished her cocktail at Jimmy Adams's estate in Greenwich, Connecticut, and was walking toward the dining room, with Winnie Corbally's assistance, when Helen announced, "I feel funny."

Mrs. Corbally made her sit down on a bench for a few moments. She seemed to feel better, and everyone felt relieved when she went into the dining room and enjoyed a hearty lunch. Later, people noticed that she had trouble standing when she returned home. Her personal physician, Dr. Morris Chick, was called. After examining Helen, he quickly concluded that she had suffered a slight stroke and put her in Bridgeport Hospital for tests.

In the hospital, Helen's mind wandered. She imagined that she was back in the old Wrentham farmhouse with Annie Sullivan and John Macy, the place where she had spent some of the happiest days of her life.

Dr. Chick swiftly reached a prognosis. "It is my opinion that Miss Keller has reached a stage in her life where she will have to completely retire from public appearances and from here on will have to be cared for with round-the-clock nursing service," he wrote to Evelyn Seide. "She is not now, and probably never will be, capable of taking long trips or attending benefits. I suppose we must all realize that Miss Helen is eighty-one years of age and old age comes to all of us. . . . Her condition is static, and I cannot offer much hope for further improvement. I think we can be glad that she seems content and is in no obvious distress."

Other minor strokes followed, which were complicated by diabetes, and for the next seven years Helen was confined to her wheelchair and bed. On the rare days when she felt up to it, Winnie and Evelyn read to her. "Miss Helen continues well, but growing older, and of course, being in the 'sunset' time of life she is no longer able to get around her home by herself," Winnie Corbally wrote a friend in 1966. "It is very important that she does not fall . . . she is like a fragile porcelain lady."

IN 1964 Helen was one of thirty Americans on whom President Lyndon Johnson conferred the Presidential Medal of Freedom, the nation's highest

At age eighty-three

civilian award. A year later, she was one of twenty women elected to the Women's Hall of Fame at the New York World's Fair. Among the hundred nominees, she and Eleanor Roosevelt received the most votes. Those around Helen sensed that she was unaware of the two honors.

AFTER SEVEN YEARS of illness and invalidism, Helen Adams Keller died on Saturday afternoon, June 1, 1968, at Arcan Ridge. She had lived almost her entire life in gray silence and comprehended the world by the manual finger language, Braille, and lipreading as well as by her senses of smell, taste, and touch. It was a few weeks before her eighty-eighth birthday. A few days earlier she had suffered a heart attack. Winnie Corbally was at her bedside when she died. The woman who had never feared death "drifted off in her sleep. She died gently," Winnie later said.

At her request, Helen's remains were cremated. Unlike Laura Bridgman, on whom Victorian doctors had performed a hasty postmortem in a search for the secrets of the soul, no autopsy was performed. This lack of a postmortem disturbed many physicians, who felt that one might have revealed "the cause and extent of the damage to her ears and eyes." At least one doctor believed that it was not scarlet fever that had caused Helen's blindness and deafness, but a rubella epidemic that had occurred in Alabama at the time of her illness, with seventeen recorded deaths.

After Polly's death, Helen had arranged for a Swedenborgian minister of The New Church in New York to officiate at her own funeral service in Westport, Connecticut. But this ceremony never took place, although the Swedenborgians later held their own memorial service for Helen in New York, which, according to one person who attended it, was beautiful and affecting.

Although Helen had been a devout Swedenborgian for most of her life, her family and trustees disregarded her wishes about their participation at her funeral. Four years before his sister's death, Phillips Keller, Helen's brother, had written Winnie Corbally that he and his wife wanted a prominent Presbyterian minister to conduct the funeral service for Helen at the Congregational Church in Westport. "The Kellers all started out as Presbyterians and Sister Mildred, her daughter, and their families [sic] are all life long Presbyterians. . . . I understand at one time Sister Helen was more or less interested in the Swedenborgian faith with which none of us are very familiar, and I am also sure that she has had little connection with or interest in Swedenborgian. I might also add that I do not believe those people are overly interested in Sister Helen."

Phillips was relieved when several months before his sister's death, Helen's trustees decided to cancel the service for her in Connecticut. "Just a note to express to you again the appreciation of the Keller family for the changes you are making in the funeral arrangements when and as required. We never went for the Swedenborgian stuff at all and it was hanging regretfully over our heads."

In the years following her death, Helen's radicalism would be similarly overlooked by both her family and organizations aiding the blind, and perhaps with some justification, considering the negative connotation of socialism and Communism in the last third of the twentieth century. A recent photography exhibit on her life in Montgomery, Alabama, that was sponsored by a relative did not mention her debatable political activities, nor did a traveling exhibit sponsored by the American Foundation for the Blind. Pamphlets about her life, distributed by the foundation and other institutions with which her name is associated, describe her personal victory over deafness and blindness and her work to achieve equal rights for people with handicaps. Missing from her curriculum vitae are her militant socialism and the fact that she once had to be protected by six policemen from an admiring crowd of two thousand people in New York after delivering a fiery speech protesting America's entry into World War I. The war, she had told her audience to thunderous applause, was a capitalistic ploy to further enslave the workers. As in her lifetime, Helen Keller's public image remains one of an angelic, sexless deaf-blind woman who is smelling a rose as she holds a Braille book open on her lap.

FOLLOWING HELEN'S CREMATION in Bridgeport, Connecticut, a funeral service was held in Washington, D.C., at the National Cathedral, where Woodrow Wilson was buried. Twelve hundred mourners, led by Chief Justice of the United States and Mrs. Earl Warren, honored Helen's memory in a nondenominational service. The public memorial was attended by other well-known figures as well as by many deaf and blind people, including the choir of the Perkins School, which filled the nave with a crystalline sound, and Poh Lin Chan of Singapore, a highly accomplished young deaf-blind student at Perkins who had come to be known as "the Helen Keller of Southeast Asia."

Later, in a private interment in the columbarium of the Chapel of St. Joseph of Arimathea, the urn containing Helen's ashes was deposited next to those of Annie Sullivan and Polly Thomson. Ever since Annie's demise thirty-two years before, Helen had been convinced that at the moment of her own death, she would see her teacher, the only human being she had ever truly loved. "What is so sweet as to awake from a troubled dream and behold a beloved face smiling upon you? I have to believe that such shall be our awakening from earth to heaven," she had written in *My Religion*.

Then her family and friends departed from the chapel, leaving behind the mortal remains of a woman who in death, as in life, remained the epitome of humanity's triumph over limitation and despair.

But Helen's final resting place was not destined to be soundless, like her life. All day long the Chapel of St. Joseph of Arimathea resounds with the bright chatter of schoolchildren who have come to visit her grave and to learn from their teachers about the remarkable achievements of a severely handicapped person. As they leave the predominantly Romanesque chapel, with its magnificent mural painted above the altar that tells the story of Christ's entombment, more often than not, the curious children rub their fingers across a bronze plaque that informs them in Braille that "Helen Keller and her beloved companion Anne Sullivan Macy are interred in the columbarium behind this chapel." So many children have touched and worn away the Braille dots that the plaque has been replaced twice.

CHAPTER 27

Helen's Legacy

The public must learn that the blind man is neither a genius nor a freak nor an idiot. He has a mind which can be educated, a hand which can be trained, ambitions which it is right for him to strive to realize, and it is the duty of the public to help him make the best of himself so that he can win light through work.

—HELEN KELLER, 1907

H ELEN KELLER CALLED the deaf-blind "the loneliest people on earth," yet in the thirty years since her death, two men who became deaf-blind early in life have approached her accomplishments. Although not world-famous, they have led a more autonomous, normal life, a goal that was Helen's dream. "My whole desire has been to have my own door key, and go and come like people who can see," she once told an interviewer. Unfortunately, she was never able to live independently.

At five years of age, Robert Smithdas was stricken with cerebral spinal meningitis that left him blind, and eventually deaf at twelve years old. An acclaimed poet, he was the first deaf-blind person, after Helen Keller, to graduate from college and the first deaf-blind person ever to earn a master's degree. A vital, broad-shouldered man who was an accomplished wrestler and swimmer in his youth, Smithdas was for many years in charge of the deaf-blind department at the Industrial Home for the Blind in Brooklyn, New York. Unmarried at the time, he lived alone, cooking his own meals and conversing with friends on a special phone that enabled him to receive messages in the form of electronic pulsations on his fingertips, and often traveling independently through the Brooklyn streets.

"The general public has a misconception about deaf-blind people," Smithdas once said. "Each has a definite personality all his own. We are pretty realistic. Also we don't see darkness or blackness. To me, it just appears as a void, empty of color. Others I know think of it as light without things, without objects."

Like Helen Keller and Robert Smithdas, Leonard Dowdy was born a normal, healthy, active baby until he was sticken at age nineteen months with spinal meningitis. For nine weeks he lay in a coma with a temperature between 104 and 105 degrees. When he regained consciousness, it was discovered that he had lost both sight and hearing. Dowdy, an exuberant, outgoing man with a quick wit, has recently retired after more than thirty years' employment. He is married to a woman who is also deaf-blind.

Today the deaf-blind community includes many highly accomplished people who are partially deaf and blind or have become completely deaf-blind in later life. Both Deborah G. Groeber and Georgia Griffith were born missing one sense, then became deaf-blind some years later. An attractive, athletic blonde who could be mistaken for a model or a cheerleader, Groeber was deaf as an infant. After she learned to lip-read, an operation restored her hearing. When she was eight, her eyesight deteriorated, and she was diagnosed as having Stargardt's disease, a hereditary eye disease that in some cases is accompanied by deafness. Despite her disabilities, Groeber earned an M.B.A. from the Wharton School at the University of Pennsylvania, graduated from Columbia University Law School, and currently practices at a Philadelphia law firm. She lived on her own before getting married and is an avid skier and aerobic dancer.

Griffith, whom a friend has admiringly called "the Helen Keller of the technological age," currently serves as the host for five popular Compu-Serve on-line forums on politics, current events, and religion. She works on several computers that have been adapted to let her read the screen in Braille. Griffith, who was born blind due to a damaged optical nerve and completely lost her hearing when she was thirty-nine, calls the Internet "my window on the world. Gradually it has gotten larger and I can see more and more."

Other extraordinary deaf-blind people include the late Richard Kinney,

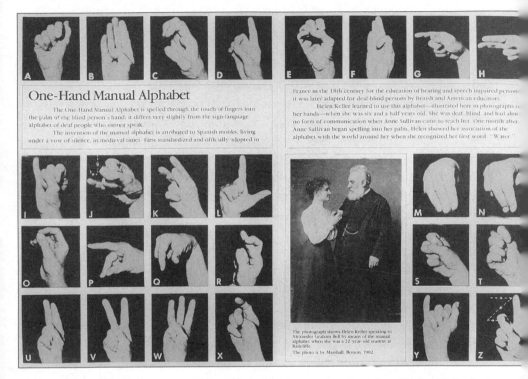

The one-hand manual alphabet, illustrated here in photographs of Helen Keller's hands, is spelled through the touch of fingers into the palm of the blind person's hand; it differs very slightly from the sign-language alphabet of deaf people who cannot speak.

The invention of the manual alphabet is attributed to Spanish monks, living under a vow of silence, in medieval times. First standardized and officially adopted in France in the eighteenth century for the education of hearing-impaired and speech-impaired persons, it was later adapted for deaf-blind persons by British and American educators.

a published poet and a summa cum laude college graduate who was the executive director of the Hadley School for the Blind and the father of a son; the late Geraldine Lawhorn, who studied piano and acting and who performed monologues onstage in the style of Ruth Draper, including a performance at Carnegie Hall; the late Helen May Martin, an accomplished deaf-blind pianist; Dolores Follett, who is married and the mother of three children; Jackie Coker, for many years a rehabilitation teacher for the blind employed by the state of California; and Michelle Smithdas, who is married to Robert Smithdas. Mrs. Smithdas, who was born hard of hearing, became deaf at sixteen and then blind as a result of a snowmobile accident during her senior year in college. Like her husband, she has a master's degree and works with him on behalf of the deaf-blind at the Helen Keller National Center for Deaf-Blind Youths and Adults.

Unlike most deaf-blind people who are educated in either a school for the blind or for the deaf, the late Helen Schultz Hayes, who lost her sight and hearing in childhood, received most of her education in New Jersey public schools. In contrast to Helen Keller, she did not have a private teacher-companion on whom she was dependent. Eventually she married the nephew of her adoptive mother and maintained her right to a normal life.

Today relatively few deaf-blind people suffer from Helen Keller's condition—that is, being completely deaf and blind from an early age. The life-threatening childhood infections such as meningitis and scarlet fever have been for the most part eradicated, and the simultaneous onset of blindness and deafness seldom occurs.

In general, deafness precedes blindness. Today 50 percent of the deaf-blind population suffer from Usher syndrome, a genetic condition characterized by hearing loss and by retinitis pigmentosa, an irreversible condition causing night blindness, progressive loss of peripheral vision, and eventual total blindness in middle age. There are two types of Usher syndrome, and both are devastating for the patient, who is typically a teenager when his or her condition is diagnosed, and their family. In Type I, the child is born profoundly deaf, with absent vestibular function, leading to a poor sense of balance, and retinitis pigmentosa. In Type II, children are born hard of hearing with retinitis pigmentosa and normal balance. Unlike people with Type I, who usually attend a school for the deaf, communicate in American Sign Language, and are part of the deaf community, those with Type II often grow up attending regular school and identify with hearing-sighted people.

People suffering from both types of Usher syndrome are faced with not only a grim prognosis but also social ostracism. As they lose their sight, people with Usher syndrome I are often shunned by the deaf community, with which they shared a common identity, language, and culture, and in many cases from their parents, many of whom refuse to learn sign language and keep secret their prognosis of eventual total blindness. Those suffering from Usher syndrome II are equally marginalized by the hearing-sighted world. Their loneliness and sense of isolation are indescribable. Despairing about the future, many contemplate or attempt suicide, and it is only through counseling and meeting other people like themselves at such rehabilitation centers as the Helen Keller Center for Deaf-Blind Youths and Adults that they are able to adjust philosophically, psychologically, and socially to the prospect of becoming completely deaf and blind.

THE EDUCATION OF deaf-blind persons has changed since the days of Helen Keller and Annie Sullivan. In the early 1930s Dr. Gabriel Farrell, the director of the Perkins Institution, changed the policy whereby a deaf-blind student was assigned to a special teacher who taught him or her exclusively. If she were a deaf-blind child being taught today, Helen Keller would be taught by several teachers, not one, to discourage a symbiotic relationship.

However, Annie Sullivan's innovative teaching method of talking into Helen's hand as a mother of a normal infant talks into a baby's ear and of instructing her in natural environments are still considered the best methods of teaching a deaf-blind person. In contrast, Dr. Howe's methods of teaching Laura Bridgman by labeling common objects with raised print have been questioned by some teachers who feel that Laura's gestures should have been used "as a starting point for beginning communication intervention."

Experts in special education generally agree that the outstanding academic and literary career of Helen Keller, an intelligent woman who was not a genius, was largely due to her teacher, who prodded her to persevere and excel. As the sociologist Herbert Rusalem once said of Annie Sullivan: "Perhaps the real miracle was a statistical one. Of all the possible teachers who could have been assigned to Helen Keller, the task fell to the one teacher in a million who was equal to the task."

But Helen's success in overcoming her disabilities was not solely due to Annie Sullivan's brilliance as a teacher. It also was related to both the nature of her handicaps and the age at which she developed them. Helen was fortunate to see and hear until she was nineteen months of age and to recover from her life-threatening illness without neurological impairment or additional handicaps. According to the following Gesell's developmental tests, her vision, by age nineteen months, would have gone through several crucial stages:

At 1 week: baby stares without fixation.

4–12 weeks: looks at mother's face, adults' hands, and own hands; face brightens.

6 weeks: starey gaze, true inspection, follows retreating figure of mother, a moment of searching, more alert, adaptive.

16 weeks: protracted moment of staring, knows mother, sobers when she sees strangers.

24 weeks: recurrence of regard.

28 weeks: perceptual behavior; interest in own abilities, can be content alone, concentrates on an object.

40–52 weeks: inquisitive visual and motor behavior; intent on regarding what other person does; perceptive moods, gives and takes.

52–56 weeks: imitates.

As far as her hearing was concerned, Helen, by nineteen months, would have been able to follow simple requests such as "Come here" and correctly identify body parts such as the nose or mouth.

Finally, according to Jean Piaget's theory of cognitive development, she would have reached the sixth stage, "Internationalization of Thought (eighteen months to two years)," in which "the child needs no longer engage in overt trial and error behavior but rather can think about possible behaviors and the effects that they would have. . . ."

HELEN KELLER'S LIFELONG DREAM was to learn to speak clearly, a goal she never accomplished despite years of laborious practice. In contrast, Robert Smithdas and Leonard Dowdy have remarkably clear, pleasant speaking voices with a different method of lipreading and speaking from the one that Helen was taught in the early 1900s. They can carry on a comprehensible conversation with anyone with whom they come in contact. The Tadoma method, as it is called, teaches deaf-blind students to speechread and to speak by placing their fingers on the speaker's mouth, jaw, and throat to feel the vibrations of speech and the placement of the lips and then to place their fingers on their own face to duplicate these movements and vibrations. The philosophy behind Tadoma, which was invented by Sophie Alcorn and named after two deaf-blind children, Tad Chapman and Oma Simpson, to whom she had taught it successfully, was that a deaf-blind person had to learn to speak to get along in a hearing society. The Tadoma method was popular in the 1930s, where it was taught by Inis Hall at the Perkins Institution to a number of deaf-blind people, and teachers came from all over the world to learn it. It eventually fell into disfavor in the mid-1960s during a rubella epidemic in which there was an enormous increase in the number of deaf-blind children with additional disabilities who could not use it. In addition, many in the deaf community who use American Sign Language as their primary mode of communication have rejected Tadoma as an oral method that is unnatural to them.

If she were alive today, Helen's life as a deaf-blind woman would be radically different from her cloistered existence in the first half of the twentieth century, in which only a select few could communicate with her directly. Like some women of succeeding generations who became deaf-blind later in life, she undoubtedly would have married, although it is debatable whether she would have borne children.

A visionary who once wrote "there are two worlds: the world that we can measure with line and rule, and the world that we feel with our heart and imagination," Helen would have been baffled by our high-tech world, with its impersonality, speed, and fragmentation. Nevertheless, she would have benefited from the technological advances that in the last quarter of the twentieth century have revolutionized the lives of the deaf-blind and the blind. For her entire life, Helen attained the majority of her knowledge about the outside world literally secondhand—first through Annie's hand and later through Polly's—and longed to be able to communicate directly with the average person who did not know the manual finger language or Braille. Today an adaptive device that is attached to a standard personal computer enables blind and deaf-blind people who read and write Braille to send and receive messages or print in Braille. With such a device Helen would have been able to communicate with anyone in the world in cyberspace, whether or not they knew Braille, without the need of an interpreter, possessive or otherwise.

ALL HER LIFE, Helen Keller envisioned not only a better tomorrow for the disabled but also a better world for everyone in which social fairness prevailed. "The highest result of education is tolerance," she observed,

Melbourne, Australia, 1948

adding, "When indeed shall we learn that we are all related to the other, that we are all members of the same body? Until the spirit of love for our fellow men, regardless of race, color, or creed, shall fill the world . . . social justice can never be attained."

In this new world of Helen's dreams, a person's handicap would not stand in the way of his or her finding employment and personal fulfillment, and the disabled would be welcomed into society whether or not they were geniuses, talented, attractive, or well-to-do.

In Helen's enlightened society, where a person's individuality and worth are considered first and his or her disability second, if at all, there would be no "Helen Kellers," no perfect symbols of a handicapped person to make us less afraid of our own human fragility. In the disabled, we would discover ourselves.

Despite Helen's dream of a better future for the handicapped, the sad truth is that with the dawn of the third millennium, the blind and other disabled people are still struggling to achieve equality and employment. Of the 9.7 million blind or visually impaired in the United States, only 26 percent of people between ages twenty-one and sixty-four have jobs.

"The only lightless dark is the night of ignorance and insensibility," Helen wrote. "We differ, blind and seeing, one from another, not in our senses, but in the use we make of them, in the imagination and courage with which we seek wisdom beyond the senses."

Works by Helen Keller

The Story of My Life, 1903

Optimism: An Essay, 1903

The World I Live In, 1908

The Song of the Stone Wall, 1910

Out of the Dark, 1913

My Religion, 1927

Midstream: My Later Life, 1929

Peace at Eventide, 1932

Helen Keller in Scotland, 1933

Helen Keller's Journal, 1938

Let Us Have Faith, 1941

Teacher: Anne Sullivan Macy, 1955

The Open Door, 1957

Helen Keller: Her Socialist Years,
edited by Philip S. Foner, 1967

Notes

HELEN KELLER'S *The Story of My Life* is still in print, but the current editions of this classic work contain only the letters that she wrote to her family and friends between 1887 and 1901 and omit the more fascinating supplementary account of her education, including the letters that Annie Sullivan wrote to Mrs. Sophia Hopkins over a fifteen-month period. When John Macy edited *The Story of My Life*, he borrowed these letters from Mrs. Sophia Hopkins, although he did not print all of them. Afterward the originals were stored in the attic of the house he shared with Annie Sullivan and Helen Keller in Wrentham, Massachusetts. Subsequently there was a leak in the roof, and the water that dripped on the letters during rainstorms reduced them to a pulp. Fortunately, Annie's absorbing account of the first days she spent with her pupil at Ivy Green in Tuscumbia, Alabama, was preserved in Macy's "Supplementary Account," and the interested reader is referred to the 1903 edition of *The Story of My Life* that was published by Doubleday, Page & Company.

Helen's papers, which she donated to the American Foundation for the Blind (AFB), present some unique problems for the researcher. Not only did she take notes in Braille, correspond with other blind persons in Braille, and have reading material translated into Braille, but she also did her own typing and often neglected to make carbon copies. In addition, the papers she kept in her home, Arcan Ridge, between 1932 and 1946 were destroyed by fire. According to Marguerite L. Levine, the former archivist at the foundation, after 1946 she transferred her papers to the AFB on a fairly regular basis. "The task of filling these many gaps is not an easy one," she noted.

Although all of Helen's own papers were supposedly destroyed in the fire, her archives at the foundation contain many personal documents predating 1947. This discrepancy prompted Miss Levine to write Nella Braddy Henney in 1971, asking her whether she had them in her custody at the time of the fire and thus was able to preserve them from destruction. Nella replied, however, that she had never held any Helen Keller documents, and they must have been given to the foundation by Helen and Annie. Annie, in fact, had donated papers to the foundation in October 1932. Unfortunately, the last four years of her life remain scantily documented, as any letters or journals she kept during this period were destroyed in the fire that destroyed Arcan Ridge fourteen years later.

ABBREVIATIONS

The following abbreviations and short titles are used in the notes:

 AFB Helen Keller Archives, American Foundation for the Blind, New York, New York
 PSB Nella Braddy Henney Collection, Perkins School for the Blind, Watertown, Massachusetts
VOLTA Alexander Graham Bell Association for the Deaf, Washington, D.C.
  AS Antiquarian Society, Worcester, Massachusetts

Preface

p. xiii "not quite seven years old," Mary Jo Salter, "Helen Keller: The Achiever," *New York Times Magazine,* Nov. 24, 1996, p. 61.

  xv "If I could see," quoted in Helen Keller's obituary, *New York Times,* June 2, 1968, p. 1.

CHAPTER 1 *Helen*

 4 "a religious figure," Georgette Leblanc, *The Girl Who Found the Bluebird* (New York: Dodd, Mead, 1914), pp. 111–12.

  "Physically she was large for her years," Laurence Hutton, *Talks in a Library with Laurence Hutton* (New York: G. P. Putnam's Sons, 1905), p. 385.

  The strange quivers, Leblanc, pp. 34–35.

 5 "It's not Teacher!," Helen Keller, *Helen Keller's Journal* (New York: Doubleday, Doran, 1938), p. 277.

  "in a great green place," PSB.

  "seeing flakes of light," ibid.

 6 skin sloughed off in patches, ibid.

  "How d'ye," Helen Keller, *The Story of My Life* (New York: Doubleday, Page, 1903), p. 6.

  "by the flickering shadows of leaves," ibid., p. 7.

  Her vision was excellent, Helen Keller, *Midstream: My Later Life* (New York: Doubleday, Doran, 1929), p. 216.

  "a gentleman farmer," PSB.

  "a man of limited ideas," ibid.

  "next to his family," Keller, *The Story of My Life,* p. 15.

 8 "Mildred Campbell," ibid., p. 6.

 11 "so dry and hot," ibid., p. 7.

  "to the wall," op. cit.

  Medical tests, Frederick Tilney, M.D., "A Comparative Sensory Analysis of Helen Keller and Laura Bridgman," *Archives of Neurology and Psychiatry* (June 1929): 1242.

  "I was too young," Keller, AFB.

  killed in infancy, Edward Waterhouse, *The Education of the Deaf-Blind in the United States of America, 1837–1967,* p. 5.

  In ancient Greece, Frances A. Koestler, *The Unseen Minority: A Social History of Blindness in the United States* (New York: David A. McKay, 1976), p. 2.

 12 pinched her Grandma Adams, Helen Keller to Mildred Keller, June 9, 1933, PSB.

  "Fate ambushed," PSB.

  crude signs, Keller, *The Story of My Life,* pp. 9–11.

  "I cannot recall," ibid., p. 9.

 13 "Sometimes I stood," ibid., p. 10.

CHAPTER 2 *Laura*

14 Medical tests, Tilney, "A Comparative Sensory Analysis of Helen Keller and Laura Bridgman," p. 1244.

15 "he so combined," quoted in Koestler, *The Unseen Minority*, p. 396.
Howe met Julia, ibid., p. 453.

17 "... blind, deaf and dumb," Charles Dickens, *American Notes, 1842, The Works of Charles Dickens*, Vol. 14, National Library Editions (New York: Bigelow, Brown, undated).
The fear, Koestler, *The Unseen Minority*, p. 3.

18 Most wills of the period, Charles Panati, *Panati's Extraordinary Endings of Practically Everything and Everybody* (New York: Harper & Row, 1989), p. 41.

19 his life and fictional world, Fred Kaplan, *Dickens: A Biography* (New York: William Morrow, 1988), pp. 94–95.
"as a real girl," Elisabeth Gitter, "Deaf-mutes and Heroines in the Victorian Era," *Victorian Literature and Culture*, Vol. 20 (New York: AMS Press, 1993), p. 186.

20 the protean idealist, Harold Schwartz, *Samuel Gridley Howe: Social Reformer, 1801–1876* (Cambridge, Mass.: Harvard University Press, 1956), p. 327.
He convinced Laura, Gitter, *Deaf-Mutes and Heroines*, p. 188.

21 An avid exerciser, Mary Swift Lamson, *Life and Education of Laura Dewey Bridgman* (Boston: New England Publishing Co., 1879), p. 143.
She loved pretty dresses, ibid., p. 85.
estimate the age of her visitors, Tilney, *A Comparative Sensory Analysis*, p. 1257.
"a remarkable sense of direction," ibid., p. 1255.
"W-A-S-H Y-O-U-R D-I-R-T-Y P-A-W-S!," Nella Braddy (Henney), *Anne Sullivan Macy: The Story Behind Helen Keller* (New York: Doubleday, Doran, 1933), p. 113.
    Like Laura Bridgman, Helen Keller hated dust. "You see too much," her friends used to tell her when she complained of noticing it.
physical and mental strain, Lamson, *Life and Education of Laura Dewey Bridgman*, p. 315.

23 "from other brains," Henry H. Donaldson, "Anatomical Observations on the Brain and Several Sense-Organs of the Blind-Deaf Mute, Laura Dewey Bridgman," *American Journal of Psychology* (Sept. 1890), pp. 293–338.

24 "There's a gentleman in Washington," Keller, *The Story of My Life*, p. 19.
Bell's mother, Eliza, Robert V. Bruce, *Alexander Graham Bell and the Conquest of Solitude* (Boston: Little, Brown, 1973), p. 14.

25 "The value of speech," ibid., p. 322.
"no uncommon occurrence," ibid., p. 321.
"But I did not dream," Keller, *The Story of My Life*, p. 19.
"chillingly empty," Bruce, *Alexander Graham Bell*, p. 400.

CHAPTER 3 *Annie*

27 "an idle, quarrelsome, and disorderly class," PSB.

28 "She would be so pretty," ibid.
"long, thin fingers," Braddy, *Anne Sullivan Macy*, p. 6.
"Mother had been taken," PSB.

30 Of the twenty-seven foundlings, Braddy, *Anne Sullivan Macy*, p. 16.
"Jimmie used to tease," ibid., p. 18.
"Jimmie tried to stand up," PSB.

31 "The light from the half-window," Braddy, *Anne Sullivan Macy*, pp. 26–27.
"longed desperately to die," ibid., p. 28.

32 "Beggars, thieves, whores," ibid., p. 45.
"a queer fascinated antagonism for men," op. cit.
"bright colors," ibid., p. 32.
"a small, incidental figure," PSB.

33 paupers' corpses, Braddy, *Anne Sullivan Macy*, p. 60.
   "trysting in courtyards," PSB.
   "sweet, virginal and inexperienced," Braddy, *Anne Sullivan Macy*, p. 66.
   "My mind was a question mark," ibid., p. 68.
34 "All of her life," PSB.
   "sitting beside her window," ibid., p. 73.
35 "always been able to see," ibid., p. 77.
   "asking one moonlight winter night," ibid., p. 82.
36 "richly musical," ibid., p. 84.
   with her curling iron, ibid., p. 93.
37 "The thought of Mrs. Hopkins' kindness," ibid., pp. 94–95.
   "Sewing and crocheting," ibid., p. 68.
38 "My Dear Annie," Michael Anagnos to Annie Sullivan, Aug. 26, 1886, PSB.
39 "in a sleeping-car," PSB.
40 "The loneliness in my heart," Annie Sullivan to Mrs. Hopkins, undated, quoted in Braddy, *Anne Sullivan Macy*, p. 118.
   "my little pupil," Annie Sullivan to Michael Anagnos, quoted in Joseph Lash, *Helen and Teacher: The Story of Helen Keller and Anne Sullivan Macy* (New York: Delacorte Press/Seymour Lawrence, 1980), p. 58.
41 "There was Helen standing by the porch-door," Anne Sullivan to Mrs. Sophia Hopkins, Mar. 4, 1888, quoted in Keller, *The Story of My Life*, p. 299.
   "an inane swaying," Richard Slaytown French, *From Homer to Helen Keller: A Social and Educational Study of the Blind* (New York: American Foundation for the Blind, 1932), pp. 20–21.
   According to Nella Braddy Henney, although Helen was almost completely free from the nervous habits known as blindisms, if she had to wait for any length of time, her body swayed from side to side almost imperceptibly. "Once at a political meeting, when all that was worth spelling had been given to her," Nella reported, "this swaying became so apparent that at least one person in the audience thought she had lost emotional control of herself."
   "If Helen had been deformed," Braddy, *Anne Sullivan Macy*, p. 119.
42 "a pale, delicate child," quoted in Keller, *The Story of My Life*, p. 304.
43 "I let her see that I was eating," ibid., p. 307.
   "She was greatly excited at first," ibid., p. 310.
44 "My heart is singing for joy," ibid., p. 311.
45 "Force was wasted," Helen Keller, *Teacher* (New York: Doubleday, 1956), pp. 49–50.
   "In a previous letter," Keller, *The Story of My Life*, p. 316.
46 "Before my teacher came to me," Keller, *The World I Live In*, p. 113.
   "nothing could be more false," John Albert Macy, PSB.
47 "There was a great rumpus," Keller, *The Story of My Life*, pp. 328–30.
49 "The experience of the deaf-blind person," Helen Keller, *The World I Live In* (New York: The Century Co., 1908).
   "overflows my soul like a tide," Annie Sullivan to Mrs. Hopkins, PSB.
51 "a child—my child," ibid.
   "nearer perfect than any human being I ever dreamed of," Annie Sullivan to Michael Anagnos, Apr. 2, 1888, AS.

CHAPTER 4 *Helen and Annie*
52 "rang, rippled, danced," Keller, *Teacher*, p. 73.
53 "normal child's capacity," Braddy, *Anne Sullivan Macy*, p. 128.
   "What happened at the well-house," Keller, *Teacher*, pp. 43–44.
   "Long before I learned to do a sum in arithmetic," AFB.
54 "came into the room one day laughing merrily," Keller, *Teacher*, p. 44.
   "the buried impressions of ages," PSB.

Notes

353

"It actually seemed," ibid.
"the most wonderful sight," Annie Sullivan to Mrs. Hopkins, undated letter, AFB.
"very fond of dress," 55th Annual Report of the Perkins Institution and Massachusetts School for the Blind, 1887.
55 "And right here," Annie Sullivan to Mrs. Hopkins, quoted in Braddy, *Anne Sullivan Macy*, p. 139.
56 "And how are we to keep her from thinking?" Annie Sullivan to Michael Anagnos, quoted in Lash, *Helen and Teacher*, p. 58.
"I do wish things would stop being born!" Annie Sullivan to Sophia Hopkins, Aug. 28, 1887, quoted in *The Story of My Life*, pp. 331–32.
57 "My work occupies my mind, heart, and body," Annie Sullivan to Sophia Hopkins, quoted in Lash, *Helen and Teacher*, p. 77.
"Have I not all my life been lonely?," Annie Sullivan to Mrs. Hopkins, Mar. 4, 1888, AFB.
58 "I got up, washed my face," Keller, *The Story of My Life*, p. 346.
When Helen first began to write, it was in pencil with the help of a board with parallel grooves to indicate the height of the letters. The letter was shaped with the right hand while the forefinger of the left hand completed the movement. It was a laborious process, especially with a perfectionist such as Annie Sullivan at her side, and a number of her early letters end with "I am tired" or "I am too tired to write more."
In the February 1995 issue of *Ziegler* magazine, it was also pointed out that "Helen was very skilled in a handwriting technique that uses the shape of a rectangle as a mental template for forming the shapes of print letters. To give you an idea of how this works, the letter 'H' in her name looks like the two sides of a rectangle with no lines at the top or base, but with a horizontal line running at the center from one side to the other. The letter 'L' is simply a vertical line with a short straight line at its base, as if forming the left side and half the baseline of a rectangle. The letter 'K' requires rather more skill, being formed by a line drawn at an angle from top and bottom right-hand corners of a rectangle to meet at the middle of a line forming the left side of the rectangle. Helen Keller used a ruler or straight-edge to align the bases of the letters. Curiously enough, this system has had a hi-tech reincarnation in electronic displays and dot matrix printers that generate the shapes of letters and numbers by means of dots or lines within a rectangular format."
Later in her life, after Helen had mastered the touch system of the typewriter, she was on equal terms with any typist, except that in the dark she could not manage carbons because they smeared. Like many correspondents of her time, she apologized for her first personal letters on the typewriter, but this was to be the method by which she wrote all her letters, except those in Braille to her blind friends. To intimate friends, even her signature was likely to be typed.
59 "she seems to live in a sort of double life," PSB.
"The years have not destroyed the magic," ibid.
learned the manual finger alphabet. The manual alphabet is as easy to learn as the ABC's. A young friend of Helen's who was a preschooler wanted to learn it so he could talk with her and was dismayed to find that he couldn't learn it until he had learned to spell.
"It was only the intellectual side of herself," PSB.
60 "this gentleman was as argumentative," ibid.
"as though a hurricane," Annie Sullivan to Michael Anagnos, undated, AS.
"The untidy, shiftless manner," PSB.
61 "I rejoice to be able to tell you," Annie Sullivan to Mrs. Hopkins, ibid.
"Miss Annie, I thank God," Keller, *The Story of My Life*, p. 343.
62 "She seemed very much troubled for a few moments," Annie Sullivan to Michael Anagnos (Jan. 13, 1888), AS.

Dorothy Burlingham, a child psychologist and associate of Anna Freud who closely observed a group of children in an institution for the blind in Vienna during the 1940s, describes an eight-year-old boy named Jacob, who had been completely blind since birth. One of Jacob's passions was collecting postcards and stamps, which he could not tell apart and that he gave away to his teachers and the seeing children in the institute. Burlingham was baffled by his avid collecting until she realized that "his presents were not a sign of friendship but rather a way of wooing and bribing people. He understood that he needed the seeing adults and children and that they would be more inclined to do something for him if he could do something for them. By giving presents, he strengthened his sense of security; he bribed people in the hope that they would lead him, take care of him and protect him from dangers.

". . . A remarkable degree of compliance is observed in all our children," Burlingham continued. "They have learned from experience how dependent they have to be on those with sight, into how many dangers they run, and how many of their wishes are unobtainable when they are on their own. But this manifest compliance is no more than a thin disguise which hides the revolt against dependency. The latter shows in a tense posture, a clenched fist, etc."

In Burlingham's opinion, "the blind are a minority in a world which is focused on the characteristics, needs, accomplishments, and behavior of the seeing. . . . It is therefore hardly possible to study the mental processes of the blind undistorted by the influences which are brought to bear on them from their sighted environment.

". . . Every one of these children realized at a very early age that the world around them was a seeing one, that he was blind, defective, and therefore an exception. . . . They tried to imitate the sighted in every possible way, thereby adjusting to this world as far as they could. They do not for a moment forget that they are blind, but their main goal in life is to make others forget it, i.e., to cover up their blindness.

". . . The reaction of seeing people to the blind is one which the blind meet at a very early age, and one which is apt to make them very much aware of their blindness and of being different from those who see. . . . Every sighted person who is not familiar with the blind through daily contact with them meets them with shyness and embarrassment, sometimes even with dislike and repulsion. . . . We know that this fear—as dread of a defect in oneself—comes into play not only in regard to the blind but in regard to all cripples.

". . . This relationship between the blind child and his seeing environment gives rise to his double life, which consumes the greater part of his psychic energies. Their constantly being in contact with the world of the sighted, which differs considerably from their own, continually interferes with their capacity to adapt to life on the basis of their limitations and abilities. . . . They speak the language of the sighted, although many words have no meaning whatsoever for them, and behave as if they recognized and understood what in reality must forever remain a mystery to them." Dorothy Burlingham, *Psychoanalytic Studies of the Sighted and the Blind* (New York: International Universities Press, 1972).

Other researchers in the field also have noted the lack or suppression of aggression in the blind child, although there is by no means universal agreement that every blind child is submissive and unassertive. There is also continuing disagreement about whether there is any qualitative difference between the personalities of the adult blind and those of sighted persons. Those who believe there are personality differences feel that they are the result of the differences in the social and physical environments of blind and of sighted children.

CHAPTER 5 *"The Eighth Wonder of the World"*

63 "But of all the blind and deaf-mute children," Michael Anagnos, *Helen Keller: A Second Laura Bridgman*, 56th Annual Report of the Perkins Institution and Massachusetts School for the Blind, 1888, pp. 10–14.

65 "never been told anything about death," Keller, *The Story of My Life*, p. 354.
  "By means of a dot and dash system," Annie Sullivan to Michael Anagnos (Mar. 1889), AS.
  "Bell followed the Tuscumbia 'miracle,' " Bruce, *Alexander Graham Bell*, pp. 401–2.
66 "Dear Mr. Bell," Keller, *The Story of My Life*, p. 148.
  According to her editors, John Macy and Nella Braddy Henney, Helen was not a natural writer and seldom felt a joyous compulsion to put her thoughts on paper. "From childhood on she was under the compulsion to write letters," Nella noted, "and since her teacher knew (if she did not) that every letter would be proudly exhibited by the one who received it, she demanded perfection. Letters were written over and over until they were without flaw and often Helen was sick of them before they were ready for the post office. Most of her letters, even to friends, are strangely impersonal. Only in letters to her family could she really let herself go. And as the years went on there was a terrible sameness in the themes: thank you letters and letters of appeal for the handicapped. Her natural style was filled with metaphors; when her heart was not in what she was writing, the metaphors became excessive in her effort to cover her lack of interest."
68 "I feel that in this child," quoted in Joseph Lash, *Helen and Teacher*, p. 172.
  "Why, one might just as well say," quoted in Braddy, *Anne Sullivan Macy*, p. 141.
69 "If you would only find it in your heart," Anne Sullivan to Michael Anagnos, AS.
  "Miss Spitfire," PSB.
  "Come with me," PSB.
  "I wish to be near you," Anne Sullivan to Michael Anagnos, AS.
70 "I consider you my daughter," Michael Anagnos to Anne Sullivan, AS.
  "I command you," quoted in Braddy, *Anne Sullivan Macy*, p. 143.
  "But remarkable and unparalleled," 56th Annual Report of the Perkins Institution and Massachusetts School for the Blind, 1888, pp. 26–27.
  "The report came last night," Annie Sullivan to Mrs. Hopkins, Jan. 9, 1888, quoted in Keller, *The Story of My Life*, p. 344.
71 "talked very fast with his fingers," 56th Annual Report of the Perkins Institution, and Massachusetts School for the Blind, 1888, p. 122.
  "We went to see Mr. Cleveland," ibid, p. 123.
  "I cannot bring myself to the mental state," Annie Sullivan to Michael Anagnos, undated letter, AS.
  "I never felt at ease with anyone," quoted in Braddy, *Anne Sullivan Macy*, pp. 164–65.
72 read a poem. Helen read with her left hand, but always held out her right hand to receive spelling.
  "So rapid were the movements," quoted in Lash, *Helen and Teacher*, p. 91.
  "Can it be possible, Madam," quoted in Lash, *Helen and Teacher*, p. 121.
  "filled with wonder," Keller, *The Story of My Life*, p. 47.
  "the sea, as if weary," ibid., p. 48.
73 "I read in my books," ibid., p. 174.
  "With all my faith" Michael Anagnos to Annie Sullivan, undated letter, AFB.
74 "Mon cher Monsieur Anagnos," Keller, *The Story of My Life*, p. 162.
  "Helen's mind," 57th Annual Report of the Perkins Institution and Massachusetts School for the Blind, 1889.
75 "If these statements are correct," Anne Sullivan to Michael Anagnos, Feb. 1, 1889, AS.
76 "Has anyone," Michael Anagnos to Anne Sullivan (Mar. 5, 1889) AS.
77 "Her voice was to me the loneliest sound," quoted in Lash, *Helen and Teacher*, p. 122.
  "The tragic fact is that Teacher," Keller, *Teacher*, pp. 61–62.
78 "She has grown amazingly fast," 60th Annual Report of the Perkins Institution and Massachusetts School for the Blind, 1891, p. 59.
  "Yes, darling," PSB.
  "Helen is not a regular pupil," ibid.

79 "The truth is," quoted in Braddy, *Anne Sullivan Macy*, p. 155.
"in the faint hope," ibid.
"she sometimes used them," Braddy, *Anne Sullivan Macy*, p. 156.
80 "Since this report was printed," 60th Annual Report of the Perkins Institution and Massachusetts School for the Blind, p. 95.
"Someone wrote Mr. Anagnos," Keller, AFB.
81 "As I myself never read this story," Anne Sullivan, *Souvenir, Volta Bureau*
"Helen said to me," quoted in *Miss Sullivan's Methods*, PSB.
82 "I cannot say positively," Anne Sullivan to Michael Anagnos (Mar. 6, 1892), AS.
"with what seemed to me," Keller, *The Story of My Life*, pp. 66–67.
83 "The extraordinary events," Edward Waterhouse, "The Lantern," spring 1980, Perkins School for the Blind, p. 20.
84 "When I went into the room," Keller, *The Story of My Life*, p. 71.
"And after we," Helen Keller to F. B. Sanborn (1906), PSB.
"Helen Keller is," Villey-Desmeserets, Pierre: *The World of the Blind* (New York: Macmillan, 1930), p. 313.
85 "It is with a kind of fear," Keller, *The Story of My Life*, p. 3.

CHAPTER 6 *"Angel Child"*

86 "where she was so captivated," Helen Keller, *Teacher*, p. 55.
87 "Caught, discovered," ibid., p. 65.
"to a calf," ibid., p. 65.
"indescribable dearness," ibid., p. 68.
"She made every word vibrant," ibid., p. 73.
"moved among the fires," ibid., p. 54.
88 "bits of talk," op. cit.
"Annie Sullivan was born," ibid., p. 55.
89 "Teacher was wounded," ibid., p. 75.
"I was very glad," Anne Sullivan to John Hitz (Nov. 1892), VOLTA.
"I wrote timidly, fearfully," Keller, *The Story of My Life*, p. 74.
"Written wholly without help," *Youth's Companion* (Jan. 4, 1894).
90 "water that I felt rushing," Keller, *The Story of My Life*, p. 217.
91 "angel visions," ibid., p. 76.
"how it is possible," ibid., pp. 76–77.
92 "More than anyone else," Bruce, *Alexander Graham Bell*, p. 406.
　　Bell was asked to administer the trust fund that was set up for Helen in 1896. He declined, although he did contribute a thousand dollars and helped organize it. When Captain Keller died, he sent Helen four hundred dollars and in 1899 sent her and Annie one hundred dollars for a country vacation. Both women were immensely grateful, and Annie wrote to Bell that he "will never know how deeply grateful I am to him for one of the richest and fullest years we have ever known." Long after Bell's death, when asked how she could have stayed with such a difficult task for many years, she replied, "I think it must have been Dr. Bell—his faith in me."
"he also observed," ibid., p. 405.
94 "He met us at the train," AFB.
95 "superior even to the creation," PSB.
"It was my wish," Annie Sullivan to John Hitz, VOLTA.
"Much has been said," quoted in Braddy, *Anne Sullivan Macy*, pp. 170–71.
97 "Miss Sullivan's cool assumption," Francis D. Clarke to Arthur Gilman, PSB.

CHAPTER 7 *"It Took the Pair of You"*

100 "no one seeing her 'copy,' " Hutton, *Talks in a Library*, p. 389.
"My time is wholly occupied," quoted in Koestler, *The Unseen Minority*, p. 462.

"willing to work night and day," AFB.

"an awareness of the universal struggle," Keller, *Teacher*, p. 61.

101 "We felt as if we were looking," Hutton, *Talks in a Library*, pp. 384–85.

"She was peculiarly affectionate," ibid., p. 392.

"her absolute dependence," ibid., pp 386–87.

102 "She knew that men and women," op. cit.

"powers of concentration," ibid., pp. 389–90.

"The teacher interested," ibid., p. 394.

103 "The wonderful child," Samuel Clemens, *Mark Twain's Autobiography*, 2 vols., ed. Albert Bigelow Paine (New York: Harper & Brothers, 1924), pp. 295–303.

104 "a lifelong guilt seeker," Justin Kaplan, *Mr. Clemens and Mark Twain* (New York: Simon & Schuster, 1966), p. 78.

"In everything," ibid., p. 308.

"Mr. Clemens, Mr. Zola," ibid., p. 336.

105 "It is one of the mysteries of our nature," ibid., p. 335.

"All the circumstances," *Mark Twain's Letters*, Vol. 2 (New York: Harper & Brothers, 1917), p. 636.

"during the fall and winter," Kaplan, *Mr. Clemens and Mark Twain*, p. 369.

" 'Sozodont and sozodont,' " op. cit.

106 "sitting upright," ibid., p. 371.

"The pattern of Livy's last years," ibid., p. 372.

"Not the kind of billiards," quoted in Ralph Martin and Richard Harrity, *The Three Lives of Helen Keller* (Garden City, N.Y.: Doubleday, 1962), p. 50.

107 "You are a wonderful creature," *Mark Twain's Letters*, p. 731.

"How she stands out in her letters!," op. cit.

"the higher life," Kaplan, *Mr. Clemens and Mark Twain*, p. 315.

"I heard the voice," quoted in Panati, *Panati's Extraordinary Endings*, p. 357.

108 "for and in behalf," *Mark Twain's Letters*, Vol. 2, p. 638.

109 Spaulding's heirs, Helen Keller to Mildren Tyson (June 9, 1933), PSB.

110 "come to believe," Annie Sullivan to John Hitz, VOLTA.

"no aptitude for emotional expression," PSB.

"He died last Saturday," quoted in Harrity and Martin, *The Three Lives of Helen Keller*, p. 42.

"Teacher has read," Helen Keller to John Hitz, VOLTA.

111 "a fraud and a humbug," quoted in Lash, *Helen and Teacher*, p. 129.

112 "To begin with," Annie Sullivan to Michael Anagnos (Aug. 17, 1892), AS.

CHAPTER 8 *"A Born Schemer"*

115 "join them," Keller, AFB.

"Their whiteness and delicacy," ibid.

116 "I think I may say," *Souvenir*, 1899, VOLTA.

"for the first time," AFB.

117 "Last week," Arthur Gilman to Eleanor Hutton, (Nov. 17, 1897), PSB.

"The issue," Mrs. Gilman to Mrs. Kate Keller (Nov. 28, 1897), PSB.

"a state of collapse," Mrs. Sophia Hopkins to Arthur Gilman (Nov. 19, 1897), PSB.

118 "She is nothing if not theatrical," PSB.

"Helen is no incident," Edward Rider to William Wade (Aug. 2, 1898), PSB.

Annie Sullivan's attitude toward menstruation, Harvey Green, *The Light of the Home: An Intimate View of the Lives of Women in Victorian America* (New York: Pantheon Books, 1983), pp. 118–19.

119 "I am much disturbed," William Wade to Arthur Gilman (Nov. 22, 1897), PSB.

"the meaning of something," William Wade to Arthur Gilman (Nov. 29, 1897), PSB.

120 "Confound it!," William Wade to Arthur Gilman (Mar. 28, 1898), PSB.

"Miss Sullivan must be separated," William Wade to Arthur Gilman (Apr. 2, 1898), PSB.
"exert my authority," Arthur Gilman to Kate Keller (1897), PSB.
121 "I thank you most sincerely," Kate Keller to Arthur Gilman (Nov. 28, 1897), PSB.
"very, very blind," Kate Keller to Arthur Gilman (Dec. 8, 1897), PSB.
"You are authorized," Kate Keller to Arthur Gilman (Dec. 8, 1897), PSB.
"at the cost of two dead bodies," Arthur Gilman to A. Bennett (Feb. 21, 1898), PSB.
122 "an angel laid a restraining hand," Keller, *Teacher*, p. 81.
"What is it, Teacher?," quoted in Lash, *Helen and Teacher*, p. 223.
"At Wrentham," PSB.
123 "in the event of any separation," PSB.
"Helen's intellect," PSB.
"Helen as partly your child," quoted in Braddy, *Anne Sullivan Macy*, p. 184.
"made very cruel use," ibid., p. 185.

CHAPTER 9 *"Half-Rome"*

124 "Miss Sullivan spelled their bright chatter," Keller, *Midstream: My Later Life* (New York: Doubleday, Doran, 1919), p. 18.
"the warm, living touch," AFB.
125 "to have people despise me," Anne Sullivan to John Hitz, VOLTA.
"Radcliffe did not desire," quoted in Lash, *Helen and Teacher*, p. 263.
126 "impersonal as Victrolas," Keller, *Midstream*, p. 15.
At Radcliffe, Helen studied French, German, English, and Latin, and took courses in government, economics, the history of medieval Europe, Shakespeare and Elizabethan literature, nineteenth-century literature, the history of philosophy, and the Bible. Her work included no independent research, fine arts, music, drawing, chemistry, botany, zoology, geology, or any other subject that involved the use of instruments and physical specimens.
"I used to have time," Keller, *The Story of My Life*, p. 97.
"When the word became public," *The Radcliffe Quarterly* (Aug. 1968).
127 "Mr. S. is too attractive," ibid.
"It seems to me, Helen," quoted in Keller, *Midstream*, pp. 133–34.
129 "The noble men and women of history," ibid., p. 10.
"so happily at home in philosophy," ibid, p. 12. As much as she loved philosophy, Helen disagreed with William James, who felt it was secondary to religion.
130 "I am always eager to learn," Helen Keller to John Hitz, VOLTA.
Helen's first instruction in religion came at age eight, fewer than two years after the scene at the water pump when she grasped the idea of language. She thought it a joke when an aunt told her that she was made of "dust," that God was her father, that God was love, and that God was everywhere. A nonbeliever, Annie Sullivan was hard pressed to answer Helen's questions, many of which she felt were unanswerable.
In later life, after she had discovered Swedenborgianism, Helen read the Bible every morning, usually the Psalms. Her favorites were the ninetieth, the ninety-eighth, the hundredth, and, of course, the twenty-third.
"I confess I get rather exasperated with ministers who think there must be a special form to one's prayers, one way of approaching God," she once wrote. "My feeling is that all prayers should spring from the Lord's prayer—after that I pray to God that I may act according to His law of life and to practice what I think and believe, not in words merely, but in acts. I really feel that there is a special bond between all earnest believers—Christians, Jews, Moslems—often I thank Him for permitting me to feel so close to him."
Every Sunday, Helen celebrated her religion privately at her home, but even her closest friends did not know the nature of the service. She did speak to them, how-

ever, of the dreariness of many of the tracts of other religions besides Swedenborgianism that were sent to her. At her request, Polly threw them away as soon as they
arrived in the mail.

"could not see much farther," Keller, *Teacher*, p. 98.

131 "I have always accepted," AFB.
"In some of her work," ibid.

132 "When she began work at her story," John Albert Macy, "Helen Keller As She Really
Is," *Ladies' Home Journal* (Oct. and Nov. 1902).

134 "The lives of teacher and pupil," ibid.

135 "nothing like it in heaven," *Mark Twain's Letters*, Vol. 2, pp. 731–32.

136 "worth reminding," *New York Sun* (1903), quoted in Braddy, *Anne Sullivan Macy*,
p. 200.
"All her knowledge is hearsay knowledge," *The Nation*, quoted in Braddy, *Anne Sullivan Macy*, p. 201.

137 "a kind of arrogance," AFB.
"The wonderful and varied imagery," John Hitz, *Arkansas Optic* (Mar. 3, 1900).

CHAPTER 10 *John*

140 "As you go hammer and tongs," John Macy to Upton Sinclair, undated, Upton Sinclair Manuscript Collection, Lilly Library, University of Indiana, Bloomington.
would have been insulted, John B. Strommer to M. Robert Barnett (Apr. 15, 1966),
AFB.
"Temperamentally I hate reformers," AFB.

141 John Macy . . . was born, *Dictionary of American Biography*, Vol. 6, p. 177.
"a bad fairy of nerves," Keller, *Teacher*, p. 122.
"rent with emotions," AFB.
"to have won a degree," quoted in Braddy, *Anne Sullivan Macy*, p. 208.

142 "most harmonious development," quoted in Green, *The Light of the Home*, p. 29.

143 "two desks," John Macy to Mr. Farrington (Apr. 12, 1904), PSB.
"Dearest Heart," Anne Sullivan to John Macy (July 2, year not given), AFB.

144 "She changed her mind," Keller, *Teacher*, p. 100.
"The lover sought," "Helen Keller ALMOST Married" (newspaper unknown),
VOLTA.

145 "too cruel," quoted in Braddy, *Anne Sullivan Macy*, p. 215.
"possibilities for you," Edward Everett Hale to Helen Keller (May 3, 1905), AFB.

146 "My cup ran over!," Keller, *Midstream*, pp. 32–33.
" 'I told you, Helen,' " ibid., p. 135.

148 "Dearest little Billy," John Macy to Helen Keller (Jan. 18, 1905), PSB.
"Annie never wholly acquiesced," Keller, *Teacher*, p. 101.

149 "the few years," ibid., p. 106.
"tried my patience," ibid., p. 107.
"met their Waterloo," Annie Sullivan to John Hitz, VOLTA.

150 "so many scolding passages," ibid., p. 116.
"kind of medieval self-mortification" Keller, *Teacher*, p. 116.
"a sort of pre-existence," Keller, *Midstream*, p. 46.
"the best critic," PSB.
"For Macy early on," John B. Strommer to M. Robert Barnett (Apr. 15, 1966), AFB.

151 "Both had a magical way," Keller, *Midstream*, pp. 33–34.

152 "smiling like a babe," ibid., pp. 34–35.

153 "Her memory of people," quoted in Keller, *The Story of My Life*, pp. 286–99.

155 "Miss Sullivan's skill," PSB.
"Not even scholarly," quoted in Lash, *Helen and Teacher*, pp. 306–11.
"in such a happy mood," Keller, *Midstream*, p. 34.

CHAPTER 11 *The World I Live In*

156 "Patiently the [deaf-blind] child," Keller, *The World I Live In*, pp. 122–23.
"Every object is associated," ibid., p. 7.
157 "Not only is the hand," ibid., p. 27.
"talked so much," ibid., pp. 108–9.
 Pink was Helen Keller's favorite color, and she said it was like "a baby's cheek" or "a gentle southern breeze." Gray she said, was like "a shawl around the shoulders." White meant "exaltation." There were two kinds of red, she said. One red was the warm blood in a healthy body and the other was of hate and hell. Lilac, which was Annie's favorite color, made Helen think of faces she had loved and kissed. Black meant hopelessness and despair, while purple was mysterious. Referring to silver, she said that she had some idea of what sparkling was because she had felt soap bubbles quivering.
"Every atom of my body," ibid., pp. 49–50.
"Footsteps," ibid., pp. 43–45.
"A slight flutter," ibid., pp. 46–47.
158 "attractive" vibrations, Diane Ackerman, *A Natural History of the Senses* (New York: Vintage Books, 1991), pp. 212–13.
"I love the instrument," Keller, *The World I Live In*, p. 52.
"beautifully alive," ibid., p. 53.
159 "hand on the piano case," ibid, pp. 52–53.
 People close to Helen felt that her love of music was often exaggerated. She could distinguish only a few compositions, such as Beethoven's Ninth Symphony. Sculpture, which is palpable as well as visual, was the art that she appreciated the most. Her friend Jo Davidson, watching her pass her hands over his busts and figures, said that she "saw" his work with deeper understanding than anyone else he had ever known. Watching her move her sensitive fingers over the great works of Donatello and Michelangelo, Davidson commented: "I have seen these sculptures before, but never so intimately as when I watched her hands wandering over the forms, peering into the slightest crevices, into the most subtle undulations."
placing her hand, ibid., pp. 54–55.
"I notice first," ibid., p. 68.
"a potent wizard," ibid., p. 64.
New studies, Matt Crenson, "Memories Triggered by Smell Another Kettle of Fish," Associated Press, *The Doylestown Intelligencer* (Sept. 16, 1996).
161 "to my childhood frolics," Keller, *The World I Live In*, p. 66.
"The odors of wood," ibid., pp. 73–74.
"had a miraculous gift," Ackerman, *A Natural History of the Senses*, pp. 44–45.
"a sensuist," ibid., p. xviii.
"Without imagination," Keller, *The World I Live In*, p. 14.
162 "of tangible white darkness," Keller, *The Story of My Life*, p. 21.
"a London fog," quoted in Koestler, *The Unseen Minority*, p. 452.
"the analogy," Rev. Thomas J. Carroll, *Blindness: What It Is, What It Does and How to Live with It* (Boston: Little, Brown, 1961), pp. 31–32.
"In my dreams," Keller, *The World I Live In*, pp. 161–62.
"The dark world," Thomas D. Cutsforth: *The Blind in School and Society* (New York: D. Appleton, 1933), p. 130.
164 "Both researchers," Donald Kirtley, *The Psychology of Blindness* (Chicago: Nelson-Hall, 1975), pp. 307–8.
165 "A typical dream," ibid., p. 209.
In contrast to Laura, ibid., p. 212.
"a sensation of cool dampness," Keller, *The World I Live In*, pp. 150–51.
 Helen told both Annie Sullivan and Nella Henney that she was not conscious of

touch in her dreams, but she "seemed to see things, as in a mirror." They were anxious to learn her thought processes and to find out what she meant by "seeing" things in her dreams. "You can't see in a mirror, Helen, any more than you can see in the back of your head," Annie told her. Then they asked her what immediately came into her mind when they said the word "horse." "His long face," said Helen, expressing length with her hands. "His big form," also with the hands. "His short hair, his mane and tail, if he has a tail." "What color?" Annie asked. "That depends upon what I am told," Helen replied. She continued her description by saying that she felt "his life," moving her hands upward to express abounding spirits.

"When I am in Dreamland," quoted in Lash, *Helen and Teacher*, pp. 275–76.

167 "paragraphs that strike them," ibid, pp. 342–43.
168 "difficult for me to get a hearing," PSB.
    "I hope to enlarge my life," quoted in Lash, *Helen and Teacher*, p. 368.
    "More than anyone else," Keller, *Midstream*, p. 66.
169 "all in white," ibid., p. 53.
    "his talk fragrant," ibid., p. 56.
    "cigars and a thermos bottle," ibid., p. 58.
    "humor was on the surface," ibid., p. 67.
    "strongest impression," ibid., p. 66
    "I am very lonely," ibid., p. 50.
170 he died en route, "A Brief History of the Last Few Hours of Mr. John Hitz" (Mar. 27, 1908), AFB.
    "Jekyll and Hyde," Kaplan, *Mr. Clemens and Mark Twain*, p. 388.
    "I reached out," Keller, *Midstream*, pp. 68–69.

CHAPTER 12 *A Fiery Radical*

171 this small volume, Harvard College Class of 1899, 5th Report, 1929.
    "The trouble with," John Albert Macy, *Socialism in America* (Garden City, N.Y.: Doubleday, Page, 1916), p. 57.
172 "The Communists disdain," quoted in *Socialism in America*, p. 163.
    "to strengthen the working class," ibid., p. 126.
    such demands as the collective ownership, ibid., pp. 126–35.
    "among the younger writers," ibid., p. 225.
173 "American socialism," Irving Howe, *Socialism and America* (New York: Harcourt Brace Jovanovich, 1985), p. 16.
    the Wobblies' songbooks, Oliver Jensen, Joan Paterson Kerr, and Murray Belsky, *American Album* (New York: American Heritage Publishing Company, 1968), p. 258.
    "I shall not soon forget," ibid., p. 258.
    "a dusty army," Macy, *Socialism in America*, p. 182.
175 "an orator able," Howe, *Socialism and America*, p. 42.
    "some index of Goldman's power," *American Album*, p. 262.
    "the supreme honor," Harvard College Class of 1899, 5th Report, 1924.
176 "I am a militant suffragette," AFB.
    "from the time she was twelve," Van Wyck Brooks, *Helen Keller: Sketch for a Portrait* (New York: E. P. Dutton, 1956), p. 87.
177 "The soul of the German people," quoted in William Shirer, *The Rise and Fall of the Third Reich: A History of Nazi Germany* (New York: Simon & Schuster, 1960), p. 241.
    "in the cause of the deaf," Keller, *Midstream*, pp. 81–82.
178 "Only red-handed workmen," quoted in Lash, *Helen and Teacher*, p. 469.
    "She was not a woman suffragist," Keller, *Teacher*, p. 105.
    "the windows had to be guarded," AFB.
179 "this warmhearted reception," ibid.

CHAPTER 13 *"More of an Institution Than a Woman"*

181 photographed in right profile. The public conjectured why Helen was always photographed from her right side. An explanation that avoided mention of her obvious
blindness was offered by O. O. McIntyre, a famous columnist of the period. He speculated that "when younger there was a question to have or not have a blemish on her
cheek removed and it was finally decided it might cause her mental anguish to tell
her about it. The same council of friends persuaded her never to marry."
"big, wide, open, blue eyes." The date is uncertain when Helen Keller began to wear
artificial glass eyes, but in the Helen Keller Archives at the American Foundation for
the Blind there is a bill to Anne Sullivan, dated 1911, from a Boston manufacturer of
prostheses for "one artificial eye." In the 1920s Helen's artificial eyes would be made
of glass by a German firm based in New York. In later life they were probably made of
hard acrylic. Acrylic eyes were developed after World War II, when German-made
glass eyes were no longer available. In this country, acrylic eyes have been in widespread use since the late 1950s. That Helen's eyes, which seemed so intelligent, were
artificial, made some of her friends speculate that a person's expressiveness was
largely due to the facial muscles.
"Sometimes he would set me stark naked," quoted in the *New York Times* (Oct. 16,
1995).
182 "I am sure you will find him," quoted in Lash, *Helen and Teacher*, p. 374.
"perpetual stumbling block," quoted in Braddy, *Anne Sullivan Macy*, p. 232.
183 "my voice soaring," Keller, *Midstream*, p. 97.
184 "From the moment, therefore," Leblanc, *The Girl Who Found the Bluebird*, pp.
26–27.
"Helen is tall," ibid., pp. 29–30.
"to observe the girl," ibid., pp. 32–33.
"At moments of direct communication," ibid., pp. 34–35.
185 "Helen's silence," ibid., pp. 40–41.
"Helen had been speaking," ibid., pp. 81–82.
186 "I rise absent-mindedly," ibid., pp. 111–12.
"Helen is the example," ibid., pp. 129–30.
187 "a young American," ibid., p. 30.
"Is she not there," ibid., pp. 66–67.
"more of an institution," quoted in Braddy, *Anne Sullivan Macy*, p. 223.
189 "we were going on a lecture tour," Helen Keller to John Macy, PSB.
190 "You are wrong, John," Helen Keller to John Macy, PSB.
191 "You, her husband," Helen Keller to John Macy, PSB.
192 "You know, John," Helen Keller to John Macy (Mar. 4, 1914), PSB.
193 "things were ruined," Helen Keller to Mildred Tyson (June 9, 1933), PSB.
"taken Mr. Fagan as your secretary," Helen Keller to John Macy, PSB.

CHAPTER 14 *"A Little Island of Joy"*

194 "her presence sweetened," Keller, *Midstream*, p. 177.
195 "a woman of talent and charm," *Dictionary of American Biography*, Vol. 6, p. 178.
"married an institution," PSB.
"demanding my love," Keller, *Teacher*, pp. 126–28.
196 "I saw more clearly," Keller, *Midstream*, p. 178.
"held my hand in silence," ibid., p. 179.
"doing with that creature," ibid., p. 180.
197 "It was after she got to Montgomery," PSB.
198 "The memory of her sorrow," Keller, *Midstream*, p. 181.
"The brief love," ibid., p. 182.
199 "if Mrs. Macy had been there," ibid., p. 181.

CHAPTER 15 *Separation*

200 her own "joy isle." Although Annie Sullivan invited Helen and Mrs. Keller to visit her in Puerto Rico, they did not accept her invitation. Helen wanted to come, but her mother was threatened by Annie's new, relaxed life on the island, where she mingled freely with the black population. Annie was perplexed by Mrs. Keller's rigid attitude. She wrote Helen about her mother's "prejudice against Puerto Rico. . . . I wonder that she can have such strong opinions of a place she really doesn't know."

201 to her startled biographer, PSB. Helen once described Annie Sullivan as talking less about herself than any person she had ever known with the exception of her mother, and it appears that Annie was also less than forthcoming with her biographer. Nella Braddy Henney was not permitted to see the letters that Annie and Helen exchanged while Annie was recuperating in Puerto Rico, and, of course, she never confided to Nella "the secret" that made her so driven and reckless.

"didn't inherit the New England conscience," Anne Sullivan Macy to Helen Keller, undated letter, AFB.

202 "strange experience here," ibid.

"It distresses me to think," Helen Keller to Anne Sullivan Macy, AFB.

203 "I do want to get well," Anne Sullivan Macy to Helen Keller, undated letter, AFB.

"her liberal views," AFB.

"In the East," Philip S. Foner, ed., *Helen Keller: Her Socialist Years* (New York: International Universities Press, 1967), p. 123.

204 "Already countless mothers," ibid., p. 71.

"like Joan of Arc," AFB.

"ever since childhood," ibid.

"The outrages against the colored people," quoted in Lash, *Helen and Teacher*, p. 454.

In *Double Blossoms*, a collection of tributes to Helen and Annie by famous writers of the period that was published in 1931, the black American educator and writer W. E. B. DuBois, contributed the following reminiscence: "When I was studying philosophy at Harvard under William James, we made an excursion one day out to the Roxbury. We stopped at the Blind Asylum and saw a young girl who was blind and deaf and dumb, and yet who, by infinite pains and loving sympathy, had been made to speak without words and to understand without sound. She was Helen Keller. Perhaps just because she was blind to color differences in this world, I was intensely interested in her, and all through my life I have followed her career. Finally there came the thing which I had somehow sensed would come: Helen Keller was in her own state, Alabama, being feted and made much of by her fellow citizens. And yet courageously and frankly she spoke out of the iniquity and foolishness of the color line. It cost her something to speak. They wanted her to retract, but she sat serene in the consciousness of the truth that she had uttered. And so it was proven, as I knew it would be, that this woman who sits in darkness has a spiritual insight clearer than that of many wide-eyed people who stare uncomprehendingly at this prejudiced world."

205 "The people who did," AFB.

"a phrase that justifies," quoted in Lash, *Helen and Teacher*, pp. 454–55.

"I haven't taken sides," ibid., p. 415.

one of her defenders, Braddy, *Anne Sullivan Macy*, p. 257.

206 "I have one or two plain questions," Helen Keller to Anne Sullivan Macy, AFB.

"never out of my thoughts," Anne Sullivan Macy to Helen Keller (1916), AFB.

207 "From the year 1905," Helen Keller to Mildred Tyson (1933), PSB.

"the game of words," Anne Sullivan Macy to Helen Keller, AFB.

208 "Just think, last Friday," Helen Keller to Anne Sullivan Macy, AFB.

"on the ghastly battle-fields," Helen Keller to Anne Sullivan Macy (Mar. 16, 1917), AFB.

209 "It pains me deeply," Anne Sullivan Macy to Helen Keller (1917), AFB.
"little to tell," Helen Keller to Anne Sullivan Macy (Apr. 9, 1917), AFB.
"so endeared to me," Keller, *Midstream*, p. 185.

CHAPTER 16 *Hollywood*

211 "tap, tap, tap," Keller, *Midstream*, p. 189.
212 "strife and social injustice," ibid., p. 187.
214 "Such a strange thing has happened!," Keller, *My Religion* (New York: Doubleday, Page, 1927), p. 33.
215 "I was glad," Keller, *Midstream*, p. 208.
"I felt as if I had died," ibid., p. 193.
216 spontaneously scream, ibid., pp. 204–5.
217 "I thought my heart would burst," ibid., p. 205.
"Was I afraid?," ibid., pp. 199–200.
"Few, if any," ibid., pp. 146–47.
218 "they had both endured poverty," Keller, *Teacher*, p. 147.
"Nothing refreshed me," Keller, *Midstream*, p. 188.
"I thought I could visit," PSB.

CHAPTER 17 *"The Star of Happiness"*

221 The curtain rises. The complete script for Helen Keller's vaudeville act is located in the Helen Keller Archives, the American Foundation for the Blind.
223 "rush, glare, and noise," Keller, *Midstream*, p. 215.
the highest-paid performers. The reason that Helen received as high a salary as any star in vaudeville was that E. F. Albee and other executives in the Keith vaudeville firm were of the opinion that at various times "persons of no worth received large sums to enter vaudeville on the strength of mere notoriety and that Miss Keller was entitled to as much whether her appearance was a success as vaudeville entertainment or not."
A typical advertisement for her vaudeville appearance reads as follows:

Next Week the Greatest of All
The Most-Talked-Of Woman in the World
The Brightest Star of Happiness and Optimism
HELEN KELLER
(IN PERSON)
BLIND-DEAF-AND FORMERLY DUMB
In The Sweetest Story Ever Told, Constituting
A Remarkable Portrayal of the Triumph of Miss Keller's Life Over
the Greatest Obstacles That Ever Confronted a Human Being
Assisted by Anne Sullivan Macy
Her Life Long Friend and Devoted Teacher

"vaudeville much more amusing," ibid., pp. 210–11.
224 "claimed cruelty," Joe Laurie, Jr.: *Vaudeville: From the Honky Tonks to the Palace* (New York: Henry Holt, 1953), p. 219.
Billed as "the Man-Woman," ibid., p. 225.
225 "the greatest of all the odd and interesting acts," op. cit.
"I have sat in her room," AFB.
"a large company," *B. F. Keith Theatre News* (May 24, 1920).
226 Mad Harry, as the press dubbed him. Helen wrote Harry Thaw at a Pittsburgh mental hospital after his mother's death, asking him for a donation to the American Foundation for the Blind "as a memorial to your mother who was deeply interested in the sightless. . . . You, too, have walked along a road of sorrow, and known how precious it was to feel her hand in yours." Helen Keller to Harry Thaw (Oct. 30, 1930), AFB.
As a publicity stunt, Laurie, *Vaudeville*, pp. 390–91.

"Vulgarity will not be tolerated," ibid., p. 483.

"Her life seemed always to turn," Keller, *Teacher*, pp. 155–57.

question-and-answer period. "Questions asked Helen Keller by her Vaudeville Audiences ca. 1922" (AFB).

228 "On the vaudeville stage," Karen Payne Malone, "An Historical Study for a Production Reconstructing Helen Keller's Vaudeville and Lecture Performances." Master's thesis, Southwest Missouri State University (1994), pp. 50–51.

"Every fiber of my being," Keller, *Midstream*, p. 222.

229 "Yes, life was good," ibid., p. 217.

"My mother talked intelligently," ibid., p. 220.

230 "just as she was leaving me," Helen Keller to Mildred Tyson, undated letter, AFB.

"I had absolute faith," Keller, *Midstream*, p. 223.

CHAPTER 18 *"The Dreadful Drama Is Finished"*

231 her eyesight deteriorated, PSB.

232 "I seldom think of my limitations," ibid.

"one of the sensitive spirits," Keller, *Teacher*, p. 159.

"afraid of people in the flesh," Anne Sullivan Macy, "Foolish Remarks of a Foolish Woman," AFB.

"a futile fight of it," obituary, Anne Sullivan Macy, *New York Times* (Oct. 21, 1936).

233 "she would make friends," Keller, *Teacher*, p. 185.

"She loved perfection and nonsense," ibid., p. 189.

"none of the lack-luster look," Robert M. Coates, Profiles, *The New Yorker* (Jan. 25, 1930), p. 26.

234 "All the primitive instincts," AFB.

235 "I never think about money," Anne Sullivan Macy, "Foolish Remarks," AFB.

"They had only one story to tell," Koestler, *The Unseen Minority*, p. 57.

236 "Teacher and I felt real shame," Keller, *Teacher*, p. 175.

socialism was the answer, Foner, *Helen Keller's Socialist Years*, p. 16.

"Try to imagine," Koestler, *The Unseen Minority*, pp. 65–66.

238 "If Teacher had been left free," Keller, *Teacher*, p. 168.

"Left to herself," Braddy, *Anne Sullivan Macy*, p. 292.

239 "a bon vivant," Koestler, *The Unseen Minority*, p. 62.

240 "illegitimate daughter to the office," Lash, *Helen and Teacher*, p. 515.

"humanness of his nature," *The National Encyclopedia of American Biography*, pp. 108–9.

"Last night you came to me," PSB.

"I felt humiliated," Keller, *Teacher*, p. 180.

241 "Annie never cast the shadow," PSB.

"it terrifies me," Keller, *Midstream*, pp. 343–44.

"I just want to say this," PSB.

Helen's singular world, Tilney, "A Comparative Sensory Analysis of Helen Keller and Laura Bridgman," p. 1239.

243 "poignant memories," ibid., p. 1241.

"The sense of smell," ibid., p. 1240.

"Not only is she able," ibid.

"this was the one touch of nature," ibid.

"One feature," ibid.

244 "But, however brilliant," ibid.

245 "four long afternoons," PSB.

"nothing extraordinary," Helen Keller to Effendi Doubleday, AFB.

246 "Was or was not Helen Keller," Thomas Cutsforth, *The Blind in School and Society* (New York: D. Appleton, 1933), pp. 22–23.

"We followed a tributary," ibid., p. 52.

"The paragraph conveys," ibid.
247 "Critics . . . assume," Keller, *The World I Live In*, p. 127.
"Dr. Cutsforth," Helen Keller to Nella Braddy Henney (Sept. 24, 1933), PSB.
248 "If Annie was drowned," PSB.
"All the bitterness," Braddy, *Anne Sullivan Macy*, p. 323.
"their waywardness," PSB.
"was held fast," Keller, *Teacher*, p. 195.
"You must see Killarney," Helen Keller to Nella Braddy (July 27, 1930), AFB.
249 "the thought of age," Anne Sullivan Macy, "Foolish Remarks," AFB.
last will and testament, AFB.
"An engagement," ibid.
250 "When I think," ibid.
"Honors which," Anne Sullivan Macy, "Foolish Remarks," AFB.
Recently the trustees, Braddy, *Anne Sullivan Macy*, p. 340.
251 "I have never thought," Keller, *Teacher*, p. 211.
"not a shrew," Helen Keller, *Helen Keller in Scotland* (London: Methuen, 1933), p. 34.
252 "Their Majesties were both," ibid., pp. 41–42.
"soothing quiet of deep heather," PSB.
253 "As we drove up in front," Anne Sullivan Macy, "Foolish Remarks," AFB.
254 "Why did you not ask your questions," ibid.
"a new lamp," Keller, *Teacher*, p. 217.
255 "like a naughty child," ibid., p. 219.
"That was our desperate last effort," ibid., pp. 226–27.
Anne Sullivan Macy died, Certificate of Death, City of New York, Department of Health, AFB.
256 "At Annie Sullivan's funeral," Alexander Woollcott, *Long, Long Ago* (New York: Viking Press, 1943), p. 87.

Alexander Woollcott was a great admirer of Annie Sullivan, believing that Helen was "her great work that will live after her as *A Christmas Carol* will live after Charles Dickens." When Annie was in Doctor's Hospital in New York, he visited her often and sent her a daily bouquet of flowers. After Annie's death, he broadcast a tribute to her on his radio show, in which he announced that it was "a memorial to one of the great women of our time — or any time." Helen cried when Polly spelled his words into her hand.

257 for cremation, *New York Herald Tribune* (Oct. 23, 1936).
"Good-bye John Macy," AFB.
"taken out." Throughout their long relationship, Annie regarded herself as Helen's collaborator. "Of course you know that whatever Helen writes represents my labour as well as hers," she wrote Eleanor Hutton, one of Helen's benefactors. "The genius is hers, but much of the drudgery is mine. The conditions are such that she could not prepare a paper for publication without my help. The difficulties under which she works are so unsurmountable. Someone must always be at her side to read to her, to keep her typewriter in order, to read over her manuscripts, make corrections, and look up words for her, and do the many things which she could do for herself if she had her sight. I make this statement because Helen's friends have not always understood what the relations between her and me really are. They have thought her earning capacity independent of me, and one person at least has hinted that financially she might be better off without me. Helen feels very differently, and when the book contracts were made, she insisted that they should revert to me on her death. It is also her wish to divide equally with me, during her life, all the money that comes to her as our joint earnings. I am willing to accept one third." Quoted in Braddy, *Anne Sullivan Macy*, pp. 212–13.

The Russian artist, ibid., p. 341.
"Helen would be nothing," PSB.

CHAPTER 19 *Helen Without Annie*

258 "I ache all over," Keller, *Helen Keller's Journal* (Garden City, N.Y.: Doubleday, 1938), pp. 277–80.
259 "consider it a privilege," Anson Phelps Stokes to Mr. Brock (Oct. 21, 1936), AFB.
"somnambulist," Keller, *Helen Keller's Journal*, p. 2.
   On December 2, 1937, Polly Thomson became a citizen of the United States. Helen Keller was one of her character witnesses, and when the ceremony was over, Helen grasped her companion's hand and said, "Now that Miss Thomson is a citizen I have a new feeling of safety because I shall know that she will always be with me." The news to their friends in this announcement was that Polly's real name was Mary Agnes.
260 "What earthly consolation," ibid., p. 3.
"tantalizing almost beyond endurance," ibid., p. 6.
261 "that country would not now be emerging," ibid., pp. 87–88.
"anti-Semitic atrocities," ibid., p. 105.
"I doubt whether His Majesty," ibid , pp. 57–58.
"Only through experiences," ibid., p. 60.
262 "Airmen flying blind in a fog," ibid., pp. 33–34.
"work is the only sure bulwark," ibid., p. 37.
263 "This repels me," ibid., pp. 182–83.
she liked to attend films and the theater. Famed actor David Warfield was one of many celebrities who never forgot the sensation Helen made when she appeared at the theater. He recalled her as being "a tall, splendid figure wrapped in a beautiful evening cloak of pale blue." A member of her theater party observed, "As her companions spelled the action into her hand, her face became a mirror of a thousand fleeting expressions. . . . On it there are registered shades of expression, fine shades of feeling, which the face of the normal human being is incapable of reflecting." It took both Annie Sullivan and a friend to convey the action onstage to her. "Quickly their fingers work as they play upon the hands, wrists and arms of the girl at their side. But not more quickly than their lips, which Miss Keller lightly touches with her fingertips, sometimes caressing the throat, eyelids, cheek and forehead of Mrs. Macy— these latter movements being made always when there is an extraordinary emotional crisis going on in the scene onstage." *New York Sun* (Oct. 6, 1913).
264 "I had watched the darkness," ibid., p. 194.
"a likeness snatched," ibid., p. 243.
"Pink! . . . Blue!," ibid., p. 43.
265 Many of her blind contemporaries, Cutsforth, *The Blind in School and Society*, p. 134.

CHAPTER 20 *Polly and Nella*

266 "sinewy and overdeveloped," PSB.
   Using no shortcuts, Polly Thomson interpreted to Helen at the rate of eighty-five words per minute at top speed when they went to the movies, describing the scenes and giving snatches of dialogue sufficient for Helen to follow the film. In everyday life, however, when Helen realized what she was about to tell her, she took her hand away to save Polly unnecessary work.
   Nella Braddy Henney had a sister and two brothers. The family was close. In her journal she observed that in her old age her mother had remarked, "You do not get the children you dream of, but you learn to be satisfied with what you have." Her mother had wanted "two pretty, lighthearted, frivolous and immensely popular girls."

According to Nella, neither she nor her sister qualified. "They were not pretty," she wrote, "though my six-foot sister was very handsome, they were serious and bookish and not at all to the taste of the young men in our small Georgia town. But they were brought up on poetry and had as much right as the next to picture themselves as blessed damozels, a rather bloodless substitute for popularity but it was the best they could do and it served. My mother's second statement came after my father's death. 'I want you to know that I loved your father more than I did any of you.' "
"the devoted sisters," ibid.

267 "Polly was a complex person," ibid.
"Polly was a lady," ibid.

268 "Dear Teacher," ibid.
"lifeline in keeping," Maguerite Levine to Keith Henney (Nov. 15, 1977), AFB.

269 "Helen not original," PSB.

270 "the Helen I know," ibid.
"For all her love of mankind," ibid.

271 "I feel confident," Franklin Roosevelt to Helen Keller (Mar. 20, 1937), AFB.
"It would be wonderful," Keller, *Helen Keller's Journal*, pp. 268–69.
"Please, dear Mr. Roosevelt," Helen Keller to Franklin Delano Roosevelt (Feb. 7, 1929), AFB.

272 "More than any other president," Keller, *Helen Keller's Journal*, p. 130.
"No longer belonging," Doris Kearns Goodwin, *No Ordinary Time* (New York: Simon & Schuster, 1994), p. 17.
"Anything Helen Keller is for, I am for."
At a dinner given by John Nance Garner, Roosevelt's vice president, the humorist Will Rogers—at the request of Helen Keller—broadcast an appeal to supply blind people with Talking Book reading machines with which to read the Talking Books that were being placed by the Library of Congress in the libraries for the blind throughout the United States. Before Will Rogers left the room to broadcast, Roosevelt wrote a brief note on a card, which he permitted Rogers to read on the air. It said, "Dear Will: Anything Helen Keller is for, I am for. I say this because of the splendid work for humanity which she has done these many years."
Sometime later, Franklin Roosevelt designated Thursday, March 3, 1938, as National Helen Keller Day. In his proclamation, Roosevelt wrote: ". . . The day now set apart, March 3, 1938, will mark the fiftieth anniversary of the first meeting between Helen Keller and her great teacher—a day which Miss Keller regards as her spiritual birthday. In honoring Helen Keller, the nation honors all who are today achieving happy and successful lives in spite of physical handicap, and in honoring the memory of the late Anne Sullivan Macy, the nation extols all who, like her, work to bring light to those who sit in darkness." AFB.

273 "Eleanor considered," Blanche Wiesen Cook, *Eleanor Roosevelt*, Vol. 1 (New York: Penguin Books, 1992), p. 313.

274 "I thought how wonderfully," quoted in Lash, *Helen and Teacher*, p. 687.

275 In her last will and testament, Panoti, *Extraordinary Endings*, p. 124.
"I who am blind," Keller, "Three Days to See," *Atlantic Monthly* (Jan. 1933).

276 This phenomenon was first observed, Oliver Sacks, *An Anthropologist on Mars* (New York: Random House, 1995), p. 110.

277 "an extensive field of light," Annie Dillard, *Pilgrim at Tinker Creek* (New York: Harper's Magazine Press, 1974), p. 26.
"In the newly sighted," Sacks, *An Anthropologist on Mars*, p. 141.
"One must die," ibid., pp. 141–42.
"Sound, for them," ibid., p. 142.

278 "Remember that when a blind man," Keller, *The World I Live In*, p. 21.
David Warren and other researchers, however, believe "that much of the evi-

dence supports that notion that a period of early vision may provide an integrative basis for spatial relations that endures even after vision is lost, providing the later blind person with substantial advantage over the person blind from birth." David H. Warren, *Blindness and Early Childhood Development*, 2d ed., rev. (New York: American Foundation for the Blind, 1989), p. 79.

different short speeches. To deliver a speech, Helen first typed her message on an ordinary typewriter, and then the typescript was spelled to her and any necessary corrections were made. Then the speech was rewritten by her in Braille, from which version she read until she was memory-perfect and ready to deliver it.

"utterly selfish creature," Keller, *Helen Keller's Journal*, p. 281.

"He is one," ibid., p. 296.

279 "the degrading poverty," ibid., pp. 298–99.

"The spirit, like the sea," ibid., pp. 302–303.

280 "The doctors advise me," PSB.

CHAPTER 21 *"A Source of Embarrassment"*

282 "Helen Keller's habit," quoted in Lash, *Helen and Teacher*, p. 703.

283 "Finally, I am on Soviet soil!," Federal Bureau of Investigation file on Helen Keller.

"At the Larry Adler opening," quoted in Ed Sullivan's column, the *New York Daily News* (Nov. 26, 1947).

According to Nella Braddy Henney, "The American Foundation for the Blind was 'somewhat disturbed' by Pegler's insinuations that both Helen and Jo Davidson were Communists without ever accusing them directly. There are several reasons," she wrote. "One is that Helen is an international saint, and we demand austerity of our saints. The other is that she is begging for money, and the group that Pegler represents has more of it than any other. Helen called Pegler 'a dung-beetle' and the rest of us called him worse names than that. I told her that Café Society Uptown was one of the most celebrated entertainment places in New York. 'But Nella,' she said, 'it is not evil.' " (PBS). It was reported, however, that Pegler considered both Café Society Uptown and Café Society Downtown as hotbeds of Communism.

never conducted an investigation, letter to the author from the Federal Bureau of Investigation.

284 "I was glad of the subway ride," Keller, *Helen Keller's Journal*, p. 200.

286 "The charming relations," Helen Keller, introduction to *Taffy and Tuffy* by Mildred Seybert and Lyla M. Olson, (New York: D. Appleton-Century, 1942).

Helen doted on her dogs, and when horsemeat was first bought for them, she would not allow them to have it until she had tasted it herself and had pronounced it "good clean meat."

When she had visited Japan, *New York Times* (June 17, 1939).

Kamikaze-Go soon died of distemper, N. Rhoden and J. Hooper, "Helen Keller and the Forgotten Story of her Akitas," *The Akita Journal*, Yearbook Issue (1978).

Jo Davidson. He made two busts of Helen, allowing her to touch the material as he worked and entertaining her with amusing stories about others for whom he had made busts. When the first one of her was finished, Helen "saw" it with her hands. "It's me," she said with a smile.

287 "Pearl Harbor extinguished," Lash, *Helen and Teacher*, pp. 675–76.

289 "Never have I felt as diffident," AFB.

"She was her own best walking testimonial," Harrity and Martin, *The Three Lives of Helen Keller*, p. 135.

"You are the most impressive," quoted in Koestler, *The Unseen Minority*, p. 274.

"The crowning experience of my life," PSB.

"The company went mute," Brooks, *Helen Keller: Sketch for a Portrait*, p. 137.

290 "a panther," PSB.
291 "That murderous furnace," ibid.
    "Something broke in Polly," ibid.
292 "The undercurrent of distress," ibid.

CHAPTER 22 *"In a Black, Silent Hole"*

293 "Not one tall building," Helen Keller to Nella Braddy Henney (Oct. 14, 1948), PSB.
    "scorched a deep scar," ibid.
295 "They should be trained," quoted in Lash, *Helen and Teacher*, p. 729.
296 "Helen Keller, then in her seventies," Lilli Palmer, *Change Lobsters and Dance* (New York: Macmillan, 1975), pp. 223–29.
    Something of a gourmet, Helen loved food, and she and Polly were often obliged to watch the scales. In preparing the menu, her household staff always kept in mind her blindness. A broiled spring chicken, for example, would be replaced by a casserole. Helen's meat and bacon and eggs were always cut for her, but otherwise she required no assistance at the table.
297 "He is not the first," PSB.
299 "Annie and Polly's careless attitude towards money," ibid.
300 "some degree of embarrassment," ibid.
    "Oh, Katharine," Helen Keller to Katharine Cornell, undated, AFB.
    "His wife and daughter," PSB.
301 "for the colored blind," ibid.
    "This revolt has slumbered," Helen Keller to Nella Braddy Henney (Sept. 22, 1946), PSB.
302 "Suppose Polly did become very ill," PSB.
    "The belief in immortality," ibid. Like Annie Sullivan, Polly was an nonbeliever, but after her death, Helen believed that Polly, along with Teacher, was in heaven, smiling down upon her.
    "never think of Helen," ibid.

CHAPTER 23 *"A Witness of God"*

303 "handling" Helen, PSB.
304 "She allows no ego," ibid.
    "Main point," ibid.
306 "How the flames pursue me," ibid.
    "Helen's face was dead," ibid.
307 "To this day," ibid.
308 "real nobility," ibid.
    "to love life," ibid.
309 "there were no crooks," quoted in Harrity and Martin, *The Three Lives of Helen Keller*, p. 144.
310 "in the Hall of Fame," Adela Rogers St. Johns, *Some Are Born Great* (New York: New American Library, 1974), pp. 272–73.
312 "bordering on madness," PSB.
    "handicapped to look nice," ibid.
    Polly always carefully selected Helen's clothes to enhance her public image. She made sure that she was simply but fashionably dressed, and anything too flossy was immediately vetoed.

CHAPTER 24 *"I Am in Agony"*

313 "We started downstairs," PSB.
    In 1952, a device called a Telerapid was attached to the telephone in Helen's home in Connecticut so she could call the police in case of an emergency. To sum-

mon help, she would take the receiver from the telephone, turn a lever on the Tele-rapid, say into the phone two or three times, "Helen Keller, help, Helen Keller, help," then replace the receiver and rest her hands on the telephone until she felt the vibration of a ring that would indicate that help was on the way. In a businesslike manner she learned to send out the alarm, but Nella reported that "more than one person had to leave the room, so vivid was the picture of what might happen if she were doing it in earnest."

316 "It does give her some ease of mind," ibid.
317 "Polly does not like," ibid.
"It won't do," ibid.
318 "Who is she?" ibid.
The inscription on Polly's urn read, "Polly Thomson's heart has been the most precious treasure to Teacher and me," while the engraving on Anne Sullivan Macy's urn read, "Teacher and Life Long Friend of Helen Keller. Greater Love Hath No Man Than This."

CHAPTER 25 *The End of a Friendship*

320 "When I first saw Helen," Patty Duke, *Call Me Anna: The Autobiography of Patty Duke* (New York: Bantam Books, 1987), pp. 85–86.
321 Then Gibson wrote, *The Miracle Worker* was not filmed in Tuscumbia, Alabama, Helen's birthplace, but in an old house near Middletown, New Jersey.
323 "the fights that," Duke, *Call Me Anna*, pp. 72–73.
"wah-wah," ibid., p. 71.
"My emotional identification," Patty Duke, *A Brilliant Madness* (New York: Bantam Books, 1992), pp. 155–56.
"What had troubled her," PSB.
324 "Never did I dream," ibid.
Polly's attitude. Nella felt that the reason why Polly did not like *The Miracle Worker* was that any treatment of Teacher's early life made her uncomfortable and she "cringed" at some of the words that were put into Teacher's mouth. Nella had a few misgivings about this herself, but she felt that Teacher was crude when she first went to Alabama and "Mr. Gibson's deviations from the canon were justified for dramatic emphasis." Nella Braddy Henney to Ken McCormick (Oct. 15, 1956), AFB.
She also agreed with Gibson when he wrote that Annie's style was finer than Helen's and remarkably contemporary today. "This has always been my opinion and I think Mr. Gibson and I would be at one on most points," she wrote in her journal. "Helen's style, even in *Teacher*, is rather ornate and dated. . . . I think Helen was won-derfully objective, but I do think her style, quite properly in view of her mysticism, lacks sharpness of definition."
"If Mrs. Henney telephones," ibid.
"Due to Polly's illness," Helen Keller to Nella Braddy Henney (Jan. 15, 1960), AFB.
"reconsidered the matter," Helen Keller to James S. Adams (Feb. 22, 1960), AFB.
325 "[Adams] had his part," PSB.
money had been the issue. Friends often noted that when discussions of money were in progress or when compliments were paid to her, Helen took her hand away.
"Back in 1934," Lash, *Helen and Teacher*, p. 764.
"a luxurious captive," PSB.
327 "women who liked men," ibid.
"utterly out of place," ibid.
328 "always low-rated Helen Keller," ibid.
drink her martinis. Both Helen and Polly liked their cocktails. At five they and their guests would gather around the fire for a "wee drappie." Helen never let go of her glass until she had completely drained it, and Nella always asked her if she was ready

for a refill a little before the glass was empty just for the fun of watching her do "bot-
toms up" before she released it.

"the dancing over Polly's grave," PSB.

"Those were the fun years," quoted in Lash, *Helen and Teacher*, p. 769.

329 "Problems," PSB.
330 "Polly would never have allowed," ibid.
331 "going downhill," AFB.

At Helen's eightieth-birthday party, which Nella did not attend, fearing that she
"might easily have run the risk of public repudiation," Evelyn Seide spelled into
Helen's hand. When a telegram of congratulations from Vice President Nixon was
spelled into her hand, Helen immediately jerked her hand away as soon as she realized who had sent it.

CHAPTER 26 *"A Fragile Porcelain Lady"*

332 Helen's mind wandered, James S. Adams to Jansen Noyes, Jr. (Nov. 13, 1961), AFB.
"a stage in her life," Forris B. Chick to Evelyn Seide (Nov. 6, 1961), AFB.
333 "A fragile porcelain lady," Winnie Corbally to Mrs. Isabel Thomson (June 18, 1966),
AFB.
334 a rubella epidemic, ibid.
arranged for a Swedenborgian minister, memo from Evelyn Seide, ibid.
"The Kellers all started out," Phillips B. Keller to Winifred Corbally (Sept. 30, 1964),
AFB.
335 "Just a note," Phillips B. Keller to James S. Adams (Oct. 21, 1967), AFB.
336 "What is so sweet," Keller, *My Religion*, Swedenborg Foundation (1960), p. 109.

CHAPTER 27 *Helen's Legacy*

337 "My whole desire," Coates, "Profiles," *The New Yorker* (Jan. 25, 1930), p. 26.
338 "The general public," interview with author.
"An attractive, athletic blonde," "Blind, Deaf Lawyer Has the Last Laugh," *Indi-
anapolis Star* (June 22, 1995).
"the Helen Keller of the technological age," "Georgia on My Screen," *People* (Sept.
1995), pp. 91–92.
340 two types of Usher syndrome, Ilene Minor, "People with Usher Syndrome, Type II:
Issues and Adaptation," *Journal of Visual Impairment and Blindness*, Nov–Dec, 1997,
pp. 579–89.
341 "changed the policy," Koester, *The Unseen Minority*, p. 458.
questioned by some teachers, Barbara A. B. McLetchie, "Teacher Preparation," in
Welcoming Students Who Are Deaf-Blind into Typical Classrooms. (Baltimore: Paul
H. Brookes, 1995), pp. 89–93.

Although they would not have been of use to Helen personally, there are other
machines that enable the blind or visually impaired to be independent. One is an
optical scanner, or personal reading machine, that "reads" print out loud, using a synthetic voice, thus enabling a person with little or no vision to read books, newspapers,
and other material without the assistance of a sighted reader. There are also closed-
circuit television systems that magnify print or pictures, and devices that enable a
blind writer, using a computer, to hear a synthetic voice telling him or her the words
the person has written that are appearing on the visual display.

"Perhaps the real miracle," quoted in Koestler, *The Unseen Minority*, p. 477.
342 Gesell's developmental tests, quoted in Burlingham, *Psychoanalytic Studies of the
Sighted and the Blind*, p. 308.
Jean Piaget's theory, quoted in Warren, *Blindness and Early Childhood Development*,
p. 32.

According to David Warren, the period from three to six months "may be especially critical, since it is then that significant visual control of manual behavior emerges in the infant with sight." Warren, p. 182.

343 "The highest result of education," quoted in *The Open Door*, (New York: Doubleday), p. 19.

345 Despite Helen's dream, "Outlook," *U.S. News & World Report*, Mar. 11, 1996.
"The only lightless dark," quoted in *The Open Door*, p. 96.

Selected Bibliography

Ackerman, Diane. *A Natural History of the Senses*. New York: Vintage Books, 1991.

Blaxall, Arthur William. *Helen Keller under the Southern Cross*. Cape Town and Johannesburg: Juta, 1952.

Braddy, Nella (Henney). *Anne Sullivan Macy: The Story Behind Helen Keller*. Garden City, N.Y.: Doubleday, Doran, 1933.

Brooks, Van Wyck. *Helen Keller: Sketch for a Portrait*. New York: E. P. Dutton, 1956.

Brownlow, Kevin. *The Parade's Gone By*. New York: Alfred A. Knopf, 1968.

Bruce, Robert V. *Alexander Graham Bell and the Conquest of Solitude*. Boston: Little, Brown, 1973.

Burlingham, Dorothy. *Psychoanalytic Studies of the Sighted and the Blind*. New York: International Universities Press, 1972.

Carroll, Rev. Thomas J. *Blindness: What It Is, What It Does and How to Live with It*. Boston: Little, Brown, 1961.

Clemens, Samuel. *Mark Twain's Letters*, Vol. 2, arranged with comment by Albert Bigelow Paine. New York: Harper & Brothers, 1917.

Coates, Robert M. "Profiles." *The New Yorker*, Jan. 25, 1930, pp. 26–27.

Cook, Blanche Wiesen. *Eleanor Roosevelt*, Vol. 1. New York: Penguin Books, 1992.

Cutsforth, Thomas D. *The Blind in School and Society: A Psychological Study*. New York: American Foundation for the Blind, 1951.

Davidson, Jo. *Between Sittings*. New York: The Dial Press, 1951.

Dickens, Charles. *American Notes, 1842. The Works of Charles Dickens*, Vol. 14, National Library Editions. New York: Bigelow, Brown, undated.

Dillard, Annie. *Pilgrim at Tinker Creek.* New York: Harper's Magazine Press, 1974.

Duke, Patty, and Gloria Hochman. *A Brilliant Madness.* New York: Bantam Books, 1992.

Duke, Patty, and Kenneth Turan. *Call Me Anna: The Autobiography of Patty Duke.* New York: Bantam Books, 1987.

Faber, Doris. *The Life of Lorena Hickok: E.R.'s Friend.* New York: William Morrow, 1980.

Foner, Philip S., ed. *Helen Keller: Her Socialist Years.* New York: International Universities Press, 1967.

French, Richard Slayton. *From Homer to Helen Keller: A Social and Educational Study of the Blind.* New York: American Foundation for the Blind, 1932.

Gibson, William. *The Miracle Worker: A Play for Television.* New York: Alfred A. Knopf, 1957.

———. *Monday After the Miracle, A Play in Three Acts.* New York: Dramatists Play Service, 1983.

Gitter, Elisabeth. "Deaf-mutes and heroines in the Victorian era." In *Victorian Literature and Culture*, Vol. 20. New York: AMS Press, 1993.

Goodwin, Doris Kearns. *No Ordinary Time.* New York: Simon & Schuster, 1994.

Harrity, Richard, and Ralph G. Martin. *The Three Lives of Helen Keller.* Garden City, N.Y.: Doubleday, 1962.

Helen Keller Souvenir, Vol. 1. Washington, D.C.: Volta Bureau, 1892.

Helen Keller Souvenir, Vol. 2, 1892–99. *Commemorating the Harvard Final Examination to Radcliffe College, June 29–30, 1899.* Washington, D.C.: Volta Bureau, 1899.

Hitz, John. *Helen Keller*, repr. *American Anthropologist* 8: 308–24. Lancaster, Pa.: New Era Printing Co., 1906.

Howe, Irving. *Socialism and America.* New York: Harcourt Brace Jovanovich, 1985.

Hutton, Laurence. *Talk in a Library with Laurence Hutton.* New York: G. P. Putnam's Sons, 1905.

Jastrow, Joseph. "Helen Keller: A Psychological Autobiography." *Popular Science Monthly*, May 1903.

Jensen, Oliver. *American Album.* New York: American Heritage, 1968.

Kaplan, Justin. *Mr. Clemens and Mark Twain.* New York: Simon & Schuster, 1966.

Kates, Linda, and Jerome D. Schein. *A Complete Guide to Communication with Deaf-Blind Persons.* Silver Spring, Md.: National Association of the Deaf, 1980.

Keller, Helen. *Light in My Darkness*, rev. and ed. Ray Silverman. West Chester, Pa.: Chrysalis Books, 1994.

———. *The Story of My Life. With Her Letters (1887–1901) and A Supplementary Account of Her Education, Including Passages from the Reports and Letters of Her Teacher, Anne Mansfield Sullivan by John Albert Macy. Special Edition, Illustrated.* New York: Grosset & Dunlap, 1904.

Kirtley, Donald. *The Psychology of Blindness.* Chicago: Nelson-Hall, 1975.

Lamson, Mary. *Life and Education of Laura Dewey Bridgman: The Deaf, Dumb and Blind Girl.* Boston: New England Publishing Co., 1879.

Lash, Joseph. *Helen and Teacher: The Story of Helen Keller and Anne Sullivan Macy.* New York: Delacorte Press/Seymour Lawrence, 1980.

Laurie, Joe, Jr. *Vaudeville: From the Honky Tonks to the Palace.* New York: Henry Holt, 1953.

Leblanc, Georgette. *The Girl Who Found the Bluebird.* New York: Dodd, Mead, 1914.

Macy, John Albert. "Helen Keller As She Really Is." *Ladies' Home Journal,* November 1902.

———. "Helen Keller at Radcliffe College." *Youth's Companion,* June 2, 1905, 267–68.

———. *Socialism in America.* Garden City, N.Y.: Doubleday, Page, 1916.

———. *The Spirit of American Literature.* Garden City, N.Y.: Doubleday, Page, 1913.

Malone, Karen Payne. "An Historical Study for a Production Reconstructing Helen Keller's Vaudeville and Lecture Performances." M.A. thesis, Southwest Missouri State University, 1994.

McDonald, William Lindsey. "Helen Keller's Father." *Shoals Magazine* 5, no. 4 (1994): 10.

McInnes, J. M., and J. A. Treffry. *Deaf-Blind Infants and Children: A Developmental Guide.* Toronto: University of Toronto Press, 1982.

Michael Anagnos. Boston: Wright and Potter, 1907.

Miner, Ilene. "The Impact of Usher Syndrome, Type I, on Adolescent Development. *Journal of Vocational Rehabilitation* 6 (1996): 159–66.

———. "People with Usher Syndrome, Type II: Issues and Adaptations." *Journal of Visual Impairment and Blindness* (Nov–Dec. 1997): 579–89.

———. "Psychosocial Implications of Usher Syndrome, Type I, Throughout the Life Cycle." *Journal of Visual Impairment and Blindness* (May–June 1995): 287–96.

Mitchell, Arthur. *About Dreaming, Laughing and Blushing.* Edinburgh: William Green & Sons, 1905.

Palmer, Lilli. *Change Lobsters and Dance.* New York: Macmillan, 1975.

Panati, Charles. *Panati's Extraordinary Endings of Practically Everything and Everybody.* New York: Harper & Row, 1989.

Percy, Walker. *The Message in the Bottle: How Queer Man Is, How Queer Language Is, and What One Has to Do with the Other.* New York: Farrar, Straus & Giroux, 1975.

Ridley, Peter. *Helen Keller: Revolutionary Socialist.* New York: Touchstone/Simon & Schuster, 1979.

Sacks, Oliver. *An Anthropologist on Mars.* New York: Alfred A. Knopf, 1995.

———. *Seeing Voices: A Journey into the World of the Deaf.* Berkeley/Los Angeles: University of California Press, 1989.

Scapini, J. Georges. *A Challenge to Darkness.* New York: Doubleday, Doran, 1929.

Schwartz, Harold. *Samuel Gridley Howe: Social Reformer, 1801–1876.* Cambridge, Mass.: Harvard University Press, 1956.

Stahlecker, James E., Laurel E. Glass, and Steven Machalow. *State-of-the-Art: Research Priorities in Deaf-Blindness.* San Francisco: University of California, San Francisco, Center on Mental Health and Deafness, 1985.

St. Johns, Adela Rogers. *Some Are Born Great.* New York: New American Library, 1974.

Swan, Jim. "Touching Words: Helen Keller, Plagiarism, Authorship." *Cardozo Arts & Entertainment Law Journal* 10, no. 2 (1992): 321–64.

Tilney, Frederick. "A Comparative Sensory Analysis of Helen Keller and Laura Bridgman." *Archives of Neurology and Psychiatry* (June 1929): 1227–69.

Twain, Mark. *Mark Twain's Autobiography,* ed. Albert Bigelow Paine, 2 vols. New York: Harper & Brothers, 1924.

———. *Mark Twain's Letters,* Vol. 2, arranged with comment by Albert Bigelow Paine. New York: Harper & Brothers, 1917.

Villey-Desmeserets, Pierre. *The World of the Blind.* New York: Macmillan, 1930.

Walsh, Sara R., and Robert Holzberg. *Understanding and Educating the Deaf-Blind/Severely and Profoundly Handicapped: An International Perspective.* Springfield, Ill.: Charles C. Thomas, 1981.

Warren, David H. *Blindness and Early Childhood Development,* 2d ed., rev. New York: American Foundation for the Blind, 1989.

Woollcott, Alexander. *Long, Long Ago.* New York: Viking Press, 1930–43.

Yoken, Carol. *Living with Deaf-Blindness: Nine Profiles.* Washington, D.C.: The National Academy of Gallaudet College, 1979.

Young, Art. *On My Way.* New York: Horace Liveright, 1928.

Acknowledgments

INTERPRETING THE LIFE of a deaf-blind person was a challenging project for a biographer, and I am especially indebted to the following people for helping me shed light on Helen Keller's extraordinary life and career.

My deepest gratitude goes to Kenneth Stuckey, research librarian of the Samuel P. Hayes Research Library at the Perkins School for the Blind in Watertown, Massachusetts, for his help in my research and for his continuing friendship. Upon her death, Nella Braddy Henney left her unpublished notes and journals with her private observations of Helen Keller, Annie Sullivan, and their circle to the Perkins School. I am grateful to Ken for allowing me full access to this key archive and for spending countless hours answering my questions and giving me the benefit of his interpretations.

To Allison M. Bergmann, formerly of the American Foundation for the Blind, my deepest appreciation for sharing her insightful analysis of Helen Keller and Annie Sullivan and for becoming a mentor and friend during the arduous years when I was trying to reconstruct Helen's world.

For her generous assistance in helping me research the relationships among Alexander Graham Bell and Annie Sullivan and Helen Keller, I am grateful to Judith Anderson, the archivist at the Alexander Graham Bell Association for the Deaf (formerly the Volta Bureau) in Washington, D.C.

My special thanks also to Carl R. Augusto, the president and executive director of the American Foundation for the Blind, for granting me access to the Helen Keller Archives and to Leslie Rosen, Elga Joffee, Diane Wolf, and Julie Tucker for their help in my research.

I would also like to express my appreciation to Robert Smithdas for the invigorating afternoon I spent with him at the Helen Keller National Center for Deaf-Blind Youths and Adults at Sands Point, New York, and for sharing his reminiscences of Helen Keller.

In Tuscumbia, Alabama, I am indebted to Helen's nephew, William T. Johnson, for his reminiscences of his famous aunt. I am also grateful to the Helen Keller Property Board of Ivy Green, her birthplace and childhood home, and to the board of the Helen Keller Festival. This annual four-day event celebrates her birthday on June 27, and I would like to thank the people of Tuscumbia for the warm hospitality they showed me during my visit several summers ago.

My deepest thanks also to Reverend Robert Junge of The New Church in Ivyland, Pennsylvania, for pointing out to me that Helen's faith was a large part of her overcoming the obstacles in her life and to Ray Silverman, a minister in the New Church in Bryn Athyn, Pennsylvania, who has revised and expanded Helen Keller's *My Religion*. His new version, titled *Light in My Darkness*, which is published by Chrysalis Books, an imprint of the Swedenborg Foundation, presents an inspiring portrait of this remarkable woman's affirmation of the power and triumph of the spirit.

Many other people have contributed to this biography, sharing their recollections in interviews or offering leads and encouragement. To all of them I am especially grateful: Jill Alexander and Cafer T. Barkus of the Perkins School for the Blind; Sylvia Cooper, Prudence Crowther, Nancy Daughtery, Dr. Richard Dolins, Liz Foster, Elizabeth Hargrove, Andrea Jolles, Joy Jurnovoy, Carol Klein, Donna McNear; Ilene D. Miner of the Helen Keller National Center for Deaf-Blind Youths and Adults; Charlotte Parks, Lisa Patterson, and Sue Pilkilton, director of Ivy Green; Hazel Rhodes, Carl Rollyson, Bette and Bob Silverman, Katharine Sims, Janet Smallwood, Dr. Loren Southern, and Mary Jean Spanspree of "Very Special Arts"; Gunilla Stenberg, director of the Tomteboda Resource Centre for Children and Youth with Visual Impairment, Solna, Sweden; the staff of the National Cathedral in Washington, D.C.; the staff of the Alabama Institute for the Deaf and Blind; and the students and staff of the Perkins School for the Blind.

Under a Freedom of Information Act request, the Federal Bureau of Investigation released to me their file on Helen Keller. These documents shed considerable light on her political activities.

To the libraries and librarians who assisted me in documenting Helen Keller's life, I am most grateful: the New York Public Library; the Mercantile Library in New York; the New Hope and Doylestown public libraries; and the Roscoe L. West Library, Trenton State College, Trenton, New Jersey.

Several prior biographies of Anne Sullivan Macy and Helen Keller provided useful information. Of these works, Nella Braddy Henney's *Anne Sullivan Macy* remains the primary source of information about Teacher's life and personality, although it omits the more fascinating observations about her private life that Nella reserved for her notes and journals.

Another informative work is Joseph Lash's *Helen and Teacher*. Although overly detailed, this 850-page dual biography provides many interesting insights into their relationship, as well as a complete analysis of Helen Keller's politics, religion, and her lesser literary works that are not discussed in this text.

For readers interested in learning more about Helen's work for the American Foundation for the Blind, no work is more informative than Frances Koestler's *The Unseen Minority*, the definitive social history of the blind in the United States.

For his friendship and wise counsel throughout the years, I owe a special debt of gratitude to Owen Laster, my literary agent at the William Morris Agency.

I am also fortunate to have as my editor Victoria Wilson at Alfred A. Knopf. Her keen editorial sense coupled with her meticulous eye for the right photograph to enhance the text were invaluable in helping me shape this biography. I am also grateful to her assistant, Lee Buttala, and to Karen Deaver, Louise Collazo, and Karla Knight for their help with the production of the manuscript.

Friends and family have sustained me during the writing of this biography. The willingness of my husband, Lance Silverman, to read every draft was a spur to finish. My friend and fellow biographer Marion Meade has encouraged me by her interest in my work, as have my sister and brother-in-law, Wendy and Jon Harlow.

Finally, my thanks to my mother, Lucille Fletcher Wallop. A suspense novelist and playwright, it is she who has taught me by her lifelong dedication and example what it means to be a writer. At age eighty-five, despite the disability of memory loss, she is writing a play, and I can only continue to applaud her for her imagination and courage.

DOROTHY HERRMANN
New Hope, Pennsylvania
1998

Index

Matteawan State Hospital, New York, 181, 226
Maurois, André, *Life of Disraeli*, 260–1
Mayo Clinic, Rochester, Minnesota, 280, 295, 305
McCarthy, Joseph, 308, 309
McCarthyism, 283, 309
McClintic, Guthrie, 286, 287
McCloskey General Hospital, Temple, Texas, 289
McCormack, John, 298
McCormack, Patty, 321
McKinley, William, 309
Meir, Golda, 305
Melchior, Lauritz, 160
Memorial Hospital, New York, 313
Memory Cottage, Kent, England, 252
Mencken, H. L., 151
Ménière's disease, 107n.
meningitis, 9, 337, 338
menstruation, 107, 117–18 and n.
mental illness, 19
Mentor, The, 79
Metropolitan Opera House, New York, 160
Michelangelo, *David*, 295
Michigan School for the Deaf, 97
Midstream: My Later Life (Keller), 152, 162, 198, 199, 217, 236, 239–41, 264; German edition withdrawn, 261; publication, 236
Migel, Moses Charles, 238–9, 250, 270, 290, 297, 299, 317, 324, 325
Migel Committee, 270
Migel Medal, 247
Miller, Francis Trevelyan, 213–15
Milton, John, 126
mines, Keller in, 262
Miracle Worker, The (film), xiii, 310, 321
Miracle Worker, The (play), 214, 310, 320–3, 324; royalties, 325
Mitchell, Margaret, *Gone with the Wind*, 278
Molière, 126
Monday After the Miracle (play), 321–2
Monsarrat, Nicholas, *The Story of Esther Costello*, 327
Montclair, New Jersey, 183
Moon type, 177
Moore, Colonel Alexander, 9
Morgan, J. P., 171
Morgan, Mrs. John Pierpont, 94
Morris, William, 172
Morrow (William) & Company, 239
Mount Vernon, New York, 222
movies, 263, 276; on Keller, 211–16, 216, 217–20, 288, 303–4, 304, 305, 310, 311, 321
music, 152–3, 158–9, 160
Myla, 195
My Religion (Keller), 239, 336
"My Story" (Keller), 89–90

Nagasaki, 293–4
Nation, The, 136–7, 239, 240

National Association for the Advancement of Colored People, 204–5
National Cathedral, Washington, D.C., 259, 319, 335–6
National Institute of Social Sciences, Gold Medal Award, 309
National Institution for the Blind, Paris, 15
Nazism, 176–7, 251, 260; Keller on, 260, 261, 283, 287, 288
Neal, Patricia, 321
Nehru, Jawaharlal, 308
Neilson, William Allan, 125, 127
Nesbit, Evelyn, 181, 225–6
New Church, New York, 334
New Church, Washington, D.C., 239
New Deal, 282
New Orleans, 145
New Republic, The, 213
Newton, Cora, 35
New York, 91, 98, 174, 276; *Deliverance* opening, 218, 220; World Council for the Blind (1931), 249; Wright-Humason School, 99–101
New York *Call*, 203
New York Point, 177
New York Public Library, 135
New York state, 182, 271
New York Sun, 136, 306
New York Times, 176, 301
New York Times Book Review, 135
New York World's Fair (1965), Women's Hall of Fame, 334
Nixon, Richard, 308
North Alabamian, 8
Nova Scotia, 127, 128
Noyes, Jansen, Jr., 324, 325

opera, 160, 224
ophthalmia neonatorum, 177; Keller's articles on, 177
oral language, 24–5, 63, 96, 342–3; vs. sign language, 24–5; *see also* speech
Orwell, George, 176
Out of the Dark (Keller), 176

Palmer, Lilli, 295–7; *Change Lobsters and Dance*, 295–6
parapsychology, 308; *see also* supernatural
Paris, 15
Park Avenue Presbyterian Church, New York, 256
Pearl Harbor, attack on, 288–9
Pegler, Westbrook, 283
Penn, Arthur, 321, 323
Perkins Institution for the Blind (Boston, later Watertown, Massachusetts), 15–23, 26, 63, 66, 67, 68, 89, 115, 126, 238, 335, 341, 343; Laura Bridgman at, 16–22; Henney (Nella Braddy) collection, 192, 331; Keller at, 68–73, 78–85, 93, 119, 235–6, 307; public exhibition of blind

Photographic Credits

The photographs in this book are used by permission and courtesy of the following:

Alexander Graham Bell Association for the Deaf: pp. 7 (top and bottom), 29, 48, 50, 91, 108, 111, 112, 116, 128, 147, 189, 220

American Foundation for the Blind, Helen Keller Archives: pp. 10 (top and bottom), 74, 96, 103, 125, 132, 142, 160 (top and bottom), 216, 219 (bottom), 220, 229, 233, 242, 253, 269, 274, 280, 285, 288, 289, 291, 294, 298, 304, 311, 322, 326, 329, 333, 339, 344

Culver Pictures: p. 219 (top)

Library of Congress: pp. 135, 138, 153, 158, 163

New York Public Library Photograph Collection: pp. 16, 37

Perkins School for the Blind: pp. 18, 22, 64, 67, 88

My gratitude to Galowitz Photographics in New York, which rephotographed pictures in the public domain on pp. 151, 185, 212, and 224

A NOTE ON THE TYPE

The text of this book was set in Electra, a typeface designed by
W. A. Dwiggins (1880–1956). This face cannot be classified as
either modern or old style. It is not based on any historical model,
nor does it echo any particular period or style. It avoids
the extreme contrasts between thick and thin elements that
mark most modern faces, and it attempts to give a feeling of
fluidity, power, and speed.

Composed by North Market Street Graphics,
Lancaster, Pennsylvania

Printed and bound by Quebecor Printing,
Martinsburg, West Virginia

Designed by Cassandra J. Pappas